Mathematics
Today

Curriculum and Instruction

Janet S. Abbott
Coordinator of Mathematics
Chula Vista City School District
Chula Vista, California

David W. Wells
Formerly Director of Instruction
and Mathematics Education
Oakland Schools
Pontiac, Michigan

Consulting Educators

Elizabeth H. Abbott
Formerly Teacher of Title I
Computer Assisted Instruction
Greenville Public Schools
Greenville, Mississippi

Wilma B. Blossman
LaSalle Elementary School
Baton Rouge, Louisiana

Dr. Barbara Branch
Principal
White Station Junior High School
Memphis, Tennessee

Barbara Brunjes
Fourth Grade Teacher
St. James Elementary School
St. James, New York

Dr. Phillip E. Duren
Mathematics Consultant, K-12
Stark County Department of
Education
Louisville, Ohio

Dr. E. Alma Flagg
Educational Consultant
Newark, New Jersey

Betty Jean Gould
Learning Development Specialist
Sachem Central School District
Holbrook, New York

William Ezra Hansen
Supervisor of Math and Science
Kindergarten through 12
Davis County School District
Farmington, Utah

Ann Helms
Elementary Principal
Clubview Elementary School
of Muscogee County
Columbus, Georgia

Terri Katsulis
Administrator
Chicago Public School
Chicago, Illinois

Alice D. Lombardi
Formerly Mathematics Specialist
Division of Curriculum & Instruction
New York City Board of Education
New York, New York

Wallace Manning
Director of Federal Programs
District 91
Idaho Falls, Idaho

Robert D. Postman
Mercy College
Westchester County, New York

Leonard E. Thomas
Parent
Flint Community Schools
Flint, Michigan

Yvonne Tomlinson
Classroom Teacher
Riverdale High School
Jefferson, Louisiana

Mathematics
Today

HBJ Harcourt Brace Jovanovich, Publishers

Orlando   New York   Chicago   San Diego   Atlanta   Dallas

PHOTO CREDITS
Key: Top(t); Center(c); Bottom(b); Left(l); Right(r).

Ken Karp: Cover
The Bettmann Archives: 11, 216, 315. *Black Star:* Richard Howard: 46; *NASA:* 7(t). C.H. Brinton: 210, 275(r), 344(t). *Carnegie Hall Press Office:* 373. *Earth Scenes:* Jack Wilburn: 123(t). Halley Ganges: 55, 81, 133, 153, 243, 307, 329, 359. *Girl Scouts of U.S.A.:* Joel Gordon: 91. Ingert Gruttner: 95, 127, 128, 131, 223, 228, 264, 301, 317, 336(c). HBJ PHOTO: 205, 241. Michal Heron: 21, 107, 122, 191, 219, 224, 281, 296. *The Image Bank:* Roger Miller: 34, 35. Mark Solomon: 330(tc). Harald Sund: 330(b). *Magnum Photos:* Wayne Miller: 66. *MTA:* Don Forschmidt: 110. Roy Morsch: 5, 56, 74, 88(t), 172, 185, 188, 239, 245(c), 251, 266, 267, 275(t), 282, 284, 288, 294, 308, 318, 323, 325, 300(t), 331, 336(b), 337, 344(b), 347, 351, 364. *Photo Researchers:* Linda Bartlett: 17. Van Buchner: 145. Junebug Clark: 366(b). Jerry Cooke: 3. Townsend Dickenson: 369. William A. Graham: 88(b). Eunice Harris: 135(c). David O. Hill: 76. Tom Hollyman: 208. Mel Ingber: 336(b). Robert A. Isaacs: 64(b). Mac Jamieson: 372. Calvin Larsen: 123(b). Edward Lettau: 262(r). Jan Lukas: 314. Larry Mulvehill: 29. *NASA:* 6(t). Joseph Nettis: 135(t). Kjell B. Sandved: 38. William E. Townsend: 169. Catherine Ursillo: 215. C. Vergara: 340. *Shostal Associates:* 6, 7(b), 64(l), 320. Sid Avery: 99. Ernest Bernard: 36. Eric Carle: 41, 116, 183, 262(l), 314. Don Curtis: 135(b). Art D'Arazien: 319. D.J. Forbert: 124, 275(l). W.D. McKinney: 38. Herbert Lanks: 64(r). *Manley Photo:* 262(c). August Upitis: 13,165. *Sports Photofile:* David Lissy: 336(t). Chuck Muhlstock: 247, 334. *Stock Boston:* Daniel Brody: 30. *The Stock Market:* Peter B. Kaplan: 330(bc). *Wide World Photo:* 216(b). *Woodfin Camp and Associates:* Craig Aurness: 252. Robert Frerck: 134. George Hall: 1, 36. Michal Heron: 263.

ART CREDITS
Key: Top(t); Center(c); Bottom(b); Left(l); Right(r).

Susan Banta: 10(l), 24, 25(b), 96, 97, 111, 136(l), 162, 174, 209(b), 226, 227, 250(c). Wendy Biggins: 67, 87, 93, 164(b), 175, 194(b), 195, 234, 331(t), 360(b). Eulala Conner: 44, 145(tr), 256, 312. Ric Del Rossi: 62, 287, 353(bl). Andrea Eberbach: 8(t), 9, 47(bl), 59, 103, 110(b), 194(t), 201, 232, 349(b), 361(b). Pam Ford: 168, 210(t), 211, 311, 338, 339(bl), 360(t). Thomas Hamilton Jr.: 41, 261(b). John Killgrew: 105, 135(b), 182(b). Claude Martinot: 52, 70, 82, 101, 116, 125, 156, 157, 187, 246(b), 260(b), 261(t), 310, 365. Verlin Miller: 22, 33, 39, 40, 51, 72, 73, 100, 139(r), 183(tr), 225, 248(tl,t), 258(t), 260(tc). Sara Mintz Zwicker: 258(b), 259(t,b), 266(c), 267(b), 270(b), 271, 285(b), 290(t), 303, 363, 366(c). Michael O'Reilly: 47(tr), 77, 118, 222. Patricia Perleberg: 270(t), 272(t), 283, 362. Ondre Pettingill: 173, 369. Tom Powers/Dave Hannum: 182(tl). Nancy Shill: 28, 95, 114, 115, 143, 154, 165, 176, 181, 322, 371. Dennis Schofield: 13, 90, 102, 126, 196(t), 204, 290(b), 298, 323, 339(tr). Samantha Smith: 108, 109, 112, 262. Judith Sutton: 63, 92, 154, 163, 198, 200, 244(b), 245, 266(b), 272(b), 273, 308(t), 316, 341, 375(b), 379. Gary Undercuffler: 31, 38, 86, 98, 113, 120, 266(tr), 292, 324. Jan Watkins: 8(b), 164(t), 230, 231, 237. Yerkes: 32, 42, 60, 61, 68, 69, 71, 94, 192, 193, 206, 215.

Technical art, charts, graphs and maps: Dave Hannum
Glossary Art: Vantage Art Inc.

Printed in the United States of America
ISBN: 0-15-350707-1

CONTENTS

chapter 4 Dividing by One-Digit Numbers

chapter 5 Dividing by Two-Digit Numbers

chapter **9** Fractions: Multiplication and Division

chapter **10** Measurement

chapter **14** # Ratio and Percent

Numeration

Expanded Form • Place Value • Millions and Billions • Comparing and Ordering Numbers • Rounding Numbers • Problem Solving: Using a Table • Roman Numerals

Expanded Form

We use ten **digits** to name numbers.

0 1 2 3 4 5 6 7 8 9

We use only ten digits because we group by tens.

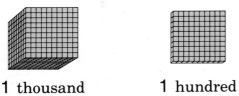

1 thousand	1 hundred	1 ten	1 one
(10 hundreds)	(10 tens)	(10 ones)	

We can show a number such as two thousand, three hundred fifty-two in **expanded form**.

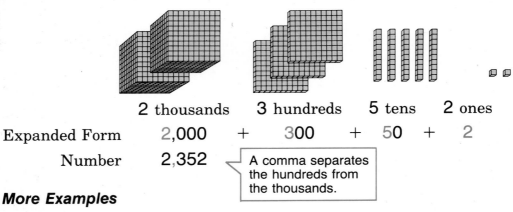

	2 thousands	3 hundreds	5 tens	2 ones
Expanded Form	2,000 +	300 +	50 +	2
Number	2,352			

A comma separates the hundreds from the thousands.

More Examples

Expanded Form   4,000 + 70 + 6

Number   4,076

Practice • Write the numbers.

1.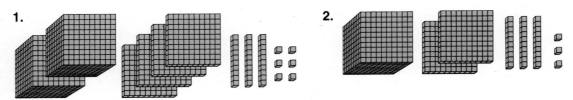

3. six thousand, seven hundred forty-two

4. 200 + 7   5. 3,000 + 600 + 20 + 4

Write the expanded forms.

6. 378   7. 937   8. 406   9. 5,281   10. 2,940

Mixed Practice • Write the numbers.

11.

12.

13.

14.

15. five thousand, six hundred eighty-two

16. nine thousand, six hundred sixty

17. seven thousand, eighty-four

18. 100 + 70 + 4   19. 300 + 50 + 6

20. 7,000 + 300 + 10 + 9   21. 6,000 + 50 + 2

22. 5,000 + 400 + 80 + 3   23. 9,000 + 10 + 6

Write the expanded forms.

24. 594   25. 862   26. 703   27. 9,730   28. 3,504

29. 4,375   30. 6,075   31. 4,077   32. 9,002   33. 3,080

Write the numbers in words.

34. 916   35. 250   36. 2,486   37. 5,443   38. 8,300

39. 768   40. 9,821   41. 4,023   42. 7,309   43. 1,008

Here is another way to write the expanded form for 2,438.

$(2 \times 1,000) + (4 \times 100) + (3 \times 10) + (8 \times 1)$

Write the expanded form as shown above.

★ 44. 672   ★ 45. 503   ★ 46. 2,127   ★ 47. 5,785   ★ 48. 9,436

PROBLEM SOLVING • APPLICATIONS

Write the numbers.

49. The Fair Park Coliseum in Dallas has a seating capacity of seven thousand, five hundred ninety-three.

50. The seating capacity of the Denver Coliseum is nine thousand, thirty-eight.

Place Value

hundred thousands 10 × 10,000 100,000	ten thousands 10 × 1,000 10,000	thousands 10 × 100 1,000	hundreds 10 × 10 100	tens 10 × 1 10	ones 1
					5
				5	0
			5	0	0
		5	0	0	0
	5	0	0	0	0
5	0	0	0	0	0

In the ones place, the 5 names the number 5.
In the tens place, the 5 names the number 50.
In the hundreds place, the 5 names the number 500.

What number does the 5 name in the thousands place?
What number does the 5 name in the ten-thousands place?
What number does the 5 name in the hundred-thousands place?

*Each place in a numeral has a value
ten times the value of the place to its right.*

Practice • What number does the 3 name in each exercise?

	hundred thousands	ten thousands	thousands	hundreds	tens	ones
1.			5	3	4	2
2.		6	8	4	3	7
3.	5	1	3	6	0	2
4.	3	4	7	9	6	8
5.	8	3	5	4	2	1

In which place is the blue digit?

6. 142   7. 476,103   8. 52,188   9. 942,581

10. 3,768   11. 4,636   12. 753,214   13. 76,894

Mixed Practice • What number does the blue digit name?

14. 4,658   **15.** 307   **16.** 29,654   **17.** 35,820

18. 72,135   **19.** 697,384   **20.** 321,756   **21.** 8,957

22. 304,627   **23.** 548,209   **24.** 746   **25.** 941,207

In what place is the blue digit?

26. 6,257   **27.** 183,249   **28.** 20,431   **29.** 4,582

30. 581,469   **31.** 784   **32.** 39,502   **33.** 137,954

34. 35,462   **35.** 8,950   **36.** 658,254   **37.** 397,802

In which number does the 3 have the greater place value?

38. 3,256 or 2,356   **39.** 10,316 or 11,237   **40.** 2,543 or 6,382

41. 1,372 or 4,613   **42.** 347 or 103   **43.** 53,209 or 49,365

44. 743,621 or 436,107   **45.** 54,103 or 79,365   **46.** 839,704 or 982,534

PROBLEM SOLVING • APPLICATIONS

Use all the digits. Write the greatest number possible.

★ **47.** 2, 9 and 5   ★ **48.** 1, 8 and 6   ★ **49.** 4, 3, 8 and 2   ★ **50.** 6, 0, 4 and 3

Use all the digits. Write the least number possible.

★ **51.** 1, 2 and 5   ★ **52.** 8, 4 and 6   ★ **53.** 3, 6, 7 and 9   ★ **54.** 5, 2, 1 and 9

Skills Maintenance

Add.

1. 8
   +6

2. 4
   +4

3. 5
   +9

4. 3
   +4

5. 7
   +5

6. 9
   +3

7. 2
   +9

8. 4
   +8

9. 6
   +5

10. 4
   +6

Millions and Billions

The distance between the sun and the earth is about one hundred forty-nine million, five hundred ninety thousand kilometers.

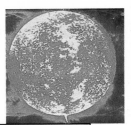

Billions Period			Millions Period			Thousands Period			Ones Period		
hundred billions	ten billions	billions	hundred millions	ten millions	millions	hundred thousands	ten thousands	thousands	hundreds	tens	ones
			1	4	9	5	9	0	0	0	0

Large numbers are separated into **periods** by commas.

Read: ⟶ 149 million, 590 thousand
Write: ⟶ 149,590,000

Here is another large number.

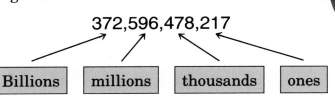

372,596,478,217

Billions millions thousands ones

Read: ⟶ 372 billion, 596 million, 478 thousand, 217

Practice • Write the numbers.

1. 109 million, 723

2. 743 million, 166

3. 28 billion, 629 million, 219

4. 530 billion, 317 thousand, 748

Write the digits that are in the millions period.

5. 38,046,172

6. 458,212,874

7. 24,172,000,142

Write the digits that are in the billions period.

8. 7,116,295,101

9. 162,792,100,631

10. 19,764,963,400

Mixed Practice • Write the numbers.

11. 402 million, 358 thousand, 794

12. 908 billion, 21 thousand

13. 763 billion, 529 million, 408 thousand, 642

14. five hundred seventy-eight million, three hundred eighty-four thousand, nine hundred twenty-two

15. one hundred seven billion, three hundred fifteen million, six hundred fifty-three

Write the digits that are in the millions period.

16. 52,175,983

17. 197,461,803

18. 326,963,147,197

Write the digits that are in the billions period.

19. 4,421,834,112

20. 82,147,632,109

21. 794,805,392,104

Name 1,000 more.

22. 142,764,000

23. 965,173,040,174

24. 62,437,852

Name 1,000,000 more.

25. 762,371,425

26. 10,475,429,471

★ 27. 99,400,000

Name 1,000,000,000 more.

28. 432,000,000,000

29. 72,416,349,146

★ 30. 769,142,973,761

PROBLEM SOLVING • APPLICATIONS

Use the table to answer the questions.

31. Which planet is the farthest from the Sun?

32. Which planet is the second closest to the Sun?

33. Which planet is farther from the Sun, Mercury or Earth?

★ 34. How far is Pluto from the Sun?

★ 35. How far is Neptune from the Sun? Is it farther away than Saturn?

Planet	Distance from Sun (km)
Earth	149,590,000
Jupiter	778,120,000
Mars	227,720,000
Mercury	57,900,000
Neptune	4,492,100,000
Pluto	5,914,300,000
Saturn	1,428,300,000
Uranus	2,872,700,000
Venus	108,230,000

Comparing and Ordering Numbers

Simon keeps a record of the number of dogs registered with kennels. Was the greater number of dogs registered in the first or the fourth year?

Dogs Registered with Kennels	
Year	Number of Dogs
First	1,022,849
Second	1,048,648
Third	1,013,650
Fourth	960,750

> means "is greater than," < means "is less than," and = means "is equal to."

Compare: 1,022,849 ● 960,750

Think: Millions are greater than thousands.
So 1,022,849 > 960,750.
The greater number of dogs was registered in the first year.

Compare: 1,048,648 ● 1,013,650

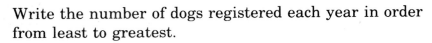

Think: Same number of millions.
Same number of hundred thousands.
Compare the ten thousands. 4 > 1
So 1,048,648 > 1,013,650.

Write the number of dogs registered each year in order from least to greatest.

Think: 960,750 < 1,013,650
1,013,650 < 1,022,849
1,022,849 < 1,048,648
So 960,750 < 1,013,650 < 1,022,849 < 1,048,648.

Practice • Use >, <, or = to write a true sentence.

1. 696 ● 696

2. 4,634 ● 1,962

3. 27,421,046 ● 27,542,017

4. 316,475,326 ● 471,304,129

Write in order from least to greatest.

5. 358; 349; 502; 384

6. 6,725; 7,941; 5,930

7. 258,402; 85,402; 528,402

8. 392,485; 485,392; 439,285; 458,926

8

Mixed Practice • Use >, <, or = to write a true sentence.

9. 4,832  8,432   10. 975 ● 2,175   11. 43,721 ● 42,819

12. 38,924 ● 39,824   13. 572,118 ● 572,118   14. 892,904 ● 892,409

15. 4,721,925 ● 8,365,147   16. 725,109 ● 2,406,118

17. 2,177,824 ● 2,274,132   18. 9,392,174 ● 9,392,174

Write in order from least to greatest.

19. 458; 259; 249

20. 85,412; 85,335; 85,548

21. 907,135,268; 49,320,004; 974,629,330; 705,000,672

22. 487,349,602; 487,349,553; 87,449,671; 87,962,555

★ 23. 1,285,352,604; 1,274,389,665; 1,274,369,208; 989,657,304

PROBLEM SOLVING • APPLICATIONS

Use the table to answer the questions.

24. In which year were more poodles registered?

25. Were there more Dobermans or German shepherds registered in the first year?

★ 26. Is the information on the table listed in rank order? If so, how?

Dogs Registered for Two Years		
	First Year	**Second Year**
Poodles	101,100	112,300
Doberman Pinschers	81,964	79,254
German Shepherds	61,783	67,072

Midchapter Review

Write the expanded forms.

1. 463   2. 509   3. 8,052   4. 5,196

Write the numbers.

5. 743 thousand, 166   6. 500 billion, 457 thousand, 604

In what place is the blue digit?

7. 139,701   8. 6,724,351   9. 852,962,074,256

Rounding Numbers

Christine travels 53 kilometers from Wilmington, Delaware, to Vineland, New Jersey. To the nearest ten, about how many kilometers does she travel?

53 is between 50 and 60.
It is nearer to 50.
53 rounded to the nearest ten is 50.

Christine travels about 50 kilometers.

Bruce travels 532 kilometers.
532 is between 500 and 600.
It is nearer to 500. 532 rounded to the nearest hundred is 500.

Sylvia travels 550 kilometers.
550 is halfway between 500 and 600.
Round 550 up to 600. 550 rounded to the nearest hundred is 600.

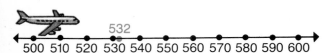

You can round numbers without using a number line.

Round 4,326 to the nearest thousand.

The digit in the thousands place is 4.
The digit to the right of the 4 is less than 5.
Keep the digit in the thousands place the same.

thousands place
↓
4,326
↑

4,326 rounded to the nearest thousand is 4,000.

Round 2,837,079 to the nearest ten thousand.

The digit in the ten-thousands place is 3.
The digit to the right of the 3 is 5 or greater.
Increase the digit in the ten-thousands place by 1.

ten-thousands place
↓
2,837,079
↑

2,837,079 rounded to the nearest ten thousand is 2,840,000.

Practice • Round to the nearest ten.

1. 47   2. 53   3. 45   4. 58

Round to the nearest hundred.

5. 683   6. 558   7. 7,204   8. 9,181

Round to the nearest thousand.

9. 4,725   10. 5,429   11. 30,892   12. 73,624

More Practice • Round to the nearest ten.

13. 61	**14.** 143	**15.** 794	**16.** 1,939
17. 4,732	**18.** 865	**19.** 3,799	**20.** 4,627

Round to the nearest hundred.

21. 496	**22.** 547	**23.** 4,854	**24.** 16,925
25. 7,526	**26.** 3,974	**27.** 2,859	**28.** 65,555

Round to the nearest thousand.

29. 35,121	**30.** 17,721	**31.** 172,914	**32.** 29,571
33. 62,548	**34.** 392,804	**35.** 459,274	**36.** 642,941

Round to the nearest ten thousand.

37. 26,410	**38.** 83,572	**39.** 115,721	**40.** 4,398,194
41. 58,394	**42.** 285,473	**43.** 9,034,671	**44.** 3,425,643

Round to the nearest hundred thousand.

45. 493,804	**46.** 625,158	**47.** 3,379,213	**48.** 7,495,800
49. 2,620,591	**50.** 7,754,063	**51.** 125,306,000	**52.** 643,651,499

Round to the nearest million.

★ **53.** 6,942,108	★ **54.** 2,047,591	★ **55.** 4,593,226	★ **56.** 6,451,602
★ **57.** 253,710,884	★ **58.** 27,694,005	★ **59.** 199,842,384	★ **60.** 639,107,853

PROBLEM SOLVING • APPLICATIONS

United States Presidential Election of 1892	
Grover Cleveland	5,554,414
Benjamin Harrison	5,190,802
James Weaver	1,027,329

61. What would the vote totals be if they all were rounded to the nearest ten thousand?

62. What would the vote totals be if they all were rounded to he nearest hundred thousand?

★ **63.** What would the vote totals be if they all were rounded to the nearest million? Who won?

PROBLEM SOLVING • STRATEGIES

Using a Table

Sometimes you must locate information in a table in order to solve a problem. Use the headings to help you find the information you need.

Land Area of Some States			
State	Area in Square Kilometers	State	Area in Square Kilometers
Alaska	1,527,464	North Dakota	183,022
California	411,013	South Carolina	80,432
Indiana	93,993	Tennessee	109,411
Michigan	150,779	Texas	692,402
New York	128,401	Wyoming	253,596

What is the land area of North Dakota?

Use these four steps to help you solve the problem.

Step 1
Read the problem. What does it ask?

What is the land area of North Dakota?

Step 2
Make a plan.

Use the headings to find the state and land area.

Step 3
Find the answer.

Find North Dakota on the list of states. Read across to find the land area. The answer is 183,022 square kilometers.

Step 4
Check the answer.

Read the question again. Does the information answer the question?

Use the table to answer the questions.

1. Name the state listed that has the largest area.

2. Name the state listed that has the smallest area.

3. Is the area of New York closer to 120,000 or 130,000 square kilometers?

4. Is the area of Indiana closer to 90,000 or 100,000 square kilometers?

5. What states have an area between 100,000 square kilometers and 200,000 square kilometers?

6. What state has an area of about 700,000 square kilometers?

7. Which state has the smaller area, Michigan or Alaska?

8. Which state has the larger area, New York or North Dakota?

9. Round each number in the table to the nearest ten thousand.

10. What states have an area larger than 500,000 square kilometers when rounded to the nearest ten thousand?

11. What states have an area smaller than 100,000 square kilometers when rounded to the nearest ten thousand?

Remember to round up if the digit is 5 or more.

12. The area of New Mexico is about 100,000 square kilometers less than the area of California. What is the area of New Mexico rounded to the nearest ten thousand?

13. The area of Wyoming is about 100,000 square kilometers more than the area of Georgia. What is the area of Georgia rounded to the nearest ten thousand?

★ 14. List the states shown in the table in order from the smallest to the largest area.

★ 15. Find the total amount of land area occupied by the states listed in this table.

REVIEW

Write the numbers. (pages 2–3)

1. four thousand, one hundred five.   2. one thousand, seven hundred eight.

3. 2000 + 600 + 80 + 4   4. 900 + 50

Write the expanded forms. (pages 2–3)

5. 726   6. 309   7. 8,253   8. 6,044

What number does the blue digit name? (pages 4–5)

9. 871   10. 86,529   11. 100,181   12. 806,367

In what place is the blue digit? (pages 4–5)

13. 256   14. 6,418   15. 594,181   16. 24,925

Write the numbers. (pages 6–7)

17. 35 million, 261 thousand, 835   18. 426 billion, 900 million, 48 thousand, 15

Use 496,831,070,695. Write the digits that are in the (pages 4–7)

19. billions period.   20. millions period.   21. thousands period.

Write >, <, or =. (pages 8–9)

22. 1,986 ● 1,006   23. 29,622 ● 29,622   24. 6,241,305 ● 6,242,305

Write in order from least to greatest. (pages 8–9)

25. 630; 295; 800; 703   26. 40,957; 39,529; 40,769

Round 572,586 to the nearest (pages 10–11)

27. hundred.   28. thousand.   29. ten thousand.   30. hundred thousand.

Solve.

31. In Smithtown there are 755,483 people. There are 600,483 people in Johnston. Which place has more people? (p. 8)

32. Uranus is 2,872,700,000 miles from the Sun. Neptune is 4,492,100,000 miles from the Sun. Which planet is farther from the Sun? (p. 8)

PROJECT

Symbols Past and Present

Other cultures, past and present, have used different words or symbols to name numbers. We say *one* and those who speak Spanish say *uno*. The decimal system we use is based on ten. The Mayan Indians of Central America used a system based on twenty.

Look up the numbers named in the table. Fill in the words or symbols. Then make a large poster to display the information.

Words				Symbols				
English	Spanish	French		Arabic	Chinese	Egyptian	Greek	Mayan
one	uno		1					
two			2					
three			3					
four			4					
five			5					
six			6					
seven			7					
eight			8					
nine			9					
ten			10					

TEST

Write the numbers.

1. six thousand, five hundred ninety-two

2. one thousand, eight

3. 700 + 6

4. 3,000 + 600 + 70 + 3

Write the expanded forms.

5. 934   **6.** 237   **7.** 5,010   **8.** 9,256

What number does the blue digit name?

9. 962   **10.** 65,206   **11.** 364,295   **12.** 840,609

In what place is the blue digit?

13. 357   **14.** 3,294   **15.** 120,531   **16.** 308,955

Write the numbers.

17. 91 million, 27 thousand, 305   **18.** 529 billion, 396 million, 10 thousand, 778

Use, 2,399,421,990. Write the digits that are in the

19. millions period.   **20.** thousands period.   **21.** billions period.

Write >, <, or =.

22. 7,057 ● 6,943   **23.** 1,216 ● 1,218   **24.** 845,117 ● 845,117

Write in order from least to greatest.

25. 6,245; 6,605; 7,683; 5,962   **26.** 31,406; 30,995; 31,156

Round 402,135,739 to the nearest

27. hundred.   **28.** thousand.   **29.** ten thousand.   **30.** hundred thousand.

Solve.

31. Earth is 149,590,000 kilometers from the Sun. Saturn is 1,428,300,000 kilometers from the Sun. Which is closer to the Sun?

32. In a primary election 845,711 people voted. In the general election 954,117 people voted. In which did more people vote?

ENRICHMENT

Roman Numerals

The ancient Romans used these symbols to name numbers.

I	V	X	L	C	D	M
1	5	10	50	100	500	1000

Their system was not a place value system. To find the value of a Roman numeral you either add or subtract.

You add when the symbols are alike or when they decrease in value from left to right.

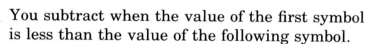

XVII = 10 + 5 + 1 + 1, or 17
MDLX = 1,000 + 500 + 50 + 10, or 1,560

You subtract when the value of the first symbol is less than the value of the following symbol.

In the number IV, I is less than V, and so IV = 5 − 1, or 4.
In the number XC, X is less than C, and so XC = 100 − 10, or 90.

What number is named?

1. II
2. VI
3. IV
4. XVI
5. XXIII
6. XXXVII
7. XL
8. LX
9. LXXVI
10. CCXIII
11. CCCLXV
12. DCXXI
13. MMCCXII
14. MDCLXVI
15. MDCXLIV

Write the Roman numerals.

16. 6
17. 8
18. 11
19. 17
20. 26
21. 33
22. 44
23. 89
24. 92
25. 128
26. 765
27. 956
28. 1,999
29. 1,492
30. 2,783

COMPUTER

Computer Vocabulary

A **computer** is a machine that works with numbers and letters.
Computer hardware is the metal and plastic machinery of the computer itself.
A **computer system** includes input, output, hardware, and software.
A **programmer** is a person who writes instructions to the computer in a program. A **program** is a list of step-by-step input to a computer.
Computer software includes all the programs and data in the computer hardware.

Data are the numbers, letters, and instructions with which the computer works. A **datum** is a single number or letter. The plural of *datum* is *data*.
A computer works with, or **processes**, data. That is why a computer system is sometimes called a **data-processing system**.
A computer can get **input** from a keyboard, punched cards, tape, or disks.
A **keyboard** is a typewriter that is attached to a computer.

A computer can place **output** on any or all of these types of output devices:
> A **cathode-ray tube (CRT)** displays output on a television screen.
> A **printer** can print output on paper to make a permanent document.
> **Punched cards** can save output for years.
> **Magnetic tapes** hold output data in a very condensed form.
> **Diskettes**, sometimes called **floppy disks**, are very portable.
> **Hard disks** can hold millions of letters or numbers.

Input and output **devices** are usually shown by the following symbols.

> for a keyboard. The shape is that of a keyboard viewed from the side.

> for punched cards.   for printer.

> for magnetic tapes. The line at the bottom represents tape.

> for a CRT display. It represents the tube as seen from the side.

> for disks or diskettes or other forms of storage devices.

A computer is shown by a box. Input devices have arrows pointing into a computer. Output devices have arrows pointing out of a computer.
A computer stores a program in its **storage**, or **memory**.

Now you can put together a picture of a computer system. All the parts are shown in the diagram. Each of the parts has a label. The label shows the first letter of the name of that part. Make a list of numbers from 1 through 16 on a sheet of paper and complete the name for each part.

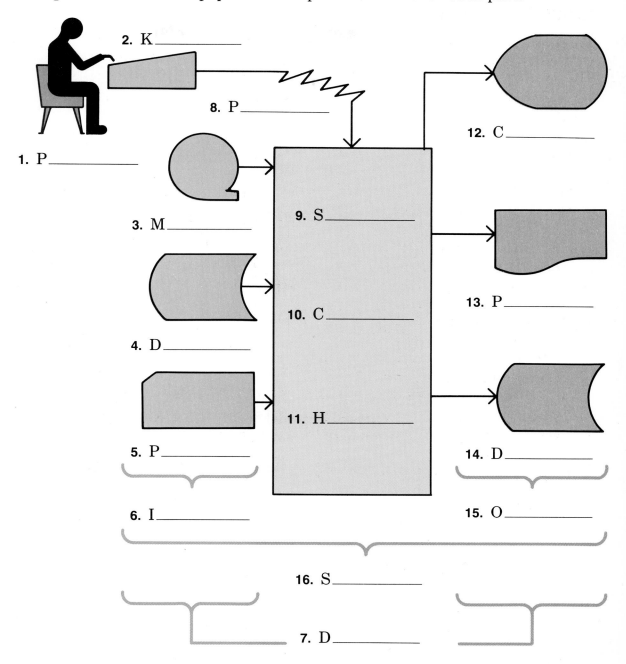

2. K_____

8. P_____

1. P_____

3. M_____

9. S_____

10. C_____

4. D_____

11. H_____

5. P_____

6. I_____

12. C_____

13. P_____

14. D_____

15. O_____

16. S_____

7. D_____

Choose your names from the following list:
Keyboard, Program, Cathode-ray tube, Programmer, Software, Magnetic tape, Computer, Printer, Disk, Hardware, Punched cards, Input, Output, System, Data. Names may be used more than once.

Choose the correct answers.

1. Write the number.

2,000 + 50 + 6

    A. 56
    B. 2,056
    C. 2,560
    D. not here

2. Write the expanded form.

967

    A. 900 + 60 + 7
    B. 9,000 + 600 + 70
    C. 90 + 60 + 7
    D. not here

3. In what place is the blue digit?

49,327

    A. ten thousand
    B. million
    C. thousand
    D. not here

4. What number does the blue digit name?

15,463

    A. 4
    B. 40
    C. 400
    D. not here

5. Write the digits that are in the millions period.

26,372,967,340

    A. 967
    B. 372
    C. 26
    D. not here

6. Name 1,000 more.

65,872,546

    A. 66,872,546
    B. 65,882,546
    C. 65,872,646
    D. not here

7. Compare.

2,396 ◯ 3,269

    A. >
    B. <
    C. =
    D. not here

8. Write in order from least to greatest.

268; 286; 249

    A. 249; 268; 286
    B. 268; 249; 286
    C. 249; 286; 268
    D. not here

9. Round 216,756 to the nearest ten thousand.

    A. 210,000
    B. 217,000
    C. 220,000
    D. not here

10. Cline receives 430,500 votes in a state election. Jarit receives one million more votes. How many votes does Jarit receive?

    A. 430,500   **B.** 1,430,500
    C. 10,430,500   **D.** not here

11. Evelyn travels 645 kilometers while she is on vacation. To the nearest hundred, about how many kilometers does she travel?

    A. 500   **B.** 700
    C. 600   **D.** not here

Addition and Subtraction

Addition • Related Facts • Facts Drill • Estimating
Sums • Addition with Regrouping • Adding
Greater Numbers • Column Addition • Estimating
Differences • Subtraction with Regrouping • Problem
Solving: Adding and Subtracting Money
• Regrouping More Than Once • Zeros in Subtraction
• Problem Solving: Making Change

Addition

There are 8 starships on
a trip to Alpha Centauri.
Then 6 other starships join them.
How many starships are there in all?

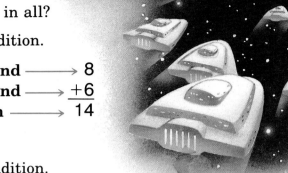

Here are two ways to show addition.

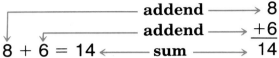

$$\text{addend} \longrightarrow 8$$
$$\text{addend} \longrightarrow \underline{+6}$$
$$8 + 6 = 14 \longleftarrow \text{sum} \longrightarrow 14$$

There are 14 starships in all.

Here are some properties of addition.

Order Property of Addition You can add two numbers in either order. The sum is always the same.	$9 + 5 = 14$ $5 + 9 = 14$

Zero Property of Addition When one of two addends is 0, the sum equals the other addend.	$4 + 0 = 4$ $0 + 0 = 0$ $0 + 6 = 6$

Grouping Property of Addition You can group addends differently. The sum is always the same.	$(5 + 3) + 7 = ?$ $5 + (3 + 7) = ?$ $8\quad + 7 = 15$ $5 + \quad 10 \quad = 15$

> Work inside the
> parentheses first.

Practice • Add.

1. $9 + 9 = \underline{\ ?\ }$ **2.** $7 + 7 = \underline{\ ?\ }$ **3.** $9 + 0 = \underline{\ ?\ }$

4. $\begin{array}{r} 6 \\ +5 \\ \hline \end{array}$ **5.** $\begin{array}{r} 5 \\ +8 \\ \hline \end{array}$ **6.** $\begin{array}{r} 8 \\ +0 \\ \hline \end{array}$ **7.** $\begin{array}{r} 4 \\ +8 \\ \hline \end{array}$ **8.** $\begin{array}{r} 6 \\ +7 \\ \hline \end{array}$ **9.** $\begin{array}{r} 6 \\ +8 \\ \hline \end{array}$ **10.** $\begin{array}{r} 5 \\ +4 \\ \hline \end{array}$

11. $9 + 8 = \underline{\ ?\ }$ **12.** $8 + 9 = \underline{\ ?\ }$ **13.** $0 + 7 = \underline{\ ?\ }$

14. $(8 + 1) + 7 = \underline{\ ?\ }$ **15.** $8 + (1 + 7) = \underline{\ ?\ }$ **16.** $(7 + 0) + 9 = \underline{\ ?\ }$

Mixed Practice • Add.

17. 6 +0	18. 4 +7	19. 7 +8	20. 6 +6	21. 8 +5	22. 9 +8	23. 5 +5
24. 6 +3	25. 8 +7	26. 4 +9	27. 7 +6	28. 9 +5	29. 7 +4	30. 0 +0
31. 5 +0	32. 5 +7	33. 8 +8	34. 5 +6	35. 8 +4	36. 9 +6	37. 8 +6

38. $8 + 7 = $ ___?___

39. $7 + 8 = $ ___?___

40. $4 + 0 = $ ___?___

41. $6 + 9 = $ ___?___

42. $9 + 6 = $ ___?___

43. $6 + 8 = $ ___?___

44. $9 + 7 = $ ___?___

45. $7 + 9 = $ ___?___

46. $0 + 6 = $ ___?___

47. $(2 + 8) + 1 = $ ___?___

48. $2 + (8 + 1) = $ ___?___

49. $(7 + 3) + 5 = $ ___?___

50. $(6 + 4) + 8 = $ ___?___

51. $9 + (2 + 6) = $ ___?___

★ 52. $3 + 5 + 4 = $ ___?___

Use the numbers in the INPUT column. Follow the rule. List the OUTPUTS.

★ 53.

Add 4

INPUT	OUTPUT
8	?
7	?
9	?
6	?

★ 54.

Add 8

INPUT	OUTPUT
9	?
6	?
7	?
4	?

★ 55.

Add 9

INPUT	OUTPUT
3	?
7	?
5	?
6	?

PROBLEM SOLVING • APPLICATIONS

56. In space 2 freighters are searching for wrecks. The first ship found 7 wrecks on Venus and 1 on Mercury. The second freighter found 9 on Mars. How many wrecks in all did they find?

★ 57. One day 9 spaceships left earth. The first 2 went to Venus. The next 4 went to Mars. The rest went to Jupiter. How many ships went to Jupiter?

23

Related Facts

At the loading dock are 4 trucks.
Then 3 more drive up.
How many are there now?

$$4 + 3 = 7 \leftarrow \text{The \textbf{sum} is the answer in addition.}$$

Soon 3 drive away.
How many are there now?

$$7 - 3 = 4 \leftarrow \text{The \textbf{difference} is the answer in subtraction.}$$

You can write four number sentences using 4, 3, and 7.

$$4 + 3 = 7 \qquad 7 - 3 = 4$$
$$3 + 4 = 7 \qquad 7 - 4 = 3$$

These four related number sentences make up a **family of facts**.

Practice • Complete the sentence.

Write three other number sentences that belong to the family of facts.

1. $7 + 3 = \underline{?}$ **2.** $13 - 7 = \underline{?}$ **3.** $9 + 5 = \underline{?}$ **4.** $11 - 8 = \underline{?}$

Use the three numbers. Write four number sentences that make up a family of facts.

5. 3, 5, 8   **6.** 9, 4, 13   **7.** 5, 7, 12   **8.** 6, 4, 10

Mixed Practice • Complete the sentences.

Write three other number sentences that belong to the family of facts.

9. $6 + 5 = \underline{?}$ **10.** $9 + 4 = \underline{?}$ **11.** $16 - 9 = \underline{?}$ **12.** $14 - 8 = \underline{?}$

Use the three numbers. Write four number sentences that make up a family of facts.

13. 7, 4, 11   **14.** 3, 7, 10   **15.** 8, 4, 12   **16.** 5, 9, 14

17. 7, 8, 15   **18.** 9, 7, 16   **19.** 5, 8, 13   **20.** 4, 5, 9

21. 9, 2, 11   **22.** 6, 8, 14   **23.** 9, 8, 17   **24.** 5, 6, 11

Find the missing numbers.

25. $15 - 8 = \underline{\ ?\ }$ **26.** $\underline{\ ?\ } + 5 = 12$ **27.** $16 - 7 = \underline{\ ?\ }$ **28.** $\underline{\ ?\ } + 7 = 11$

29. $8 + \underline{\ ?\ } = 17$ **30.** $6 + \underline{\ ?\ } = 13$ **31.** $13 - 8 = \underline{\ ?\ }$ **32.** $4 + \underline{\ ?\ } = 13$

33. $\underline{\ ?\ } + 4 = 12$ **34.** $11 - 6 = \underline{\ ?\ }$ **35.** $8 + \underline{\ ?\ } = 14$ **36.** $5 + \underline{\ ?\ } = 13$

37. $14 - 6 = \underline{\ ?\ }$ **38.** $13 - 9 = \underline{\ ?\ }$ **39.** $11 - 7 = \underline{\ ?\ }$ **40.** $9 + \underline{\ ?\ } = 12$

Subtract to find how many are left.

41. Fred has 7 boxes.
He puts 3 boxes on the truck.
How many does he have left?

$7 - 3 = ?$

Subtract to find how many you need.

42. Carmela needs 7 boxes.
She has 3 boxes.
How many more does she need?

$3 + ? = 7 \text{ or } 7 - 3 = ?$

Subtract to compare.

43. Joan has 7 boxes.
Carole has 3 boxes.
How many more does Joan have?

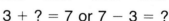

$7 - 3 = ?$

PROBLEM SOLVING • APPLICATIONS

44. Aaron had 9 packages to deliver. He has delivered 6. How many packages does he have left to deliver?

★ **45.** Perry has 13 boxes to pack. Violet has 7 boxes to pack, and Nina has 5. How many more boxes does Perry have to pack than Violet and Nina together?

Addition and Subtraction Facts Drill

Add.

1. 9
+1

2. 4
+0

3. 1
+4

4. 8
+6

5. 2
+3

6. 6
+9

7. 0
+7

8. 3
+6

9. 2
+5

10. 6
+7

11. 2
+1

12. 3
+9

13. 0
+2

14. 5
+4

15. 7
+3

16. 4
+2

17. 0
+4

18. 5
+3

19. 7
+0

20. 3
+1

21. 4
+9

22. 1
+2

23. 6
+4

24. 0
+0

25. 8
+1

26. 1
+6

27. 9
+2

28. 1
+0

29. 5
+7

30. 7
+8

31. 3
+0

32. 9
+9

33. 2
+0

34. 5
+6

35. 2
+7

36. 8
+2

37. 4
+1

38. 0
+5

39. 8
+8

40. 3
+3

41. 4
+8

42. 5
+0

43. 1
+1

44. 3
+5

45. 2
+4

46. 8
+5

47. 6
+3

48. 1
+8

49. 7
+6

50. 0
+6

51. 7
+4

52. 4
+3

53. 6
+2

54. 0
+3

55. 4
+6

56. 5
+8

57. 1
+7

58. 2
+8

59. 3
+2

60. 1
+3

61. 5
+1

62. 4
+5

63. 6
+1

64. 2
+6

65. 6
+5

66. 7
+2

67. 0
+1

68. 5
+5

69. 6
+8

70. 7
+9

71. 4
+7

72. 8
+0

73. 3
+4

74. 5
+2

75. 4
+4

76. 7
+1

77. 0
+8

78. 1
+5

79. 8
+4

80. 9
+0

81. 8
+7

82. 2
+2

83. 7
+5

84. 0
+9

85. 9
+4

86. 3
+8

87. 9
+6

88. 1
+9

89. 3
+7

90. 8
+3

91. 6
+0

92. 9
+3

93. 8
+9

94. 5
+9

95. 9
+7

96. 6
+6

97. 9
+5

98. 2
+9

99. 7
+7

100. 9
+8

Subtract.

1. 14 − 5	**2.** 10 − 7	**3.** 15 − 7	**4.** 7 −4	**5.** 11 − 5	**6.** 8 −7	**7.** 13 − 6	**8.** 12 − 8
9. 2 −0	**10.** 9 −1	**11.** 4 −4	**12.** 7 −2	**13.** 10 − 1	**14.** 11 − 9	**15.** 11 − 3	**16.** 4 −2
17. 7 −2	**18.** 10 − 8	**19.** 6 −0	**20.** 9 −2	**21.** 5 −0	**22.** 11 − 6	**23.** 7 −6	**24.** 8 −3
25. 13 − 7	**26.** 4 −0	**27.** 14 − 7	**28.** 6 −0	**29.** 12 − 5	**30.** 8 −4	**31.** 1 −1	**32.** 5 −2
33. 11 − 4	**34.** 2 −1	**35.** 9 −7	**36.** 11 − 2	**37.** 7 −0	**38.** 3 −1	**39.** 5 −4	**40.** 17 − 8
41. 12 − 3	**42.** 9 −0	**43.** 8 −1	**44.** 10 − 5	**45.** 4 −3	**46.** 7 −3	**47.** 8 −5	**48.** 10 − 2
49. 1 −0	**50.** 4 −1	**51.** 12 − 9	**52.** 14 − 6	**53.** 17 − 9	**54.** 13 − 4	**55.** 8 −8	**56.** 14 − 8
57. 6 −1	**58.** 8 −2	**59.** 6 −4	**60.** 5 −1	**61.** 12 − 7	**62.** 13 − 9	**63.** 2 −2	**64.** 5 −3
65. 14 − 9	**66.** 11 − 8	**67.** 6 −5	**68.** 16 − 9	**69.** 9 −5	**70.** 3 −3	**71.** 13 − 5	**72.** 5 −5
73. 15 − 8	**74.** 3 −2	**75.** 9 −4	**76.** 15 − 9	**77.** 16 − 7	**78.** 15 − 6	**79.** 12 − 4	**80.** 11 − 7
81. 7 −1	**82.** 10 − 6	**83.** 9 −3	**84.** 16 − 8	**85.** 3 −0	**86.** 10 − 4	**87.** 10 − 3	**88.** 7 −7
89. 12 − 6	**90.** 10 − 9	**91.** 9 −0	**92.** 8 −0	**93.** 8 −2	**94.** 13 − 8	**95.** 9 −8	**96.** 6 −3
97. 18 − 9	**98.** 0 −0	**99.** 6 −2	**100.** 9 −6				

Estimating Sums

Students from the Madison School are cleaning the schoolyard. There are 28 students from the fourth grade. There are 45 students from the fifth grade. About how many students are working to clean the schoolyard?

Estimate: 28 + 45 = ?

Think: Round each addend to the nearest ten. Add.

Nearest Ten

$$\begin{array}{r} 28 \longrightarrow 30 \\ +45 \longrightarrow +50 \\ \hline 80 \end{array}$$

About 80 students are working to clean the schoolyard.

Estimate: 637 + 250 = ?

Think: Round each addend to the nearest hundred.

Nearest Hundred

$$\begin{array}{r} 637 \longrightarrow 600 \\ +250 \longrightarrow +300 \\ \hline 900 \end{array}$$

Estimate: 7,592 + 3,846 = ?

Think: Round each addend to the nearest thousand.

Nearest Thousand

$$\begin{array}{r} 7,592 \longrightarrow 8,000 \\ +3,846 \longrightarrow +4,000 \\ \hline 12,000 \end{array}$$

Practice • Estimate. Round to the nearest ten. Then add.

1. 85	2. 93	3. 72	4. 64	5. 59	6. 31
+67	+27	+53	+69	+92	+94

More Practice • Estimate. Round to the nearest ten. Then add.

7. 45	8. 82	9. 73	10. 92	11. 55	12. 91
+59	+44	+29	+37	+85	+66

13. 52	14. 67	15. 35	16. 72	17. 82	18. 72
+67	+83	+85	+49	+33	+45

Estimate. Round to the nearest hundred. Then add.

19. 243	20. 478	21. 738	22. 923	23. 753	24. 863
+852	+625	+365	+501	+750	+282

25. 493 +910	26. 805 +916	27. 259 +167	28. 483 +729	29. 351 +650	30. 946 +194

Estimate. Round to the nearest thousand. Then add.

31. 8,547 +8,323	32. 9,291 +4,762	33. 6,437 +4,428	34. 5,563 +7,727	35. 7,346 +6,930	36. 3,618 +5,681
37. 9,282 +6,507	38. 5,754 +5,257	39. 4,323 +8,646	40. 9,271 +7,214	41. 7,256 +7,675	42. 8,562 +6,458

PROBLEM SOLVING • APPLICATIONS

Estimate the sums. Round to the nearest hundred. Then add.

43. Simone and Thomas are collecting aluminum cans for recycling. Simone collects 262 cans. Thomas collects 318 cans. How many cans do they collect in all?

44. Sylvia collects glass bottles for recycling. She collects 284 green bottles and 457 clear bottles. How many bottles does she collect in all?

45. Students who help with recycling receive awards at an assembly. Awards are given to 178 girls and 137 boys. How many awards are presented in all?

★ **46.** Kuni takes 135 bottles to the recycling center. Karen takes 378 bottles, and Mr. Lamar takes 54 bottles. How many bottles do Kuni and Karen take in all?

Skills Maintenance

Round to the nearest ten.

1. 56   **2.** 438   **3.** 1,412   **4.** 72,361   **5.** 408,909

Round to the nearest thousand.

6. 3,576   **7.** 5,478   **8.** 78,449   **9.** 104,265   **10.** 116,987

Addition with Regrouping

The Hiho Circus is performing in Warrenville on Saturday. 56 tickets are sold for the afternoon show. 27 tickets are sold for the evening show. How many tickets are sold in all?

56 + 27 = ?

Step 1
Add the ones.
Regroup 13 ones as
1 ten 3 ones.

```
  1
  5 6
+ 2 7
───────
    3
```

Step 2
Add the tens.

```
  1
  5 6
+ 2 7
───────
  8 3
```

83 tickets are sold in all.

Add: 765 + 189.

Step 1
Add the ones.
Regroup 14 ones as
1 ten 4 ones.

```
    1
  7 6 5
+ 1 8 9
───────
      4
```

Step 2
Add the tens.
Regroup 15 tens as
1 hundred 5 tens.

```
  1 1
  7 6 5
+ 1 8 9
───────
    5 4
```

Step 3
Add the
hundreds.

```
  1 1
  7 6 5
+ 1 8 9
───────
  9 5 4
```

Practice • Add.

1. 37 +26	**2.** 65 +62	**3.** 589 + 67	**4.** 708 +396	**5.** 89 +964
6. 745 +408	**7.** 574 +326	**8.** 37 +65	**9.** 445 + 65	**10.** 925 +943

Mixed Practice • Add.

11. 35 +46	**12.** 46 +27	**13.** 773 + 52	**14.** 578 +662	**15.** 478 +314

16. 653 +154	17. 792 +322	18. 99 +202	19. 303 +958	20. 576 +632
21. 769 +232	22. 477 +235	23. 88 +735	24. 403 +896	25. 89 +942
26. 672 +758	27. 920 +279	28. 348 +526	29. 575 +461	30. 876 +765
31. 352 +876	32. 697 +836	33. 185 +427	34. 234 +513	35. 539 +862

36. 26 + 964 = ___?___

37. 967 + 877 = ___?___

38. 583 + 792 = ___?___

39. 285 + 412 = ___?___

40. 583 + 498 = ___?___

41. 462 + 622 = ___?___

42. 280 + 834 = ___?___

43. 498 + 209 = ___?___

44. 638 + 279 = ___?___

Use the numbers in the INPUT column. Follow the rule. List the OUTPUTS.

★ 45.

Add 9

INPUT	OUTPUT
7	?
6	?
8	?
9	?

★ 46.

Add 7

INPUT	OUTPUT
6	?
9	?
7	?
8	?

★ 47.

Subtract 8

INPUT	OUTPUT
17	?
15	?
14	?
16	?

PROBLEM SOLVING • APPLICATIONS

48. Red the Clown is 167 centimeters tall. In her circus act she wears stilts. The stilts add 128 centimeters to her height. How tall is Red when she is wearing stilts?

★ 49. A circus truck has 2 cages on it. A lion in one cage weighs 176 kilograms. The lioness in the other cage weighs 129 kilograms. What is the total weight of the animals? How much more does the lion weigh than the lioness?

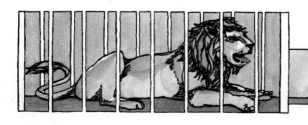

31

Adding Greater Numbers

The table shows the distances between cities on a Pacific Coast cruise. One nautical mile is about two kilometers.

| Cities | | Distance in Nautical Miles |
From	To	
San Francisco, California	Seattle, Washington	807
Seattle, Washington	Vancouver, British Columbia	126
Vancouver, British Columbia	Anchorage, Alaska	1,444
Anchorage, Alaska	San Francisco, California	1,879

Mr. and Mrs. Sanders took the cruise from Vancouver to Anchorage and then to San Francisco. How far did they travel?

1,144 + 1,879 = ___?___

Step 1
Add the ones.
Regroup.

```
    1
  1,4 4 4
 +1,8 7 9
 ─────────
        3
```

Step 2
Add the tens.
Regroup.

```
   1 1
  1,4 4 4
 +1,8 7 9
 ─────────
      2 3
```

Step 3
Add the hundreds.
Regroup.

```
  1 1 1
  1,4 4 4
 +1,8 7 9
 ─────────
    3 2 3
```

Step 4
Add the thousands.

```
  1 1 1
  1,4 4 4
 +1,8 7 9
 ─────────
  3,3 2 3
```

Mr. and Mrs. Sanders traveled 3,323 nautical miles.

Practice • Add.

1. 1,582 +3,479	2. 6,384 + 216	3. 5,602 +4,899	4. 2,546 +7,158	5. 4,062 +3,985
6. 8,543 + 297	7. 5,329 +9,687	8. 3,982 +5,341	9. 6,824 + 748	10. 3,762 +5,834

Mixed Practice • Add.

11. 3,574 +2,059	12. 6,213 + 974	13. 4,837 +2,594	14. 8,219 + 602	15. 7,983 +5,246
16. 59,765 +61,327	17. 60,989 +70,598	18. 67,905 +21,495	19. 87,502 + 4,639	20. 53,421 + 659

21. 62,583 +35,297	22. 56,235 +40,752	23. 93,728 + 4,362	24. 84,985 +30,359	25. 52,978 +53,410
26. 673,298 +485,117	27. 935,408 +257,624	28. 731,842 +225,153	29. 942,316 + 28,759	30. 594,633 +173,628
31. 438,276 +394,802	32. 536,491 +274,328	33. 409,582 +384,963	34. 375,806 +795,438	35. 952,704 +325,746

36. $6,358 + 907 =$ ___?___

37. $3,582 + 9,201 =$ ___?___

38. $38,764 + 3,572 =$ ___?___

39. $27,941 + 582 =$ ___?___

40. $568,209 + 531,778 =$ ___?___

41. $367,241 + 625,784 =$ ___?___

What are the next two numbers in the pattern?

★ 42.

3	27	51	?	?

★ 43.

4	40	76	?	?

★ 44.

201	305	409	?	?

★ 45.

400	532	664	?	?

PROBLEM SOLVING • APPLICATIONS

Use the table on page 32 to answer the questions.

46. Byron takes a cruise from San Francisco to Vancouver. How far does he travel?

47. Mr. and Mrs. Whitney began a cruise in Seattle. They left the cruise in Anchorage. How far did they travel by sea?

48. Elvira takes a cruise from San Francisco to Vancouver. She visits in Vancouver until the ship returns from Anchorage. She boards the ship and returns to San Francisco. How many nautical miles does she travel?

★ 49. Jason traveled from Seattle to Anchorage. Then he traveled to San Francisco. How far did he travel in all?

Column Addition

A telegraph message is sent from Bynard to Latham. It is then sent to Naveth. From Naveth it is sent to Ritlor. Finally the message is sent to Warif. How far does the message travel?

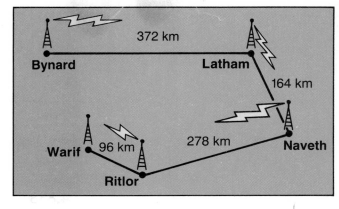

$372 + 164 + 278 + 96 = ?$

Step 1
Add the ones.
Regroup.

```
  2
 372
 164
 278
+ 96
   0
```

Step 2
Add the tens.
Regroup.

```
 3 2
 372
 164
 278
+ 96
  1 0
```

Step 3
Add the hundreds.

```
 3 2
 372
 164
 278
+ 96
 9 1 0
```

The message travels 910 kilometers.

You can check by adding up. Compare the sums.

```
 910          910
 372          372
 164          164
 278          278
+ 96         + 96
              910
```

Practice • Add.

1.	2.	3.	4.	5.
7	59	94	856	245
9	38	659	759	65
+86	+ 6	+723	34	347
			+123	95
				+234

Mixed Practice • Add.

6.	7.	8.	9.	10.
8	97	6	7	95
9	5	62	88	61
+96	+18	+31	+18	+22

34

11. 72	12. 82	13. 35,294	14. 4,689	15. 172
83	493	1,378	2,493	283
+952	+597	+ 181	+ 571	+491

16. 32	17. 304	18. 995	19. 621,692	20. 254,308
123	207	342	41,045	946,143
+492	+397	+127	+857,171	+ 27,896

21. 56	22. 7	23. 375	★ 24. 1,449	★ 25. 6,509
20	69	4,838	692,425	57,402
86	325	75,142	2,527	482,147
49	479	2,589	408,189	31,189
+53	+625	+63,972	+ 1,256	+724,567

26. 4,075 + 2,786 + 3,457 = __?__

27. 5,403 + 279 + 1,273 = __?__

★ 28. 8,982 + (3,798 + 29) + 4,006 = __?__

★ 29. 6,925 + (80,143 + 937) + 9,287 = __?__

PROBLEM SOLVING • APPLICATIONS

30. The following numbers of messages were sent over four weeks: 178 the first week; 365 the second week; 592 the third week; and 241 the fourth week. How many messages were sent in all?

31. Elaine recorded the number of telegraph messages sent each year for 4 years. The totals were 782,957; 827,468; 902,187; and 947,779. How many messages were sent in all?

Midchapter Review

Estimate. Round to the nearest hundred. Then add.

| 1. 187 | 2. 475 | 3. 268 | 4. 583 | 5. 509 |
| +224 | +356 | +341 | +920 | +391 |

Add.

6. 349	7. 586	8. 4,653	9. 72,641	10. 498
+228	+170	+3,887	+27,588	24
				+733

Estimating Differences

The table shows the number of radio and TV stations operating in some states during a recent year.

About how many more TV stations operated in California than in Florida?

Radio and TV Stations			
State	AM	FM	TV
California	228	170	54
Florida	199	97	29
Iowa	74	59	13
Michigan	126	98	21
Rhode Island	15	8	2
Texas	287	146	56

Nearest Tens

Estimate: 54 − 29 = ?

Think: Round each number to the nearest ten. Subtract.

$$\begin{array}{r} 54 \\ -29 \\ \end{array} \longrightarrow \begin{array}{r} 50 \\ -30 \\ \hline 20 \end{array}$$

About 20 more TV stations operated in California than in Florida.

Nearest Hundreds

Estimate: 750 − 482 = ?

Think: Round each number to the nearest hundred.

$$\begin{array}{r} 750 \\ -482 \\ \end{array} \longrightarrow \begin{array}{r} 800 \\ -500 \\ \hline 300 \end{array}$$

Nearest Thousands

$$\begin{array}{r} 8{,}493 \\ -6{,}028 \\ \end{array} \longrightarrow \begin{array}{r} 8{,}000 \\ -6{,}000 \\ \hline 2{,}000 \end{array}$$

Estimate: 8,493 − 6,028 = ?

Think: Round each number to the nearest thousand.

Practice • Estimate. Round to the nearest ten. Then subtract.

1. 94	2. 78	3. 59	4. 64	5. 35	6. 57
−75	−64	−29	−35	−23	−18

More Practice • Estimate. Round to the nearest ten. Then subtract.

7. 35	8. 34	9. 48	10. 69	11. 87
−24	−19	−35	−38	−36

12. 63	13. 72	14. 79	15. 57	16. 83
−39	−33	−35	−29	−42

Estimate. Round to the nearest hundred. Then subtract.

17. 593	18. 835	19. 927	20. 450	21. 469
−143	−524	−543	−256	−138

22. 457	23. 634	24. 629	25. 695	26. 283
−342	−219	−350	−457	−142

Estimate. Round to the nearest thousand. Then subtract.

27. 3,693	28. 9,727	29. 7,648	30. 8,395	31. 7,431
−2,522	−2,243	−4,257	−5,201	−3,876

32. 6,392	33. 7,869	34. 5,058	35. 9,672	36. 7,391
−4,943	−2,624	−3,229	−7,238	−2,852

Write two plus signs to the left of the equal sign to make a true sentence.

Example: 5 9 + 3 8 6 + 2 = 447

★**37.** 3 8 4 3 7 8 = 429   ★**38.** 5 6 2 4 8 7 = 554

★**39.** 9 7 2 7 5 6 = 792

PROBLEM SOLVING • APPLICATIONS

Use the table on the opposite page to answer the questions.
Estimate the answer. Round to the nearest ten.

40. How many more FM radio stations operated in Iowa than in Rhode Island?

★ **41.** What is the difference between the total number of radio stations and the total number of TV stations shown?

Estimate the answer. Round to the nearest hundred.

42. How many more AM radio stations operated in Texas than in California?

★ **43.** How many more AM radio stations than FM radio stations operated in the states shown?

Subtraction with Regrouping

The trip to Mount Rainier in Washington is 83 kilometers from home. The Leongs drive 26 kilometers and stop for lunch. How much farther do they have to drive?

$83 - 26 = ?$

Step 1
Look at the ones.
$6 > 3$. Regroup 8 tens 3 ones as 7 tens 13 ones.

```
  7 13
  8̸ 3̸
- 2 6
```

Step 2
Subtract the ones.

```
  7 13
  8̸ 3̸
- 2 6
      7
```

Step 3
Subtract the tens.

```
  7 13
  8̸ 3̸
- 2 6
  5 7
```

They have to drive 57 kilometers farther.

Subtract: $857 - 274$.

Step 1
Look at the ones.
No need to regroup.
Subtract the ones.

```
  857
 -274
    3
```

Step 2
Look at the tens.
Regroup 8 hundreds 5 tens as 7 hundreds 15 tens.
Subtract the tens.

```
   7 15
   8̸ 5̸ 7
 - 2 7 4
     8 3
```

Step 3
Subtract the hundreds.

```
   7 15
   8̸ 5̸ 7
 - 2 7 4
   5 8 3
```

Practice • Subtract.

1.	82	2.	92	3.	84	4.	78	5.	46
	−69		−87		−35		−59		− 7

6.	561	7.	815	8.	427	9.	661	10.	737
	− 82		−473		−253		−326		− 86

Mixed Practice • Subtract.

11. 36 −29	12. 51 −29	13. 75 −38	14. 63 −54	15. 53 −24
16. 295 −158	17. 247 − 29	18. 897 − 8	19. 462 −355	20. 323 − 19
21. 716 −683	22. 513 − 3	23. 728 − 78	24. 770 −310	25. 559 − 73
26. 254 − 37	27. 467 −358	28. 923 −712	29. 727 −144	30. 736 − 86

31. $316 - 52 =$?

32. $785 - 543 =$?

33. $657 - 483 =$?

34. $946 - 572 =$?

35. $619 - 76 =$?

36. $873 - 238 =$?

★ 37. $648 -$? $= 319$

★ 38. $873 -$? $= 293$

★ 39. $742 -$? $= 81$

PROBLEM SOLVING • APPLICATIONS

40. The volcanoes Mauna Loa in Hawaii and Masaya in Nicaragua both erupted in 1978. Mauna Loa is 4,168 meters high. Masaya is 635 meters high. How much higher is Mauna Loa?

★ 41. Mount Rainier is 4,392 meters high. Lassen Peak in California is 3,187 meters high. How much higher is Mount Rainier than Lassen Peak?

Skills Maintenance

Write >, <, or =.

1. 496 ● 469

2. 32,419 ● 32,419

3. 820,130 ● 821,030

4. 7,008 ● 7,080

5. 608,009 ● 68,020

6. 39,987 ● 39,987

Write in order from least to greatest.

7. 3,846; 3,486; 3,492

8. 5,421; 5,922; 5,293; 5,329

9. 15,847; 10,487; 1,121

10. 58, 313; 58,331; 58,133

PROBLEM SOLVING • STRATEGIES

Adding and Subtracting Money

Add or subtract amounts of money as if you were adding or subtracting whole numbers. Remember to write the dollar sign and cents point in the answer.

Jan pays $4.55 for hyacinth bulbs and $9.87 for tulip bulbs. How much money does he spend in all?

$4.55 + $9.87 = ?

Use these four steps to help you solve the problem.

Step 1 Read the problem. What does it ask?

Step 2 Make a plan. You must add.

Step 3 Find the answer.

Step 4 Check the answer. Add up to check.

$$\begin{array}{r} \$4.55 \\ +\ 9.87 \\ \hline \$14.42 \end{array}$$

Jan spends $14.42.

$$\begin{array}{r} \$14.42 \\ 4.55 \\ +\ 9.87 \\ \hline \$14.42 \end{array}$$

Subtract: $8.75 − $3.94.

Think:
$$\begin{array}{r} 875 \\ -394 \\ \hline 481 \end{array}$$

Write:
$$\begin{array}{r} \$8.75 \\ -\ 3.94 \\ \hline \$4.81 \end{array}$$

These should be the same.

Check:
$$\begin{array}{r} \$4.81 \\ +\ 3.94 \\ \hline \$8.75 \end{array}$$

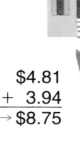

How would you solve? Write ADD or SUBTRACT.

1. Juliana has $7.25. She spends $4.80 on daffodils. How much money does she have left?

2. Chris had $5.00. He earns $3.50 working after school. How much money does he have now?

Read the question carefully. Did you choose the correct operation?

3. Nero had $4.78. He spent $2.87. How much money did he have left?

Solve.

4. Peter had $4.50. His mother gives him $3.50 to help pay for a pair of wooden shoes. How much can he spend on his shoes?

5. Juliana had $4.35. She spends $3.84 on cheese. How much money does she have left?

Estimate to see if your answer makes sense.

---

6. Chris wants to buy a bag of tulip bulbs that costs $4.29. He has $2.85. How much more money does he need?

7. Mrs. DeVries shops at the Amsterdam Market. She spends $15.97 on a set of mugs and $39.25 on a knitted sweater. How much money does she spend in all?

8. A dozen hyacinths cost $7.40. A dozen tulips cost $3.90. How much more do the hyacinths cost?

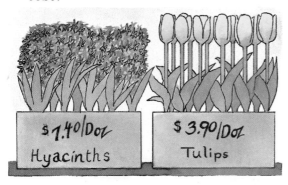

9. The repair work on Peter's bicycle will cost $9.85. He has $7.40. How much more money does he need to pay for the repair work?

10. The price of an adult ticket for a canal cruise is $4.00. The price of a child's ticket is $2.65. Mr. Vermeer takes his young son on the cruise. How much does he pay for the tickets?

11. Anne buys a clay pot for $2.25, a saucer for $.97, and bulbs for $1.89. How much money does she spend?

★ 12. Peter spends $3.45 on a reflector for his bicycle and $.85 on a decal. He gives the clerk $4.50. How much change does he receive?

★ 13. Mr. Vermeer had $45.00. He receives $29.59 when he sells some of his flowers. Then he buys a new sign for $7.82. How much money does he have now?

Regrouping More Than Once

A record dealer has 2,735 country-western albums.
He also has 1,168 folk-music albums.
How many more country-western albums does he have?

2,735 − 1,168 = ?

Step 1
Look at the ones.
8 > 5. Regroup 3 tens
5 ones as 2 tens 15 ones.
Subtract the ones.

$$\begin{array}{r} {}^{2}\,{}^{15} \\ 2,7\,\cancel{3}\,\cancel{5} \\ -\,1,1\,6\,8 \\ \hline 7 \end{array}$$

Step 2
Look at the tens.
6 > 3. Regroup 7 hundreds
2 tens as 6 hundreds 12
tens. Subtract the tens.

$$\begin{array}{r} {}^{12} \\ {}^{6}\,{}^{2}\,{}^{15} \\ 2,\cancel{7}\,\cancel{3}\,\cancel{5} \\ -\,1,1\,6\,8 \\ \hline 6\,7 \end{array}$$

Step 3
Subtract the
hundreds. Subtract
the thousands.

$$\begin{array}{r} {}^{12} \\ {}^{6}\,{}^{2}\,{}^{15} \\ 2,\cancel{7}\,\cancel{3}\,\cancel{5} \\ -\,1,1\,6\,8 \\ \hline 1,5\,6\,7 \end{array}$$

The record dealer has 1,567 more country-western albums.
Check your answer.
You subtracted 1,168. So now add 1,168 to your answer.
You should be back where you started.

Problem

$$\begin{array}{r} 2,735 \\ -1,168 \\ \hline 1,567 \end{array}$$

← These should be the same.

Check

$$\begin{array}{r} 1,567 \\ +1,168 \\ \hline 2,735 \end{array}$$

Practice • Subtract.

1. $\begin{array}{r} 572 \\ -377 \\ \hline \end{array}$

2. $\begin{array}{r} 492 \\ -295 \\ \hline \end{array}$

3. $\begin{array}{r} 4,625 \\ -2,832 \\ \hline \end{array}$

4. $\begin{array}{r} 652 \\ -\ 95 \\ \hline \end{array}$

5. $\begin{array}{r} 438 \\ -239 \\ \hline \end{array}$

6. $\begin{array}{r} 6,573 \\ -2,956 \\ \hline \end{array}$

7. $\begin{array}{r} 3,714 \\ -\ 885 \\ \hline \end{array}$

8. $\begin{array}{r} 631 \\ -453 \\ \hline \end{array}$

9. $\begin{array}{r} 19,528 \\ -\ 6,759 \\ \hline \end{array}$

10. $\begin{array}{r} 26,215 \\ -\ 431 \\ \hline \end{array}$

Mixed Practice • Subtract.

11. 6,435 −3,146	12. 8,547 − 8	13. 9,623 −4,245	14. 7,326 − 837	15. 5,623 − 57
16. 69,437 − 3,549	17. 84,124 −44,982	18. 62,552 −34,487	19. 17,286 − 8,859	20. 25,379 −10,483
21. 38,475 −24,665	22. 27,539 − 6,301	23. 94,714 −87,375	24. 62,347 −25,468	25. 95,124 −38,046
26. 224,599 −187,429	27. 857,895 − 51,497	28. 835,241 −236,897	29. 483,794 −190,468	30. 567,500 −306,600

31. $7{,}384 - 4{,}526 = \underline{\ ?\ }$

32. $6{,}208 - 4{,}107 = \underline{\ ?\ }$

33. $39{,}542 - 7{,}652 = \underline{\ ?\ }$

34. $98{,}215 - 63{,}739 = \underline{\ ?\ }$

35. $584{,}925 - 467{,}098 = \underline{\ ?\ }$

36. $654{,}286 - 15{,}839 = \underline{\ ?\ }$

What are the next two numbers in the pattern?

★37. | 49 | 46 | 43 | ? | ? |

★38. | 97 | 77 | 57 | ? | ? |

★39. | 879 | 769 | 659 | ? | ? |

★40. | 999 | 988 | 977 | ? | ? |

PROBLEM SOLVING • APPLICATIONS

41. During the first week in November, 567 jazz records were sold. How many jazz records are left?

42. On November 1, 1,075 of the country-western records were on sale. How many were not on sale?

★43. In October, 4,646 rock records and 785 classical records were sold. How many more rock records were sold?

Records in Stock as of November 1	
Type	**Number**
Classical	1,145
Country-Western	2,236
Folk Music	2,188
Jazz	3,241
Rock	5,367

★44. During the month of November, 9,748 records were sold and 6,320 were added to the stock list. How many records were left at the end of November?

Zeros in Subtraction

A clerk stacked 905 cans of vegetables on the shelves in the Foods Supermarket. 247 of the cans were sold. How many cans were left?

$905 - 247 = ?$

Step 1
7 > 5. You must regroup. There are 0 tens. Regroup 9 hundreds 0 tens as 8 hundreds 10 tens.

```
 8 10
 9 Ø 5
-2 4 7
```

Step 2
Regroup 10 tens 5 ones as 9 tens 15 ones. Subtract the ones.

```
     9
 8 10 15
 Ø Ø 5
-2 4 7
      8
```

Step 3
Subtract the tens.

```
     9
 8 10 15
 Ø Ø 5
-2 4 7
   5 8
```

Step 4
Subtract the hundreds.

```
     9
 8 10 15
 Ø Ø 5
-2 4 7
 6 5 8
```

There were 658 cans of vegetables left.

Subtract: 8,000 − 3,762.

Step 1
2 > 0. Regroup. There are 0 tens and 0 hundreds. 8 thousands 0 hundreds is 7 thousands 10 hundreds.

```
 7 10
 8,0 0 0
-3,7 6 2
```

Step 2
Regroup 10 hundreds as 9 hundreds 10 tens. Regroup 10 tens as 9 tens 10 ones.

```
    9 9
 7 10 10 10
 8,0 0 0
-3,7 6 2
```

Step 3
Subtract the ones. Subtract the tens.

```
    9 9
 7 10 10 10
 8,Ø Ø Ø
-3,7 6 2
     3 8
```

Step 4
Subtract the hundreds. Subtract the thousands.

```
    9 9
 7 10 10 10
 8,Ø Ø Ø
-3,7 6 2
 4,2 3 8
```

Practice • Subtract.

1. 600
   −275

2. 403
   −249

3. 800
   − 95

4. 700
   −693

5. 506
   −409

6. 4,000
   −3,074

7. 6,080
   − 999

8. 5,021
   −3,768

9. 8,000
   − 427

10. 9,000
   −8,163

Mixed Practice • Subtract.

11. 500 -327	12. 800 -702	13. 600 $-\ 14$	14. 700 -603	15. 900 -693
16. 6,020 $-4,394$	17. 7,120 $-6,246$	18. 4,090 $-\ 431$	19. 3,020 $-2,075$	20. 5,000 $-2,087$
21. 47,005 $-27,232$	22. 15,000 $-\ 7,079$	23. 96,645 $-53,282$	24. 27,000 $-\ 3,384$	25. 34,030 $-\ 2,496$
26. 502,530 $-\ 61,985$	27. 800,000 $-452,971$	28. 620,001 $-389,492$	29. 465,762 $-327,565$	30. 390,060 $-153,384$
31. 259,000 $-168,237$	32. 407,000 $-\ 9,386$	33. 813,927 $-\ 37,619$	34. 350,605 $-152,389$	35. 400,000 $-139,765$

36. $5,000 - 2,630 = $ _?_

37. $10,202 - 7,375 = $ _?_

38. $905,002 - 545,961 = $ _?_

39. $940,030 - 87,632 = $ _?_

Complete the tables.

⭐ **40. Subtract 237**

INPUT	OUTPUT
566	329
422	?
345	?
904	?
600	?

⭐ **41. Subtract 1,483**

INPUT	OUTPUT
4,344	?
2,476	?
3,002	?
5,033	?
7,000	?

⭐ **42. Subtract 6,598**

INPUT	OUTPUT
9,688	?
7,243	?
8,010	?
27,582	?
82,954	?

PROBLEM SOLVING • APPLICATIONS

Add or subtract to solve the problem.

43. How many more cans of Brand B beans are sold than cans of Brand A beans?

44. How many more cans of Brand A corn are sold than cans of Brand B corn?

Number of Cans Sold			
	Beans	Asparagus	Corn
Brand A	5,449	2,208	4,346
Brand B	6,540	1,191	3,233

45. How many more cans of corn are sold than cans of asparagus?

PROBLEM SOLVING · STRATEGIES

Making Change

Always figure how much change you should receive. If you must make change yourself, be sure you understand how.

Read the problem.

You are a clerk in a store that sells magic tricks. A customer buys a magic lamp for $14.33. The customer gives you $20.00. How much change should you give?

Start with the cost, $14.33.
Count on to reach $20.00.

Start	$14.33
Count 2 pennies ⟶	14.35
Count 1 nickel ⟶	14.40
Count 1 dime ⟶	14.50
Count 2 quarters or	
1 half-dollar ⟶	15.00
Count 5 dollars ⟶	20.00

You should give $5.67 in change:
5 dollars, 2 quarters or 1 half-dollar,
1 dime, 1 nickel, and 2 pennies.

OR
Subtract the cost, $14.33, from the amount given. Then give the correct change, using the least number of bills and coins.

$$\begin{array}{r} \$20.00 \\ -\ 14.33 \\ \hline \$\ 5.67 \end{array}$$

What coins and bills should you give in change?

1. A magic slipper costs $12.88.
You are given $15.00.

Start	$12.88
Count __?__ pennies	12.90
Count __?__ dimes	13.00
Count __?__ dollars	15.00

Start with coins of the least value to make change.

2. A ring trick costs $6.77. You are given $10.00.

Start	$ 6.77
Count __?__ pennies	6.80
Count __?__ dimes	7.00
Count __?__ dollars	10.00

3. A book about magic costs $6.59.
You are given $7.00.

Solve. What coins and bills should you give in change?

4. A magician's candle costs $4.73. You are given $10.00.

5. A magic wand costs $14.29. A customer gives you $20.00.

6. A customer buys 6 scarves for $9.38. You are given $10.00.

7. A set of rings costs $18.85. The customer gives you $20.00.

Use the fewest number of coins to make change.

8. A magician buys a top hat for $7.78. The magician gives you $10.00.

9. A magician buys a toy rabbit for $5.63. The magician gives you $10.00.

10. A customer buys 5 magic eggs for $3.29. You are given $5.00.

★ 11. A magician buys 2 boxes for $7.98 and a magic rope for $3.95. He gives you $15.00.

★ 12. A magician buys a cape for $18.95 and a pair of gloves for $2.55. You are given $25.00.

REVIEW

Add. (pages 22–23)

1. $9 + 3 =$ ___?___

2. $0 + 8 =$ ___?___

3. $(7 + 1) + 6 =$ ___?___

4. 5
  $+5$

5. 1
  $+4$

6. 9
  $+6$

7. 4
  $+8$

8. 9
  $+8$

Use the three numbers. Write four number sentences that make up a family of facts. (pages 24–25)

9. 7, 9, 16

10. 6, 8, 14

11. 6, 5, 11

Add. (pages 30–35)

12.   67
  $+24$

13. 342
  $+591$

14. 493
  $+278$

15. 8,954
  $+6,829$

16. 3,978
  $+1,856$

17. 26,865
  $+19,527$

18. 136,509
  $+\ 78,627$

19.   327
  6,562
  $+\ \ 919$

20.   564
  84,075
  2,996
  $+351,408$

Subtract. (pages 38–39, 42–45)

21. 75
  -26

22. 534
  $-\ 72$

23. 822
  -409

24. 236
  -179

25. 3,148
  $-\ 765$

26. 58,162
  $-49,758$

27. 365,381
  $-144,675$

28. 6,500
  $-1,372$

29. 700,401
  $-293,256$

Solve.

30. The Rileys are moving to a new town. The population there is 48,824. There are 26,958 people where they used to live. How many more people live in the new town? (p. 42)

31. The Rileys are driving to their new home. They drive 160 kilometers before lunch and 265 kilometers after lunch. How far do they drive in all? (p. 30)

PROJECT

Magic Cross-Out

Step 1
Draw a 4-by-4 square.

Step 2
Choose any eight numbers. Write them lightly alongside the square on the left and across the top, as shown.

Step 3
Find the sum of the 8 numbers. Write it on an index card. Place the card so that it cannot be seen.

Step 4
Add the numbers as you would in an addition table, and write the sums in the square. Then erase the numbers you wrote on the outside of the square.

Step 5
Play Magic Cross-Out with a friend. Have your friend circle any number in the square. Then have the friend cross out the other numbers in the same row and column.

Step 6
Repeat Step 5 until all the numbers are circled or crossed out. Ask your friend to find the sum of the circled numbers. Then have your friend look at the card. The two sums should be the same.

	7	3	5	2
6				
9				
1				
4				

$7 + 3 + 5 + 2 + 6 + 9 + 1 + 4 = ?$

37

13	9	11	8
16	12	14	11
8	4	6	3
11	7	9	6

13	9	11	8
16	12	14	11
8	4	6	3
11	7	9	6

$$\begin{array}{r} 13 \\ 12 \\ 3 \\ +\ 9 \\ \hline 37 \end{array}$$

TEST

Add.

1. 4 + 9 = __?__   **2.** 8 + 2 = __?__   **3.** 5 + (3 + 1) = __?__

4. 3	**5.** 6	**6.** 8	**7.** 9	**8.** 0
+2	+8	+8	+1	+4

Use the three numbers.
Write four number sentences that make up a family of facts.

9. 6, 4, 10   **10.** 9, 5, 14   **11.** 8, 1, 9

Add.

12. 29	**13.** 651	**14.** 289	**15.** 9,454	**16.** 3,689
+38	+ 87	+527	+7,772	+2,567

17. 29,486	**18.** 189,337	**19.** 19	**20.** 256,783
+62,764	+ 45,826	3,745	10,421
		+ 288	552
			+671,831

Subtract.

21. 78	**22.** 273	**23.** 629	**24.** 781	**25.** 4,502
−19	− 35	− 84	−125	− 796

26. 54,236	**27.** 70,506	**28.** 104,040	**29.** 435,227
−18,757	− 9,798	− 18,299	−194,958

Solve.

30. At a printing plant, 159 people work during the day. At night 247 people work there. How many people work at the printing plant in all?

31. Every day 4,000 copies of the morning newspaper have to be printed. So far there are 1,569 copies. How many more copies have to be printed?

Calendar Sums

			March			
	1	2	3	4	5	6
7	8	9	10	11	12	13
14	15	16	17	18	19	20
21	22	23	24	25	26	27
28	29	30	31			

Look at the 2-by-2 square on the calendar.

Add along the diagonals.

$9 + 17 = $ _?_
$16 + 10 = $ _?_

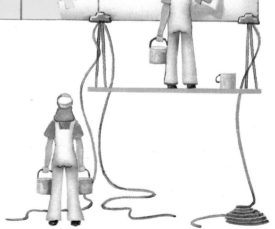

What do you notice?
Try it with some other squares.

Choose a 3-by-3 square
from the calendar.
Add along the diagonals.

$$10 + 18 + 26 = \underline{?}$$
$$24 + 18 + 12 = \underline{?}$$

Add the middle column.
Add the middle row.

$$11 + 18 + 25 = \underline{?}$$
$$17 + 18 + 19 = \underline{?}$$

What do you notice?
Try it with some other squares.

Choose a 4-by-4 square.
Add along the diagonals.
Are the sums the same?

Can you find any rows or
columns that have that same sum?

Add the numbers shown
in the four corners.

$$7 + 10 + 28 + 31 = \underline{?}$$

Add the numbers shown
in the middle.

$$15 + 16 + 22 + 23 = \underline{?}$$

What do you notice?
Try this with other calendars.

CALCULATOR

Calculator Basics

A calculator has **number** buttons and **command** buttons.

⑦ ⑧ ⑨

④ ⑤ ⑥

① ② ③

⓪

÷ DIVIDE

× TIMES

⊖ MINUS

+ PLUS

= EQUALS

First turn the calculator on.

To add 6 and 8, push ⑥ ⊕ ⑧ ⊜ . Look at the screen: The answer is 14. | 14. |

Addition and Subtraction Facts Drill

1. 6 − 6 = __?__   **2.** 7 + 2 = __?__   **3.** 9 + 4 = __?__   **4.** 3 + 8 = __?__

5. 3 + 0 = __?__   **6.** 9 − 4 = __?__   **7.** 8 − 1 = __?__   **8.** 6 − 5 = __?__

Press the *CLEAR* Ⓒ button to start over. You want to add 9 and 3.

You push ⑨ ⊖ ③ . That is wrong. Press Ⓒ to start over.

An *entry* is any button (number or command) that you push.

Push the *CLEAR ENTRY* ⒸⒺ button to clear only the *last* entry.

You want to add 9 and 3. You push ⑨⊕② . Look at the screen: | 2. |

That is not the entry you want. Push ⒸⒺ . Look at the screen: | 0. |

The last entry has been cleared. The calculator has stored 9 + from before.

Now enter the second addend. Push ③ . Look at the screen: | 3. |

That is the entry you want. Push ⊜ . Look at the screen: | 12. |
The correct sum of 9 and 3 is 12.

Calculate. If you make a mistake, use the Ⓒ or the ⒸⒺ button.

9. 845 + 148 = __?__   **10.** 999 − 998 = __?__   **11.** 432 + 234 = __?__

Turn the calculator off.

SKILLS MAINTENANCE
Chapters 1 Through 2

Choose the correct answers.

1. What number does the blue digit name.

256,947

A. 50
B. 50,000
C. 5,000
D. not here

2. Write the digits that are in the billions period.

62,357,296,400

A. 296
B. 357
C. 62
D. 400

3. Name 100 more.

967

A. 977
B. 1,967
C. 1,067
D. not here

4. Round 4,528 to the nearest thousand.

A. 4,000
B. 5,000
C. 4,500
D. not here

5. Add.

$4 + (8 + 5) = $ ___?___

A. 7
B. 16
C. 17
D. not here

6. Estimate. Round to the nearest hundred.

479
+368

A. 700
B. 900
C. 800
D. not here

7. Add.

$39 + 634 = $ ___?___

A. 673
B. 665
C. 663
D. not here

8. Add.

84,265
297
+ 1,763

A. 85,952
B. 85,335
C. 86,235
D. not here

9. Subtract.

4,024
− 867

A. 4,167
B. 3,157
C. 4,881
D. not here

10. Arthur buys a shirt for $17.29. He gives the clerk $20.00. How much change does Arthur get?

A. $3.81
B. $3.71
C. $2.71
D. not here

11. Adrian owns a bookstore. He had 4,590 books in stock. He receives a shipment of 3,758 books. What is the total number of books in Adrian's store?

A. 7,248
B. 8,348
C. 1,248
D. not here

54

Multiplication

Multiplication

There are 5 boxes of crayons.
There are 8 crayons in each box.
How many crayons are there in all?

You can add to find the answer.

$$8 + 8 + 8 + 8 + 8 = 40$$

When the addends are all the same,
you can multiply.

$$5 \times 8 = 40$$

There are 40 crayons in all.

Here are two ways to show multiplication.

$$
\begin{array}{l}
8 \longleftarrow \text{factor} \longrightarrow \\
\times 5 \longleftarrow \text{factor} \longrightarrow 5 \times 8 = 40 \\
\overline{40} \longleftarrow \text{product} \longrightarrow
\end{array}
$$

These properties of multiplication will help you.

Order Property of Multiplication You can multiply two numbers in either order. The product is always the same.	$8 \times 7 = 56$ $7 \times 8 = 56$
Grouping Property of Multiplication You can group factors differently. The product is always the same.	$(3 \times 2) \times 5 = 3 \times (2 \times 5)$ $6 \quad \times 5 = 3 \times \quad 10$ $30 = 30$
Property of One for Multiplication When one of two factors is 1, the product equals the other factor.	$6 \times 1 = 6 \qquad 1 \times 6 = 6$ $1 \times 1 = 1 \qquad 1 \times 4 = 4$
Property of Zero for Multiplication When a factor is 0, the product is 0.	$6 \times 0 = 0 \qquad 0 \times 6 = 0$ $0 \times 0 = 0 \qquad 4 \times 0 = 0$

Practice • Multiply.

1. $\begin{array}{r} 8 \\ \times 9 \\ \hline \end{array}$
2. $\begin{array}{r} 4 \\ \times 4 \\ \hline \end{array}$
3. $\begin{array}{r} 6 \\ \times 7 \\ \hline \end{array}$
4. $\begin{array}{r} 9 \\ \times 6 \\ \hline \end{array}$
5. $\begin{array}{r} 8 \\ \times 4 \\ \hline \end{array}$
6. $\begin{array}{r} 5 \\ \times 4 \\ \hline \end{array}$
7. $\begin{array}{r} 9 \\ \times 1 \\ \hline \end{array}$

8. $3 \times 6 = \underline{\ \ ?\ \ }$

9. $2 \times 9 = \underline{\ \ ?\ \ }$

10. $3 \times 7 = \underline{\ \ ?\ \ }$

Mixed Practice • Multiply.

11.	12.	13.	14.	15.	16.	17.
9 ×5	7 ×7	9 ×8	8 ×6	9 ×9	6 ×9	3 ×4

18. $7 \times 6 =$ __?__

19. $8 \times 5 =$ __?__

20. $7 \times 4 =$ __?__

21. $4 \times 9 =$ __?__

22. $9 \times 4 =$ __?__

23. $5 \times 0 =$ __?__

24. $(4 \times 1) \times 6 =$ __?__

25. $4 \times (1 \times 6) =$ __?__

26. $(2 \times 2) \times 3 =$ __?__

27. $2 \times (2 \times 3) =$ __?__

28. $(2 \times 4) \times 7 =$ __?__

29. $2 \times (4 \times 7) =$ __?__

Find the missing factors.

30. $5 \times$ __?__ $= 30$

31. $3 \times$ __?__ $= 24$

32. $6 \times$ __?__ $= 18$

33. $7 \times$ __?__ $= 56$

34. $8 \times$ __?__ $= 0$

35. $7 \times$ __?__ $= 7$

Complete. Multiply inside the parentheses first.

36. $(2 \times 5) + 7 =$ __?__

37. $(5 \times 3) + 8 =$ __?__

38. $(4 \times 6) - 8 =$ __?__

39. $(5 \times 9) + 12 =$ __?__

40. $(8 \times 5) + 21 =$ __?__

41. $(9 \times 4) - 28 =$ __?__

Complete the table.

★ **42. Multiply by 8**

INPUT	OUTPUT
5	40
7	?
?	24
?	16
4	?

★ **43. Multiply by 9**

INPUT	OUTPUT
5	?
?	27
6	?
?	36
9	?

★ **44. Multiply by 7**

INPUT	OUTPUT
4	?
6	?
?	56
?	35
?	63

PROBLEM SOLVING • APPLICATIONS

45. Aponi works in a supermarket. She unpacked 7 boxes of shampoo. There were 8 bottles in each box. How many bottles of shampoo did she unpack?

★ **46.** Heta works in a hardware store. She unpacked 6 boxes of wall paint and 4 boxes of ceiling paint. There were 4 cans of paint in each box. How many cans of paint did she unpack?

Multiplying Tens, Hundreds, and Thousands

If you can multiply ones, you can multiply tens.

4	4 **tens**	40
×3	×3	× 3
12	12 **tens**	120

You can multiply hundreds.

7	7 **hundreds**	700
×5	×5	× 5
35	35 **hundreds**	3,500

You can multiply thousands, too.

6	6 **thousands**	6,000
×4	×4	× 4
24	24 **thousands**	24,000

7×1	$= 7$	9×4	$= 36$
7×10	$= 70$	9×40	$= 360$
7×100	$= 700$	9×400	$= 3,600$
$7 \times 1,000$	$= 7,000$	$9 \times 4,000$	$= 36,000$

Practice • Multiply.

1. 70 × 8	**2.** 600 × 9	**3.** 8,000 × 6	**4.** 700 × 9	**5.** 9,000 × 7
6. 700 × 7	**7.** 50 × 6	**8.** 6,000 × 7	**9.** 80 × 8	**10.** 8,000 × 9

Mixed Practice • Multiply.

11. 80 × 9	**12.** 900 × 5	**13.** 7,000 × 2	**14.** 40 × 5	**15.** 4,000 × 2
16. 700 × 9	**17.** 6,000 × 6	**18.** 50 × 9	**19.** 900 × 7	**20.** 8,000 × 7

21. 30
× 4

22. 700
× 6

23. 70
× 3

24. 5,000
× 2

25. 900
× 8

26. 200
× 9

27. 800
× 4

28. 900
× 9

29. 4,000
× 9

30. 400
× 6

31. 8 × 50 = ___?___

32. 3 × 5,000 = ___?___

33. 9 × 300 = ___?___

34. 6 × 2,000 = ___?___

35. 4 × 800 = ___?___

36. 5 × 50 = ___?___

Find the missing factors.

37. 9 × ___?___ = 2,700

38. 6 × ___?___ = 300

39. 7 × ___?___ = 2,800

★40. 5 × ___?___ = 35,000

★41. 6 × ___?___ = 48,000

★42. 9 × ___?___ = 63,000

PROBLEM SOLVING • APPLICATIONS

43. A flea is 3 millimeters long. It can jump 100 times its length. How far can it jump?

44. An ant in the driveway is 4 millimeters long. The driveway is 2,000 times as long. How long is the driveway?

★45. A butterfly beats its wings 4 times each second. A housefly beats its wings 50 times as fast. A midge beats its wings 5 times as fast as the housefly. How many times does the midge beat its wings each second?

Skills Maintenance

1. 37
+86

2. 472
+918

3. 960
+508

4. 6,908
+5,087

5. 4,237
+3,596

6. 32,980
+47,099

7. 61,437
+49,856

8. 51,030
7,908
+ 615

9. 4,156
982
+11,207

10. 10,003
54,982
+61,876

Multiplying by One-Digit Numbers

Some pirates buried 6 treasure chests. In each chest there are 27 pieces of jewelry. How many pieces of jewelry are there in all?

$6 \times 27 = ?$

Here is a way to think about the product.

$$6 \times 27 = 6 \times (20 + 7)$$
$$= (6 \times 20) + (6 \times 7)$$
$$= \quad 120 \quad + \quad 42$$
$$= \quad\quad\quad 162$$

Here is how you show the work.

Step 1
Multiply the ones by 6.
Regroup 42 as
4 tens 2 ones.

$$\begin{array}{r} 4 \\ 2\,7 \\ \times\ \ 6 \\ \hline 2 \end{array}$$

Step 2
Multiply the tens by 6.
Add the 4 tens.

$$\begin{array}{r} 4 \\ 2\,7 \\ \times\ \ 6 \\ \hline 1\,6\,2 \end{array}$$

There are 162 pieces of jewelry.

Practice • Multiply.

1. $\begin{array}{r} 87 \\ \times\ 9 \end{array}$	2. $\begin{array}{r} 23 \\ \times\ 6 \end{array}$	3. $\begin{array}{r} 38 \\ \times\ 8 \end{array}$	4. $\begin{array}{r} 62 \\ \times\ 4 \end{array}$	5. $\begin{array}{r} 79 \\ \times\ 9 \end{array}$	6. $\begin{array}{r} 86 \\ \times\ 7 \end{array}$
7. $\begin{array}{r} 53 \\ \times\ 3 \end{array}$	8. $\begin{array}{r} 45 \\ \times\ 8 \end{array}$	9. $\begin{array}{r} 73 \\ \times\ 5 \end{array}$	10. $\begin{array}{r} 91 \\ \times\ 7 \end{array}$	11. $\begin{array}{r} 62 \\ \times\ 9 \end{array}$	12. $\begin{array}{r} 88 \\ \times\ 6 \end{array}$

Mixed Practice • Multiply.

13. $\begin{array}{r} 87 \\ \times\ 2 \end{array}$	14. $\begin{array}{r} 32 \\ \times\ 9 \end{array}$	15. $\begin{array}{r} 23 \\ \times\ 4 \end{array}$	16. $\begin{array}{r} 32 \\ \times\ 3 \end{array}$	17. $\begin{array}{r} 67 \\ \times\ 4 \end{array}$	18. $\begin{array}{r} 55 \\ \times\ 5 \end{array}$
19. $\begin{array}{r} 78 \\ \times\ 8 \end{array}$	20. $\begin{array}{r} 67 \\ \times\ 5 \end{array}$	21. $\begin{array}{r} 45 \\ \times\ 4 \end{array}$	22. $\begin{array}{r} 87 \\ \times\ 9 \end{array}$	23. $\begin{array}{r} 23 \\ \times\ 2 \end{array}$	24. $\begin{array}{r} 37 \\ \times\ 8 \end{array}$

25. 64 × 6	26. 39 × 8	27. 26 × 9	28. 83 × 3	29. 36 × 7	30. 23 × 5
31. 54 × 3	32. 52 × 7	33. 93 × 2	34. 73 × 8	35. 48 × 9	36. 56 × 7

37. $4 \times 61 = $ ___?___

38. $7 \times 77 = $ ___?___

39. $5 \times 83 = $ ___?___

40. $6 \times 47 = $ ___?___

41. $3 \times 58 = $ ___?___

42. $4 \times 76 = $ ___?___

43. $7 \times 93 = $ ___?___

44. $5 \times 86 = $ ___?___

45. $3 \times 37 = $ ___?___

Multiply. Then write >, <, or =.

★ 46. $6 \times 43 \bigcirc 8 \times 36$

★ 47. $4 \times 76 \bigcirc 3 \times 92$

★ 48. $7 \times 52 \bigcirc 9 \times 41$

★ 49. $5 \times 47 \bigcirc 6 \times 43$

★ 50. $4 \times 53 \bigcirc 2 \times 88$

★ 51. $4 \times 97 \bigcirc 8 \times 32$

PROBLEM SOLVING • APPLICATIONS

52. Some pirates buried 9 treasure chests. In each chest there are 42 pieces of jewelry. How many pieces are there in all?

53. The pirates find 3 treasure chests. There are 58 pieces of gold in each chest. How many pieces of gold are there in all?

54. There are 7 pirates who are sharing a treasure equally. Each receives 64 pieces of silver. How many pieces of silver are in the treasure?

★ 55. Would you rather find:
4 bags of treasure with 26 pieces of silver in each
or
5 bags of treasure with 16 pieces of silver in each?

Multiplying Greater Numbers

The elevation of Cheaha Mountain in Alabama is 734 meters.
The elevation of Mount Elbert in Colorado is 6 times as high.
What is the elevation of Mount Elbert?

$6 \times 734 = ?$

Step 1
Multiply the ones.
Regroup.

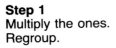
```
  2
  7 3 4
×     6
-------
      4
```

Step 2
Multiply the tens.
Add. Regroup.

```
  2 2
  7 3 4
×     6
-------
    0 4
```

Step 3
Multiply the hundreds. Add.

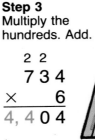
```
  2 2
  7 3 4
×     6
-------
4, 4 0 4
```

The elevation of Mount Elbert is 4,404 meters.

More Examples

```
  1 3 2
3, 4 8 6
×       4
---------
1 3, 9 4 4
```

```
  2 3 3
2 0, 3 4 5
×         7
-----------
1 4 2, 4 1 5
```

```
4 6 6 4
6 5, 7 8 6
×         8
-----------
5 2 6, 2 8 8
```

Practice • Multiply.

1. 576
    × 2

2. 906
    × 9

3. 894
    × 5

4. 579
    × 8

5. 239
    × 7

6. 2,012
    × 4

7. 6,452
    × 9

8. 2,907
    × 6

9. 7,323
    × 3

10. 4,486
     × 7

Mixed Practice • Multiply.

11. 413
     × 3

12. 654
     × 6

13. 602
     × 4

14. 256
     × 7

15. 786
     × 7

16. 9,732
     × 5

17. 9,746
     × 4

18. 8,007
     × 9

19. 4,659
     × 6

20. 3,568
     × 7

21. 78,009
     × 4

22. 16,892
     × 8

23. 42,479
     × 7

24. 36,789
     × 9

25. 19,753
     × 5

Multiply.

26. 8 × 406 = ___?___

27. 6 × 532 = ___?___

28. 4 × 2,586 = ___?___

29. 8 × 7,520 = ___?___

30. 5 × 39,772 = ___?___

31. 3 × 62,857 = ___?___

Find the products.

★**32.** 609,256	★**33.** 786,204	★**34.** 423,975	★**35.** 435,398	★**36.** 468,579
× 6	× 8	× 3	× 9	× 5

PROBLEM SOLVING • APPLICATIONS

37. The elevation of Denver, Colorado, is 4 times the height of a World Trade Center building in New York City. The World Trade Center building is 405 meters high. What is the elevation of Denver?

38. Humphreys Peak in Arizona is 2 times as high as Mount Washington in New Hampshire. The elevation of Mount Washington is 1,917 meters. What is the elevation of Humphreys Peak?

★**39.** High Point in New Jersey has an elevation of 550 meters. Mount Rainier in Washington is 8 times as high. What is the elevation of Mount Rainier? What is the difference between their elevations?

★**40.** Nina's group of hikers climbs 136 meters on the south side of Bear Mountain. Paul's group climbs 5 times as far on the north side of the mountain. How many more meters does Paul's group climb?

Midchapter Review

1. 60	**2.** 800	**3.** 4,000	**4.** 53	**5.** 92
× 9	× 7	× 8	× 4	× 5

6. 174	**7.** 325	**8.** 6,873	**9.** 2,094	**10.** 18,937
× 6	× 3	× 9	× 7	× 8

Multiplying by Tens and Hundreds

Look for a pattern.

12	12	12	12
×10	×20	×30	×40
120	240	360	480

When multiplying by tens, write 0 in the ones place. Then multiply by the number of tens.

Multiply: 50 × 37.

Step 1
Write zero.

```
  37
×50
   0
```

Step 2
Multiply by 5.

```
   37
×  50
1,850
```

Look for a pattern.

12	12	12	12
×100	×200	×300	×400
1,200	2,400	3,600	4,800

When multiplying by hundreds, write 0 in the ones place and 0 in the tens place. Then multiply by the number of hundreds.

Multiply: 500 × 37.

Step 1
Write two zeros.

```
   37
×500
   00
```

Step 2
Multiply by 5.

```
    37
× 500
18,500
```

Practice • Multiply the numbers by 10.

1. 7   **2.** 18   **3.** 46   **4.** 70   **5.** 384   **6.** 732

Multiply the numbers by 100.

7. 7   **8.** 18   **9.** 46   **10.** 70   **11.** 384   **12.** 732

Mixed Practice • Multiply.

13. 42
    ×30

14. 61
    ×70

15. 86
    ×40

16. 53
    ×30

17. 78
    ×40

18. 25
    ×70

19. 89
    ×90

20. 67
    ×50

21. 750
    × 30

22. 229
    × 60

23. 924
    × 50

24. 435
    × 40

25. 340
    × 90

26. 537
    × 40

27. 35
    ×80

28. 68
    ×700

29. 23
    ×900

30. 52
    ×200

31. 38
    ×600

32. 56
    ×400

33. 48
    ×800

34. 86
    ×500

35. 860
    ×300

36. 623
    ×900

37. 457
    ×700

38. 967
    ×600

39. 769
    ×800

40. 240
    ×400

41. 535
    ×900

42. 374
    ×200

43. 50 × 34 = ___?___

44. 70 × 49 = ___?___

45. 80 × 920 = ___?___

★46. 600 × 889 = ___?___

★47. 700 × 986 = ___?___

★48. 900 × 781 = ___?___

★49. Fill in the pearls.

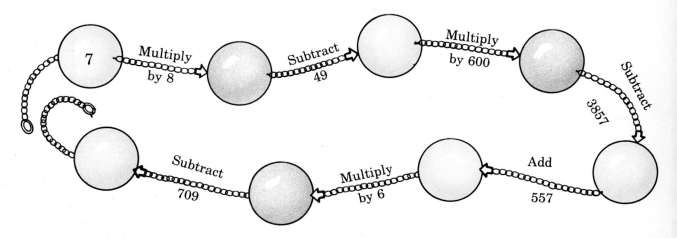

PROBLEM SOLVING • APPLICATIONS

50. Cultured pearls are found in oysters. About 20 oysters must be opened before one valuable pearl is found. How many oysters are opened if 458 pearls are found?

★51. One worker can string 20 pearl necklaces in one day. How many necklaces can be strung in 7 weeks if the person works 5 days a week?

Multiplying by Two-Digit Numbers

Each carton contains 36 books.
How many books are in 24 cartons?

Estimate: 36 × 24 = ?

Think: Round 36 to 40.
Round 24 to 20.
Multiply.

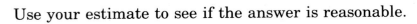

	Nearest Tens
36 ⟶	40
×24 ⟶	×20
	800

There are about 800 books.

Use your estimate to see if the answer is reasonable.

Multiply: 24 × 36.

Step 1
Think of 24 as 20 + 4.
Multiply by 4.

```
  36
 ×24
 144  ← 4 × 36
```

Step 2
Multiply by 20.

```
  36
 ×24
 144
 720  ← 20 × 36
```

Step 3
Add the products.
Compare the answer
with your estimate.

```
  36
 ×24
 144
 720
 864  ← 144 + 720
```

There are 864 books.

More Examples

```
      258            4,509          35,824
    ×  36          ×     32        ×     53
    1 548            9 018         107 472
    7 740          135 270       1 791 200
    9,288          144,288       1,898,672
```

Practice • Estimate the product, and then multiply.

Compare the answer with your estimate.

1. 69
   ×19

2. 82
   ×39

3. 56
   ×34

4. 378
   × 94

5. 886
   × 62

6. 806
   × 94

7. 465
   × 84

8. 6,870
   × 73

9. 12,357
   × 82

10. 86,723
    × 56

Mixed Practice • Choose the best estimate for the product.

11. $62 \times 85 =$ ___?___
    a. 5,400   b. 540   c. 54,000

12. $29 \times 86 =$ ___?___
    a. 27,000   b. 2,700   c. 270

13. $72 \times 904 =$ ___?___
    a. 63,000   b. 630,000   c. 6,300

14. $89 \times 394 =$ ___?___
    a. 360   b. 36,000   c. 3,600

Multiply.

15. 76
  ×43

16. 76
  ×25

17. 69
  ×67

18. 89
  ×46

19. 68
  ×69

20. 5,723
  × 68

21. 7,650
  × 70

22. 6,789
  × 48

23. 6,587
  × 25

24. 6,875
  × 78

25. 83,559
  × 67

26. 67,008
  × 89

27. 69,732
  × 46

28. 77,945
  × 77

29. 90,734
  × 60

30. 59,207
  × 19

31. 21,456
  × 97

32. 70,098
  × 28

33. 27,442
  × 85

34. 39,425
  × 76

35. $73 \times 29 =$ ___?___
    36. $86 \times 347 =$ ___?___
    37. $96 \times 893 =$ ___?___

★ 38. $36 \times 1,235 =$ ___?___
  ★ 39. $84 \times 724,558 =$ ___?___
  ★ 40. $86 \times 926,784 =$ ___?___

PROBLEM SOLVING • APPLICATIONS

Complete the table.

	Science Order			
	Book	**Number in carton**	**Number of cartons**	**Total**
41.	Text	24	34	?
42.	Workbook	60	14	?
43.	Test booklet	200	94	?
44.	Lab Manual	64	83	?

45. The warehouse shipped 97 boxes of books. There were 36 books in each box. How many books were shipped in all?

★ 46. The bookstore received 47 boxes of books on Monday and 87 boxes on Tuesday. There are 24 books in each box. How many books did the store receive on the two days?

PROBLEM SOLVING • STRATEGIES

Multiplying Money

Multiply amounts of money as if you
were multiplying whole numbers.
Remember to write the dollar sign
and cents point in your answer.

Daniel Thompkins owned his own
barber shop from 1882 to 1898.

Daniel ordered 3 pairs of barber's
shears. Each pair cost $1.18. How
much money did he spend?

Think:	118	Write:	$1.18
	× 3		× 3
	354		$3.54

Daniel spent $3.54.

Solve.

1. A high-quality shaving brush
   cost $.29. Daniel purchased 12 of
   them. How much money did he
   spend?

> **Remember to write the dollar sign
> and cents point in the answer.**

2. A hanging wall mirror with
   leather trim cost $5.75. Daniel
   needed 3 of them for his shop.
   How much did he spend on
   mirrors?

3. Daniel bought shaving cases to
   sell to his customers. Each case
   cost him $2.58. How much money
   did Daniel spend if he bought 24
   cases?

4. Daniel had to buy 4 hanging
   lamps when he remodeled his
   shop. Each lamp cost $5.45. How
   much money did he spent on
   lamps?

5. Daniel needed 4 wash basins
   when he remodeled the barber
   shop. Each basin cost $2.67. How
   much did Daniel spend on wash
   basins?

6. Each cane waiting chair cost
   $3.75. Daniel purchased 6 of

them. How much did he spend on chairs?

7. Daniel sold pocket combs to his customers. Each comb cost Daniel $.04. Daniel ordered 72 combs. How much money did he spend?

Use the facts you have learned to multiply amounts of money.

---

8. The barber's shears Daniel liked cost $.78 each. How much did 4 pairs cost him?

9. Daniel sold shaving mugs for $.52. He sold 15 of them one month. What was the total amount of money he collected from his customers who purchased mugs?

10. Mr. Emery bought 4 brushes from Daniel. Each brush cost $.55. How much money did Mr. Emery spend?

★ 11. Daniel sold hand mirrors for $.39 and manicure sets for $1.25. Mrs. Card bought 2 mirrors and 2 manicure sets. How much money did she spend?

★ 12. Mr. Ward had his hair cut by Daniel once each month for 3 years. A haircut cost $.15. How much money had Mr. Ward spent at Daniel's barber shop?

Multiplying by Three-Digit Numbers

Everyday a mail plane flies 729 kilometers from Kansas City, Missouri, to Indianapolis, Indiana. How many kilometers are flown on this route in one year (365 days)?

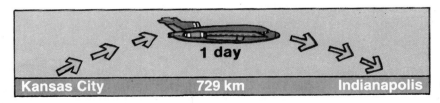

$365 \times 729 = ?$

Step 1
Multiply by 5.

```
  729
×365
 3645  ← 5 × 729
```

Step 2
Multiply by 60.

```
   729
 ×365
  3645
 43740  ← 60 × 729
```

Step 3
Multiply by 300.

```
    729
  ×365
   3645
  43740
 218700  ← 300 × 729
```

Step 4
Add the products.

```
    729
  ×365
   3645
  43740
 218700
 266,085
```

266,085 kilometers are flown on this route in one year.

More Examples

```
   7,432
 ×  657
  52024
 371600
4459200
4,882,824
```

```
  62,430
 ×   650
 3121500
37458000
40,579,500
```

```
   $62.34
 ×   507
   43638
 3117000
$31,606.38
```

Practice • Multiply.

1. 432
   ×302

2. 312
   ×214

3. 900
   ×456

4. 123
   ×203

5. 543
   ×926

6. 2,578
   × 534

7. 6,291
   × 408

8. 3,502
   × 726

9. 4,629
   × 385

10. 9,482
    × 607

Mixed Practice • Multiply.

11. 320
    ×403

12. 780
    ×680

13. 348
    ×627

14. 647
    ×432

15. 427
    ×806

70

16. 5,423
× 143

17. 8,234
× 203

18. 7,312
× 241

19. 3,512
× 298

20. 6,313
× 422

21. 2,746
× 825

22. 4,313
× 693

23. 9,615
× 981

24. 4,530
× 705

25. 7,622
× 234

26. 35,923
× 904

27. 12,543
× 742

28. 94,317
× 419

29. 71,418
× 378

30. 20,726
× 480

31. $3.20
× 456

32. $14.02
× 736

33. $34.09
× 607

34. $578.06
× 274

35. $384.29
× 508

36. 813 × 543 = __?__

37. 700 × 408 = __?__

38. 705 × 4,852 = __?__

39. 594 × 3,961 = __?__

★ 40. 372 × 62,548 = __?__

★ 41. 857 × 50,295 = __?__

PROBLEM SOLVING • APPLICATIONS

42. A mail-order company sends out 536 sets of mugs. It costs $1.89 to mail each set. What is the total cost of mailing the sets?

43. Each day about 75,000 Mailgrams are sent in the United States. At this rate about how many are sent in 268 days?

★ 44. Heta mailed 750 catalogs a day for five days. Each catalog cost $2.19 to mail. What was the total cost to mail all the catalogs?

★ 45. Willis mails catalogs to customers. He mails 1,342 catalogs at a cost of $.98 each. He mails 743 catalogs at a cost of $1.19 each. How much does it cost Willis to mail these catalogs?

Skills Maintenance

1. 95
−44

2. 72
−19

3. 725
−368

4. 429
−340

5. 6,113
− 968

6. 7,000
−3,428

7. 9,050
−8,170

8. 47,186
− 297

9. 46,916
−17,088

10. 96,000
− 7,038

PROBLEM SOLVING • STRATEGIES

Do You Have Enough Money?

When you are planning to make a purchase,
knowing how to estimate will help.
You will be able to tell whether you have
enough money to buy what you need.
Read the problem.

Glass Container	$ 3.25
Pebbles (bag)	$ 1.79
Charcoal (bag)	$ .94
Soil Mixture (bag)	$ 1.59
Fern	$ 2.29
Moss (bag)	$ 1.09
Velvet Plant	$ 2.98
Baby Tears (bunch)	$ .79
Ivy Plant	$ 1.29
Clay Pot	$ .59
Plastic Pot	$ 1.19

Bill and Ben are making a terrarium. Together they have $2.50.
Do they have enough money to buy 3 bunches of baby tears?

You can estimate.

$$\begin{array}{r} \$.80 \\ \times\ \ \ 3 \\ \hline \$2.40 \end{array}$$

You can multiply to find the actual cost.

$$\begin{array}{r} \$.79 \\ \times\ \ \ 3 \\ \hline \$2.37 \end{array}$$

Yes, they have enough money.

Estimate. Do you have enough money? Write YES or NO.

1. You have $3.50.
   You want 6 clay pots.

   > Remember to round in order to
   > estimate the answer.

2. You have $2.75.
   You want 2 ivy plants.

3. You have $4.00.
   You want 6 bunches of baby
   tears.

Find the total cost. Do you have enough money? Write YES or NO.

4. You have $7.75.
You want 7 bags of moss.

5. You have $5.25.
You want 3 bags of pebbles.

6. You have $9.00.
You want 4 ferns.

7. You have $5.75.
You want 2 velvet plants.

8. You have $7.00.
You want a glass container, a fern, and a bag of moss.

Make sure you are using the correct price for each item.

---

9. You have $9.00.
You want 3 plastic pots, 4 clay pots, and a velvet plant.

10. You have $3.25.
You want 5 bunches of baby tears.

11. You have $3.25.
You want 2 bags of soil mixture.

12. You have $2.50.
You want 3 bags of charcoal.

13. You have $3.75.
You want 3 ivy plants.

★**14.** You have $14.50.
You want a bag of charcoal, 2 velvet plants, 1 fern, a bag of soil mixture, a bag of pebbles, and a bunch of baby tears.

★**15.** You have $17.00.
You want 2 ivy plants, a velvet plant, 3 glass containers, and 3 bags of soil mixture.

REVIEW

Multiply. (pages 56–71)

1. 9 ×5	**2.** 6 ×6	**3.** 7 ×3	**4.** 2 ×9	**5.** 7 ×8

6. $5 \times 0 = $ _____?_____

7. $4 \times 1 = $ _____?_____

8. $(2 \times 3) \times 2 = $ _____?_____

9. 60 × 3	**10.** 80 × 9	**11.** 400 × 7	**12.** 5,000 × 4	**13.** 7,000 × 7
14. 34 × 6	**15.** 95 × 2	**16.** 415 × 8	**17.** 3,762 × 7	**18.** 89,754 × 9
19. 29 ×30	**20.** 85 ×400	**21.** 375 ×600	**22.** 58 ×43	**23.** 402 × 87
24. 9,367 × 41	**25.** 41,327 × 63	**26.** $7.26 × 18	**27.** 415 ×243	**28.** 2,908 × 527

Solve.

29. There are 24 marbles in each package. A carton has 48 packages. How many marbles are in the carton? (p. 64)

30. A factory makes 12,000 marbles in one hour. How many marbles can it make in 42 hours? (p. 66)

31. Jones's Variety Store sells marbles for $.89 a package. On Monday the store sold 9 packages. How much money was this in all? (p. 68)

32. Harvey's Toy Store ordered 7 cartons of marbles. If each carton costs $29.76, how much did the 7 cartons cost? (p. 68)

PROJECT

Napier's Rods

This method of multiplication was invented by John Napier in the early seventeenth century.

Use eleven strips of cardboard to make a set of Napier's Rods.

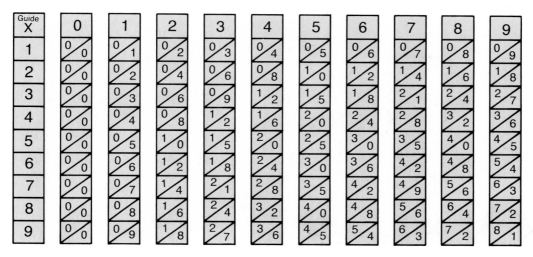

Use them to multiply: 32 × 4,967.

Line up the guide rod and the rods for 4, 9, 6, and 7.

To find the product of 2 × 4,967 use the numbers in the 2 row. Start at the right and add as shown by the arrows.

To find the product of 30 × 4,967 use the numbers in the 3 row. Start at the right and add as shown by the arrows. Remember to place a 0 at the end of 14901 since you are multiplying by 30.

Now add the products.

$$\begin{array}{r} 9{,}934 \\ +149{,}010 \\ \hline 158{,}944 \end{array}$$

32 × 4,967 = 158,944

Use your set of Napier's Rods to find the product.

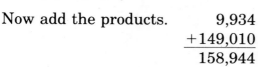

1. 3,841	**2.** 1,609	**3.** 5,137	**4.** 1,684	**5.** 9,047
× 28	× 36	× 59	× 80	× 71

Multiply.

1. 8
    ×4

2. 7
    ×7

3. 5
    ×6

4. 3
    ×4

5. 6
    ×1

6. $8 \times 9 =$ _?_

7. $2 \times 0 =$ _?_

8. $(4 \times 2) \times 2 =$ _?_

9. 20
    × 7

10. 50
    × 8

11. 500
    × 3

12. 6,000
    × 8

13. 9,000
    × 5

14. 65
    × 9

15. 83
    × 6

16. 239
    × 7

17. 2,941
    × 8

18. 49,103
    × 4

19. 36
    ×80

20. 95
    ×200

21. 529
    ×600

22. 51
    ×78

23. 439
    × 47

24. 4,206
    × 39

25. 71,388
    × 62

26. $6.94
    × 37

27. 619
    ×281

28. 3,477
    × 589

Solve.

29. A jumbo jet can carry 249 passengers. On 183 flights all the seats were filled. How many passengers were on the flights in all?

30. The top cruising speed of the jumbo jet is 625 miles per hour. If it flies at top speed for 5 hours, how far does it fly?

31. There were 34 passengers who had to pay an airport tax. The tax was $7.82 for each person. What was the total amount of taxes paid?

32. A jumbo jet was carrying 249 passengers. If each passenger paid a tax of $9.87, what was the total amount of taxes paid?

ENRICHMENT

Hidden Multiplication Digits

Try to find the hidden digits.

```
  ■ 3 7
×     4
  5 4 ■
```

■ What number is 4 × 7?
Then the digit under ■ is 8.

■ Could the digit under ■ be 2? Why not?
Why must the digit be 1?

Now find the hidden multiplication digits in this example.
Take one step at a time.

```
  ■ 1 5
×   2 ■
  6 4 5
4 ■ 0 0
4 9 ■ 5
```

■ First find the digit under ■.
Why must it be 1, 3, 5, 7, or 9?
Think: ■ × 15 = 45.

■ **Think:** ■ × 3 = 6.
The digit under ■ is 2.

Now it will be easy to finish.
What is under ■? What is under ■?

Find the hidden digits.

```
1.  ■ 1 3        2.  ■ 0 5        3.  ■ 2 3        4.  8 0 ■        5.  7 ■ 3
  ×   3 4          ×     4 ■        ×   ■ 5          ×   ■ 3          ×   4 ■
    8 5 2          2 8 3 5          6 1 5          2 4 0 6          2 1 3 9
  ■ 3 ■ 0        1 ■ 2 0 0        ■ 9 2 0        1 ■ 0 4 0        2 8 ■ 2 0
  7 2 ■ 2        1 ■ 0 3 5        ■ 5 3 5        1 ■ 4 4 6        3 0 ■ 5 9
```

77

COMPUTER

Computer Review

Computers use binary numbers. **Binary numbers** have only zeros and ones. Each 0 or 1 is called a **bit**. A group of *four* bits is called a **nibble**. A group of *eight* bits is called a **byte**. Each byte can have one of 256 different decimal values. Each byte can be translated into one of 256 different characters.

A **character** can be a number, a letter, a command, or a special symbol such as a question mark or a dollar sign or a parenthesis.

A computer can use a cathode-ray tube (CRT) for display. The smallest square of light on a CRT is called a **pixel**. All digits, letters, and special symbols can be made from groups of pixels.

Computer **storage** is measured in **K**. K stands for a storage of 1,024 bytes. A 32K computer can hold about as much as 16 pages like this one.

Hard disks contain **megabytes**, millions of bytes, of storage. A 12-megabyte hard disk can hold as much information as 6,000 pages.

In the future, storage devices such as floppy disks will be storing more characters. Today a $5\frac{1}{4}$-inch floppy disk stores 850,000 characters.

The surface of the disk is like a long spiral of 850,000 tiny magnets linked up end to end. Its surface is similar to the surface of a phonograph record.

Top view   **Side view**

Soon a process of **vertical recording** will stand the magnets on end. These new disks will be able to store 5,000,000 characters.

Choose the correct answers.

1. A group of eight bits is
   a. a bit.
   b. a nibble.
   c. a byte.
   d. None of the above

2. K stands for a storage of
   a. 1,000 bytes.
   b. 1,024 bytes.
   c. 6,000 bytes.
   d. None of the above

3. Megabytes are
   a. 1,024 bytes.
   b. 6,000 bytes.
   c. 1,000,000 bytes.
   d. None of the above

4. The surface of a floppy disk is
   a. like a phonograph record.
   b. like a spiral of magnets.
   c. Both of the above
   d. Neither a nor b

Choose the correct answers.

1. Write three thousand, six as a number.

- **A.** 306
- **B.** 3,006
- **C.** 3,060
- **D.** not here

2. What number does the blue digit name?

746,285

- **A.** 400,000
- **B.** 40,000
- **C.** 4,000
- **D.** not here

3. Round 18,509 to the nearest ten thousand.

- **A.** 20,000
- **B.** 19,000
- **C.** 18,000
- **D.** not here

4. Compare.

98,657 ⬤ 98,657

- **A.** >
- **B.** <
- **C.** =
- **D.** not here

5. Add.

$82 + 9 + 175 = \underline{\ ?\ }$

- **A.** 156
- **B.** 256
- **C.** 247
- **D.** not here

6. Add.

$$\begin{array}{r} \$62.95 \\ 3.54 \\ + \ 19.25 \\ \hline \end{array}$$

- **A.** $85.74
- **B.** $84.84
- **C.** $176.47
- **D.** not here

7. Find the missing number.

$14 - \underline{\ ?\ } = 6$

- **A.** 6
- **B.** 9
- **C.** 8
- **D.** not here

8. Subtract.

$$\begin{array}{r} 4,672 \\ -1,909 \\ \hline \end{array}$$

- **A.** 6,851
- **B.** 3,773
- **C.** 2,763
- **D.** not here

9. Subtract.

$$\begin{array}{r} \$18.00 \\ - \ \ 6.42 \\ \hline \end{array}$$

- **A.** $24.42
- **B.** $11,58
- **C.** $12.58
- **D.** not here

10. Find the missing factor.

$6 \times \underline{\ ?\ } = 0$

- **A.** 6
- **B.** 1
- **C.** 0
- **D.** not here

11. Multiply.

$$\begin{array}{r} 3,768 \\ \times \ \ \ \ 9 \\ \hline \end{array}$$

- **A.** 33,912
- **B.** 32,502
- **C.** 28,462
- **D.** not here

12. Multiply.

$$\begin{array}{r} 682 \\ \times \ 59 \\ \hline \end{array}$$

- **A.** 41,408
- **B.** 39,338
- **C.** 40,238
- **D.** not here

Choose the correct answers.

13. Ralph buys a shovel for $17.98, a bag of fertilizer for $8.95, and a package of seeds for $ .89. How much money does Ralph spend in all?

    A. $17.73   **B.** $27.82
    C. $25.61   **D.** not here

14. Willy's Garden Center has 4,000 tomato plants. Willy sells 750 tomato plants to one customer. How many tomato plants does Willy have left?

    A. 3,300   **B.** 4,250
    C. 3,250   **D.** not here

15. Jason buys 9 packages of notebook paper. Each package costs $ .89. How much money does Jason spend?

    A. $8.01   **B.** $7.81
    C. $9.80   **D.** not here

16. There are 42 cartons packed with paperback books. Each carton contains 144 books. How many paperback books are in the cartons?

    A. 5,946   **B.** 6,048
    C. 6,184   **D.** not here

17. Julianna has 86 stamps in her collection. She buys 24 more. Her mother gives her 7 more stamps. How many stamps does Julianna have in all?

    A. 93   **B.** 107
    C. 69   **D.** not here

18. Mr. Bijon buys a new sport jacket for $67.89. How much change should he get from $80.00?

    A. $147.80   **B.** $12.11
    C. $12.01   **D.** not here

19. In the year 1900, 94,883 students graduated from high school. About 33 times that many graduated in 1980. About how many students graduated from high school in 1980?

    A. 3 thousand   **B.** 3 million
    C. 3 hundred thousand   **D.** not here

20. Violet sold 186 magazine subscriptions in June. In July she sold 324. How many more subscriptions were sold in July?

    A. 510   **B.** 242
    C. 138   **D.** not here

Dividing by One-Digit Numbers

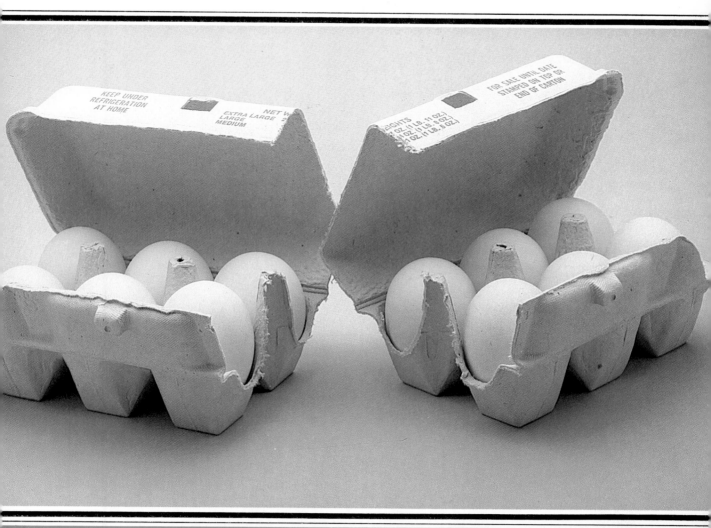

Division and Related Facts • Facts Drill • Quotients and Remainders • Dividing Two-Digit Numbers • Dividing Three-Digit Numbers • Dividing Greater Numbers • Problem Solving: Dividing Amounts of Money • Zero in the Quotient • Averages • Short Form of Division

Division and Related Facts

There are 24 students.
There are 4 tables.
The same number of students sit at each table.
How many students sit at each table?

$$24 \div 4 = ?$$

Think: $? \times 4 = 24.$
Since $6 \times 4 = 24,$
then $24 \div 4 = 6.$

Use division to find **how many are in each group.**

6 students sit at each table.

There are 24 students.
6 will sit at each table.
How many tables are needed?

$$24 \div 6 = ?$$

Think: $? \times 6 = 24.$
Since $4 \times 6 = 24,$
then $24 \div 6 = 4.$

Use division to find **how many groups there are.**

4 tables are needed.

You can write four related number sentences using 4, 6, and 24.

$$6 \times 4 = 24 \qquad 4 \times 6 = 24$$
$$24 \div 6 = 4 \qquad 24 \div 4 = 6$$

These four number sentences make up a **family of facts**.

Here are two ways to show division.

$$24 \div 6 = 4 \qquad 6)\overline{24}$$

quotient ⟶ 4
divisor
dividend

Practice • Divide.

1. $64 \div 8 = \underline{\quad?\quad}$

2. $48 \div 6 = \underline{\quad?\quad}$

3. $24 \div 4 = \underline{\quad?\quad}$

4. $4)\overline{32}$ 5. $2)\overline{18}$ 6. $9)\overline{45}$ 7. $7)\overline{56}$ 8. $6)\overline{36}$ 9. $8)\overline{72}$

Use the three numbers. Write four number sentences.

10. 3, 5, 15

11. 7, 4, 28

12. 9, 5, 45

82

Mixed Practice • Divide.

13. $24 \div 6 =$ ___?___   **14.** $36 \div 4 =$ ___?___   **15.** $32 \div 8 =$ ___?___

16. $21 \div 7 =$ ___?___   **17.** $81 \div 9 =$ ___?___   **18.** $24 \div 3 =$ ___?___

19. $7\overline{)35}$ **20.** $5\overline{)25}$ **21.** $2\overline{)14}$ **22.** $9\overline{)27}$ **23.** $4\overline{)28}$ **24.** $3\overline{)18}$

25. $5\overline{)40}$ **26.** $6\overline{)42}$ **27.** $9\overline{)36}$ **28.** $9\overline{)54}$ **29.** $5\overline{)15}$ **30.** $4\overline{)24}$

Write four number sentences.

31. 8, 5, 40   **32.** 9, 6, 54   **33.** 4, 5, 20

34. 8, 9, 72   **35.** 7, 8, 56   **36.** 3, 8, 24

When you divide a number by 1, the quotient is the same as the dividend.

$$3 \div 1 = 3 \qquad 1\overline{)7}^{\,7} \qquad 1 \div 1 = 1$$

Divide.

37. $1\overline{)8}$ **38.** $3\overline{)6}$ **39.** $1\overline{)5}$ **40.** $1\overline{)9}$ **41.** $4\overline{)12}$ **42.** $1\overline{)7}$

When you divide zero by a number other than 0, the quotient is always 0.

$$0 \div 8 = 0 \qquad 5\overline{)0}^{\,0} \qquad 0 \div 1 = 0$$

You cannot divide any number by 0.

Divide.

43. $4\overline{)0}$ **44.** $1\overline{)6}$ **45.** $2\overline{)0}$ **46.** $7\overline{)0}$ **47.** $1\overline{)4}$ **48.** $9\overline{)0}$

PROBLEM SOLVING • APPLICATIONS

49. There are 28 students. There are 7 tables. The same number of students sit at each table. How many students sit at each table?

50. There are 14 air-hockey players. There are 7 tables. The same number play at each table. How many play at each table?

★**51.** Match the quotient with a letter to find the answer to the riddle. What breaks when you say its name? Write your answer on separate paper.

___ ___ ___ ___ ___ ___ ___

$6\overline{)54}$ $8\overline{)64}$ $9\overline{)36}$ $7\overline{)35}$ $4\overline{)12}$ $3\overline{)21}$ $5\overline{)25}$

4	5	9	3	7	8
L	E	S	N	C	I

Multiplication and Division Facts Drill

Multiply.

1. 8 ×5	2. 0 ×4	3. 6 ×4	4. 1 ×1	5. 4 ×9	6. 2 ×8	7. 1 ×0	8. 3 ×8
9. 2 ×4	10. 9 ×6	11. 7 ×1	12. 0 ×2	13. 3 ×7	14. 6 ×0	15. 4 ×6	16. 2 ×7
17. 5 ×6	18. 3 ×0	19. 6 ×9	20. 8 ×1	21. 5 ×9	22. 1 ×2	23. 5 ×0	24. 3 ×3
25. 2 ×0	26. 3 ×9	27. 7 ×7	28. 0 ×6	29. 2 ×1	30. 5 ×4	31. 8 ×2	32. 0 ×9
33. 6 ×7	34. 1 ×5	35. 3 ×2	36. 6 ×5	37. 4 ×3	38. 8 ×0	39. 5 ×8	40. 4 ×1
41. 4 ×4	42. 8 ×4	43. 0 ×1	44. 2 ×3	45. 1 ×7	46. 7 ×4	47. 8 ×3	48. 2 ×2
49. 7 ×9	50. 4 ×2	51. 8 ×6	52. 4 ×0	53. 3 ×4	54. 3 ×1	55. 5 ×5	56. 0 ×0
57. 7 ×0	58. 9 ×5	59. 4 ×5	60. 1 ×9	61. 2 ×6	62. 7 ×5	63. 0 ×3	64. 1 ×3
65. 5 ×3	66. 6 ×1	67. 0 ×8	68. 7 ×2	69. 4 ×7	70. 2 ×9	71. 5 ×1	72. 6 ×8
73. 1 ×8	74. 3 ×5	75. 8 ×9	76. 0 ×5	77. 6 ×3	78. 9 ×0	79. 7 ×8	80. 2 ×5
81. 9 ×3	82. 5 ×7	83. 5 ×2	84. 6 ×6	85. 1 ×4	86. 4 ×8	87. 1 ×6	88. 3 ×6
89. 6 ×2	90. 7 ×6	91. 9 ×7	92. 7 ×3	93. 9 ×4	94. 9 ×1	95. 8 ×7	96. 9 ×9

97. 0
    ×7

98. 8
    ×8

99. 9
    ×2

100. 9
     ×8

Divide.

1. 8)24   2. 7)14   3. 3)9   4. 9)0   5. 1)4

6. 2)4   7. 1)3   8. 8)48   9. 5)10   10. 6)18

11. 9)81   12. 6)24   13. 2)16   14. 8)40   15. 3)24

16. 5)25   17. 3)0   18. 1)5   19. 8)56   20. 6)6

21. 7)56   22. 8)16   23. 2)2   24. 4)20   25. 4)28

26. 1)3   27. 5)35   28. 9)18   29. 8)32   30. 1)9

31. 9)36   32. 7)21   33. 9)45   34. 1)2   35. 3)12

36. 7)7   37. 4)12   38. 6)12   39. 7)28   40. 3)18

41. 4)4   42. 4)36   43. 1)1   44. 2)0   45. 1)8

46. 6)0   47. 5)30   48. 3)6   49. 9)9   50. 2)14

51. 5)0   52. 6)36   53. 3)21   54. 8)72   55. 4)24

56. 1)7   57. 9)54   58. 7)49   59. 2)6   60. 1)0

61. 6)48   62. 5)20   63. 8)0   64. 9)72   65. 2)10

66. 7)63   67. 2)18   68. 4)0   69. 6)54   70. 9)27

71. 5)5   72. 4)32   73. 2)8   74. 5)45   75. 1)6

76. 5)15   77. 7)35   78. 6)42   79. 8)64   80. 5)40

81. 4)8   82. 6)30   83. 7)42   84. 4)16   85. 9)63

86. 3)15   87. 8)8   88. 3)27   89. 2)12   90. 7)0

Quotients and Remainders

Susan is making party favors.
She has 22 peanuts.
She puts 4 in each bag.
How many bags does she need?
How many peanuts are left over?

$22 \div 4 = ?$

How many fours are in 22?

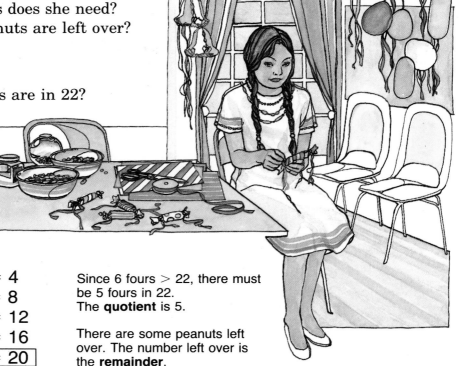

Think:

$$1 \times 4 = 4$$
$$2 \times 4 = 8$$
$$3 \times 4 = 12$$
$$4 \times 4 = 16$$
$$\boxed{5 \times 4 = 20}$$
$$6 \times 4 = 24$$

Since 6 fours > 22, there must be 5 fours in 22.
The **quotient** is 5.

There are some peanuts left over. The number left over is the **remainder**.

Use the multiplication fact to divide.

Step 1
Write 5 above 22.

$$4\overline{)22}^{\;5}$$

Step 2
Multiply 5 × 4.

$$4\overline{)22}^{\;5}$$
$$20$$

Step 3
Subtract.
Show the remainder in the answer.

The remainder must be less than the divisor 4.

$$\begin{array}{r} 5\ \text{r}2 \\ 4\overline{)22} \\ -20 \\ \hline 2 \end{array}$$

Susan needs 5 bags. She has 2 peanuts left over.

Practice • Find the quotient and the remainder.

1. $8\overline{)67}$ 2. $6\overline{)45}$ 3. $9\overline{)47}$ 4. $7\overline{)50}$ 5. $8\overline{)43}$ 6. $6\overline{)38}$

7. $4\overline{)37}$ 8. $4\overline{)29}$ 9. $3\overline{)23}$ 10. $6\overline{)41}$ 11. $3\overline{)17}$ 12. $5\overline{)49}$

Mixed Practice • Divide.

13. $4\overline{)34}$ 14. $7\overline{)31}$ 15. $3\overline{)20}$ 16. $9\overline{)19}$ 17. $5\overline{)48}$ 18. $7\overline{)25}$

19. $5\overline{)23}$ 20. $9\overline{)84}$ 21. $4\overline{)27}$ 22. $7\overline{)59}$ 23. $3\overline{)29}$ 24. $8\overline{)19}$

25. $8\overline{)60}$ 26. $8\overline{)35}$ 27. $5\overline{)44}$ 28. $9\overline{)48}$ 29. $5\overline{)19}$ 30. $2\overline{)17}$

31. $6\overline{)33}$ 32. $7\overline{)18}$ 33. $3\overline{)26}$ 34. $9\overline{)31}$ 35. $8\overline{)50}$ 36. $7\overline{)45}$

37. $5\overline{)22}$ 38. $6\overline{)39}$ 39. $5\overline{)38}$ 40. $8\overline{)27}$ 41. $9\overline{)57}$ 42. $5\overline{)13}$

43. $6\overline{)58}$ 44. $7\overline{)46}$ 45. $9\overline{)64}$ 46. $7\overline{)39}$ 47. $5\overline{)34}$ 48. $6\overline{)26}$

49. $8\overline{)30}$ 50. $9\overline{)89}$ 51. $4\overline{)30}$ 52. $7\overline{)43}$ 53. $9\overline{)75}$ 54. $5\overline{)28}$

55. $52 \div 6 = \underline{\quad?\quad}$ 56. $32 \div 5 = \underline{\quad?\quad}$ 57. $58 \div 7 = \underline{\quad?\quad}$

58. $63 \div 8 = \underline{\quad?\quad}$ 59. $78 \div 8 = \underline{\quad?\quad}$ 60. $39 \div 5 = \underline{\quad?\quad}$

61. $29 \div 9 = \underline{\quad?\quad}$ 62. $69 \div 7 = \underline{\quad?\quad}$ 63. $86 \div 9 = \underline{\quad?\quad}$

When you divide by 4, the remainder can be 0.
It can also be 1, 2, or 3.
It cannot be 4. Why?

What remainders can you get when you divide by

★ **64.** 2?   ★ **65.** 3?   ★ **66.** 5?   ★ **67.** 6?   ★ **68.** 7?   ★ **69.** 8?   ★ **70.** 9?

PROBLEM SOLVING • APPLICATIONS

71. Bill is making cookies. He has 18 bags of peanuts. He uses 3 bags of peanuts in each batch. How many batches can he make?

72. Rhona has 68 bags of peanuts. She packs 9 bags into each carton. How many cartons does she fill? How many bags are left over?

★ 73. There are 35 bags of peanuts in 5 cartons. How many bags do 8 cartons contain?

Dividing Two-Digit Numbers

There are 97 tickets for a concert.
4 clubs want tickets. Each club
receives the same number of tickets.
How many tickets does each club receive?
How many tickets are left over?

$97 \div 4 = ?$

Step 1
Divide the tens.
Think: $4\overline{)9}$.
Multiply. Subtract.

The remainder must be less than the divisor.

$$\begin{array}{r} 2 \\ 4\overline{)97} \\ -8 \\ \hline 1 \end{array}$$

Step 2
Divide the ones.
Bring down the next digit.
Think: $4\overline{)17}$.
Multiply. Subtract.
Show the remainder.

$$\begin{array}{r} 24 \text{ r1} \\ 4\overline{)97} \\ -8\downarrow \\ \hline 17 \\ -16 \\ \hline 1 \end{array}$$

Check your answer.

Multiply the quotient by the divisor. →
Add the remainder. →
Should equal the dividend. ↗

$$\begin{array}{r} 24 \\ \times\ 4 \\ \hline 96 \\ +\ 1 \\ \hline 97 \end{array}$$

Each club receives 24 tickets. There is 1 ticket left over.

More Examples

$$\begin{array}{r} 12 \\ 7\overline{)84} \\ -7 \\ \hline 14 \\ -14 \\ \hline 0 \end{array}$$

$$\begin{array}{r} 22 \text{ r2} \\ 3\overline{)68} \\ -6 \\ \hline 8 \\ -6 \\ \hline 2 \end{array}$$

$$\begin{array}{r} 11 \text{ r6} \\ 8\overline{)94} \\ -8 \\ \hline 14 \\ -8 \\ \hline 6 \end{array}$$

Practice • Divide. Check your answer.

1. $4\overline{)93}$　　2. $6\overline{)87}$　　3. $7\overline{)79}$　　4. $3\overline{)54}$　　5. $5\overline{)69}$　　6. $8\overline{)92}$

7. $9\overline{)99}$　　8. $2\overline{)58}$　　9. $6\overline{)73}$　　10. $4\overline{)63}$　　11. $7\overline{)95}$　　12. $5\overline{)58}$

Mixed Practice • Divide.

13. $8\overline{)98}$ 14. $3\overline{)76}$ 15. $5\overline{)87}$ 16. $2\overline{)75}$ 17. $6\overline{)84}$ 18. $7\overline{)86}$

19. $3\overline{)38}$ 20. $6\overline{)68}$ 21. $2\overline{)37}$ 22. $5\overline{)92}$ 23. $7\overline{)91}$ 24. $4\overline{)78}$

25. $8\overline{)89}$ 26. $3\overline{)47}$ 27. $4\overline{)46}$ 28. $6\overline{)28}$ 29. $8\overline{)90}$ 30. $8\overline{)88}$

31. $6\overline{)73}$ 32. $9\overline{)58}$ 33. $5\overline{)74}$ 34. $4\overline{)56}$ 35. $3\overline{)35}$ 36. $7\overline{)93}$

37. $2\overline{)53}$ 38. $6\overline{)76}$ 39. $8\overline{)47}$ 40. $7\overline{)78}$ 41. $5\overline{)60}$ 42. $2\overline{)67}$

43. $3\overline{)71}$ 44. $4\overline{)53}$ 45. $2\overline{)29}$ 46. $6\overline{)89}$ 47. $9\overline{)32}$ 48. $5\overline{)82}$

49. $74 \div 3 = \underline{\quad?\quad}$ 50. $72 \div 5 = \underline{\quad?\quad}$ 51. $45 \div 2 = \underline{\quad?\quad}$

52. $49 \div 7 = \underline{\quad?\quad}$ 53. $64 \div 4 = \underline{\quad?\quad}$ 54. $93 \div 8 = \underline{\quad?\quad}$

Complete.

★ 55. $(\underline{\quad?\quad} \times 5) + 7 = 62$ ★ 56. $(\underline{\quad?\quad} \times 9) + 3 = 39$ ★ 57. $(\underline{\quad?\quad} \times 6) + 5 = 83$

★ 58. $(\underline{\quad?\quad} \times 4) + 2 = 94$ ★ 59. $(\underline{\quad?\quad} \times 8) + 1 = 89$ ★ 60. $(\underline{\quad?\quad} \times 7) + 6 = 90$

PROBLEM SOLVING • APPLICATIONS

61. Felix fills ticket orders. He makes up envelopes with 4 tickets in each. He uses 68 tickets. How many envelopes does he fill?

★ 62. Juan had 89 tickets to sell. He gave 43 to Mary and the rest to Joan. Mary shared her tickets equally with 6 people and gave the leftovers to Joan. How many tickets did Joan have to share?

Skills Maintenance

Multiply.

1. 400×7 2. 519×5 3. 306×4 4. 147×18 5. 608×46

6. 981×70 7. 702×58 8. 123×900 9. 468×870 10. 567×982

Dividing Three-Digit Numbers

The scouts are going camping. They take 176 feet of rope to use to set up their tents. There are 5 teams. Each team receives the same amount of rope to set up a tent. How much rope does each team receive? How much rope is left over?

$176 \div 5 = ?$

5)176   There are not enough hundreds to divide.

5)176   There are enough tens to divide.

The first digit of the quotient is the tens place.

Step 1
Divide the tens.
Think: 5)17.
Multiply. Subtract.

The remainder must be less than the divisor.

$$\begin{array}{r} 3 \\ 5)\overline{176} \\ -15 \\ \hline 2 \end{array}$$

Step 2
Divide the ones.
Think: 5)26.
Multiply. Subtract.
Show the remainder.

$$\begin{array}{r} 35 \text{ r}1 \\ 5)\overline{176} \\ -15\downarrow \\ \hline 26 \\ -25 \\ \hline 1 \end{array}$$

Check your answer.

Multiply the quotient by the divisor. →

$$\begin{array}{r} 35 \\ \times\ 5 \\ \hline 175 \end{array}$$

Add the remainder. →

$$\begin{array}{r} + 1 \\ \hline 176 \end{array}$$

Should equal the dividend.

Each team receives 35 feet of rope. There is 1 foot of rope left over.

More Examples

$$\begin{array}{r} 31 \text{ r}3 \\ 4)\overline{127} \\ -12 \\ \hline 7 \\ -4 \\ \hline 3 \end{array} \qquad \begin{array}{r} 318 \\ 3)\overline{954} \\ -9 \\ \hline 5 \\ -3 \\ \hline 24 \\ -24 \\ \hline 0 \end{array} \qquad \begin{array}{r} 127 \text{ r}4 \\ 7)\overline{893} \\ -7 \\ \hline 19 \\ -14 \\ \hline 53 \\ -49 \\ \hline 4 \end{array}$$

Practice • Divide.

1. 2)171   **2.** 7)853   **3.** 8)194   **4.** 7)253   **5.** 5)135

6. 9)851   **7.** 4)275   **8.** 4)351   **9.** 5)645   **10.** 6)824

Mixed Practice • Divide.

11. $7\overline{)195}$ 12. $8\overline{)608}$ 13. $7\overline{)325}$ 14. $5\overline{)794}$ 15. $6\overline{)275}$

16. $4\overline{)327}$ 17. $6\overline{)462}$ 18. $8\overline{)653}$ 19. $4\overline{)584}$ 20. $9\overline{)657}$

21. $5\overline{)442}$ 22. $3\overline{)854}$ 23. $5\overline{)632}$ 24. $4\overline{)278}$ 25. $3\overline{)47}$

26. $9\overline{)198}$ 27. $7\overline{)57}$ 28. $3\overline{)945}$ 29. $9\overline{)315}$ 30. $8\overline{)895}$

31. $7\overline{)804}$ 32. $8\overline{)510}$ 33. $9\overline{)392}$ 34. $5\overline{)89}$ 35. $8\overline{)357}$

36. $5\overline{)473}$ 37. $3\overline{)777}$ 38. $5\overline{)64}$ 39. $8\overline{)477}$ 40. $9\overline{)568}$

41. $400 \div 9 = \underline{\ ?\ }$ 42. $214 \div 6 = \underline{\ ?\ }$ 43. $93 \div 8 = \underline{\ ?\ }$

44. $52 \div 3 = \underline{\ ?\ }$ 45. $329 \div 8 = \underline{\ ?\ }$ 46. $780 \div 5 = \underline{\ ?\ }$

47. $477 \div (5 + 4) = \underline{\ ?\ }$ ★ 48. $744 \div (4 + 2) = \underline{\ ?\ }$ ★ 49. $846 \div (2 + 5) = \underline{\ ?\ }$

PROBLEM SOLVING • APPLICATIONS

50. The scouts ride 15 miles in 3 hours. They ride about the same distance each hour. How many miles do they ride each hour?

51. There are 7 scouts who are trying to earn money to go on a trip. They sell 287 boxes of nuts. If each scout sells the same number of boxes, how many does each scout sell?

★ 52. Today 8 scouts are having a cookout. They buy 3 pounds of hamburger to be divided evenly among them. How many ounces of meat does each scout get? (1 pound = 16 ounces)

Midchapter Review

1. $6\overline{)49}$ 2. $8\overline{)59}$ 3. $9\overline{)58}$ 4. $5\overline{)84}$ 5. $4\overline{)95}$

6. $8\overline{)96}$ 7. $7\overline{)629}$ 8. $7\overline{)240}$ 9. $6\overline{)948}$ 10. $4\overline{)857}$

Dividing Greater Numbers

Larry owns a gift shop. He has 2,338 postcards. He is arranging them all on 4 racks. He wants to put an equal number on each rack. How many postcards go on each rack? How many are left over?

$2,338 \div 4 = ?$

$4\overline{)2,338}$ There are not enough thousands to divide.

$4\overline{)2,338}$ There are enough hundreds to divide.

The first digit of the quotient is in the hundreds place.

Step 1 Divide the hundreds.
Think: $4\overline{)23}$.
Multiply. Subtract.

$$
\begin{array}{r}
5 \\
4\overline{)2,338} \\
-20 \\
\hline
3
\end{array}
$$

Step 2 Divide the tens.
Think: $4\overline{)33}$.
Multiply. Subtract.

$$
\begin{array}{r}
58 \\
4\overline{)2,338} \\
-20 \\
\hline
33 \\
-32 \\
\hline
1
\end{array}
$$

Step 3 Divide the ones.
Think: $4\overline{)18}$.
Multiply. Subtract.

$$
\begin{array}{r}
584 \text{ r}2 \\
4\overline{)2,338} \\
-20 \\
\hline
33 \\
-32 \\
\hline
18 \\
-16 \\
\hline
2
\end{array}
$$

584 postcards go on each rack. There are 2 postcards left over.

More Examples

$$
\begin{array}{r}
1,424 \text{ r}1 \\
4\overline{)5,697} \\
-4 \\
\hline
16 \\
-16 \\
\hline
9 \\
-8 \\
\hline
17 \\
-16 \\
\hline
1
\end{array}
$$

$$
\begin{array}{r}
6,553 \text{ r}1 \\
5\overline{)32,766} \\
-30 \\
\hline
27 \\
-25 \\
\hline
26 \\
-25 \\
\hline
16 \\
-15 \\
\hline
1
\end{array}
$$

Check your answer.

$$
\begin{array}{r}
6,553 \\
\times \quad 5 \\
\hline
32,765 \\
+1 \\
\hline
32,766
\end{array}
$$

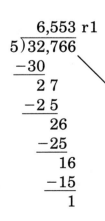

Practice • Divide.

1. $7\overline{)1,853}$ 2. $9\overline{)8,474}$ 3. $4\overline{)3,658}$ 4. $6\overline{)9,575}$ 5. $8\overline{)6,049}$

6. $9\overline{)8,424}$ 7. $5\overline{)6,457}$ 8. $6\overline{)4,575}$ 9. $4\overline{)7,435}$ 10. $9\overline{)4,029}$

Mixed Practice • Divide.

11. $7\overline{)3,164}$ 12. $9\overline{)7,526}$ 13. $5\overline{)2,895}$ 14. $8\overline{)5,699}$ 15. $4\overline{)8,654}$

16. $9\overline{)6,475}$ 17. $6\overline{)4,986}$ 18. $5\overline{)8,415}$ 19. $8\overline{)2,497}$ 20. $5\overline{)9,365}$

21. $8\overline{)2,748}$ 22. $9\overline{)567}$ 23. $8\overline{)1,528}$ 24. $5\overline{)776}$ 25. $7\overline{)4,500}$

26. $2\overline{)18,351}$ 27. $8\overline{)61,837}$ 28. $5\overline{)32,207}$ 29. $7\overline{)20,706}$ 30. $9\overline{)75,824}$

31. $8\overline{)52,436}$ 32. $7\overline{)39,540}$ 33. $9\overline{)76,829}$ 34. $3\overline{)26,952}$ 35. $9\overline{)64,273}$

36. $583 \div 4 = \underline{\ ?\ }$ 37. $4,182 \div 6 = \underline{\ ?\ }$ 38. $9,753 \div 6 = \underline{\ ?\ }$

39. $768 \div 9 = \underline{\ ?\ }$ 40. $357 \div 8 = \underline{\ ?\ }$ 41. $3,714 \div 4 = \underline{\ ?\ }$

★42. $19,754 \div (2 + 1) = \underline{\ ?\ }$ ★43. $59,283 \div (4 + 5) = \underline{\ ?\ }$ ★44. $29,547 \div (2 + 2) = \underline{\ ?\ }$

Is it possible to divide by zero?

Problem: $4 \div 0 = ?$
Think: $? \times 0 = 4$

Can you find a number that will make the sentence true?

Problem: $12 \div 0 = ?$
Think: $? \times 0 = 12$

There is no number that will make the sentence true.

You cannot divide by zero.

Divide. Write NO ANSWER for division by 0.

★45. $0\overline{)5}$ ★46. $2\overline{)0}$ ★47. $7\overline{)0}$ ★48. $0\overline{)9}$ ★49. $0\overline{)6}$

PROBLEM SOLVING • APPLICATIONS

50. Laura's Gift Shop receives a shipment of 3,782 key chains. Laura divides them equally into 4 boxes. How many key chains are in each box? How many are left over?

★51. Tara chooses 126 different picture postcards from a catalog. She orders 4 dozen of each kind. When she receives the order she puts the postcards into packets of 8. How many packets can she make?

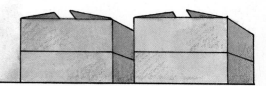

PROBLEM SOLVING · STRATEGIES

Dividing Amounts of Money

Divide amounts of money as if you were dividing whole numbers. Remember to write the dollar sign and cents point in the answer.

Yoko owns a chain of music stores called Cymbals. She orders a case of harmonicas for $35.70. There are 6 harmonicas in the case. How much does each harmonica cost?

Think:
```
      595
  6)3570
   -30↓|
     57|
    -54↓
      30
     -30
       0
```

Write:
```
    $ 5.95
  6)$35.70
   -30 ↓|
     5 7|
    -5 4↓
       30
      -30
        0
```

Each harmonica costs $5.95.

Solve.

1. A piano teacher buys 8 copies of her favorite songbook at Cymbals. She spends $30.32. How much does each book cost?

2. Metronomes are packed 4 to a case. Yoko orders one case for $88.60. How much does each metronome cost?

3. A customer signs up for 6 guitar lessons. She pays the cashier $76.50. How much does each lesson cost?

Use multiplication to check division.

4. Mrs. Budd buys 2 clarinets that cost the same amount. She spends $453.70. How much does each clarinet cost?

5. Brass cymbals come packed 8 to a case. Yoko orders one case for $70.80. How much does each cymbal cost?

6. A choral director buys 9 copies of sheet music for $8.01. How much does each copy of sheet music cost?

Remember to write the dollar sign and cents point in the answer.

---

7. Cymbals is having a special sale on tapes. They are selling any 3 tapes for $19.77. How much does each tape cost?

8. A case of electronic guitar tuners cost Yoko $226.50. There are 6 tuners in each case. How much does Yoko pay for each tuner?

9. The Westbrook School wants to buy 2 studio-size student guitars. Yoko charges the school $138.64. What is the price of each guitar?

10. Country and western albums are on sale, 5 for $26.95. What is the price of each album?

★11. The padded seats that drummers use come packed 4 to a case. Yoko orders 2 cases. She spends a total of $123.44. How much does each seat cost?

★12. The regular price for 5 organ lessons is $78.75. Cymbals is having a special this week—5 lessons for $66.45. How much money can you save on each lesson?

Zero in the Quotient

A truck arrives at a lumber yard with 2,437 pieces of wood paneling. The paneling is unloaded and put into 6 equal piles. How many pieces of paneling are in each pile? How many pieces are left over?

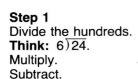

$2,437 \div 6 = ?$

Step 1
Divide the hundreds.
Think: 6)24.
Multiply.
Subtract.

```
      4
6)2,437
 -2 4
```

Step 2
Divide the tens.
Think: 6)3.
Multiply.
Subtract.

```
     40
6)2,437
 -2 4↓
      3
     -0
      3
```

Step 3
Divide the ones.
Think: 6)37.
Multiply.
Subtract.

```
    406 r1
6)2,437
 -2 4
     3
    -0↓
    37
   -36
     1
```

Check your answer.

Multiply the quotient by the divisor. ⟶
Add the remainder. →
Should equal the dividend.

```
   406
 ×   6
 2,436
 +   1
 2,437
```

406 pieces of paneling are in each pile. There is 1 piece left over.

More Examples

```
    870 r3
4)3,483
 -3 2
   28
  -28
    3
   -0
    3
```

```
  $ 3.09
8)$24.72
 -24
   7
  -0
  72
 -72
   0
```

```
   6,207 r4
6)37,246
 -36
   1 2
  -1 2
     4
    -0
    46
   -42
     4
```

Practice • Divide.

1. 7)4,219   **2.** 3)1,224   **3.** 7)765   **4.** 8)4,800   **5.** 5)4,152

6. 4)1,750   **7.** 4)1,240   **8.** 6)4,207   **9.** 3)925   **10.** 9)4,558

96

Mixed Practice • Divide.

11. $4\overline{)1,231}$ **12.** $6\overline{)4,325}$ **13.** $2\overline{)861}$ **14.** $5\overline{)3,018}$ **15.** $7\overline{)1,964}$

16. $7\overline{)4,253}$ **17.** $5\overline{)4,506}$ **18.** $9\overline{)6,339}$ **19.** $4\overline{)3,622}$ **20.** $2\overline{)1,821}$

21. $5\overline{)3,263}$ **22.** $8\overline{)3,247}$ **23.** $9\overline{)63,538}$ **24.** $6\overline{)24,577}$ **25.** $8\overline{)40,786}$

26. $8\overline{)\$57.60}$ **27.** $3\overline{)\$24.27}$ **28.** $6\overline{)\$78.42}$ **29.** $4\overline{)\$25.12}$ **30.** $9\overline{)\$345.87}$

31. $1,418 \div 2 = \underline{\ ?\ }$ **32.** $1,876 \div 3 = \underline{\ ?\ }$ **33.** $1,354 \div 5 = \underline{\ ?\ }$

34. $3,000 \div 5 = \underline{\ ?\ }$ **35.** $2,157 \div 6 = \underline{\ ?\ }$ **36.** $3,675 \div 9 = \underline{\ ?\ }$

★ **37.** $15,674 \div (4 + 3) = \underline{\ ?\ }$ ★ **38.** $71,636 \div (3 + 1) = \underline{\ ?\ }$ ★ **39.** $81,247 \div (4 + 2) = \underline{\ ?\ }$

Look for a pattern.

40. $10,000,008 \div 9 = \underline{\ ?\ }$

$20,000,007 \div 9 = \underline{\ ?\ }$

$30,000,006 \div 9 = \underline{\ ?\ }$

$40,000,005 \div 9 = \underline{\ ?\ }$

$50,000,004 \div 9 = \underline{\ ?\ }$

$60,000,003 \div 9 = \underline{\ ?\ }$

$70,000,002 \div 9 = \underline{\ ?\ }$

$80,000,001 \div 9 = \underline{\ ?\ }$

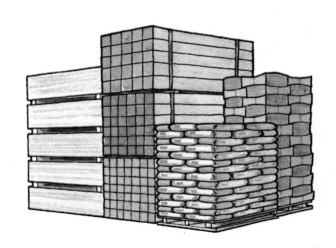

PROBLEM SOLVING • APPLICATIONS

41. In a lumberyard 1,043 planks are put into 5 equal piles. How many planks are in each pile? How many are left over?

★ **42.** Andrew buys 3 boxes of wall-covering tiles for $24.12. Each box contains 6 tiles. How much does each tile cost?

Skills Maintenance

1. $\begin{array}{r} 60 \\ -25 \\ \hline \end{array}$ **2.** $\begin{array}{r} 320 \\ -\ 80 \\ \hline \end{array}$ **3.** $\begin{array}{r} 400 \\ -\ 96 \\ \hline \end{array}$ **4.** $\begin{array}{r} 3,219 \\ -\ 499 \\ \hline \end{array}$ **5.** $\begin{array}{r} 6,384 \\ -\ 235 \\ \hline \end{array}$

6. $\begin{array}{r} 11,428 \\ -\ 519 \\ \hline \end{array}$ **7.** $\begin{array}{r} 51,414 \\ -\ 3,600 \\ \hline \end{array}$ **8.** $\begin{array}{r} 62,081 \\ -\ 3,992 \\ \hline \end{array}$ **9.** $\begin{array}{r} 87,000 \\ -58,914 \\ \hline \end{array}$ **10.** $\begin{array}{r} 91,141 \\ -66,059 \\ \hline \end{array}$

Averages

Althea visits an amusement park while she is on vacation. In one game she throws 5 balls. Her **average** score for a throw is 29. This does not mean that she gets a score of 29 on each throw. These are Althea's scores.

$$27, 31, 28, 30, 29$$

To find the **average**:

Step 1 Find the sum of the scores.

$$27 + 31 + 28 + 30 + 29 = 145$$

Step 2 Divide the sum by the number of scores.

```
                           29 ← average
number of scores ⟶  5 ) 145 ← sum of scores
                         −10↓
                          45
                         −45
                           0
```

The average score is 29.

Practice • Find the averages.

1. 20, 18, 16

2. 48, 39, 30, 55

3. 37, 19, 56, 30, 23

4. 34, 22, 28

5. 27, 38, 42, 17

6. 27, 23, 26, 24

More Practice • Find the averages.

7. 87, 11, 19

8. 84, 60, 74, 70

9. 100, 67, 129, 96

10. 32, 25, 30, 28, 35

11. 17, 36, 46

12. 13, 29, 45, 11, 47

13. 18, 6, 11, 15, 9, 13

14. 67, 29, 87, 49

15. 34, 160, 85

16. 80, 105, 87, 94, 69

17. 17, 8, 12, 5, 8, 4

18. 121, 87, 95, 121, 97, 85

⋆**19.** 52, 34, 62, 23, 71, 52

⋆**20.** 7, 8, 6, 3, 11, 9, 5

PROBLEM SOLVING • APPLICATIONS

Cindy and her family are on vacation. They keep a record of the distance they travel and the money they spend.

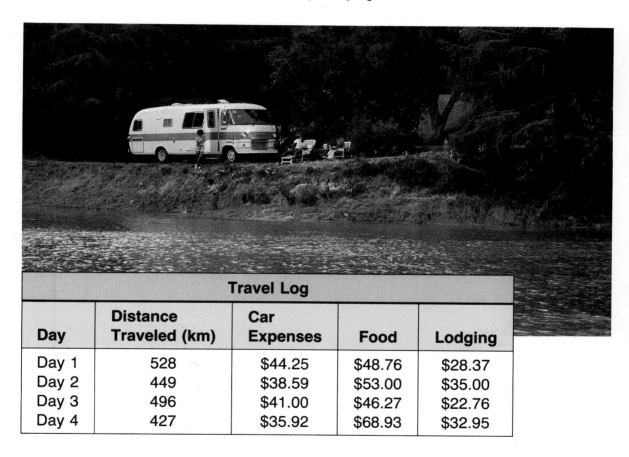

Travel Log				
Day	Distance Traveled (km)	Car Expenses	Food	Lodging
Day 1	528	$44.25	$48.76	$28.37
Day 2	449	$38.59	$53.00	$35.00
Day 3	496	$41.00	$46.27	$22.76
Day 4	427	$35.92	$68.93	$32.95

What is the average number of

21. kilometers traveled each day?

22. dollars spent on car expenses each day?

23. dollars spent on food each day?

24. dollars spent on lodging each day?

⋆**25.** What is the average cost per day for the vacation?

Divide. (pages 82–83, 86–93, 96–97)

1. $4\overline{)16}$ 2. $7\overline{)35}$ 3. $9\overline{)27}$ 4. $6\overline{)42}$

5. $2\overline{)15}$ 6. $5\overline{)39}$ 7. $4\overline{)34}$ 8. $7\overline{)60}$

9. $3\overline{)81}$ 10. $3\overline{)77}$ 11. $5\overline{)67}$ 12. $7\overline{)98}$

13. $5\overline{)119}$ 14. $4\overline{)288}$ 15. $6\overline{)894}$ 16. $2\overline{)831}$

17. $8\overline{)2,730}$ 18. $5\overline{)9,347}$ 19. $9\overline{)30,836}$ 20. $8\overline{)41,129}$

21. $3\overline{)327}$ 22. $7\overline{)2,145}$ 23. $6\overline{)16,259}$ 24. $5\overline{)\$45.30}$

Find the averages. (pages 98–99)

25. 17, 25, 42

26. 116, 95, 62, 47, 70

27. 19, 27, 47, 23

28. 4, 17, 28, 17, 89

29. 86, 52, 29, 53

30. 6, 26, 116, 118, 38, 92

Solve.

31. A satellite makes 9 orbits of the earth each day. The satellite has made 873 orbits. How many days has the satellite been in orbit? (p. 90)

32. The lengths of the last four Apollo space flights were 9 days, 12 days, 11 days, and 12 days. What was the average length of each flight? (p. 98)

33. A satellite orbits the moon 9,576 times. If the satellite orbits the moon 6 times each day, how many days has the satellite orbited the moon? (p. 92)

34. One morning 5 people visited the space center. The cost was $47.25. If each person paid the same amount, how much did the visit cost per person? (p. 94)

PROJECT

What Day of the Week Was It?

Follow the steps to find the day of the week for any date from 1753 to 1999.

Table 1	Month Number			
January	1	June	5	
leap year	0	July	0	
February	4	August	3	
leap year	3	September	6	
March	4	October	1	
April	0	November	4	
May	2	December	6	

Table 2	Year Number
1900–1999	0
1800–1899	2
1753–1799	4

What day of the week was May 13, 1969?

Step 1

Write the last two digits of the year. 69

Find the quotient of the last two digits of the year divided by 4, without the remainder. (If there is no remainder, the year is a leap year.) 17
Write the month number from Table 1 (May: 2), the day of the month, 2
and the year number from Table 2. (1900–1999: 0) 13

Step 2

Find the sum. 0

Sum: 101

Step 3

Divide the sum by 7. $101 \div 7 = 14 \text{ r} 3$

Step 4

Use the remainder to find the day.

Sun.	Mon.	Tues.	Wed.	Thurs.	Fri.	Sat.
1	2	3	4	5	6	0

May 13, 1969, was a Tuesday.

Find the day of the week for each date.

1. July 4, 1776

2. January 1, 1960

3. February 14, 1859

4. December 31, 1999

5. July 20, 1769

6. Your birthdate

TEST

Divide.

1. $2\overline{)18}$ **2.** $8\overline{)32}$ **3.** $5\overline{)25}$ **4.** $9\overline{)81}$

5. $9\overline{)50}$ **6.** $4\overline{)38}$ **7.** $6\overline{)45}$ **8.** $7\overline{)59}$

9. $4\overline{)92}$ **10.** $6\overline{)83}$ **11.** $3\overline{)56}$ **12.** $8\overline{)59}$

13. $6\overline{)138}$ **14.** $8\overline{)579}$ **15.** $5\overline{)895}$ **16.** $7\overline{)278}$

17. $7\overline{)3,559}$ **18.** $9\overline{)5,589}$ **19.** $6\overline{)17,679}$ **20.** $9\overline{)29,862}$

21. $4\overline{)826}$ **22.** $3\overline{)1,770}$ **23.** $7\overline{)16,142}$ **24.** $6\overline{)\$275.76}$

Find the averages.

25. 69, 43, 55, 25

26. 86, 92, 105, 100, 80, 89

27. 25, 37, 86, 195, 602

28. 76, 27, 34, 49, 57, 21

29. 195, 376, 487, 526

30. 101, 207, 95, 46, 128, 65

Solve.

31. The school marching band buys 5 new trumpets. The total cost is $439.75. What is the cost of each trumpet?

32. There are 6 marching bands in the parade. There are 210 band members in all. What is the average number of people in each band?

33. Carl spent $7.71 on reeds for his clarinet. If he bought 3 reeds, how much did he spend for each reed?

34. There were 17,256 people in the arena watching the band competition. If there are 8 seating sections, how many people were in each section?

ENRICHMENT

Short Form of Division

You can use a shortcut to divide.

Divide: 1,014 ÷ 4.

Step 1
Find the hundreds.
Think: 4)‾10.
2 × 4 = 8
10 − 8 = 2
Write the remainder
by the tens.

$$\begin{array}{r} 2 \\ 4\overline{)1{,}0\,{}^21\ 4} \end{array}$$

Step 2
Find the tens.
Think: 4)‾21.
5 × 4 = 20
21 − 20 = 1
Write the remainder
by the ones.

$$\begin{array}{r} 2\ 5 \\ 4\overline{)1{,}0\,{}^21\,{}^14} \end{array}$$

Step 3
Find the ones.
Think: 4)‾14.
3 × 4 = 12
14 − 12 = 2
Show the remainder
in the answer.

$$\begin{array}{r} 2\ 5\ 3\ r2 \\ 4\overline{)1{,}0\,{}^21\,{}^14} \end{array}$$

1014 ÷ 4 = 253 r2

Divide. Use the short form of division.

1. 7)‾2,593   2. 4)‾1,682   3. 5)‾3,692   4. 8)‾7,140   5. 3)‾2,673

6. 9)‾7,384   7. 6)‾5,102   8. 2)‾1,375   9. 7)‾4,831   10. 9)‾5,930

Divide. Use short division to find the thousands first.

11. 6)‾8,392   12. 9)‾9,107   13. 3)‾5,426   14. 8)‾9,721   15. 5)‾7,466

16. 4)‾6,751   17. 7)‾8,572   18. 2)‾7,908   19. 9)‾9,726   20. 4)‾8,573

CALCULATOR

Dividing and Multiplying with a Calculator

Calculators are helpful in finding averages.

Find the average of these prices: $47, $36, and $82.
Follow the method carefully.

Push **4 7**. Check the screen to be sure you have 47.

Push **+ 3 6**. Check the screen to be sure you have 36.

Push **+**. The screen shows 83. Over 40 plus over 30 is about 80.

Push **8 2**. Check the screen to be sure you have 82.

Push **÷**. The screen shows 165. 83 plus 82 is 165.

You have your sum. You have started to divide it by the number of purchases.

Push **3**. Check 3 on the screen. Then push **=**.

The average is $55. You do not have to write down the sum.

The calculator saves it for you.

Use your calculator to find the averages. Be sure to write the dollar signs.

1. $92, $98, $94, $96
2. $75, $82, $50, $44, $49
3. $100, $92, $60
4. $25, $63, $84, $52
5. $14, $8, $24, $6, $15, $5
6. $80, $74, $33, $61
7. $248, $372, $301
8. $1, $5, $4, $6, $3, $7, $2, $9, $8

Now use the calculator to divide amounts of money. $5\overline{)\$8.50} = ?$

First estimate that the answer is about $2.00.

Push **8 · 5 0 ÷ 5 =**.   The screen shows 1.7.
The calculator will not show any ending zero or zeros after a decimal point.

The calculator does not have dollar signs. Write dollar signs and the zero or zeros in the answer. Write the answer as $1.70.

Divide using the calculator.

9. $7)\overline{\$22.40}$ **10.** $9)\overline{\$9.81}$ **11.** $4)\overline{\$82.52}$ **12.** $2)\overline{\$46.22}$

13. $3)\overline{\$94.41}$ **14.** $6)\overline{\$5.82}$ **15.** $8)\overline{\$92.08}$ **16.** $1)\overline{\$98.23}$

Use your calculator to find the averages.

17. $88, $22, $99, $11   **18.** $422, $224, $50

19. $14, $15, $16, $17, $18   **20.** $743, $342, $437, $478

21. $853, $1, $1, $1, $1, $1   **22.** $100, $100, $100, $0

Divide.

23. $1)\overline{\$83.94}$ **24.** $7)\overline{\$0.84}$ **25.** $5)\overline{\$47.70}$ **26.** $9)\overline{\$97.56}$

27. $56.40 ÷ 6 = __?__   **28.** $36.96 ÷ 8 = __?__

29. $49.72 ÷ 2 = __?__   **30.** $17.52 ÷ 3 = __?__

31. $9)\overline{\$43.83}$ **32.** $7)\overline{\$91.00}$ **33.** $5)\overline{\$0.00}$ **34.** $2)\overline{\$88.88}$

The calculator also makes it easy to multiply amounts of money.
Remember to check the display for each number you enter.

$\begin{array}{r} \$42.45 \\ \times \quad 23 \end{array}$ Push

Write a dollar sign in the answer.

Your answer should be $976.35.

Estimate to check: $40 times 20 is about $800.
The answer looks correct.

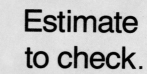

Estimate to check.

Multiply using the calculator. Estimate to check.

35. $\begin{array}{r} \$76.34 \\ \times \quad 99 \end{array}$ **36.** $\begin{array}{r} \$8.02 \\ \times \quad 70 \end{array}$ **37.** $\begin{array}{r} \$43.89 \\ \times \quad 84 \end{array}$ **38.** $\begin{array}{r} \$96.23 \\ \times \quad 23 \end{array}$

39. $\begin{array}{r} \$40.00 \\ \times \quad 73 \end{array}$ **40.** $\begin{array}{r} \$99.99 \\ \times \quad 48 \end{array}$ **41.** $\begin{array}{r} \$50.12 \\ \times \quad 93 \end{array}$ **42.** $\begin{array}{r} \$19.63 \\ \times \quad 51 \end{array}$

SKILLS MAINTENANCE

Chapters 1 Through 4

Choose the correct answers.

1. Write the expanded form.

2,096

- **A.** 2,000 + 900 + 60
- **B.** 2,000 + 900 + 6
- **C.** 2,000 + 90 + 6
- **D.** not here

2. Add.

$$6 + (3 + 5) = \underline{\ ?\ }$$

- **A.** 14
- **B.** 90
- **C.** 21
- **D.** not here

3. Estimate. Round to the nearest ten.

$$\begin{array}{r} 86 \\ +48 \\ \hline \end{array}$$

- **A.** 120
- **B.** 140
- **C.** 130
- **D.** not here

4. Add.

$$1,367 + 89 + 657 = \underline{\ ?\ }$$

- **A.** 1,987
- **B.** 1,914
- **C.** 2,113
- **D.** not here

5. Subtract.

$$\begin{array}{r} \$645.00 \\ -\ 126.74 \\ \hline \end{array}$$

- **A.** $521.36
- **B.** $518.26
- **C.** $771.74
- **D.** not here

6. Find the missing factor.

$$8 \times \underline{\ ?\ } = 56$$

- **A.** 5
- **B.** 6
- **C.** 9
- **D.** not here

7. Multiply.

$$80 \times 200 = \underline{\ ?\ }$$

- **A.** 1,600
- **B.** 16,000
- **C.** 160,000
- **D.** not here

8. Divide.

$$34 \div 8 = \underline{\ ?\ }$$

- **A.** 4 r2
- **B.** 3 r6
- **C.** 4 r4
- **D.** not here

9. Divide.

$$7\overline{)3,865}$$

- **A.** 553 r4
- **B.** 564 r3
- **C.** 552 r1
- **D.** not here

10. The lumberyard had 600 bags of gravel. Mr. Monte buys 186 bags. How many bags of gravel are left?

- **A.** 504
- **B.** 414
- **C.** 786
- **D.** not here

11. Mrs. Starr buys 9 pieces of paneling. The total cost is $89.55. What is the price of each piece of paneling?

- **A.** $9.85
- **B.** $805.95
- **C.** $9.95
- **D.** not here

Dividing by Two-Digit Numbers

SPECIAL
10 FOR 90¢

Dividing by Tens

You can use a basic fact to help you divide by tens.

$$1\overline{)6} \;\; 6 \qquad 10\overline{)60} \;\; 6$$

$$2\overline{)8} \;\; 4 \qquad 20\overline{)80} \;\; 4$$

$$3\overline{)21} \;\; 7 \qquad 30\overline{)210} \;\; 7$$

$$6\overline{)30} \;\; 5 \qquad 60\overline{)300} \;\; 5$$

Lois has collected 367 stamps. She pastes 40 stamps on each page of a stamp album. How many pages does she use? How many stamps are left over?

$$367 \div 40 = ?$$

Step 1
Think: $4\overline{)36}$.
Write 9 in the ones place.

$$40\overline{)367} \;\; 9$$

Step 2
Multiply.
$9 \times 40 = 360$

$$40\overline{)367} \;\; 9$$
$$360$$

Step 3
Subtract.
Show the remainder.

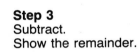
Is the remainder less than 40?

$$40\overline{)367} \;\; 9\ r7$$
$$-360$$
$$7$$

Lois uses 9 pages. There are 7 stamps left over.

Practice • Divide.

1. $10\overline{)80}$ 2. $70\overline{)210}$ 3. $50\overline{)300}$ 4. $30\overline{)90}$ 5. $80\overline{)240}$

6. $70\overline{)235}$ 7. $30\overline{)147}$ 8. $50\overline{)374}$ 9. $10\overline{)56}$ 10. $40\overline{)256}$

Mixed Practice • Divide.

11. $20\overline{)40}$ 12. $60\overline{)360}$ 13. $70\overline{)490}$ 14. $50\overline{)450}$ 15. $10\overline{)70}$

16. $70\overline{)360}$ 17. $10\overline{)50}$ 18. $80\overline{)720}$ 19. $60\overline{)180}$ 20. $90\overline{)720}$

21. $90\overline{)197}$ **22.** $70\overline{)586}$ **23.** $90\overline{)494}$ **24.** $80\overline{)286}$ **25.** $90\overline{)321}$

26. $70\overline{)406}$ **27.** $80\overline{)511}$ **28.** $90\overline{)393}$ **29.** $50\overline{)247}$ **30.** $80\overline{)358}$

31. $60\overline{)480}$ **32.** $30\overline{)204}$ **33.** $10\overline{)94}$ **34.** $90\overline{)630}$ **35.** $70\overline{)560}$

36. $80\overline{)320}$ **37.** $50\overline{)433}$ **38.** $40\overline{)240}$ **39.** $30\overline{)254}$ **40.** $40\overline{)320}$

41. $540 \div 90 = \underline{?}$ **42.** $654 \div 80 = \underline{?}$ **43.** $400 \div 50 = \underline{?}$

44. $307 \div 40 = \underline{?}$ **45.** $97 \div 30 = \underline{?}$ **46.** $350 \div 70 = \underline{?}$

47. $76 \div 20 = \underline{?}$ **48.** $378 \div 60 = \underline{?}$ **49.** $360 \div 90 = \underline{?}$

What are the next two numbers in the pattern?

★ **50.**

4	32	256	?	?

★ **51.**

3	21	147	?	?

★ **52.**

5	30	180	?	?

★ **53.**

8	24	72	?	?

PROBLEM SOLVING • APPLICATIONS

54. Honora spends $2.70 for 30 stamps. Each stamp costs the same amount. How much does each stamp cost?

55. Sal has 490 stamps to paste in an album. He pasted an equal number of stamps on each of 70 pages. How many stamps are on each page?

56. A stamp dealer makes up packets of stamps. He has 156 stamps to use. He puts 20 stamps in each packet. How many packets does he have? How many stamps are left over?

★ **57.** The owner of a stamp and coin shop has 140 French stamps. She buys 180 more French stamps at an auction. She wants to display them in cases. She puts 40 stamps in each case. How many cases does she use?

Rounding Divisors Down

Each day a dispatcher sends 336 buses out on their routes. There are 42 different routes. The same number of buses serve each route. How many buses serve each route?

$336 \div 42 = ?$

You can estimate to help you find the quotient. Round the divisor to the nearest ten.

$42\overline{)336}$  $40\overline{)336}$

Step 1
Think: $4\overline{)33}.$
Try 8.

$\begin{array}{r} 8 \\ 42\overline{)336} \end{array}$

Step 2
Multiply.
$8 \times 42 = 336.$

$\begin{array}{r} 8 \\ 42\overline{)336} \\ 336 \end{array}$

Step 3
Subtract.

$\begin{array}{r} 8 \\ 42\overline{)336} \\ -336 \\ \hline 0 \end{array}$

8 buses serve each route.

Check your answer.

Multiply the quotient and the divisor. ⟶

Add the remainder. ⟶

Should equal the dividend. →

$\begin{array}{r} 42 \\ \times\ 8 \\ \hline 336 \\ +\ \ \ 0 \\ \hline 336 \end{array}$

Practice • Divide. Check your answers.

1. $31\overline{)227}$
2. $72\overline{)364}$
3. $93\overline{)197}$
4. $64\overline{)512}$
5. $42\overline{)138}$

6. $53\overline{)283}$
7. $44\overline{)98}$
8. $23\overline{)76}$
9. $22\overline{)176}$
10. $31\overline{)190}$

Mixed Practice • Divide.

11. $63\overline{)189}$
12. $82\overline{)358}$
13. $41\overline{)215}$
14. $31\overline{)81}$
15. $43\overline{)217}$

16. $91\overline{)642}$ 17. $62\overline{)372}$ 18. $44\overline{)352}$ 19. $92\overline{)739}$ 20. $53\overline{)374}$

21. $24\overline{)79}$ 22. $81\overline{)597}$ 23. $73\overline{)302}$ 24. $51\overline{)295}$ 25. $60\overline{)265}$

26. $42\overline{)388}$ 27. $40\overline{)394}$ 28. $82\overline{)656}$ 29. $43\overline{)307}$ 30. $91\overline{)675}$

31. $32\overline{)207}$ 32. $41\overline{)264}$ 33. $52\overline{)443}$ 34. $33\overline{)86}$ 35. $50\overline{)357}$

36. $90\overline{)179}$ 37. $72\overline{)607}$ 38. $91\overline{)484}$ 39. $82\overline{)276}$ 40. $71\overline{)504}$

41. $656 \div 72 = \underline{?}$ 42. $502 \div 83 = \underline{?}$ 43. $451 \div 64 = \underline{?}$

44. $465 \div 93 = \underline{?}$ 45. $438 \div 50 = \underline{?}$ 46. $608 \div 73 = \underline{?}$

47. $547 \div 80 = \underline{?}$ 48. $298 \div 33 = \underline{?}$ 49. $373 \div 71 = \underline{?}$

Find the missing numbers.

★ 50.
$$\begin{array}{r} 9\ r\ \blacksquare\,7 \\ \blacksquare\,3\overline{)\blacksquare\,7\,\blacksquare} \\ -8\,3\,7 \\ \hline \blacksquare\,7 \end{array}$$

★ 51.
$$\begin{array}{r} 8\ r\ \blacksquare\,6 \\ 3\,\blacksquare\overline{)2\,5\,\blacksquare} \\ -2\,\blacksquare\,0 \\ \hline \blacksquare\,6 \end{array}$$

★ 52.
$$\begin{array}{r} 8\ r3\,\blacksquare \\ \blacksquare\ \blacksquare\overline{)4\,\blacksquare\,9} \\ -3\,\blacksquare\,4 \\ \hline 3\,\blacksquare \end{array}$$

PROBLEM SOLVING • APPLICATIONS

53. Today 264 senior citizens want to go to the shopping mall by bus. Each bus seats 44 people. How many buses are needed?

★ 54. The bus company orders 112 new tires. There are 12 tires for each bus. How many buses can get new tires? How many more tires must be ordered to put new tires on one more bus?

★ 55. The Theater Club hires a bus to go to a play. It costs $224 to hire the bus. There are 32 club members who plan to go on the trip. How much will each person pay for the bus? If 4 people cannot go, how much does each person have to pay?

111

Rounding Divisors Up

Mrs. Domingo has 250 roses. She puts 36 in each box to ship them to the dealers. How many boxes does she fill? How many roses are left over?

$250 \div 36 = ?$

Estimate the quotient. $36\overline{)250}$

$40\overline{)250}$

Step 1
Think: $4\overline{)25}$.
Try 6.

$$36\overline{)250}^{6}$$

Step 2
Multiply.

$$36\overline{)250}^{6}$$
$$216$$

Step 3
Subtract.
Show the remainder.

$$36\overline{)250}^{6\ r34}$$
$$-216$$
$$34$$

Mrs. Domingo fills 6 boxes. There are 34 roses left over.

Practice • Divide.

1. $35\overline{)204}$ 2. $58\overline{)369}$ 3. $66\overline{)567}$ 4. $37\overline{)83}$ 5. $89\overline{)821}$

6. $46\overline{)213}$ 7. $77\overline{)659}$ 8. $59\overline{)449}$ 9. $45\overline{)62}$ 10. $68\overline{)374}$

Mixed Practice • Divide.

11. $38\overline{)87}$ 12. $56\overline{)557}$ 13. $39\overline{)368}$ 14. $67\overline{)649}$ 15. $49\overline{)423}$

16. $57\overline{)257}$ 17. $58\overline{)379}$ 18. $26\overline{)91}$ 19. $69\overline{)439}$ 20. $55\overline{)490}$

21. $65\overline{)507}$ 22. $87\overline{)649}$ 23. $70\overline{)579}$ 24. $78\overline{)744}$ 25. $79\overline{)268}$

26. $37\overline{)282}$ 27. $53\overline{)194}$ 28. $48\overline{)176}$ 29. $79\overline{)427}$ 30. $65\overline{)227}$

31. $47\overline{)304}$ 32. $68\overline{)529}$ 33. $27\overline{)94}$ 34. $57\overline{)554}$ 35. $77\overline{)320}$

36. $85\overline{)403}$ 37. $40\overline{)371}$ 38. $66\overline{)516}$ 39. $79\overline{)610}$ 40. $38\overline{)373}$

41. $657 \div 80 = \underline{\ ?\ }$ 42. $603 \div 78 = \underline{\ ?\ }$ 43. $334 \div 57 = \underline{\ ?\ }$

44. $251 \div 39 = \underline{\ ?\ }$ ★ 45. $7{,}341 \div 81 = \underline{\ ?\ }$ ★ 46. $3{,}782 \div 68 = \underline{\ ?\ }$

PROBLEM SOLVING • APPLICATIONS

47. Mrs. Domingo has 182 carnations. She puts 28 in each vase. How many vases can she fill? How many carnations will be left over?

48. There are 312 daisies. Sharon uses 48 to make each wreath. How many wreaths can she make? How many daisies will be left over?

★ 49. The Blancs are planning a wedding. They want to spend no more than $400 for centerpieces. How many $45 centerpieces can they buy?

★ 50. Monroe is making wreaths. He cuts pieces of wire 58 centimeters long. How many pieces can he cut from 437 centimeters of wire? How much wire is left over?

★ 51. For each wreath Monroe uses ten pieces that are each 58 centimeters long. How many more 58-centimeter pieces of wire does he need to make one wreath?

Skills Maintenance

1. $\begin{array}{r} 51 \\ \times\ 3 \\ \hline \end{array}$ 2. $\begin{array}{r} 4{,}875 \\ \times\ \ \ \ 8 \\ \hline \end{array}$ 3. $\begin{array}{r} 98 \\ \times 10 \\ \hline \end{array}$ 4. $\begin{array}{r} 63 \\ \times 25 \\ \hline \end{array}$ 5. $\begin{array}{r} 200 \\ \times\ 16 \\ \hline \end{array}$

6. $\begin{array}{r} 800 \\ \times\ 30 \\ \hline \end{array}$ 7. $\begin{array}{r} 238 \\ \times 800 \\ \hline \end{array}$ 8. $\begin{array}{r} 8{,}645 \\ \times\ \ \ 56 \\ \hline \end{array}$ 9. $\begin{array}{r} 230 \\ \times 471 \\ \hline \end{array}$ 10. $\begin{array}{r} 3{,}412 \\ \times\ 475 \\ \hline \end{array}$

PROBLEM SOLVING • STRATEGIES

Multiply or Divide?

Division problems usually ask you to separate something into groups or to tell how many are in each group. Multiplication problems ask you to find a total amount. Make sure you read the problem carefully before you decide whether to multiply or divide.

The 12 members of the art club are making papier mâché cats. They will use 48 sheets of newspaper. How many sheets will each member use?

How many in each group? Divide to solve.

$$12\overline{)48} \quad \overset{4}{}$$

Each member will use 4 sheets of newspaper.

The members will put 120 sequins on each cat. How many sequins are needed for 8 cats?

How many in all? Multiply to solve.

$$\begin{array}{r} 120 \\ \times 8 \\ \hline 960 \end{array}$$

To make 8 cats, 960 sequins are needed.

Write MULTIPLY or DIVIDE. Then solve.

1. There are 4 packs of pipe cleaners. There are 140 pipe cleaners in each. How many pipe cleaners are there in all?

   Use division to check multiplication.

2. There are 156 pieces of felt. They will be shared equally by 12 members. How many pieces will each get?

3. There are 12 class members. Each 2 will share a pair of scissors. How many pairs of scissors are needed?

Solve.

4. There are 672 strips of newspaper. They will be shared equally by 8 members. How many strips will each get?

Multiplication problems ask you to find how many in all.

---

5. Each member makes 2 bowls of papier-mâché. There are 12 members. How many bowls of papier-mâché will be prepared?

6. It takes 25 minutes to put on a layer of papier-mâché. To make a cat 3 layers are needed. How many minutes will it take to put on the papier-mâché?

7. There are 40 cups that are filled with paint. An equal number of cups are filled with 5 different colors. How many cups of each color are there in all?

8. There are 16 paintbrushes in a box. There are 4 boxes. How many paintbrushes are there in all?

9. Each member needs 5 paintbrushes. There are 12 members. How many paintbrushes are needed in all?

★ 10. Small jars of paint cost $1.90 each. Leonard buys 9 jars. The cost is shared by 5 people. How much money does each person spend?

★ 11. Evelyn spends $24.64 each for 6 packages of felt squares. The cost is shared by 12 people. How much money does each person spend?

Correcting Estimates

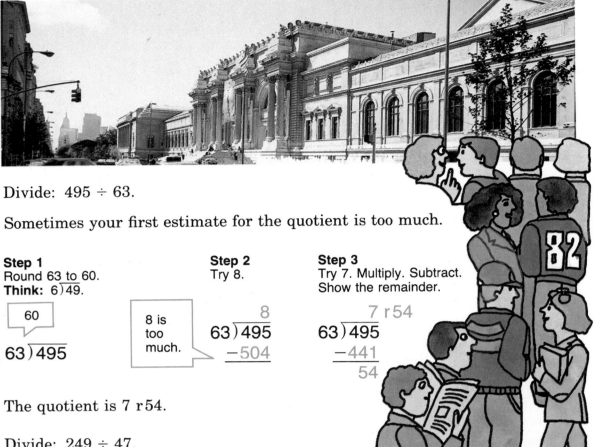

Divide: $495 \div 63$.

Sometimes your first estimate for the quotient is too much.

Step 1
Round 63 to 60.
Think: $6\overline{)49}$.

60
$63\overline{)495}$

Step 2
Try 8.

8 is too much.

$$63\overline{)495} \atop -504$$ 8

Step 3
Try 7. Multiply. Subtract.
Show the remainder.

7 r54
$$63\overline{)495} \atop \underline{-441} \atop 54$$

The quotient is 7 r54.

Divide: $249 \div 47$.

Sometimes your first estimate for the quotient is not enough.

Step 1
Round 47 to 50.
Think: $5\overline{)24}$.

50
$47\overline{)249}$

Step 2
Try 4.

4 is not enough.

4
$$47\overline{)249} \atop \underline{-188} \atop 61$$

Step 3
Try 5.
Multiply. Subtract.
Show the remainder.

5 r14
$$47\overline{)249} \atop \underline{-235} \atop 14$$

The quotient is 5 r14.

Practice • Divide.

1. $34\overline{)256}$ 2. $43\overline{)342}$ 3. $63\overline{)427}$ 4. $23\overline{)193}$ 5. $54\overline{)369}$

6. $55\overline{)495}$ 7. $69\overline{)485}$ 8. $77\overline{)475}$ 9. $26\overline{)193}$ 10. $57\overline{)470}$

Mixed Practice • Divide.

11. $85\overline{)342}$ 12. $88\overline{)704}$ 13. $24\overline{)94}$ 14. $42\overline{)409}$ 15. $73\overline{)507}$

16. $48\overline{)348}$ 17. $76\overline{)532}$ 18. $76\overline{)610}$ 19. $35\overline{)314}$ 20. $92\overline{)637}$

21. $74\overline{)449}$ 22. $86\overline{)579}$ 23. $82\overline{)339}$ 24. $79\overline{)239}$ 25. $62\overline{)427}$

26. $23\overline{)160}$ 27. $53\overline{)421}$ 28. $53\overline{)384}$ 29. $52\overline{)482}$ 30. $65\overline{)229}$

31. $41\overline{)290}$ 32. $59\overline{)413}$ 33. $54\overline{)476}$ 34. $62\overline{)276}$ 35. $24\overline{)174}$

36. $368 \div 45 = \underline{\ ?\ }$ 37. $561 \div 65 = \underline{\ ?\ }$ 38. $547 \div 56 = \underline{\ ?\ }$

39. $271 \div 34 = \underline{\ ?\ }$ 40. $473 \div 66 = \underline{\ ?\ }$ 41. $284 \div 72 = \underline{\ ?\ }$

42. $368 \div 48 = \underline{\ ?\ }$ 43. $546 \div 93 = \underline{\ ?\ }$ 44. $428 \div 79 = \underline{\ ?\ }$

Each letter represents a digit. In each exercise, each time a letter is used it represents the same digit.

Find the missing digits.

★ 45.
```
        8 r20
  A2)B5C
   -BBC
     20
```

★ 46.
```
        7 rGG
  E8)FG9
   -F06
     GG
```

★ 47.
```
        K r8
  8J)JKL
   -J83
      8
```

PROBLEM SOLVING • APPLICATIONS

48. On Tuesday 162 students take a guided tour of the museum. There are 18 students in each group. How many guides are needed?

★ 49. On the same day 14 buses arrive at the museum. There are 45 people on each bus. If the people are separated into groups of 18, how many groups are there?

Midchapter Review

1. $90\overline{)810}$ 2. $41\overline{)173}$ 3. $23\overline{)94}$ 4. $50\overline{)487}$ 5. $47\overline{)311}$

6. $39\overline{)325}$ 7. $30\overline{)251}$ 8. $72\overline{)504}$ 9. $83\overline{)422}$ 10. $68\overline{)491}$

Two-Digit Quotients

Mr. White is the school custodian.
He sets up 821 chairs for a movie.
He puts 34 chairs in each row.
How many rows are made? How
many chairs are left over?

$821 \div 34 = ?$

$34\overline{)821}$ There are not enough hundreds to divide.

$34\overline{)821}$ There are enough tens to divide.

The first digit of the quotient is in the tens place.

Step 1
Divide the tens.
Think: $3\overline{)8}$. Try 2.

$$\begin{array}{r} 2 \\ 34\overline{)821} \\ -68 \\ \hline 14 \end{array}$$

Step 2
Divide the ones.
Think: $3\overline{)14}$. Try 4.

$$\begin{array}{r} 24\,r5 \\ 34\overline{)821} \\ -68\downarrow \\ \hline 141 \\ -136 \\ \hline 5 \end{array}$$

There are 24 chairs in each row. There are 5 chairs left over.

More Examples

$$\begin{array}{r} 19\,r23 \\ 38\overline{)745} \\ -38 \\ \hline 365 \\ -342 \\ \hline 23 \end{array}$$

$$\begin{array}{r} 35\,r18 \\ 24\overline{)858} \\ -72 \\ \hline 138 \\ -120 \\ \hline 18 \end{array}$$

$$\begin{array}{r} 20\,r13 \\ 46\overline{)933} \\ -92 \\ \hline 13 \\ -\;0 \\ \hline 13 \end{array}$$

Practice • Divide.

1. $42\overline{)938}$ 2. $52\overline{)851}$ 3. $37\overline{)846}$ 4. $67\overline{)802}$ 5. $20\overline{)685}$

6. $23\overline{)385}$ 7. $34\overline{)958}$ 8. $16\overline{)763}$ 9. $38\overline{)892}$ 10. $41\overline{)895}$

Mixed Practice • Divide.

11. $21\overline{)987}$
12. $46\overline{)892}$
13. $30\overline{)958}$
14. $73\overline{)952}$
15. $34\overline{)768}$

16. $47\overline{)685}$
17. $73\overline{)870}$
18. $43\overline{)989}$
19. $28\overline{)570}$
20. $63\overline{)800}$

21. $78\overline{)957}$
22. $40\overline{)873}$
23. $39\overline{)897}$
24. $17\overline{)357}$
25. $24\overline{)174}$

26. $21\overline{)532}$
27. $56\overline{)712}$
28. $28\overline{)576}$
29. $63\overline{)748}$
30. $25\overline{)782}$

31. $30\overline{)938}$
32. $48\overline{)495}$
33. $54\overline{)973}$
34. $78\overline{)712}$
35. $33\overline{)926}$

36. $57\overline{)851}$
37. $46\overline{)684}$
38. $27\overline{)653}$
39. $70\overline{)392}$
40. $42\overline{)652}$

41. $939 \div 44 = \underline{\quad?\quad}$
42. $589 \div 28 = \underline{\quad?\quad}$
43. $267 \div 34 = \underline{\quad?\quad}$

44. $770 \div 35 = \underline{\quad?\quad}$
45. $985 \div 30 = \underline{\quad?\quad}$
46. $741 \div 53 = \underline{\quad?\quad}$

47. $392 \div 49 = \underline{\quad?\quad}$
48. $999 \div 67 = \underline{\quad?\quad}$
49. $605 \div 31 = \underline{\quad?\quad}$

★ 50. Write the answer for each frame.

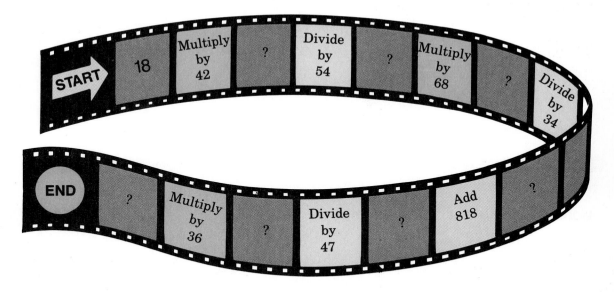

PROBLEM SOLVING • APPLICATIONS

51. On a class trip 768 students go to see a movie. There is an average of 32 students in each class. How many classes see the movie?

★ 52. A movie projector can show 360 frames in 15 seconds. How many frames can it show in one minute?

Dividing Greater Numbers

An electrician has 5,763 meters of wire. She uses the same amount of wire in each of 68 new apartments. How many meters of wire are used in each apartment? How much wire is left over?

$5{,}763 \div 68 = ?$

$68\overline{)5{,}763}$ There are not enough thousands to divide.

$68\overline{)5{,}763}$ There are not enough hundreds to divide.

$68\overline{)5{,}763}$ There are enough tens to divide.

The first digit of the quotient is in the tens place.

Step 1
Divide the tens.
Think: $7\overline{)57}$. Try 8.

$$
\begin{array}{r}
8 \\
68\overline{)5{,}763} \\
-5\ 44 \\
\hline
32
\end{array}
$$

Step 2
Divide the ones.
Think: $7\overline{)32}$. Try 4.

$$
\begin{array}{r}
84\ \text{r}51 \\
68\overline{)5{,}763} \\
-5\ 44\downarrow \\
\hline
323 \\
-272 \\
\hline
51
\end{array}
$$

84 meters of wire are used in each apartment.
51 meters of wire are left over.

More Examples

$$
\begin{array}{r}
43\ \text{r}17 \\
34\overline{)1{,}479} \\
-1\ 36 \\
\hline
119 \\
-102 \\
\hline
\end{array}
\qquad
\begin{array}{r}
74\ \text{r}40 \\
46\overline{)3{,}444} \\
-3\ 22 \\
\hline
224 \\
-184 \\
\hline
40
\end{array}
\qquad
\begin{array}{r}
70\ \text{r}48 \\
53\overline{)3{,}758} \\
-3\ 71 \\
\hline
48 \\
-\ 0 \\
\hline
48
\end{array}
$$

Practice • Divide.

1. $58\overline{)4{,}128}$ 2. $24\overline{)1{,}968}$ 3. $50\overline{)3{,}361}$ 4. $62\overline{)5{,}420}$

5. $22\overline{)1{,}628}$ 6. $50\overline{)2{,}317}$ 7. $21\overline{)1{,}323}$ 8. $31\overline{)1{,}736}$

120

Mixed Practice • Divide.

9. $46\overline{)4,193}$ 10. $68\overline{)5,440}$ 11. $40\overline{)2,140}$ 12. $51\overline{)3,428}$

13. $81\overline{)1,894}$ 14. $32\overline{)2,324}$ 15. $25\overline{)1,535}$ 16. $53\overline{)3,657}$

17. $63\overline{)3,664}$ 18. $35\overline{)2,488}$ 19. $47\overline{)3,359}$ 20. $65\overline{)455}$

21. $52\overline{)2,239}$ 22. $70\overline{)3,159}$ 23. $43\overline{)3,375}$ 24. $26\overline{)1,872}$

25. $31\overline{)1,994}$ 26. $79\overline{)854}$ 27. $48\overline{)3,499}$ 28. $90\overline{)5,048}$

29. $55\overline{)4,899}$ 30. $33\overline{)789}$ 31. $60\overline{)3,545}$ 32. $73\overline{)4,246}$

33. $3,078 \div 81 = \underline{\ ?\ }$ 34. $2,294 \div 37 = \underline{\ ?\ }$ 35. $4,358 \div 50 = \underline{\ ?\ }$

36. $3,443 \div 44 = \underline{\ ?\ }$ 37. $951 \div 47 = \underline{\ ?\ }$ 38. $3,159 \div 39 = \underline{\ ?\ }$

39. $3,960 \div 55 = \underline{\ ?\ }$ 40. $3,684 \div 72 = \underline{\ ?\ }$ 41. $4,063 \div 64 = \underline{\ ?\ }$

What are the next two numbers in the pattern?

★ 42.

10	90	810	?	?

★ 43.

12	96	768	?	?

★ 44.

15	105	735	?	?

★ 45.

27	135	675	?	?

PROBLEM SOLVING • APPLICATIONS

46. Leslie is putting wall outlets in a new building. She uses 1,152 outlets in 72 apartments. What is the average number of outlets used in each apartment?

★ 47. Twice a year $3,600 is collected from 48 apartment owners for the use of the pool. What is the average amount paid yearly by each apartment owner?

Skills Maintenance

1. 384
    $+973$

2. 659
    $+204$

3. 726
    $+217$

4. 638
    $+466$

5. 656
    $+991$

6. $7,431$
    $+2,325$

7. $6,192$
    $+1,238$

8. $9,476$
    $+8,524$

9. $99,400$
    $+\ 2,036$

10. $39,778$
    $+98,161$

PROBLEM SOLVING · STRATEGIES

Thinking About the Remainder

Often when you divide, there is a remainder in your answer. In some problems, however, the answer should be a whole number. Sometimes the answer to the problem will be the quotient. Other times the answer will be the next greater whole number.

Read the problems.

Fran is a travel agent. Her company offers a special See America Trip. 96 people will take this bus trip. Each bus can carry 53 people. How many buses are needed?

$$\begin{array}{r} 1\ r43 \\ 53\overline{)96} \\ \underline{53} \\ 43 \end{array}$$

Think: The 43 remaining people need a place to ride.

2 buses are needed.

For every 50 persons who take the trip, Fran earns a bonus of a one-week vacation. 96 people take the tour. How many weeks of vacation does Fran earn?

$$\begin{array}{r} 1\ r46 \\ 50\overline{)96} \\ \underline{50} \\ 46 \end{array}$$

Think: 46 is less than 50.

She earns 1 week of vacation.

Is the answer 3 or is it 4?

1. A group of 55 people are going on a tour. Fran must arrange for tour guides. There will be one guide for every 15 people. How many guides must Fran get?

   Read the problem carefully to decide how you will use the remainder.

2. Fran can travel at special rates. She has 25 days she can use for vacations. Each trip that she wants to take lasts 7 days. How many of these trips can she take?

3. There are 23 people on a tour. They plan to take a side trip by car. Each car can carry 6 people. How many cars are needed?

Solve.

4. Fran must change some reservations. She will use the telephone. Each call will take 3 minutes. She has only 50 minutes. How many calls can she make?

5. Fran works 5 days every week. She has worked 148 days so far this year. How many work weeks is this?

6. Fran wants to earn a bonus. She must find 24 people to take a tour. She has 5 days in which to do this. What is the average number of people she must find each day?

7. There are 66 people at a restaurant on one tour stop. Only 10 people can sit at a table. How many tables do they need?

8. There are 35 tourists waiting to take a plane trip over a canyon. The plane can carry 12 people on each trip. How many trips must the plane make?

Sometimes the answer will be the next greater whole number.

9. A printer ships 1,000 pamphlets. They must be put into packages of 45 pamphlets each. How many packages can be made?

10. A new tour is being planned. It is limited to 24 people on each trip. However, 136 people would like to take the tour. How many tours must be planned?

★11. Fran signs up 68 people for a trip through a grotto. Each boat can carry 12 people. How many boats are needed? Will there be any empty seats, and if so how many?

★12. A group of 88 people signed up to go on a canyon tour. There will be one guide for each 6 people. How many guides are needed? If 97 people go, how many guides will be needed?

Three- and Four-Digit Quotients

A company pays $6,864 to have new tires put on its 22 cars. How much does this cost for each car?

$6,864 ÷ 22 = ?

$22\overline{)6,864}$ There are not enough thousands to divide.

$22\overline{)6,864}$ There are enough hundreds to divide.

The first digit of the quotient is in the hundreds place.

Step 1
Divide the hundreds.
Think: $2\overline{)6}$. Try 3.

```
      3
22)6,864
  -6 6
     2
```

Step 2
Divide the tens.
Think: $2\overline{)2}$.

```
     31
22)6,864
  -6 6↓
     26
    -22
      4
```

Step 3
Divide the ones.
Think: $2\overline{)4}$.

```
    312
22)6,864
  -6 6|
     26|
    -22↓
      44
     -44
       0
```

It costs $312 to put new tires on each car.

More Examples

```
      207 r19
23)4,780
  -4 6
    18
   - 0
   180
  -161
    19
```

```
      643 r5
68)43,729
  -40 8
    2 92
   -2 72
     209
    -204
       5
```

```
     2,608
37)96,496
  -74
   22 4
  -22 2
     29
    - 0
    296
   -296
      0
```

Practice • Divide.

1. $25\overline{)2,975}$ 2. $46\overline{)6,079}$ 3. $31\overline{)6,609}$ 4. $28\overline{)8,665}$

5. $49\overline{)5,488}$ 6. $55\overline{)25,829}$ 7. $26\overline{)6,275}$ 8. $37\overline{)7,721}$

Mixed Practice • Divide.

9. $38\overline{)8,092}$ 10. $64\overline{)16,535}$ 11. $89\overline{)9,125}$ 12. $27\overline{)8,829}$

13. $54\overline{)9{,}637}$ **14.** $94\overline{)9{,}696}$ **15.** $28\overline{)7{,}365}$ **16.** $52\overline{)35{,}543}$

17. $38\overline{)24{,}973}$ **18.** $41\overline{)3{,}219}$ **19.** $34\overline{)8{,}038}$ **20.** $48\overline{)5{,}718}$

21. $51\overline{)7{,}126}$ **22.** $66\overline{)9{,}288}$ **23.** $69\overline{)17{,}942}$ **24.** $52\overline{)1{,}674}$

25. $65\overline{)7{,}345}$ **26.** $39\overline{)41{,}246}$ **27.** $44\overline{)3{,}173}$ **28.** $47\overline{)56{,}817}$

29. $83\overline{)85{,}042}$ **30.** $36\overline{)72{,}230}$ **31.** $75\overline{)88{,}925}$ **32.** $48\overline{)89{,}862}$

33. $9{,}702 \div 77 = \underline{\quad?\quad}$ **34.** $5{,}398 \div 93 = \underline{\quad?\quad}$ **35.** $8{,}494 \div 62 = \underline{\quad?\quad}$

36. $9{,}637 \div 16 = \underline{\quad?\quad}$ **37.** $9{,}296 \div 83 = \underline{\quad?\quad}$ **38.** $9{,}545 \div 78 = \underline{\quad?\quad}$

39. $82{,}736 \div 38 = \underline{\quad?\quad}$ **40.** $79{,}735 \div 76 = \underline{\quad?\quad}$ **41.** $59{,}099 \div 64 = \underline{\quad?\quad}$

Estimate and then divide. Round the divisor to the nearest hundred.

```
      ⌐ 300 ⌐
275)370,150
      1,346
275)370,150
    −275
      95 1
    −82 5
      12 65
    −11 00
      1 650
    −1 650
          0
```

★ **42.** $175\overline{)67{,}725}$

★ **43.** $253\overline{)19{,}987}$

★ **44.** $629\overline{)580{,}497}$

★ **45.** $439\overline{)700{,}092}$

★ **46.** $358\overline{)597{,}628}$

PROBLEM SOLVING • APPLICATIONS

47. The Wilel Company pays $6,545 to have 17 cars serviced. What is the average cost for each car?

★ **48.** Michael pays a total of $9,599 for a new car, including interest charges. He makes a down payment of $1,895. The rest of the cost is paid in 36 equal payments. How much is each payment?

★ **49.** Ms. Jones sells tires to garages. She has 7,392 tires. She sends an equal number to each of 56 garages. How many tires does each garage receive? How many sets of 4 tires does each garage receive?

Divide. (pages 108–113, 116–121, 124–125)

1. $30\overline{)60}$
2. $40\overline{)251}$
3. $70\overline{)490}$
4. $60\overline{)214}$

5. $51\overline{)357}$
6. $28\overline{)83}$
7. $33\overline{)198}$
8. $48\overline{)151}$

9. $63\overline{)532}$
10. $89\overline{)652}$
11. $41\overline{)98}$
12. $67\overline{)455}$

13. $67\overline{)611}$
14. $32\overline{)245}$
15. $74\overline{)603}$
16. $89\overline{)445}$

17. $17\overline{)656}$
18. $32\overline{)628}$
19. $28\overline{)764}$
20. $66\overline{)938}$

21. $62\overline{)2,178}$
22. $79\overline{)1,980}$
23. $44\overline{)1,628}$
24. $57\overline{)3,554}$

25. $52\overline{)17,524}$
26. $74\overline{)15,123}$
27. $69\overline{)31,884}$
28. $37\overline{)4,487}$

Solve.

29. The students at Lincoln School order 6,000 pencil sets to sell to raise money. The sets are packed 48 in a carton. How many cartons do the students order? (p. 116)

30. When 8,486 school banners arrive, each of the 32 classes receives the same number of banners to sell. How many banners does each class receive? How many banners are left over? (p. 124)

31. One Saturday 2,640 people travel by bus to the game. If each bus holds 44 people, how many buses are needed? (p. 124)

32. A crowd of 6,780 people were at the school game. If 30 people sit in each row, how many rows of seats are filled? (p. 124)

PROJECT

Sales Slips

When you buy something you usually receive a **sales slip**. This gives you a record of the sale. In most cases, when you want to return an item, you must have the sales slip with you.

Joe's Nursery
Red River Valley

Date __4/2/85__

NAME __Harold Reed__

ADDRESS __12-85 Chestnut Street__

Quantity	Item	Unit Price	Amount
22	Vegetable pack		56.98
18	Geraniums		40.50
4	Azaleas		43.00
1	Watering can		4.89

Subtotal $ _____

Tax $ __11.63__

Total $ _____

Returns must be accompanied by this sales slip.

Copy the sales slip. Then answer the questions.

1. Where was the purchase made?

2. On what date was the purchase made?

3. The amount for 22 vegetable packs is $56.98. Divide to find the price of one pack. Write the quotient in the unit price column.

4. Complete the unit price column for the other items.

5. The subtotal is the sum of the prices in the amount column. Add to find the subtotal.

6. The tax for this purchase is $11.63. Add the subtotal and the tax to find the total amount of this purchase.

Collect some sales slips. See what information is found on each slip.

TEST

Divide.

1. $10\overline{)90}$ 2. $70\overline{)562}$ 3. $60\overline{)240}$ 4. $80\overline{)430}$

5. $62\overline{)248}$ 6. $34\overline{)87}$ 7. $81\overline{)405}$ 8. $53\overline{)495}$

9. $38\overline{)325}$ 10. $49\overline{)284}$ 11. $27\overline{)94}$ 12. $56\overline{)421}$

13. $46\overline{)291}$ 14. $83\overline{)485}$ 15. $22\overline{)163}$ 16. $79\overline{)158}$

17. $62\overline{)983}$ 18. $44\overline{)939}$ 19. $29\overline{)898}$ 20. $38\overline{)997}$

21. $65\overline{)4,638}$ 22. $71\overline{)1,633}$ 23. $52\overline{)4,108}$ 24. $44\overline{)3,036}$

25. $74\overline{)8,369}$ 26. $34\overline{)73,927}$ 27. $29\overline{)86,429}$ 28. $56\overline{)16,235}$

Solve.

29. Barry orders 864 salad bowls for Lipman Department Stores. The bowls are packed 24 to a carton. How many cartons does Barry order?

30. Lipman Department Stores orders 3,420 electric blankets. The blankets are packed 12 to a carton. How many cartons are ordered?

31. A shipment of 3,030 coasters is received. They are repacked into 56 cartons. The same number of coasters is in each carton. How many coasters are in each carton? How many coasters are left over?

32. A shipment of 1,872 sheets is received. They are packed 48 to a carton. How many cartons are received?

Mean and Median

Here are Cindy's bowling scores
for 9 games.
39, 90, 95, 90, 92, 95, 90, 94, 98
What is Cindy's **mean** or average score?

$783 \div 9 = ?$

Here are Cindy's scores arranged in order
from least to greatest.
39, 90, 90, 90, 92, 94, 95, 95, 98
Which score is in the middle?
The middle score, 92, is the **median**.

All but one of Cindy's scores are in the nineties.
Find the mean of these 8 scores.
Compare it with the mean of the 9 scores.
How does one low score affect the mean score?
Did the one low score affect her median score?

Find the mean and the median.

1. 82, 43, 131, 94, 85

2. 69, 23, 129, 83, 81

3. 82, 72, 69, 92, 95, 109, 55

4. 39, 51, 22, 68, 40, 35, 60

5. 60, 32, 96, 44, 84, 108, 24

6. 43, 63, 85, 72, 55, 88, 77

7. 37, 13, 65, 21, 57, 52, 26, 32, 48

8. 46, 23, 65, 27, 80, 13, 38, 52, 70

CALCULATOR

Calculator Regrouping

Remember that a calculator has no comma.

4,827   Push (4) (8) (2) (7) . Check to be sure you have 4827.
35,490
+651,884 Push (+) (3) (5) (4) (9) (0) . Check your addend.

Push (+) . Then look at the screen: $\boxed{40317.}$

Think: Just under 5,000 plus over 35,000 is over 40,000.
The screen shows 40,317. The answer looks correct so far.

Push (6) (5) (1) (8) (8) (4) (=). Write down the answer, 692,201.

Think: 40,000 plus about 650,000 is about 690,000. The answer looks
correct.

Check the right-hand column: $7 + 0 + 4 = 11$.
The last number, 1, also agrees with your answer. The answer looks correct.

When you add by hand, you regroup the 11 as 1 ten and 1 one. Then you
regroup tens into hundreds and tens. If you were to add this example by
hand, you would regroup four times: ones into tens and ones; tens into
hundreds and tens; hundreds into thousands and hundreds; thousands
into ten thousands and thousands.

The calculator does all regrouping for you.
It saves you regrouping four times.

Use the calculator to add. Check your numbers and subtotals.
List how many regroupings the calculator does for you.

1.	33,697	2.	4,003	3.	156,907	4.	56,304	5.	2,879
	480,214		844,488		32,498		307		114,003
	+194,550		+ 28,753		+ 93,043		+483,279		+ 7

A calculator also does all regrouping for you when you subtract large numbers.

300,000   Push ③⓪⓪⓪⓪⓪ , and check the screen for 300000.
−185,417 Push ⊖①⑧⑤④①⑦ , and check the screen for 185417.
          Push ⊜. Then write the difference with a comma: 114,583.

When you subtract by hand, you regroup many times: hundred thousands into hundred thousands and ten thousands; ten thousands into ten thousands and thousands; thousands into thousands and hundreds; hundreds into hundreds and tens; tens into tens and ones. The calculator saves you regrouping five times.

Use the calculator to subtract. Check each entry. List how many regroupings the calculator does for you.

6. 458,239 −289,443	**7.** 98,704 −19,286	**8.** 973,005 − 94,893	**9.** 741,290 −204,083	**10.** 82,473 −56,019
11. 84,375 −76,289	**12.** 215,005 − 89,557	**13.** 555,379 −429,006	**14.** 285,440 − 98,421	**15.** 704,650 − 95,238
16. 86,345 −42,143	**17.** 900,000 −899,995	**18.** 453,109 − 27,443	**19.** 775,577 −763,400	**20.** 283,401 −179,301

SKILLS MAINTENANCE

Chapters 1 Through 5

Choose the correct answers.

1. Round 3,675 to the nearest hundred.

    A. 3,000
    B. 4,000
    C. 3,700
    D. not here

2. Find the missing number.

$$12 - \underline{\ ?\ } = 5$$

    A. 6   **B.** 7
    C. 8   **D.** not here

3. Add.

$$\begin{array}{r} \$6.59 \\ .87 \\ + \ 3.64 \\ \hline \end{array}$$

    A. $11.90 **B.** $11.10
    C. $11.60 **D.** not here

4. Estimate. Round to the nearest hundred.

$$\begin{array}{r} 626 \\ -397 \\ \hline \end{array}$$

    A. 200 **B.** 900
    C. 300 **D.** not here

5. Subtract.

$$2,040 - 783 = \underline{\ ?\ }$$

    A. 1,267
    B. 1,257
    C. 1,367
    D. not here

6. Round the product to the nearest thousand.

$$\begin{array}{r} 3,867 \\ \times \quad\ 6 \\ \hline \end{array}$$

    A. 1,800 **B.** 2,300
    C. 23,000 **D.** not here

7. Multiply.

$$\begin{array}{r} 534 \\ \times \ 85 \\ \hline \end{array}$$

    A. 8,942
    B. 45,390
    C. 46,190
    D. not here

8. Divide.

$$3,009 \div 8 = \underline{\ ?\ }$$

    A. 458 r6
    B. 335 r4
    C. 367 r1
    D. not here

9. Divide.

$$86\overline{)45,754}$$

    A. 659 r17
    B. 631 r80
    C. 532 r2
    D. not here

10. Mr. Boehr orders 540 mysteries, 285 novels, 1,495 paperbacks, and 65 cookbooks for his bookstore. How many books does he order in all?

    A. 2,385   **B.** 2,470
    C. 3,195   **D.** not here

11. Mr. Boehr sells 576 cookbooks in one year. What is the average number of cookbooks he sells each month?

    A. 39   **B.** 56
    C. 48   **D.** not here

Graphing

**Pictographs • Bar Graphs • Line Graphs • Locating
Ordered Pairs • Graphing Ordered Pairs • Problem
Solving: Reading Maps • Four Quadrants**

Pictographs

Graphs are used to show and compare information.
This **pictograph** shows the farm population in the United States
from 1920 to 1980. The number of people living on farms is decreasing.

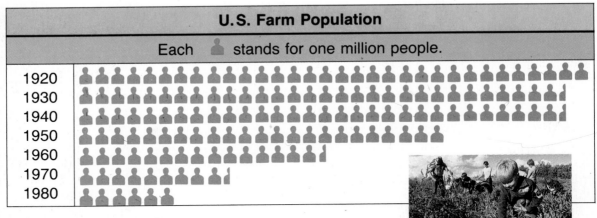

U.S. Farm Population
Each 🧍 stands for one million people.

There are 32 symbols in the 1920 row.
Each symbol stands for 1 million people.
So there were 32 × 1 million, or about 32 million, people living on farms in 1920.

Look at the symbols for 1960.
The 🧍 stands for half of 1,000,000, or 500,000 people.
There were about 15,500,000 people living on farms in 1960.
There were about twice as many people on farms in 1920 as in 1960.

Practice • Use the graph to answer questions 1 through 9.

In which year was the farm population greater,

1. 1980 or 1940?   **2.** 1980 or 1950?   **3.** 1980 or 1960?   **4.** 1980 or 1970?

5. Use the graph to make a prediction about the farm
population of the future. Do you think it will be greater than
or less than it was in 1980?

About how many people lived on farms in
6. 1950?   **7.** 1930?   **8.** 1940?   **9.** 1980?

More Practice • Use the graphs on page 135 to answer questions 10 through 22.

10. In which year were there fewer
farms, 1960 or 1970?

11. How do the number of farms in
1920 compare with the number in
1930?

12. In the future what do you think
will happen to the number of
farms?

About how many farms were there in

13. 1970?   **14.** 1960?   **15.** 1930?   **16.** 1980?

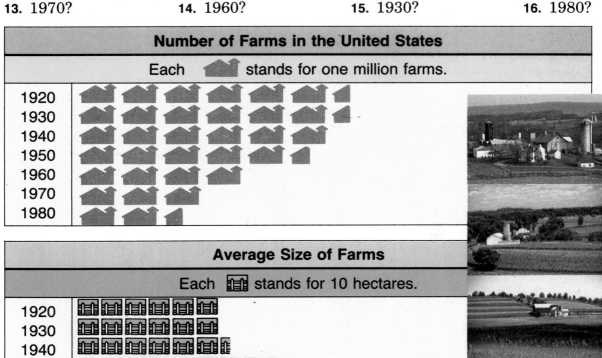

Number of Farms in the United States
Each 🏠 stands for one million farms.

1920	🏠🏠🏠🏠🏠🏠🏠
1930	🏠🏠🏠🏠🏠🏠🏠
1940	🏠🏠🏠🏠🏠🏠
1950	🏠🏠🏠🏠🏠
1960	🏠🏠🏠🏠
1970	🏠🏠🏠
1980	🏠🏠🏠

Average Size of Farms
Each 📦 stands for 10 hectares.

A hectare is equal to 10,000 square meters.

17. Is the average size of a farm increasing or decreasing?

18. The average size of a farm in the 1920s was about 60 hectares. By what year did the average size double?

About how many hectares were there in the average-size farm in

19. 1950?   **20.** 1960?   **21.** 1970?   **22.** 1980?

PROBLEM SOLVING • APPLICATIONS

23. Round each number to the nearest 10 million. Make a pictograph using the information shown in the table. Use 🐑 to stand for 10 million sheep.

Sheep on Farms in the United States	
Year	Number
1920	40,743,000
1930	51,565,000
1940	52,107,000
1950	29,826,000
1960	33,170,000
1970	20,423,000
1980	12,513,000

Bar Graphs

Dolores sells appliances. This **bar graph** gives her useful information.

The shortest bar is for dishwashers. Dolores can expect to sell fewer dishwashers than other appliances.

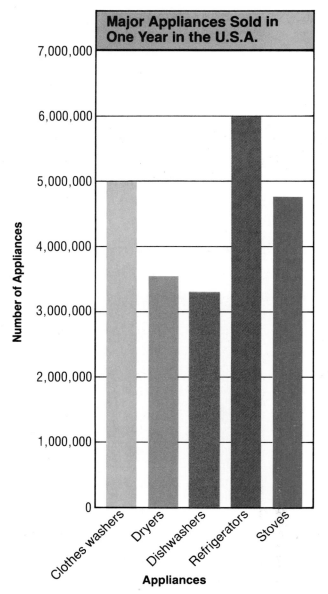

Major Appliances Sold in One Year in the U.S.A.

Number of Appliances

7,000,000
6,000,000
5,000,000
4,000,000
3,000,000
2,000,000
1,000,000
0

Clothes washers · Dryers · Dishwashers · Refrigerators · Stoves

Appliances

Practice • Use the bar graph to answer questions 1 through 5.

1. Which appliance had the greatest number of sales? *fridge*

2. Would Dolores expect to sell more stoves or more dryers? *stoves*

3. Would Dolores expect to sell fewer dishwashers or fewer stoves? *d.wash*

4. About how many clothes washers were sold? *5mil*

5. About how many refrigerators were sold? *6mil*

More Practice • Use the bar graphs to answer questions 6 through 13.

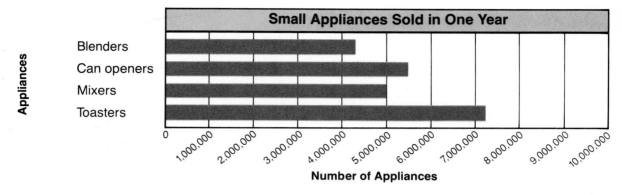

6. Which appliance had the greatest number of sales? Which had the least?

7. Were more can openers or mixers sold?

8. About how many mixers were sold?

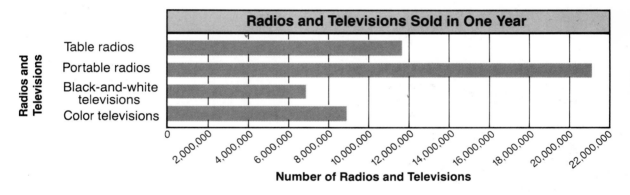

9. Which kind of radio or television had the greatest number of sales?

10. Which kind of radio or television had the least number of sales?

11. Were more color or black-and-white televisions sold?

12. Were more table or portable radios sold? About how many more?

PROBLEM SOLVING • APPLICATIONS

★ 13. Which brand had the greatest number of sales the first week?

★ 14. During which week did Brand X have the greatest number of sales?

★ 15. How many more Brand Y waffle irons were sold in the third week than in the first week?

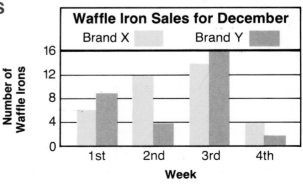

Line Graphs

The Weather Bureau recorded the temperature every two hours for a twelve-hour period. The recordings are shown in the table.

Time	Midnight	2:00 A.M.	4:00 A.M.	6:00 A.M.	8:00 A.M.	10:00 A.M.	Noon
Temperature	10°C	12°C	8°C	6°C	6°C	12°C	14°C

The results were shown on a **line graph**.
A line graph is used to show changes.

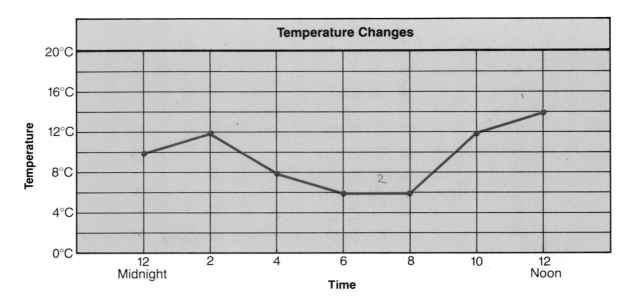

Between midnight and 2:00 A.M. the temperature increased.
Between 2:00 A.M. and 4:00 A.M. the temperature decreased.
The greatest increase was between 8:00 A.M. and 10:00 A.M.

Practice • Use the graph to answer questions 1 through 4.

1. During which other two-hour period did the temperature increase?

2. During which other two-hour period did the temperature decrease?

3. During which two-hour period was the decrease the greatest?

4. During which period did the temperature remain the same?

138

More Practice • Use the graph to answer questions 5 through 7.

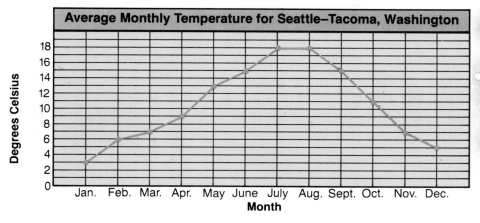

Average Monthly Temperature for Seattle–Tacoma, Washington

5. During which months did the temperature increase over the preceding month's temperature?
6. During which months did the temperature decrease from the preceding month's temperature?
7. During which month did the temperature not change from the preceding month?

PROBLEM SOLVING • APPLICATIONS

Use the graph to answer questions 8 through 11.

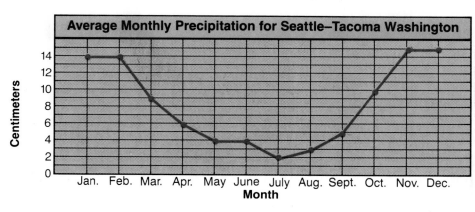

Average Monthly Precipitation for Seattle–Tacoma Washington

8. During which months did the amount of precipitation not change from the preceding month?
9. During which four months did the amount of precipitation increase over the preceding month's precipitation?
10. During which month did the amount of precipitation decrease the most from the preceding month's precipitation?
★ 11. As the average monthly temperature increased, did the amount of precipitation increase or decrease?

139

Locating Ordered Pairs

You can use an **ordered pair** of numbers to locate points on a grid.

The ordered pair (3, 2) means start at 0, move 3 spaces to the right, and then move 2 spaces up. The ordered pair (3, 2) locates point B.

D is located by the ordered pair (4, 1).

START

Practice • Use the grid to answer questions 1 through 40.

What letter is at the point?

1. (2, 1)   2. (3, 7)   3. (3, 4)   4. (4, 3)   5. (6, 6)

6. (3, 6)   7. (5, 2)   8. (5, 7)   9. (2, 8)   10. (8, 4)

11. (4, 5)   12. (1, 7)   13. (7, 0)   14. (8, 6)   15. (1, 6)

16. (5, 8)   17. (7, 5)   18. (8, 2)   19. (6, 8)   20. (6, 4)

What ordered pair tells the location of the point?

21. E   22. T   23. P   24. M   25. G

26. C   27. R   28. Z   29. U   30. K

31. I   32. F   33. X   34. J   35. S

36. A   37. O   38. Y   39. V   40. Q

140

More Practice • What ordered pair tells the location of the place?

41. Hotel

42. Restaurant

43. Television store

44. Hardware store

45. Food store

46. Train station

47. Bank

48. Post office

49. Record store

50. Bus station

51. School

52. Clothing store

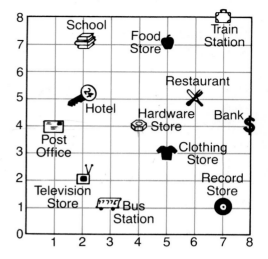

PROBLEM SOLVING • APPLICATIONS

53. Use the secret code to find a message. Go right and up to find each letter.

(2, 4) (5, 5) (1, 2) (7, 7) (5, 5)

(1, 2) (5, 5)

(6, 3) (8, 3) (7, 7) (3, 8)

(1, 7) (3, 8)

(7, 7) (5, 8) (1, 7) (0, 5) (5, 5)

(1, 2) (4, 6)   (2, 6)   (7, 2) (2, 0)

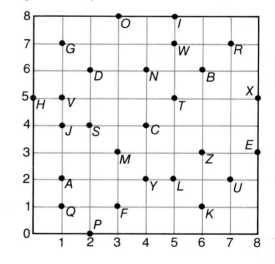

Midchapter Review

1. Which season was the favorite of the greatest number of people?

2. Which season was the favorite of the fewest number of people?

3. Did more people choose fall or winter as their favorite season?

4. How many people chose spring as their favorite season?

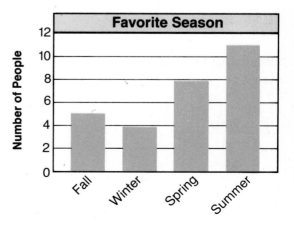

141

Graphing Ordered Pairs

Robin locates these ordered pairs.
She draws a dot at each point.

Point A is 2 spaces to the right and 3 spaces up.

Point B is 7 spaces to the right and 3 spaces up.

Point C is 7 spaces to the right and 7 spaces up.

She connects the dots to form a triangle.

Letter	Ordered Pair
A	(2, 3)
B	(7, 3)
C	(7, 7)

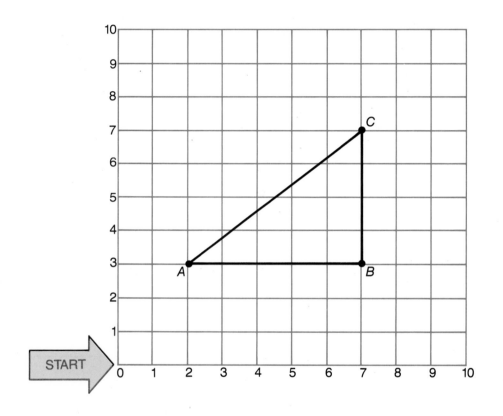

Practice • Use graph paper. Locate the ordered pair.
Draw a dot at the point. Connect the dots in order to form a figure.

1.

Letter	Ordered Pair
R	(2, 4)
S	(8, 4)
T	(8, 7)
U	(2, 7)

2.

Letter	Ordered Pair
P	(7, 5)
Q	(5, 9)
R	(1, 7)
S	(3, 3)

3.

Letter	Ordered Pair
A	(1, 7)
B	(11, 7)
C	(3, 1)
D	(6, 11)
E	(9, 1)

Mixed Practice • Use graph paper. Locate the ordered pair.
Draw a dot at the point. Connect the dots in order to form a figure.

4.

Letter	Ordered Pair
V	(6, 3)
W	(11, 8)
X	(11, 10)
Y	(9, 10)
Z	(4, 5)

5.

Letter	Ordered Pair
J	(5, 4)
K	(8, 2)
L	(8, 7)
M	(5, 10)
N	(2, 7)
O	(2, 2)

6.

Letter	Ordered Pair
L	(3, 4)
M	(6, 2)
N	(9, 4)
O	(9, 7)
P	(6, 9)
Q	(3, 7)

7. Follow the rule.
Complete the table.
List the ordered pairs.

Point	Number	Add 1	Ordered Pair
A	3	4	(3, 4)
B	4	?	?
C	2	?	?
D	1	?	?
E	0	?	?
F	5	?	?

PROBLEM SOLVING • APPLICATIONS

Use the table above.

★ **8.** Make a graph and locate the points.

★ **9.** Are the points of the graph on a straight line?

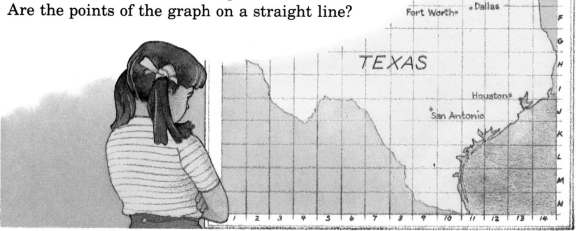

Skills Maintenance

1. 6)504   **2.** 9)197   **3.** 7)590   **4.** 8)397   **5.** 2)154

6. 6)8,823   **7.** 9)8,717   **8.** 2)1,355   **9.** 8)8,171   **10.** 5)1,882

PROBLEM SOLVING • STRATEGIES

Reading Maps

This map shows some towns, cities, and highways in a section of Alabama. The key shows us what the map symbols mean. What does 85 mean?

Look at the key. 85 is a highway marker that shows that the highway is an interstate highway. How far is it from Montgomery to Opelika using Route 85?

The small number along a highway shows the number of kilometers between arrows (↓).

It is 86 kilometers from Montgomery to Opelika using Route 85.

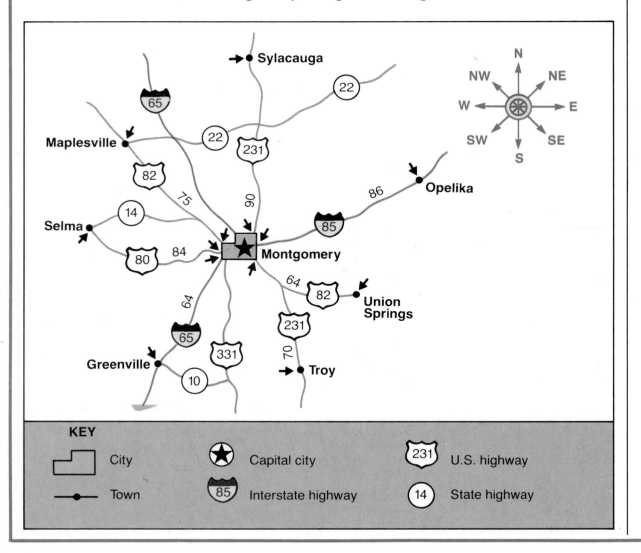

Use the map to answer the questions.

1. Name all the interstate highways.

2. Name all the U.S. highways.

3. Name all the state highways.

4. Name the capital city of Alabama.

Use the key to help you read the symbols on a map.

---

5. Name the town that is farthest north.

6. Name the town that is farthest east.

7. Name two U.S. highways that run north and south.

8. Name one U.S. highway that runs east and west.

9. Name three state highways that run east and west.

10. In which direction would you go to travel from Montgomery to Maplesville?

11. In which direction would you go to travel from Opelika to Montgomery?

12. Which highway would you use to travel from Montgomery to Greenville?

13. Which two highways would you use to travel from Union Springs to Montgomery?

Use the arrows at the top of the map to help you find the directions.

---

14. About how many kilometers is it from Montgomery to Sylacauga?

15. Start in Selma. Drive east on Route 80 to Montgomery. How far is this?

★ 16. Suppose you average 45 kilometers per hour on your drive from Sylacauga to Montgomery. About how long will it take?

★ 17. Suppose that you are driving southeast on Route 82 from Maplesville to Montgomery. You want to make the trip in one hour. What will your average rate of speed be?

Use the graphs to answer questions 1 through 8. (pages 134–139)

1. Which zoo has the fewest kinds of animals? the most?

2. In which zoo are there more kinds of animals, the Bronx or the National?

3. About how many kinds of animals are in the Denver Zoo? St. Louis Zoo?

4. Which animal is the fastest? the slowest?

5. Which is faster, a rabbit or a squirrel?

6. How fast can an elk run?

7. Which animal can run twice as fast as a rabbit?

8. Compared to the preceding day, on which days did the temperature increase? decrease? remain the same?

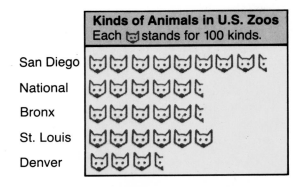

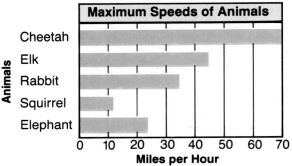

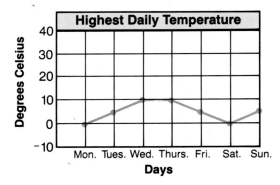

Use the grid. What letter is at the point? (pages 140–141)

9. (3, 1)   10. (5, 0)

11. (4, 4)   12. (2, 5)

Use the grid. What ordered pair locates the point? (pages 140–141)

13. B   14. E

15. H   16. G

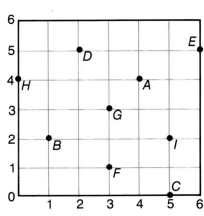

Number Cubes

When you roll a number cube, there are 6 different ways the cube can land face up.

| 1 | 2 | 3 | 4 | 5 | 6 |

Roll two number cubes.

The sum of the numbers on the faces of the cubes can be from 2 to 12.

Roll two number cubes 25 times.

Make a table like this one. After each roll, record the sum.

Sum	2	3	4	5	6	7	8	9	10	11	12
Tally											
Total											

Make a line graph to show how many times each sum was rolled.

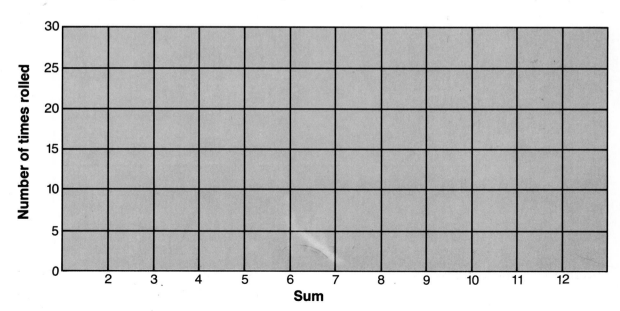

Which sums were rolled the most? Why?

TEST

Use the graphs to answer questions 1–7.

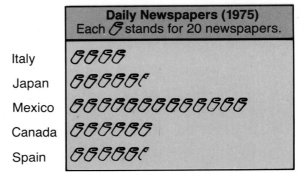

Daily Newspapers (1975)
Each ✐ stands for 20 newspapers.

Italy	✐✐✐✐
Japan	✐✐✐✐✐✐
Mexico	✐✐✐✐✐✐✐✐✐✐✐✐✐
Canada	✐✐✐✐✐✐
Spain	✐✐✐✐✐✐

1. Which country had the fewest newspapers? *Italy*

2. Were there more papers in Japan or in Canada? *canadad*

3. About how many papers were there in Mexico? in Spain? *260   120*

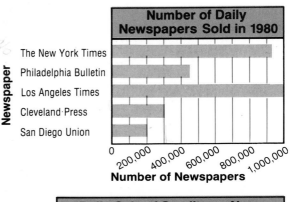

Number of Daily Newspapers Sold in 1980

4. Which newspaper sold the most copies? the fewest? *mexio + Italy*

5. Which paper sold more copies, *The New York Times* or the *Philadelphia Bulletin*? *New York*

6. How many copies were sold by the *Cleveland Press*? *Philadelphia Bulletin*? *300,000 450,000*

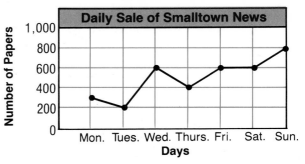

Daily Sale of Smalltown News

7. Compared to the preceding day, on which days did the sales increase? decrease? remain the same?

Use the grid. What letter is at the point?

8. (1, 0)   9. (2, 2)   10. (5, 6)

11. (3, 4)   12. (5, 2)   13. (4, 1)

Use the grid. What ordered pair locates the point?

14. H   15. E   16. B

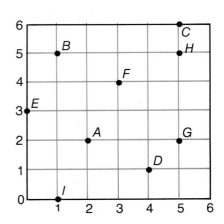

ENRICHMENT

Four Quadrants

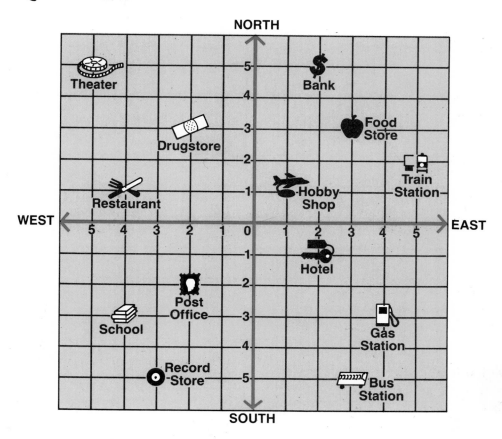

Follow these directions: east 2, north 5.

Start at 0, where the blue lines cross. Go right 2 spaces. Go up 5 spaces.

You should find the bank. Did you?

Follow the directions. What do you find?

1. east 5, north 2

2. west 2, north 3

3. east 2, south 1

4. west 4, north 1

5. east 1, north 1

6. west 2, south 2

7. east 4, south 3

8. west 4, south 3

9. east 3, south 5

10. west 5, north 5

11. east 3, north 3

12. west 3, south 5

Rainbow Island

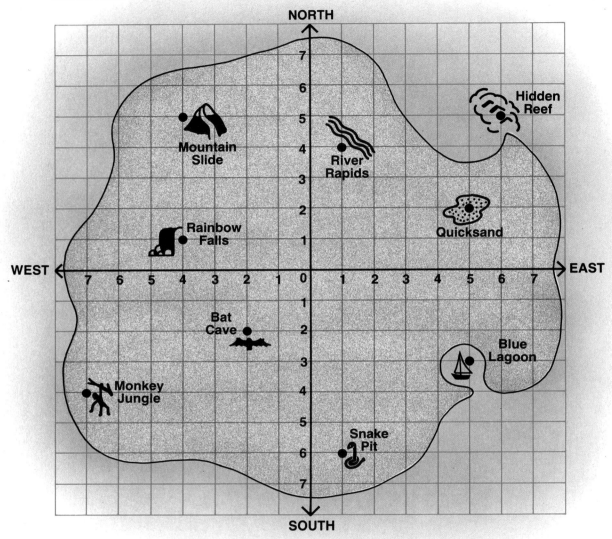

Follow the directions. What do you find on Rainbow Island?

1. east 5, south 3 _lagoon_

2. west 4, north 1 _Rainbow Falls_

3. east 6, north 5 _hidden Reef_

4. west 7, south 4 _monkey Jungle_

5. east 1, south 6 _snake pit_

6. east 1, north 4 _River rapids_

What ordered pair of directions tells the location of

7. the Bat Cave?

8. the Mountain Slide?

9. the Quicksand?

COMPUTER

More About Computers

Engineers plan, design, and build the computer hardware, which is made of metals, plastics, and other materials. Engineers help increase the speed of the computer and the amount of data that can be handled. They improve efficiency and reliability. **Efficiency** streamlines operations, and efficient operations run smoothly. **Reliability** means that the hardware operates correctly over long periods of time.

Engineers build **error-checking** into the hardware. Remember that a byte has eight bits. Suppose a byte is 01010101. There are four 1s, and so four bits are on. If an even number of bits are on, the byte is said to have **even parity**. A **check-bit** can be added to each byte. If an odd number of bits are on, then the byte has **odd parity** and the check-bit is turned on. Now the byte and the check-bit have even parity. If the byte has even parity, the check-bit is left off. The combination still has even parity. If the combination ever has odd parity, the machine signals the programmer that there is a **parity error**.

When calculations are important, as in a space shuttle, all calculations are repeated in three **parallel computers**. If computer A finds a parity error, it gets the correct data from computer B and computer C.

Hardware is continually being improved. The computer lesson in Chapter 3 described a new recording method that can increase floppy-disk capacities.

Output devices such as printers are also being improved. Most printers now print from 15 to 50 single characters per second. Faster printers print whole lines at 50 lines per second. **Ink-jet printers** "squirt" lines of print at 750 lines per second. It would take about 20 seconds to print this book.

Match the letter of the phrase with the number of the term that best fits.

1. Engineers

2. Check-bits

3. Bytes of even parity

4. Parallel computers

5. Ink-jet printers

6. New recording methods

a. squirt lines of print at a rapid rate.

b. force bytes to have even parity.

c. can increase floppy-disk capacities.

d. improve efficiency and reliability.

e. correct parity errors.

f. ensure reliability of data.

Choose the correct answers.

1. What number does the blue digit name?

89,457,342

A. 4 thousand
B. 40 thousand
C. 400 thousand
D. not here

2. Find the missing number.

$4 + \underline{\ ?\ } = 12$

A. 3
B. 8
C. 48
D. not here

3. Add.

826
175
467
+ 98

A. 1,288
B. 1,375
C. 1,566
D. not here

4. Subtract.

4,507
− 899

A. 3,608
B. 5,406
C. 3,706
D. not here

5. Multiply.

$369 \times 4 = \underline{\ ?\ }$

A. 1,236
B. 1,456
C. 1,436
D. not here

6. Multiply.

586
× 74

A. 6,466
B. 46,844
C. 43,364
D. not here

7. Find the average.

96, 55, 89

A. 80
B. 94
C. 75
D. not here

8. Divide.

$3,600 \div 40 = \underline{\ ?\ }$

A. 9
B. 90
C. 900
D. not here

9. Divide.

$62\overline{)9,468}$

A. 153
B. 152 r 44
C. 175 r 13
D. not here

10. A butterfly kite is made with tissue paper. It takes 2 sheets of paper to make each kite. How many kites can be made from 13,876 sheets of paper?

A. 6,839
B. 27,752
C. 6,938
D. not here

11. Laticia buys 18 cans of tennis balls. There are 3 balls in each can. How many tennis balls does Laticia buy?

A. 54
B. 21
C. 6
D. not here

Number Theory and Fractions

Divisibility • Factors, Primes, and Composites • Prime Factors
• Greatest Common Factor • Least Common Multiple
• Problem Solving: Choosing the Sensible Answer • Fractions
• Finding Parts of a Group • Equivalent Fractions • Finding
Equivalent Fractions • Lowest Terms • Comparing Fractions
• Whole Numbers, Mixed Numbers, and Fractions • Dividing
to Find Mixed Numbers • Problem Solving: Using a Schedule
• Probability and Predictions • Cross Products

Divisibility

Divide one number by another.
If the remainder is 0, then the first number
is **divisible** by the second.

14 is divisible by 2.   15 is not divisible by 2.

$$\begin{array}{r} 7 \\ 2\overline{)14} \\ -14 \\ \hline 0 \end{array}$$ $$\begin{array}{r} 7 \\ 2\overline{)15} \\ -14 \\ \hline 1 \end{array}$$

These rules will help you determine if a number is divisible by
2, 5, or 10.

Even numbers are divisible by 2.
Here are five even numbers. → 2, 4, 6, 8, 10
Divide each by 2. There is no remainder.

Odd numbers are not divisible by 2.
Here are five odd numbers. → 3, 5, 7, 9, 11
Divide each by 2. There is always a remainder of 1.

If there is a 0 or a 5 in the ones place,
then the number is divisible by 5.
These numbers are divisible by 5. → 5, 10, 15, 20, 25, 30

If there is a 0 in the ones place,
then the number is divisible by 10.
These numbers are divisible by 10. → 10, 20, 30, 40, 50, 60

Practice • Is the first number divisible by the second? Write YES or NO.

1. 8, 2   **2.** 36, 4   **3.** 53, 10   **4.** 17, 3   **5.** 95, 5

Is the number divisible by 2? Write YES or NO.

6. 56   **7.** 33   **8.** 27   **9.** 68   **10.** 49

More Practice • Is the first number divisible by the second? Write YES or NO.

11. 64, 9   12. 81, 8   13. 19, 3   14. 14, 2   15. 24, 5

16. 57, 7   17. 40, 4   18. 80, 10   19. 21, 6   20. 56, 9

21. 35, 4   22. 13, 2   23. 72, 8   24. 80, 6   25. 49, 7

26. 15, 5   27. 50, 10   28. 33, 3   29. 73, 10   30. 96, 6

Is the number divisible by 2? Write YES or NO.

31. 25   32. 24   33. 35   34. 60   35. 16

36. 20   37. 19   38. 40   39. 85   40. 23

Is the number divisible by 5? Write YES or NO.

41. 25   42. 24   43. 35   44. 60   45. 16

46. 20   47. 19   48. 40   49. 85   50. 23

Is the number divisible by 10? Write YES or NO.

51. 25   52. 24   53. 35   54. 60   55. 16

★ 56. 40,520   ★ 57. 56,212   ★ 58. 108,090   ★ 59. 180,605   ★ 60. 2,780,450

PROBLEM SOLVING • APPLICATIONS

Complete the table. Write YES or NO.

		Divisible by:		
	Number	**2**	**5**	**10**
61.	416	YES	NO	NO
62.	385	?	?	?
63.	260	?	?	?
64.	836	?	?	?
65.	935	?	?	?
66.	870	?	?	?
67.	797	?	?	?

Use the table. Write TRUE or FALSE.

★ 68. If a number is divisible by 5, then it is always divisible by 10.

★ 69. If a number is divisible by 10, then it is always divisible by 5.

★ 70. If a number is divisible by 10, then it is always divisible by 2 and 5.

155

Factors, Primes, and Composites

Two factors of 12 are 3 and 4.

$$3 \times 4 = 12$$

A number is divisible by its **factors**.

$$\begin{array}{r} 4 \\ 3{\overline{)}12} \\ -12 \\ \hline 0 \end{array} \qquad \begin{array}{r} 3 \\ 4{\overline{)}12} \\ -12 \\ \hline 0 \end{array}$$

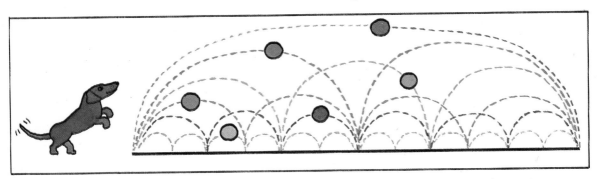

Find all the factors of 12. List them in order.

Step 1 Write 12 as the product of two whole numbers.

$$\underset{1 \times 12}{12} \qquad \underset{2 \times 6}{12} \qquad \underset{3 \times 4}{12}$$

Step 2 List the whole numbers in order. Show each only once.

Factors of 12: 1, 2, 3, 4, 6, 12

A prime number has exactly two factors: itself and 1.

The number 1 is not a prime number. It has only one factor, itself.

Factors of 3: 1, 3   3 is a prime number.

A composite number is greater than one and has more than two factors.

Factors of 4: 1, 2, 4   4 is a composite number.

Practice • Find the missing factors.

1. __?__ × 6 = 6

2. __?__ × 3 = 6

3. __?__ × 2 = 6

4. __?__ × 10 = 10

5. __?__ × 5 = 10

6. __?__ × 2 = 10

Find all the factors. List them in order.

7. 6   **8.** 10   **9.** 8   **10.** 16   **11.** 13   **12.** 22

Write PRIME or COMPOSITE.

13. 6   **14.** 9   **15.** 14   **16.** 23   **17.** 18   **18.** 15

Mixed Practice • Find the missing factors.

19. $\underline{\ ?\ } \times 4 = 20$ **20.** $\underline{\ ?\ } \times 3 = 21$ **21.** $\underline{\ ?\ } \times 3 = 33$

22. $\underline{\ ?\ } \times 12 = 36$ **23.** $\underline{\ ?\ } \times 5 = 30$ **24.** $\underline{\ ?\ } \times 5 = 25$

25. $\underline{\ ?\ } \times 10 = 50$ **26.** $\underline{\ ?\ } \times 6 = 60$ **27.** $\underline{\ ?\ } \times 8 = 32$

Find all the factors. List them in order.

28. 9   **29.** 20   **30.** 21   **31.** 15   **32.** 30   **33.** 42

34. 25   **35.** 18   **36.** 32   **37.** 27   **38.** 54   **39.** 60

40. 33   **41.** 36   **42.** 35   **43.** 40   **44.** 48   **45.** 50

46. 72   **47.** 75   **48.** 24   **49.** 31   **50.** 56   **51.** 77

Write PRIME or COMPOSITE.

52. 14   **53.** 7   **54.** 24   **55.** 39   **56.** 17   **57.** 22

58. 74   **59.** 46   **60.** 80   **61.** 53   **62.** 38   **63.** 67

64. 93   **65.** 55   **66.** 29   ★ **67.** 97   ★ **68.** 225   ★ **69.** 103

PROBLEM SOLVING • APPLICATIONS

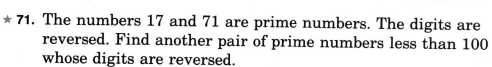

★ **70.** Some numbers have exactly 4 factors. The factors of 8 are 1, 2, 4, and 8. Find the next 3 numbers that have exactly 4 factors.

★ **71.** The numbers 17 and 71 are prime numbers. The digits are reversed. Find another pair of prime numbers less than 100 whose digits are reversed.

Prime Factors

A composite number can be shown as the product of **prime factors**.
A **factor tree** can help you find prime factors.

Step 1 Find a pair of factors for the number.

Step 2 If both factors are not prime, continue until all are prime.

Write 18 as a product of prime factors.   Write 24 as a product of prime factors.

$$18 = 2 \times 3 \times 3$$

$$24 = 2 \times 3 \times 2 \times 2$$

All the factors are prime.

Practice • Complete the factor trees.

1.
```
        30
       /  \
      2  × 15
         /   \
   ? × ? × ?
```

2.
```
        16
      /    \
     4  ×   4
    / \    / \
  ? × ? × ? × ?
```

3.
```
        27
       /  \
      ? × ?
     / \  / \
   ? × ? × ?
```

Write the number as a product of prime factors. Use a factor tree.

4. 8   **5.** 15   **6.** 28   **7.** 20   **8.** 40   **9.** 42

Mixed Practice • Complete the factor trees.

10.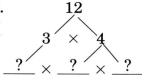
12
3 × 4
_?_ × _?_ × _?_

11. 25
_?_ × _?_

12.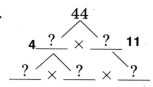
44
4 _?_ × _?_ 11
_?_ × _?_ × _?_

Write the number as a product of prime factors. Use a factor tree.

13. 45   14. 6   15. 39   16. 50   17. 75   18. 68

19. 21   20. 54   21. 81   22. 100   23. 55   24. 60

25. 35   26. 26   27. 66   28. 56   29. 63   30. 92

31. 32   32. 46   33. 36   34. 70   35. 99   36. 65

37. 14   38. 49   39. 74   40. 95   41. 34   42. 51

Draw three different factor trees for the number.
Compare the results. What do you notice?

★ 43. 24   ★ 44. 40   ★ 45. 48   ★ 46. 36   ★ 47. 64   ★ 48. 72

A number is divisible by 3 if the sum of its digits is divisible by 3.

150   1 + 5 + 0 = 6   6 is divisible by 3.
so 150 is divisible by 3.

Is the number divisible by 3? Write YES or NO.

★ 49. 18   ★ 50. 51   ★ 51. 75   ★ 52. 82   ★ 53. 43   ★ 54. 249

A number is divisible by 9 if the sum of its digits is divisible by 9.

576   5 + 7 + 6 = 18   18 is divisible by 9.
so 576 is divisible by 9.

Is the number divisible by 9? Write YES or NO.

★ 55. 54   ★ 56. 87   ★ 57. 102   ★ 58. 153   ★ 59. 648   ★ 60. 516

Greatest Common Factor

1, 2, and 4 are factors of both 8 and 12.

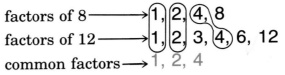

factors of 8 ⟶ 1, 2, 4, 8

factors of 12 ⟶ 1, 2, 3, 4, 6, 12

common factors ⟶ 1, 2, 4

These factors are **common factors**.

4 is the **greatest common factor** of 8 and 12.

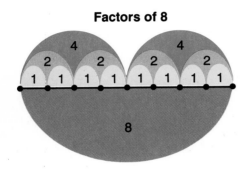

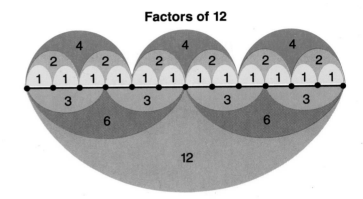

Find the **greatest common factor** of 16 and 24.

Step 1 List the factors of 16 in order. 1, 2, 4, 8, 16

Step 2 List the factors of 24 in order. 1, 2, 3, 4, 6, 8, 12, 24

Step 3 List the common factors. 1, 2, 4, 8

Step 4 Write the greatest common factor. 8

Practice • List all the factors in order.

1. 36   2. 24   3. 18   4. 12   5. 16

List the common factors in order.

6. 36, 24   7. 24, 18   8. 18, 12   9. 12, 16   10. 16, 18

Find the greatest common factors.

11. 36, 24   12. 24, 18   13. 18, 12   14. 12, 16   15. 16, 18

Mixed Practice • List all the factors in order.

16. 10   **17.** 25   **18.** 32   **19.** 21   **20.** 48

21. 72   **22.** 50   **23.** 20   **24.** 64   **25.** 54

List the common factors in order.

26. 10, 20   **27.** 32, 20   **28.** 10, 48   **29.** 21, 72   **30.** 20, 25

31. 48, 72   **32.** 64, 32   **33.** 54, 72   **34.** 50, 20   **35.** 21, 64

Find the greatest common factors.

36. 10, 20   **37.** 32, 20   **38.** 10, 48   **39.** 21, 72   **40.** 20, 25

41. 48, 72   **42.** 64, 32   **43.** 54, 72   **44.** 50, 20   **45.** 21, 64

46. 18, 54   **47.** 36, 54   **48.** 16, 48   **49.** 15, 25   **50.** 21, 42

51. 32, 72   **52.** 18, 48   ★ **53.** 9, 12, 54   ★ **54.** 27, 36, 72   ★ **55.** 16, 24, 56

PROBLEM SOLVING • **APPLICATIONS**

The factors of 8 are inside the blue circle.

The factors of 12 are inside the green circle.

The common factors are inside both circles.

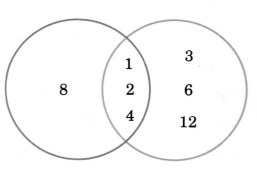

For each pair of numbers, draw circles to show the factors.
Show the common factors inside both circles.

★ **56.** 15, 25   ★ **57.** 9, 18   ★ **58.** 35, 25

★ **59.** 27, 36   ★ **60.** 16, 24   ★ **61.** 20, 30

Skills Maintenance

1. $20\overline{)400}$ **2.** $15\overline{)453}$ **3.** $28\overline{)63}$ **4.** $56\overline{)4,031}$ **5.** $82\overline{)1,640}$

6. $93\overline{)4,743}$ **7.** $45\overline{)135}$ **8.** $18\overline{)900}$ **9.** $30\overline{)9,276}$ **10.** $64\overline{)5,761}$

Least Common Multiple

When you multiply a number by 0, 1, 2, 3, and so on, the product is a multiple of that number.

0, 2, 4, 6, 8, 10, 12 are multiples of 2.
0, 3, 6, 9, 12, 15, 18 are multiples of 3.

Multiples that are the same for two or more numbers are called **common multiples**. The common multiples of 2 and 3 that are shown are 0, 6, and 12. The **least common multiple** of 2 and 3 is 6. Zero is not a least common multiple.

Find the least common multiple of 3 and 4.

Step 1 List multiples of 3. ⟶ 0, 3, 6, 9, 12, 15, 18, 21, 24, 27, . . .

Step 2 List multiples of 4. ⟶ 0, 4, 8, 12, 16, 20, 24, 28, . . .

Step 3 List the common multiples. ⟶ 0, 12, 24

Step 4 Write the least common multiple that is not zero. ⟶ 12

Practice • List six multiples in order. Start with zero.

1. 4   **2.** 5   **3.** 7   **4.** 9   **5.** 18

Find the least common multiple.

6. 4, 5   **7.** 5, 7   **8.** 9, 18   **9.** 4, 7   **10.** 4, 18

Mixed Practice • List six multiples in order. Start with zero.

11. 6   **12.** 8   **13.** 10   **14.** 11   **15.** 15

16. 20   **17.** 25   **18.** 50   **19.** 12   **20.** 100

21. 16   **22.** 32   **23.** 14   **24.** 30   **25.** 45

Find the least common multiple.

26. 6, 8   **27.** 10, 25   **28.** 12, 20   **29.** 10, 15   **30.** 16, 12
31. 8, 12   **32.** 20, 25   **33.** 20, 50   **34.** 32, 16   **35.** 50, 100
36. 12, 15   **37.** 50, 30   **38.** 30, 45   **39.** 15, 25   **40.** 20, 16
41. 8, 20   **42.** 32, 40   **43.** 15, 45   **44.** 16, 40   **45.** 10, 14
★**46.** 3, 4, 6 ★**47.** 4, 5, 8   ★**48.** 2, 5, 6   ★**49.** 3, 6, 8   ★**50.** 5, 8, 10

PROBLEM SOLVING • APPLICATIONS

51. Frank wants to buy the same number of hamburgers and rolls. There are 6 hamburgers in a package. There are 8 rolls in a package. What is the fewest number of hamburgers he must buy if he buys full packages? How many packages is this? How many packages of rolls must he buy?

★ **52.** Frank also wants to buy 72 paper plates, napkins, and cups. The plates are sold with 12 in a package. The cups are sold with 9 in a package and napkins are sold with 36 in a box. How many packages of each must he buy?

Midchapter Review

Is the number divisible by 2?
Write YES or NO.   **1.** 17   **2.** 54

Is the number divisible by 5?
Write YES or NO.   **3.** 70   **4.** 45

Find all the factors. List them in order.   **5.** 24   **6.** 29

Write PRIME or COMPOSITE.   **7.** 19   **8.** 27

Write the number as a product of prime factors.
Use a factor tree.   **9.** 36   **10.** 70

Find the greatest common factor.   **11.** 10, 75   **12.** 54, 42

Find the least common multiple.   **13.** 5, 7   **14.** 6, 8

PROBLEM SOLVING · STRATEGIES

Choosing the Sensible Answer

When solving a problem, think about whether your answer makes sense.

Bill is in charge of selling tickets to a dinner the school is having. On Monday he sold $975.15 worth of tickets. He sold $697.75 in tickets on Tuesday. How much money did he collect both days?

Which of these answers is the most sensible?

$16,729.00   or $167.29   or $1,672.90

Think: $975.15 is near $1,000.
$697.75 is near $700.

The answer is about
$1,000 + $700, or $1,700.

The sensible answer is $1,672.90.

Estimate to choose the sensible answers.

1. Phillip purchased 60 heads of lettuce. Each head cost $.79. How much did he spend for the lettuce?

   $474.00 or $47.40 or $4.74

   Make sure you round correctly.

2. Nan baked 37 trays of whole wheat rolls. There were 24 rolls on each tray. How many rolls did she bake in all?

   888 or 88 or 8,880

3. Lorraine is ordering milk for the dinner. Milk costs $1.49 for a half gallon. She needs to order 88 half gallons. How much will this cost?

   $131.12 or $13.12 or $1,311.20

164

Choose the correct answer.

4. Ms. Hinton spent $48.96 for 24 pounds of butter. How much did each pound cost?

   $.20 or $20.40 or $2.04

5. Terry is setting up chairs for the dinner. He needs 420 chairs. If the chairs are stacked in stacks of 21, how many stacks will he use?

   20 or 200 or 2.00

You can check multiplication by division and check division by multiplication.

---

6. José spent $1.47 for each table display. If there are 22 tables, how much did he spend in all?

   $3.23 or $32.34 or $323.42

7. Mike figures it will cost $1.95 to feed each person. If 407 are planning to be at the dinner, what will the total cost be?

   $79.37 or $7,937.00 or $793.65

8. Nelson is in charge of entertainment. He plans to hire 6 musicians. The expense for each will be $64.92. What will be the total cost?

   $389.52 or $3,895.20 or $649.20

9. Kim sold tickets for the door prize. She sold $625 worth of chances. If each chance cost $1.25, how many chances did she sell?

   50 or 5,000 or 500

★ 10. Three custodians will be needed for 4 hours. A custodian is paid $9.25 an hour. How much money will be paid to the custodians?

   $37.00 or $111.00 or $370.00

★ 11. Carmen listed some of the expenses for the dinner: $37.98, $247.29, $86.55, $309.47, and $219.83. What was the total of the expenses she listed?

   $901.12 or $1,011.20 or $90.11

Fractions

A garden is divided into 5 equal parts.
One part is planted with red flowers.
One-fifth of the garden is planted with red flowers.

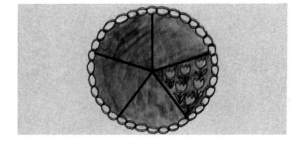

$$\frac{1}{5}\quad\frac{\textbf{numerator}}{\textbf{denominator}}\qquad\frac{\text{red part}}{\text{parts in all}}$$

The **fraction** $\frac{1}{5}$ tells what part is planted with red flowers.

10 flowers are picked from the garden.
4 of the 10 flowers are red.
Four-tenths of the flowers are red.

$$\frac{4}{10}\quad\frac{\text{red flowers}}{\text{flowers in all}}$$

Five parts are planted with flowers.
Five-fifths of the garden is planted with flowers.

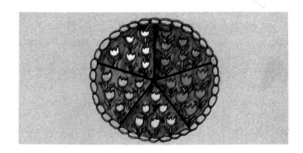

$$\frac{5}{5} = 1$$

The flowers are put into 5 vases.
Two of the vases have red flowers.
Two-fifths of the vases have red flowers.

$$\frac{2}{5}$$

Practice • Write the fraction that tells what part is blue.

1.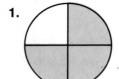
2.
3.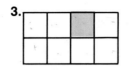
4.

Mixed Practice • Write the fraction that tells what part is blue.

5.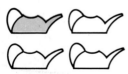
6.
7.
8.

166

The number line between 0 and 1 is divided into 4 equal parts.

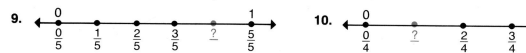

$\frac{3}{4}$ names the point. It is located three-fourths of the way from 0 to 1.

Use a fraction to name each point.

9.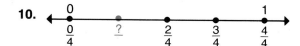

10.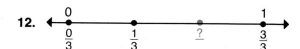

11.

12.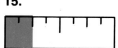

Write the fraction that tells what part is blue.

★ **13.**    ★ **14.**   ★ **15.**   ★ **16.**

★ **17.**   ★ **18.**   ★ **19.**   ★ **20.**

PROBLEM SOLVING • APPLICATIONS

Write a fraction to answer the questions.

21. A group of 5 students care for a garden. If 2 of the students plant seeds, what part of the group plants seeds?

22. José has 8 tomato plants. He sees that 3 of the plants need stakes. What part of the plants need stakes?

★ **23.** Mary buys 12 packages of seeds. She plants 5 packages in the garden. She plants 6 packages in flower boxes. What part of the packages are planted?

★ **24.** There are 6 zinnias. If 2 zinnias are yellow, what part of the zinnias are not yellow?

167

Finding Parts of a Group

There are 12 tropical fish.
Ruben owns $\frac{1}{3}$ of them. How
many belong to Ruben?

$\frac{1}{3}$ of 12 = ?

Think:
Divide them into 3 equal groups.

Ruben owns 4 tropical fish.

$12 \div 3 = 4$

$\frac{1}{3}$ of 12 = 4

There are 20 tropical fish.
Wyatt owns $\frac{3}{4}$ of them.
How many belong to Wyatt?

$\frac{3}{4}$ of 20 = ?

Think:
Divide them into 4 equal groups. $\longrightarrow$ $20 \div 4 = 5$
There are 5 in each group.
Wyatt owns 3 groups. $\longrightarrow$ $3 \times 5 = 15$

Wyatt has 15 tropical fish. $\longrightarrow$ $\frac{3}{4}$ of 20 = 15

Practice • Complete.

1.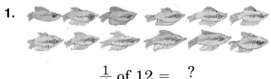

$\frac{1}{6}$ of 12 = ____?____

2.

$\frac{5}{6}$ of 12 = ____?____

3. $\frac{1}{8}$ of 24 = ____?____

4. $\frac{1}{5}$ of 15 = ____?____

5. $\frac{1}{2}$ of 16 = ____?____

6. $\frac{3}{6}$ of 24 = ____?____

7. $\frac{3}{10}$ of 30 = ____?____

8. $\frac{2}{3}$ of 18 = ____?____

Mixed Practice • Complete.

9. $\frac{1}{3}$ of 15 = ____?____

10. $\frac{5}{6}$ of 18 = ____?____

11. $\frac{2}{3}$ of 12 = ____?____

12. $\frac{1}{6}$ of 12 = ____?____

13. $\frac{1}{10}$ of 40 = ____?____

14. $\frac{1}{4}$ of 12 = ____?____

15. $\frac{4}{6}$ of 36 = ___?___

16. $\frac{5}{10}$ of 40 = ___?___

17. $\frac{1}{4}$ of 28 = ___?___

18. $\frac{5}{6}$ of 30 = ___?___

19. $\frac{7}{10}$ of 50 = ___?___

20. $\frac{3}{4}$ of 32 = ___?___

21. $\frac{3}{5}$ of 45 = ___?___

22. $\frac{3}{8}$ of 32 = ___?___

23. $\frac{4}{5}$ of 30 = ___?___

24. $\frac{1}{7}$ of 35 = ___?___

25. $\frac{1}{2}$ of 36 = ___?___

26. $\frac{3}{10}$ of 40 = ___?___

27. $\frac{4}{5}$ of 35 = ___?___

28. $\frac{7}{10}$ of 70 = ___?___

29. $\frac{7}{8}$ of 32 = ___?___

30. $\frac{3}{5}$ of 25 = ___?___

31. $\frac{5}{8}$ of 48 = ___?___

32. $\frac{3}{7}$ of 42 = ___?___

33. $\frac{1}{2}$ of 60 = ___?___

★ **34.** $\frac{5}{7}$ of 77 = ___?___

★ **35.** $\frac{4}{9}$ of 99 = ___?___

The pet store is having a sale.
The regular price is $3.
You get $\frac{1}{3}$ off.
$\frac{1}{3}$ of 3 = 1
You save $1.

How much do you save?

★ **36.** Regular price: $6
$\frac{1}{2}$ off

★ **37.** Regular price: $20
$\frac{1}{4}$ off

★ **38.** Regular price: $24
$\frac{2}{3}$ off

PROBLEM SOLVING • APPLICATIONS

39. Pat and Marty have 24 tropical fish. If $\frac{3}{4}$ of them are guppies, how many of the fish are guppies?

40. The pet store orders 20 boxes of pet food. If $\frac{1}{10}$ of them are fish food, how many of the boxes are fish food?

★ **41.** One day the pet store sells 56 tropical fish. If $\frac{4}{7}$ of them are angelfish, how many are not angelfish?

★ **42.** The pet store takes in $368. Exactly $\frac{3}{8}$ of the money is from tropical fish sales. How much is from tropical fish sales?

169

Equivalent Fractions

These two pies are the same size.

This pie is cut into thirds.

$\frac{2}{3}$ of the pie is yours.

$\frac{2}{3}$ is the same amount as $\frac{8}{12}$

$\frac{2}{3} = \frac{8}{12}$ $\frac{2}{3}$ and $\frac{8}{12}$ are **equivalent fractions.**

This pie is cut into twelfths.

$\frac{8}{12}$ of the pie is yours.

Equivalent fractions name the same number.

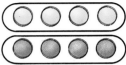

The balls are separated into 2 groups with the same number in each group.

$\frac{1}{2}$ of the balls are blue.

$\frac{1}{2} = \frac{2}{4}$ $\frac{1}{2}$ and $\frac{2}{4}$ are equivalent fractions.

Now the balls are separated into 4 groups with the same number in each group.

$\frac{2}{4}$ of the balls are blue.

Practice • Complete.

1.

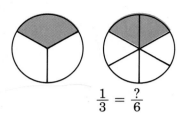

$\frac{1}{3} = \frac{?}{6}$

2.

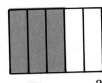

$\frac{3}{5} = \frac{?}{10}$

3.

$\frac{2}{6} = \frac{?}{3}$

4.

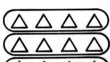

$\frac{4}{12} = \frac{?}{3}$

Mixed Practice • Complete.

5.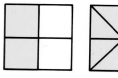

$$\frac{2}{4} = \frac{?}{8}$$

6.

$$\frac{3}{6} = \frac{?}{2}$$

7.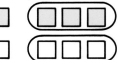

$$\frac{2}{3} = \frac{?}{6}$$

8.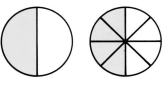

$$\frac{1}{2} = \frac{?}{8}$$

9.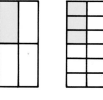

$$\frac{1}{4} = \frac{?}{12}$$

10.

$$\frac{4}{6} = \frac{?}{3}$$

Use the fraction bars. Complete.

11. $\frac{1}{2} = \frac{?}{6}$ 12. $\frac{2}{3} = \frac{?}{9}$

13. $\frac{2}{5} = \frac{?}{10}$ 14. $\frac{1}{2} = \frac{?}{10}$

15. $\frac{2}{4} = \frac{?}{2}$ 16. $\frac{4}{6} = \frac{?}{9}$

17. $\frac{2}{8} = \frac{?}{4}$ 18. $\frac{6}{8} = \frac{?}{4}$

Write two equivalent fractions.

★ 19. $\frac{1}{2}$ ★ 20. 1   ★ 21. $\frac{1}{3}$

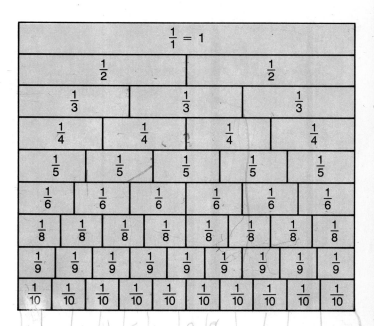

PROBLEM SOLVING • APPLICATIONS

22. Abe and Andrew go to a party. Carrot cake is served. Andrew eats $\frac{1}{5}$ of the cake. Abe eats $\frac{2}{10}$ of the cake. Who eats more cake?

★ 23. Sara has a piece of ribbon $\frac{2}{3}$ yard long. Dana has a piece of ribbon $\frac{6}{9}$ yard long and Phil has a piece $\frac{8}{12}$ yard long. Who has the longer piece of ribbon?

Finding Equivalent Fractions

David and Denise are baking a spinach pie. When it is baked, they will cut it into 8 pieces of the same size. Denise will get $\frac{3}{4}$ of the pie. How many eighths will Denise get?

$$\frac{3}{4} = \frac{?}{8}$$

Think:
What number times 4 is 8?
Since 2 times 4 = 8,
multiply the numerator by 2.
Denise will get $\frac{6}{8}$ of the pie.

$$\frac{3}{4} = \frac{2 \times 3}{2 \times 4} = \frac{6}{8}$$

To find an equivalent fraction, multiply the numerator and the denominator by the same number.

Make the fractions equivalent.

$\frac{2}{3} = \frac{?}{15}$ **Think:** ? × 3 = 15

$$\frac{2}{3} = \frac{5 \times 2}{5 \times 3} = \frac{10}{15}$$

$\frac{3}{4} = \frac{9}{?}$ **Think:** ? × 3 = 9

$$\frac{3}{4} = \frac{3 \times 3}{3 \times 4} = \frac{9}{12}$$

Practice • Multiply the numerator and the denominator by 2 to find equivalent fractions.

1. $\frac{1}{3}$ 2. $\frac{1}{6}$ 3. $\frac{1}{5}$ 4. $\frac{2}{3}$ 5. $\frac{3}{4}$ 6. $\frac{5}{8}$

Complete.

7. $\frac{1}{2} = \frac{?}{4}$ 8. $\frac{1}{6} = \frac{2}{?}$ 9. $\frac{1}{3} = \frac{?}{12}$ 10. $\frac{2}{4} = \frac{?}{8}$

Mixed Practice • Multiply the numerator and the denominator by 4 to find equivalent fractions.

11. $\frac{2}{3}$ 12. $\frac{3}{4}$ 13. $\frac{7}{10}$ 14. $\frac{3}{8}$ 15. $\frac{2}{5}$ 16. $\frac{3}{6}$

Multiply the numerator and the denominator by 10 to find
equivalent fractions.

17. $\frac{2}{8}$ **18.** $\frac{1}{2}$ **19.** $\frac{4}{5}$ **20.** $\frac{4}{6}$ **21.** $\frac{2}{3}$ **22.** $\frac{3}{4}$

Complete.

23. $\frac{2}{5} = \frac{?}{10}$ **24.** $\frac{2}{3} = \frac{6}{?}$ **25.** $\frac{1}{4} = \frac{?}{12}$ **26.** $\frac{7}{8} = \frac{?}{16}$

27. $\frac{1}{2} = \frac{?}{10}$ **28.** $\frac{4}{5} = \frac{?}{15}$ **29.** $\frac{2}{4} = \frac{?}{16}$ **30.** $\frac{4}{5} = \frac{8}{?}$

31. $\frac{1}{4} = \frac{?}{8}$ **32.** $\frac{3}{5} = \frac{?}{15}$ **33.** $\frac{1}{3} = \frac{5}{?}$ **34.** $\frac{5}{6} = \frac{?}{12}$

35. $\frac{3}{8} = \frac{6}{?}$ **36.** $\frac{2}{6} = \frac{?}{12}$ **37.** $\frac{1}{2} = \frac{?}{6}$ **38.** $\frac{2}{3} = \frac{?}{18}$

Look for a pattern. Write the next three equivalent fractions.

★ **39.** $\frac{1}{2}, \frac{2}{4}, \frac{3}{6}, \underline{\hspace{0.5cm}?}, \underline{\hspace{0.5cm}?}, \underline{\hspace{0.5cm}?}$

★ **40.** $\frac{1}{3}, \frac{2}{6}, \frac{3}{9}, \underline{\hspace{0.5cm}?}, \underline{\hspace{0.5cm}?}, \underline{\hspace{0.5cm}?}$

★ **41.** $\frac{3}{4}, \frac{6}{8}, \frac{9}{12}, \underline{\hspace{0.5cm}?}, \underline{\hspace{0.5cm}?}, \underline{\hspace{0.5cm}?}$

★ **42.** $\frac{4}{5}, \frac{8}{10}, \frac{12}{15}, \underline{\hspace{0.5cm}?}, \underline{\hspace{0.5cm}?}, \underline{\hspace{0.5cm}?}$

PROBLEM SOLVING • APPLICATIONS

43. Amy rides her bicycle to school. The distance is 2,500 meters. She is $\frac{3}{5}$ of the way there. How many meters has she ridden?

44. Ramon rides his bicycle to his friend's house. The distance is 2,700 meters. He is $\frac{4}{9}$ of the way there. How many meters has he ridden?

★ **45.** Lorraine walks 3,000 meters each day. She walks $\frac{5}{15}$ of the distance in the morning. How many meters does she walk during the rest of the day?

★ **46.** Baron is painting a fence that is 18 meters long. He has painted $\frac{24}{36}$ of the fence. How many meters does he have left to paint?

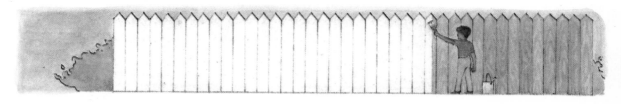

Lowest Terms

$\frac{4}{8}$, $\frac{2}{4}$, and $\frac{1}{2}$, are equivalent fractions.

To find an equivalent fraction divide the numerator and denominator by the same number.

$$\frac{4}{8} = \frac{4 \div 4}{8 \div 4} = \frac{1}{2}$$

$$\frac{2}{4} = \frac{2 \div 2}{4 \div 2} = \frac{1}{2}$$

The numerator and denominator are called the terms of a fraction.

$\frac{4}{8}$ in lowest terms is $\frac{1}{2}$.

$\frac{2}{4}$ in lowest terms is $\frac{1}{2}$.

A fraction is in lowest terms when the numerator and the denominator have no common factor greater than 1.

Write $\frac{12}{16}$ in lowest terms.

Step 1 Find the factors of 12 and 16 in order. Find the greatest common factor.

$$12 \rightarrow 1, 2, 3, 4, 6, 12$$
$$16 \rightarrow 1, 2, 4, 8, 16$$

Step 2 Divide the numerator and the denominator by the greatest common factor, 4.

$$\frac{12}{16} = \frac{12 \div 4}{16 \div 4} = \frac{3}{4}$$

$\frac{12}{16}$ in lowest terms is $\frac{3}{4}$.

Practice • Complete.

1. $\frac{2}{6} = \frac{2 \div 2}{6 \div 2} = \frac{?}{3}$

2. $\frac{6}{8} = \frac{6 \div 2}{8 \div 2} = \frac{3}{?}$

3. $\frac{3}{6} = \frac{3 \div 3}{6 \div 3} = \frac{?}{?}$

List the factors in order. Find the greatest common factors.

4. 4 and 16

5. 6 and 8

6. 12 and 16

Write the fractions in lowest terms.

7. $\frac{4}{16}$

8. $\frac{5}{10}$

9. $\frac{12}{16}$

10. $\frac{10}{12}$

11. $\frac{12}{15}$

12. $\frac{8}{10}$

Mixed Practice • Complete.

13. $\frac{3}{9} = \frac{3 \div 3}{9 \div 3} = $ ___?___   14. $\frac{10}{15} = \frac{10 \div 5}{15 \div 5} = $ ___?___   15. $\frac{8}{12} = \frac{8 \div 4}{12 \div 4} = $ ___?___

List the factors in order. Find the greatest common factors.

16. 12 and 21   **17.** 36 and 28   **18.** 16 and 24

19. 36 and 27   **20.** 12 and 32   **21.** 28 and 12

22. 26 and 42   **23.** 18 and 42   **24.** 12 and 27

Write the fractions in lowest terms.

25. $\frac{8}{12}$ **26.** $\frac{14}{16}$ **27.** $\frac{4}{10}$ **28.** $\frac{9}{12}$ **29.** $\frac{10}{15}$ **30.** $\frac{10}{20}$

31. $\frac{16}{32}$ **32.** $\frac{6}{9}$ **33.** $\frac{24}{36}$ **34.** $\frac{21}{28}$ **35.** $\frac{15}{25}$ **36.** $\frac{8}{16}$

37. $\frac{6}{8}$ **38.** $\frac{24}{27}$ **39.** $\frac{18}{32}$ ★ **40.** $\frac{96}{100}$ ★ **41.** $\frac{78}{84}$ ★ **42.** $\frac{78}{79}$

PROBLEM SOLVING • APPLICATIONS

Write the fractions in lowest terms.

43. There are 27 students in the class, and 18 of them come to school on the bus. What fraction of the students in the class comes to school on the bus?

44. There are 100 students in the lunchroom. Today 25 of them do not drink milk with their lunch. What fraction of these students do not drink milk with their lunch?

★ 45. There are 38 students in Room 7 and 34 in Room 8. Of these students, 16 go home for lunch. What fraction of the students go home for lunch?

★ 46. There are 13 boys and 11 girls in one class. If 18 of them like to ride a bicycle, what fraction of the class likes to ride a bicycle?

175

Comparing Fractions

Compare $\frac{2}{5}$ and $\frac{3}{5}$.

To compare fractions when both have the same denominator, compare the numerators.

Think: 2 is less than 3.

So $\frac{2}{5} < \frac{3}{5}$.

Compare $\frac{4}{5}$ and $\frac{2}{3}$.

To compare these fractions you can use equivalent fractions that have the same denominator.

Use the **least common denominator** for $\frac{4}{5}$ and $\frac{2}{3}$.

Step 1
Find the least common multiple of the denominators. This multiple is the least common denominator.

3   3, 6, 9, 12, 15
5   5, 10, 15

Step 2
Write equivalent fractions. Use 15 as the denominator.

$$\frac{4}{5} = \frac{3 \times 4}{3 \times 5} = \frac{12}{15} \qquad \frac{2}{3} = \frac{5 \times 2}{5 \times 3} = \frac{10}{15}$$

Since $\frac{12}{15} > \frac{10}{15}$, then $\frac{4}{5} > \frac{2}{3}$.

Practice • Find the least common multiple.

1. 4, 8

2. 5, 10

3. 6, 9

4. 10, 15

Find the least common denominator. Write equivalent fractions.

5. $\frac{3}{4}, \frac{5}{8}$

6. $\frac{2}{5}, \frac{3}{10}$

7. $\frac{5}{6}, \frac{1}{9}$

8. $\frac{7}{10}, \frac{8}{15}$

Write >, <, or =.

9. $\frac{3}{4}$ ⬤ $\frac{5}{8}$

10. $\frac{2}{5}$ ⬤ $\frac{4}{10}$

11. $\frac{5}{6}$ ⬤ $\frac{1}{9}$

12. $\frac{8}{15}$ ⬤ $\frac{7}{10}$

Mixed Practice • Find the least common multiple.

13. 5, 8   **14.** 2, 4   **15.** 6, 4   **16.** 3, 9

Find the least common denominator. Write equivalent fractions.

17. $\frac{2}{5}, \frac{7}{8}$ **18.** $\frac{1}{2}, \frac{3}{4}$ **19.** $\frac{5}{6}, \frac{3}{4}$ **20.** $\frac{2}{3}, \frac{5}{9}$

21. $\frac{2}{3}, \frac{5}{6}$ **22.** $\frac{1}{5}, \frac{1}{3}$ **23.** $\frac{1}{4}, \frac{2}{7}$ **24.** $\frac{3}{4}, \frac{2}{3}$

25. $\frac{2}{3}, \frac{1}{7}$ **26.** $\frac{3}{4}, \frac{4}{5}$ **27.** $\frac{1}{3}, \frac{5}{8}$ **28.** $\frac{2}{5}, \frac{4}{6}$

Write >, <, or =.

29. $\frac{2}{5} \bullet \frac{7}{8}$ **30.** $\frac{1}{2} \bullet \frac{3}{4}$ **31.** $\frac{5}{6} \bullet \frac{3}{4}$ **32.** $\frac{2}{3} \bullet \frac{5}{9}$

33. $\frac{2}{3} \bullet \frac{9}{15}$ **34.** $\frac{8}{12} \bullet \frac{5}{8}$ **35.** $\frac{1}{2} \bullet \frac{8}{16}$ **36.** $\frac{3}{4} \bullet \frac{7}{10}$

37. $\frac{3}{4} \bullet \frac{1}{9}$ **38.** $\frac{2}{3} \bullet \frac{2}{8}$ **39.** $\frac{3}{8} \bullet \frac{7}{8}$ **40.** $\frac{3}{7} \bullet \frac{2}{5}$

Write the fractions in order from least to greatest.
Hint: Find an equivalent fraction for each.

★ **41.** $\frac{1}{2}, \frac{1}{4}, \frac{1}{3}$ ★ **42.** $\frac{4}{9}, \frac{1}{3}, \frac{3}{6}$ ★ **43.** $\frac{2}{3}, \frac{1}{9}, \frac{5}{6}$

PROBLEM SOLVING • APPLICATIONS

44. The students in the home economics class use $\frac{1}{3}$ dozen eggs to make an omelet. They use $\frac{1}{6}$ dozen eggs to make a nut bread. Which recipe uses fewer eggs?

★ **45.** It takes Philip $\frac{3}{4}$ hour to walk to school. It takes Joanna 20 minutes to walk to school. Who spends more time walking to school, Philip or Joanna?

Skills Maintenance

1. $\begin{array}{r} 23 \\ \times 40 \\ \hline \end{array}$ **2.** $\begin{array}{r} 90 \\ \times 400 \\ \hline \end{array}$ **3.** $\begin{array}{r} 96 \\ \times 30 \\ \hline \end{array}$ **4.** $\begin{array}{r} 70 \\ \times 80 \\ \hline \end{array}$ **5.** $\begin{array}{r} 68 \\ \times 600 \\ \hline \end{array}$

6. $\begin{array}{r} 58 \\ \times 60 \\ \hline \end{array}$ **7.** $\begin{array}{r} 23 \\ \times 800 \\ \hline \end{array}$ **8.** $\begin{array}{r} 40 \\ \times 700 \\ \hline \end{array}$ **9.** $\begin{array}{r} 927 \\ \times 800 \\ \hline \end{array}$ **10.** $\begin{array}{r} 35 \\ \times 70 \\ \hline \end{array}$

Whole Numbers, Mixed Numbers, and Fractions

A fraction names 1 when the numerator and the denominator are the same. A fraction names a **whole number** when the numerator is a multiple of the denominator.

There are 4 fourths in 1.

There are 12 thirds in 4.

$$1 = \frac{4}{4}$$

$$4 = \frac{12}{3}$$

You can change a whole number to a fraction by writing an equivalent fraction.

Write the whole number over a denominator of 1.
Multiply the numerator and denominator by the same whole number.

$$1 = \frac{1}{1} = \frac{4 \times 1}{4 \times 1} = \frac{4}{4} \qquad 4 = \frac{4}{1} = \frac{3 \times 4}{3 \times 1} = \frac{12}{3}$$

Some numbers can be named with a **mixed number**.

$$2 \text{ oranges and } \frac{1}{4} \text{ orange} = 2 \text{ and } \frac{1}{4}$$

$$2\frac{1}{4}$$

You can change a mixed number to a fraction by adding.

$$2\frac{1}{4} = 2 + \frac{1}{4}$$

$$2\frac{1}{4} = \frac{8}{4} + \frac{1}{4}$$

$$2\frac{1}{4} = \frac{9}{4}$$

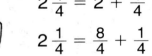 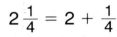

Practice • Write the whole number or the mixed number.

1.    2. 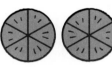   3.    4.

Complete.

5. $1 = \frac{?}{3}$ **6.** $7 = \frac{?}{2}$ **7.** $4 = \frac{?}{6}$ **8.** $1 = \frac{?}{12}$

Write as fractions.

9. $3\frac{1}{2}$ **10.** $4\frac{1}{3}$ **11.** $1\frac{4}{5}$ **12.** $2\frac{3}{8}$

178

Mixed Practice • Complete.

13. $5 = \frac{?}{3}$ **14.** $2 = \frac{?}{4}$ **15.** $1 = \frac{?}{8}$ **16.** $4 = \frac{?}{10}$

Write as fractions.

17. $1\frac{5}{8}$ **18.** $3\frac{5}{6}$ **19.** $6\frac{3}{4}$ **20.** $3\frac{3}{4}$ **21.** $4\frac{2}{3}$ **22.** $6\frac{3}{5}$

23. $5\frac{2}{3}$ **24.** $7\frac{1}{2}$ **25.** $1\frac{3}{4}$ **26.** $4\frac{4}{5}$ **27.** $2\frac{2}{3}$ **28.** $6\frac{2}{3}$

29. $2\frac{1}{5}$ **30.** $4\frac{1}{2}$ **31.** $1\frac{1}{2}$ **32.** $8\frac{1}{3}$ **33.** $1\frac{5}{6}$ **34.** $3\frac{1}{2}$

35. $2\frac{1}{2}$ **36.** $9\frac{1}{2}$ **37.** $6\frac{1}{3}$ **38.** $5\frac{1}{4}$ **39.** $3\frac{2}{5}$ **40.** $4\frac{4}{7}$

Here is another way to write $3\frac{3}{4}$ as a fraction.

Step 1
Multiply: $4 \times 3 = 12$

Step 2
Add: $12 + 3 = 15$

Step 3
Write the sum over the denominator.

$3\frac{3}{4}$ $3\frac{3}{4}$ $3\frac{3}{4} = \frac{15}{4}$

Write as fractions. Use Steps 1, 2, and 3.

41. $3\frac{1}{3}$ **42.** $4\frac{5}{7}$ **43.** $9\frac{3}{8}$ **44.** $2\frac{3}{5}$ **45.** $6\frac{4}{9}$ **46.** $5\frac{5}{6}$

47. $4\frac{3}{5}$ **48.** $6\frac{1}{8}$ **49.** $8\frac{3}{4}$ **50.** $9\frac{1}{6}$ ★ **51.** $43\frac{3}{10}$ ★ **52.** $7\frac{11}{100}$

PROBLEM SOLVING • APPLICATIONS

53. There are $6\frac{1}{2}$ dozen eggs. How many half-dozens is this?

54. There are $3\frac{1}{3}$ yards of ribbon. How many thirds of a yard is this?

★ **55.** There are $4\frac{1}{2}$ oranges. Are there enough halves for each of 10 people to have one half of an orange?

★ **56.** There are $2\frac{2}{3}$ sheets of colored paper. Are there enough thirds for each of 8 students to receive one third of a sheet?

179

Dividing to Find Mixed Numbers

Find the mixed number for $\frac{29}{8}$.
Use the pictures to help you.

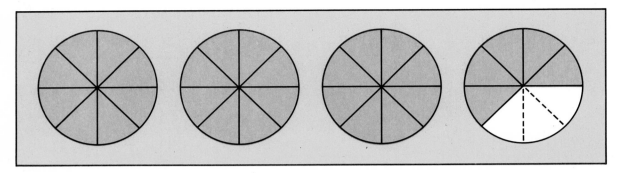

$\frac{29}{8}$ $\longrightarrow$ $\frac{24}{8} + \frac{5}{8}$ $\longrightarrow$ $3 + \frac{5}{8}$ $\longrightarrow$ $3\frac{5}{8}$

You can also divide to find the mixed number for $\frac{29}{8}$.

Step 1
Divide the numerator by the denominator.

$$\begin{array}{r} 3 \\ 8\overline{)29} \\ -24 \\ \hline 5 \end{array}$$

Step 2
Show the remainder in a fraction.
The remainder is the numerator.
The divisor is the denominator.

$$\begin{array}{r} 3\frac{5}{8} \\ 8\overline{)29} \\ -24 \\ \hline 5 \end{array}$$

The mixed number for $\frac{29}{8}$ is $3\frac{5}{8}$.

Practice • Divide. Show the remainder in a fraction.

1. $3\overline{)7}$ 2. $18 \div 5$ 3. $2\overline{)15}$ 4. $8\overline{)43}$ 5. $37 \div 6$ 6. $9\overline{)85}$

Divide to find the mixed numbers.

7. $\frac{11}{2}$ 8. $\frac{27}{4}$ 9. $\frac{35}{8}$ 10. $\frac{17}{3}$ 11. $\frac{19}{2}$ 12. $\frac{25}{4}$

Mixed Practice • Divide. Show the remainder in a fraction.

13. $6\overline{)13}$ 14. $19 \div 4$ 15. $26 \div 3$ 16. $5\overline{)38}$ 17. $8\overline{)71}$ 18. $9\overline{)86}$

180

Divide to find the numbers.

19. $\frac{11}{8}$ 20. $\frac{5}{2}$ 21. $\frac{11}{3}$ 22. $\frac{13}{5}$ 23. $\frac{7}{6}$ 24. $\frac{22}{7}$

25. $\frac{13}{2}$ 26. $\frac{20}{3}$ 27. $\frac{17}{4}$ 28. $\frac{33}{8}$ 29. $\frac{9}{2}$ 30. $\frac{10}{9}$

31. $\frac{7}{2}$ 32. $\frac{13}{2}$ 33. $\frac{13}{8}$ 34. $\frac{14}{3}$ 35. $\frac{25}{3}$ 36. $\frac{15}{2}$

37. $\frac{23}{5}$ 38. $\frac{9}{8}$ 39. $\frac{31}{5}$ 40. $\frac{25}{6}$ 41. $\frac{16}{5}$ 42. $\frac{21}{10}$

43. $\frac{19}{7}$ 44. $\frac{48}{9}$ 45. $\frac{53}{6}$ 46. $\frac{43}{10}$ 47. $\frac{37}{4}$ 48. $\frac{77}{9}$

Divide to find the numbers. Write the answers in lowest terms.

49. $\frac{14}{4} = 3\frac{2}{4} = ?$ 50. $\frac{25}{10}$ 51. $\frac{36}{8}$ 52. $\frac{51}{9}$ 53. $\frac{46}{6}$

54. $\frac{39}{12}$ 55. $\frac{42}{8}$ 56. $\frac{52}{8}$ 57. $\frac{56}{6}$ 58. $\frac{30}{9}$ 59. $\frac{38}{4}$

60. $\frac{95}{10}$ 61. $\frac{76}{8}$ 62. $\frac{27}{5}$ ★ 63. $\frac{48}{8}$ ★ 64. $\frac{63}{9}$ ★ 65. $\frac{45}{9}$

PROBLEM SOLVING • APPLICATIONS

Write the answers in lowest terms.

66. Martin has a rope 17 yards long. He cuts it into 3 pieces of the same size. How long is each piece?

67. Maria has a piece of ribbon 39 inches long. She cuts it into 4 pieces of the same size. How long is each piece?

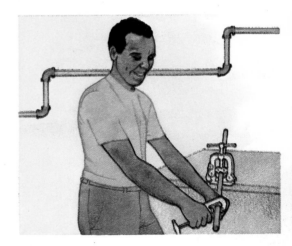

★ 68. Rhoda has a piece of wood 30 inches long. She cuts off 2 inches and then cuts what is left into 6 pieces of the same size. How long is each piece?

★ 69. Ray has a piece of pipe 88 inches long. He cuts off 4 inches and then cuts what is left into 7 pieces of the same size. How long is each piece?

181

PROBLEM SOLVING • STRATEGIES

Using a Schedule

Schedules are used for many different purposes. Two examples are bus and train information.

This is an airline schedule. It shows the times that flights are available from some of the Hawaiian Islands back to Honolulu.

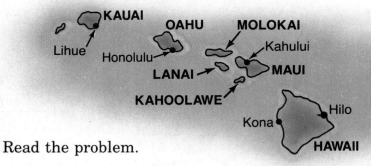

Read the problem.

What flight leaves Hilo at 1:15 P.M., and at what time does it arrive in Honolulu?

> Find the row labeled "From Hilo." Look in the first column—"Leave." Read down to find 1:15 P.M. Read across the row to find the arrival time and the flight number.

Flight 413 leaves Hilo at 1:15 P.M. and arrives in Honolulu at 1:55 P.M.

TO HONOLULU		
Leave	**Arrive**	**Flight No.**
FROM HILO		
6:55 A.M.	7:35 A.M.	41
9:00 A.M.	9:40 A.M.	43
1:15 P.M.	1:55 P.M.	413
5:55 P.M.	6:35 P.M.	47
7:30 P.M.	8:10 P.M.	49
FROM KONA		
6:57 A.M.	7:30 A.M.	81
9:05 A.M.	9:38 A.M.	83
11:12 A.M.	11:45 A.M.	105
12:27 P.M.	1:00 P.M.	85
2:52 P.M.	3:25 P.M.	109
5:25 P.M.	5:58 P.M.	87
FROM MAUI		
7:03 A.M.	7:30 A.M.	401
9:15 A.M.	9:42 A.M.	405
10:48 A.M.	11:15 A.M.	91
11:18 A.M.	11:45 A.M.	73
11:48 A.M.	12:15 P.M.	407
12:13 P.M.	12:40 P.M.	411
1:40 P.M.	2:07 P.M.	213
2:20 P.M.	2:47 P.M.	273
3:15 P.M.	3:42 P.M.	417
4:03 P.M.	4:30 P.M.	419
4:38 P.M.	5:05 P.M.	67
5:30 P.M.	5:57 P.M.	421
7:15 P.M.	7:42 P.M.	425
8:15 P.M.	8:42 P.M.	427
FROM KAUAI		
7:04 A.M.	7:30 A.M.	42
8:55 A.M.	9:21 A.M.	206
10:40 A.M.	11:06 A.M.	210
11:00 A.M.	11:26 A.M.	242
12:14 P.M.	12:40 P.M.	212
1:40 P.M.	2:06 P.M.	216
4:29 P.M.	4:55 P.M.	222
5:30 P.M.	5:56 P.M.	48
6:09 P.M.	6:35 P.M.	224
8:45 P.M.	9:11 P.M.	230

Use the airline schedule to answer the questions.

1. At what time does the 1:40 P.M. flight from Maui arrive in Honolulu?

Remember to look for A.M. or P.M. on a schedule.

2. At what time does the 10:40 A.M. flight from Kauai arrive in Honolulu?

3. At what time does flight 73 leave Maui?

4. At what time does flight 212 from Kauai arrive in Honolulu?

Solve.

5. At what time does flight 73 arrive in Honolulu?

6. At what time does flight 212 leave Kauai?

7. Theresa is leaving on flight 67. On which island is she? At what time does she arrive back in Honolulu?

8. Kameko has finished working with a client in Kona at 4:00 P.M. Which flight must she take to return to Honolulu tonight?

9. Moana has dinner on Kauai. She wants to take the last flight back to Honolulu. Which flight is this? What time does it arrive in Honolulu?

Be sure you are reading the correct line.

---

10. Theresa misses flight 47 from Hilo to Honolulu. At what time does the next flight leave?

11. Lono has a ticket for flight 85. He arrives at the airport at noon. How long must he wait for the plane to take off?

12. How many minutes does it take to fly from Maui to Honolulu on flight 421?

13. How many minutes does it take to fly from Kauai to Honolulu on flight 48?

★14. Which flight is longer, the one from Kauai to Honolulu or the one from Maui to Honolulu? How much longer?

★15. Flight 411 from Maui to Honolulu is delayed 23 minutes. At what time will it arrive in Honolulu?

REVIEW

Write the numbers as a product of prime factors. Use a factor tree. (pages 158–159)

1. 12   **2.** 20   **3.** 32   **4.** 50

Find the greatest common factor. (pages 160–161)

5. 4, 6   **6.** 15, 25   **7.** 16, 24   **8.** 32, 40

Find the least common multiple. (pages 162–163)

9. 5, 8   **10.** 8, 10   **11.** 12, 15   **12.** 4, 14

Write the fraction that tells what part is blue. (pages 166–167)

13.   **14.**   **15.**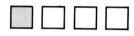

Complete. (pages 168–169, 172–173)

16. $\frac{1}{3}$ of 9 = $\underline{\quad?\quad}$ **17.** $\frac{1}{5} = \frac{?}{15}$ **18.** $\frac{3}{4} = \frac{15}{?}$

Write the fractions in lowest terms. (pages 174–175)

19. $\frac{4}{6}$ **20.** $\frac{10}{12}$ **21.** $\frac{12}{18}$

Find the least common denominator. Write the equivalent fractions. (pages 176–177)

22. $\frac{1}{2}, \frac{3}{5}$ **23.** $\frac{3}{4}, \frac{2}{5}$ **24.** $\frac{2}{9}, \frac{5}{6}$

Write as fractions. (pages 178–179)

25. $2\frac{1}{3}$ **26.** $5\frac{1}{2}$ **27.** $4\frac{5}{8}$

Divide to find mixed numbers. Write the answers in lowest terms. (pages 180–181)

28. $\frac{10}{3}$ **29.** $\frac{20}{9}$ **30.** $\frac{22}{8}$

Solve.

31. Jack had 15 postcards. He gave Ingrid $\frac{1}{3}$ of them. How many postcards did he give Ingrid? (p. 168)

32. Peggy had 21 stamps. She gave $\frac{1}{3}$ of them away. How many stamps did she give away? (p. 165)

Probability and Predictions

Make a spinner. Use a card and a pencil. Color the card as shown.

Make a prediction.

Suppose you spin it 20 times.
What do you think will happen?

A It will land on a green edge more often.

B It will land on a red edge more often.

C It will land on red and green
about the same number of times.

Investigate.

1. Spin the spinner 20 times.
   Record the color each time.

Color	Tally	Total
Red		
Green		

How do your results compare with your prediction?

2. Write a fraction for the part of the spins that were red.
   Example: If it landed on red 13 times, the fraction would be $\frac{13}{20}$.

3. Write a fraction for the part of the spins that were green.

Make a spinner like this one.
Make a prediction.

Suppose you spin it 20 times.
What part of the spins will
be red? (Write a fraction.)

Investigate.

4. Spin it 20 times.
   Record the results.

5. What part of the spins was red?
   Compare your results with your
   prediction.

Color	Prediction	Tally	Fraction
Red			
Yellow			
Blue			
Green			

TEST

Write the numbers as a product of prime factors. Use a factor tree.

1. 6   **2.** 12   **3.** 24   **4.** 60

Find the greatest common factor.

5. 6, 9   **6.** 8, 20   **7.** 10, 16   **8.** 30, 45

Find the least common multiple.

9. 2, 7   **10.** 3, 8   **11.** 10, 12   **12.** 14, 35

Write the fraction that tells what part is blue.

13. 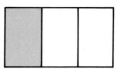   **14.**   **15.**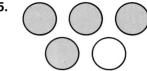

16. $\frac{5}{6}$ of 12 = ____?____   **17.** $\frac{1}{6} = \frac{?}{24}$ **18.** $\frac{5}{6} = \frac{25}{?}$

Write the fractions in lowest terms.

19. $\frac{5}{10}$ **20.** $\frac{2}{8}$ **21.** $\frac{18}{24}$

Find the least common denominator. Write equivalent fractions.

22. $\frac{1}{4}, \frac{1}{8}$ **23.** $\frac{1}{3}, \frac{2}{7}$ **24.** $\frac{5}{8}, \frac{1}{12}$

Write as fractions.

25. $3\frac{1}{4}$ **26.** $1\frac{1}{2}$ **27.** $4\frac{3}{5}$

Divide to find mixed numbers. Write the answers in lowest terms.

28. $\frac{9}{2}$ **29.** $\frac{14}{4}$ **30.** $\frac{23}{7}$

Solve.

31. Heta had 12 loaves of bread. She gave 8 of them away as presents. What fraction of the loaves did she give away?

32. Paul had made 24 plant hangers. He sold $\frac{7}{8}$ of them. How many plant hangers did he sell?

Cross Products

The photography club plans 2 trips, one in October and one in November. In October $\frac{2}{3}$ of the club plans to go on the trip. In November $\frac{4}{6}$ of the club plans to go on the trip. Is the same fraction of the club planning to go on each trip?

To answer the question, find out if the fractions are equivalent.

The **cross products** of equivalent fractions are equal.

Cross multiply.

 $2 \times 6 \bullet 4 \times 3$
$12 = 12$

Since $12 = 12$, the fractions are equivalent.
The same fraction of the club plans to go on each trip.

Compare the fractions, $\frac{3}{5}$ and $\frac{4}{9}$.

 $3 \times 9 \bullet 4 \times 5$
$27 \neq 20$ ($\neq$ means "is not equal to.")

Since $27 \neq 20$, the fractions are not equivalent.

Write = or ≠. Use cross products.

1. $\frac{4}{5} \bullet \frac{7}{8}$ 2. $\frac{3}{4} \bullet \frac{2}{3}$ 3. $\frac{1}{8} \bullet \frac{3}{24}$ 4. $\frac{3}{18} \bullet \frac{1}{6}$

5. $\frac{4}{5} \bullet \frac{5}{6}$ 6. $\frac{2}{3} \bullet \frac{6}{9}$ 7. $\frac{3}{7} \bullet \frac{7}{16}$ 8. $\frac{2}{9} \bullet \frac{8}{36}$

9. $\frac{4}{5} \bullet \frac{12}{15}$ 10. $\frac{3}{8} \bullet \frac{4}{10}$ 11. $\frac{2}{10} \bullet \frac{3}{15}$ 12. $\frac{5}{8} \bullet \frac{7}{12}$

13. $\frac{4}{9} \bullet \frac{7}{16}$ 14. $\frac{3}{15} \bullet \frac{5}{25}$ 15. $\frac{6}{14} \bullet \frac{3}{7}$ 16. $\frac{12}{20} \bullet \frac{6}{9}$

CALCULATOR

Multiples

Use repeated additions on a calculator to find multiples.
List six multiples of 17. Remember to list 0 as the first multiple.

Push 1 7 + =.   17 is the second multiple.

    Push =.   34 is the third multiple.

    Push =.   51 is the fourth multiple.

    Push =.   68 is the fifth multiple.

    Push =.   85 is the sixth multiple.

You push = one time for each nonzero multiple you want.

List six multiples in order. Start with zero.

1. 28   **2.** 7   **3.** 13   **4.** 41

List the missing multiples. Start with 0.
Then add the circled multiples to find the grand total.

5. 22: ___?___ , ___?___ , ___?___ , ___?___ , ◯ , ___?___ , ___?___ , ___?___

6. 15: ___?___ , ___?___ , ◯ , ___?___

7. 6: ◯ , ___?___ , ___?___ , ___?___ , ___?___ , ___?___

8. 1: ___?___ , ◯ , ___?___ , ___?___ , ___?___ , ___?___ , ___?___ , ___?___

9. 11: ___?___ , ___?___ , ◯

10. 9: ___?___ , ___?___ , ___?___ , ___?___ , ___?___ , ___?___ , ◯

11. grand total = ___?___

Use your calculator to help you find the least common multiple.

12. 8, 36   **13.** 5, 30   **14.** 2, 17   **15.** 28, 8

16. 1, 15   **17.** 36, 6   **18.** 28, 7   **19.** 55, 55

188

Choose the correct answers.

1. Round 6,099 to the nearest thousand.

  A. 7,000
  B. 6,000
  C. 6,100
  D. not here

2. Write in order from least to greatest.

802; 796; 820

  A. 796; 820; 802
  B. 796; 802; 820
  C. 820; 802; 796
  D. not here

3. Add.

$2,464 + 90 + 463 = \underline{\quad?\quad}$

  A. 3,827
  B. 3,465
  C. 3,017
  D. not here

4. Find the missing number.

$17 - \underline{\quad?\quad} = 9$

  A. 8
  B. 9
  C. 12
  D. not here

5. Subtract.

$$\begin{array}{r} \$80.49 \\ -\ 72.56 \\ \hline \end{array}$$

  A. $7.93
  B. $8.13
  C. $6.93
  D. not here

6. Multiply.

$300 \times 9 = \underline{\quad?\quad}$

  A. 270
  B. 2,700
  C. 27,000
  D. not here

7. Multiply.

$$\begin{array}{r} 654 \\ \times\ 78 \\ \hline \end{array}$$

  A. 47,812
  B. 50,912
  C. 51,012
  D. not here

8. Find the average.

86, 75, 90, 61

  A. 78
  B. 76
  C. 82
  D. not here

9. Divide.

$80\overline{)5,800}$

  A. 70
  B. 73
  C. 700
  D. not here

10. What is the temperature at 6:00 P.M.?

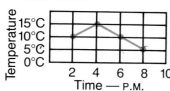

  A. 5°C   **B.** 10°C
  C. 12°C   **D.** not here

11. Find the greatest common factor.

16, 24

  A. 2
  B. 4
  C. 8
  D. not here

12. Write the fraction that tells what part is blue.

  A. $\frac{4}{6}$ **B.** $\frac{1}{2}$
  C. $\frac{4}{9}$ **D.** not here

Choose the correct answers.

13. Naomi buys a bathing suit for $16.95, a denim skirt for $9.79, and a blouse for $21.29. How much money does Naomi spend?

    A. $36.89
    B. $42.99
    C. $48.03
    D. not here

14. Melvin has 164 seashells in his collection. Marissa has 89 seashells. How many more seashells does Melvin have?

    A. 68
    B. 75
    C. 253
    D. not here

15. An auditorium has 54 rows of seats. There are 28 seats in each row. How many seats are in the auditorium?

    A. 682
    B. 1,502
    C. 1,512
    D. not here

16. One carton of orange juice serves 16 people. How many cartons are needed to serve 288 people?

    A. 18
    B. 24
    C. 16
    D. not here

17. A total of $162,000 was spent on furniture for 54 hotel rooms. What is the average amount of money spent for each room?

    A. $3,000
    B. $2,500
    C. $2,750
    D. not here

18. There are 278 people on a ship. How many 8-person lifeboats are needed?

    A. 34
    B. 35
    C. 29
    D. not here

19. Brenda wants to buy the same number of red tiles and white tiles. The red tiles are packed 8 in a box. The white tiles are packed 10 in a box. What is the fewest number of full boxes of each color she can buy?

    A. 3 red, 2 white
    B. 5 red, 4 white
    C. 4 red, 5 white
    D. not here

20. The pet shop sells 80 boxes of pet food. If $\frac{2}{5}$ of them are cat food, how many of the boxes are cat food?

    A. 40
    B. 36
    C. 32
    D. not here

Fractions: Addition and Subtraction

Adding Fractions • Subtracting Fractions • Adding Fractions with Unlike Denominators • Subtracting Fractions with Unlike Denominators • Adding and Subtracting Mixed Numbers with Like Denominators • Adding Mixed Numbers with Unlike Denominators • Subtracting Mixed Numbers with Unlike Denominators • Subtraction with Regrouping • Subtraction with Regrouping Twice • Problem Solving: Missing Information • Triangular and Square Numbers • Stock Market

Adding Fractions

Kathy and Bruce are working together on a stained-glass window.

Kathy makes $\frac{3}{8}$ of the window blue.

Bruce makes $\frac{1}{8}$ of the window blue. How much of the window is blue?

$$\frac{3}{8} + \frac{1}{8} = ?$$

Step 1
The denominators are the same. Add the numerators.

$$\frac{3}{8} + \frac{1}{8} = \frac{4}{8}$$

Step 2
Write the answer in lowest terms.

$$\frac{4}{8} = \frac{1}{2}$$

Kathy and Bruce make $\frac{1}{2}$ of the window blue.

Addition can be shown another way.

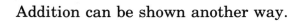

Add: $\frac{5}{8} + \frac{4}{8}$

$$\begin{array}{r} \frac{5}{8} \\ + \frac{4}{8} \\ \hline \frac{9}{8} \end{array}$$

Think: $\frac{9}{8} > 1$.

$$\frac{9}{8} = \frac{8}{8} + \frac{1}{8}$$
$$= 1 + \frac{1}{8}$$
$$= 1\frac{1}{8}$$

Practice • Add. Write the answers in lowest terms.

1. $\frac{5}{8} + \frac{2}{8} = \underline{\ ?\ }$

2. $\frac{1}{6} + \frac{3}{6} = \underline{\ ?\ }$

3. $\frac{3}{4} + \frac{3}{4} = \underline{\ ?\ }$

4. $\begin{array}{r} \frac{1}{5} \\ + \frac{3}{5} \\ \hline \end{array}$

5. $\begin{array}{r} \frac{6}{8} \\ + \frac{4}{8} \\ \hline \end{array}$

6. $\begin{array}{r} \frac{4}{5} \\ + \frac{2}{5} \\ \hline \end{array}$

7. $\begin{array}{r} \frac{1}{3} \\ + \frac{1}{3} \\ \hline \end{array}$

8. $\begin{array}{r} \frac{2}{6} \\ + \frac{1}{6} \\ \hline \end{array}$

9. $\begin{array}{r} \frac{5}{7} \\ + \frac{3}{7} \\ \hline \end{array}$

192

Mixed Practice • Add. Write the answers in lowest terms.

10. $\dfrac{3}{6} + \dfrac{2}{6} =$ _____

11. $\dfrac{1}{4} + \dfrac{2}{4} =$ _____

12. $\dfrac{2}{5} + \dfrac{2}{5} =$ _____

13. $\dfrac{5}{10} + \dfrac{7}{10} =$ _____

14. $\dfrac{3}{8} + \dfrac{3}{8} =$ _____

15. $\dfrac{4}{9} + \dfrac{2}{9} =$ _____

16. $\begin{array}{r} \frac{5}{9} \\ +\frac{3}{9} \\ \hline \end{array}$

17. $\begin{array}{r} \frac{4}{10} \\ +\frac{2}{10} \\ \hline \end{array}$

18. $\begin{array}{r} \frac{3}{7} \\ +\frac{4}{7} \\ \hline \end{array}$

19. $\begin{array}{r} \frac{7}{100} \\ +\frac{5}{100} \\ \hline \end{array}$

20. $\begin{array}{r} \frac{4}{8} \\ +\frac{1}{8} \\ \hline \end{array}$

21. $\begin{array}{r} \frac{7}{12} \\ +\frac{9}{12} \\ \hline \end{array}$

22. $\begin{array}{r} \frac{3}{4} \\ +\frac{3}{4} \\ \hline \end{array}$

23. $\begin{array}{r} \frac{7}{9} \\ +\frac{3}{9} \\ \hline \end{array}$

24. $\begin{array}{r} \frac{1}{9} \\ +\frac{1}{9} \\ \hline \end{array}$

25. $\begin{array}{r} \frac{7}{8} \\ +\frac{2}{8} \\ \hline \end{array}$

26. $\begin{array}{r} \frac{1}{3} \\ +\frac{2}{3} \\ \hline \end{array}$

27. $\begin{array}{r} \frac{5}{16} \\ +\frac{5}{16} \\ \hline \end{array}$

★ 28. $\begin{array}{r} \frac{1}{9} \\ \frac{4}{9} \\ +\frac{2}{9} \\ \hline \end{array}$

★ 29. $\begin{array}{r} \frac{2}{12} \\ \frac{5}{12} \\ +\frac{6}{12} \\ \hline \end{array}$

★ 30. $\begin{array}{r} \frac{23}{100} \\ \frac{17}{100} \\ +\frac{43}{100} \\ \hline \end{array}$

★ 31. $\begin{array}{r} \frac{5}{18} \\ \frac{7}{18} \\ +\frac{12}{18} \\ \hline \end{array}$

★ 32. $\begin{array}{r} \frac{4}{15} \\ \frac{2}{15} \\ +\frac{8}{15} \\ \hline \end{array}$

★ 33. $\begin{array}{r} \frac{2}{8} \\ \frac{3}{8} \\ +\frac{5}{8} \\ \hline \end{array}$

Find the missing numerators.

34. $\dfrac{?}{9} + \dfrac{3}{9} = \dfrac{7}{9}$

35. $\dfrac{3}{5} + \dfrac{?}{5} = \dfrac{4}{5}$

36. $\dfrac{11}{100} + \dfrac{?}{100} = \dfrac{67}{100}$

★ 37. $\dfrac{?}{8} + \dfrac{1}{8} = \dfrac{1}{2}$

★ 38. $\dfrac{4}{15} + \dfrac{?}{15} = \dfrac{2}{5}$

★ 39. $\dfrac{4}{9} + \dfrac{?}{9} = \dfrac{2}{3}$

PROBLEM SOLVING • APPLICATIONS

Write the answers in lowest terms.

40. Kathy works on a special door for $\frac{1}{5}$ hour in the morning. She works on the door $\frac{3}{5}$ hour in the afternoon. How long does she work on the door in all?

★ 41. Bruce puts flowers on $\frac{1}{8}$ of a stained-glass window. Kathy puts flowers on $\frac{5}{8}$ of the window and Carmen adds flowers on another $\frac{2}{8}$ of the window. How much of the window is flowers?

193

Subtracting Fractions

There is $\frac{4}{8}$ of a vegetable pie on a plate.
Anita eats $\frac{2}{8}$.
How much is left?

$$\frac{4}{8} - \frac{2}{8} = \,?$$

Step 1
The denominators are the same.
Subtract the numerators.

$$\frac{4}{8} - \frac{2}{8} = \frac{2}{8}$$

Step 2
Write the answer in lowest terms.

$$\frac{2}{8} = \frac{1}{4}$$

$\frac{1}{4}$ of the pie is left.

Subtraction can be shown another way.

Subtract: $\frac{3}{4} - \frac{1}{4}$.

$$\begin{array}{r} \frac{3}{4} \\ -\frac{1}{4} \\ \hline \frac{2}{4} = \frac{1}{2} \end{array}$$

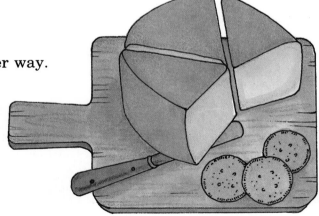

Practice • Subtract. Write the answers in lowest terms.

1. $\frac{7}{8} - \frac{3}{8} = \underline{\quad?\quad}$

2. $\frac{5}{6} - \frac{2}{6} = \underline{\quad?\quad}$

3. $\frac{7}{10} - \frac{2}{10} = \underline{\quad?\quad}$

4. $\begin{array}{r} \frac{6}{7} \\ -\frac{2}{7} \\ \hline \end{array}$

5. $\begin{array}{r} \frac{2}{3} \\ -\frac{1}{3} \\ \hline \end{array}$

6. $\begin{array}{r} \frac{39}{100} \\ -\frac{14}{100} \\ \hline \end{array}$

7. $\begin{array}{r} \frac{8}{9} \\ -\frac{2}{9} \\ \hline \end{array}$

8. $\begin{array}{r} \frac{5}{8} \\ -\frac{4}{8} \\ \hline \end{array}$

9. $\begin{array}{r} \frac{4}{6} \\ -\frac{2}{6} \\ \hline \end{array}$

Mixed Practice • Subtract. Write the answers in lowest terms.

10. $\dfrac{4}{5} - \dfrac{3}{5} = $ _____ ?

11. $\dfrac{5}{6} - \dfrac{1}{6} = $ _____ ?

12. $\dfrac{3}{4} - \dfrac{2}{4} = $ _____ ?

13. $\dfrac{8}{9} - \dfrac{5}{9} = $ _____ ?

14. $\dfrac{9}{10} - \dfrac{7}{10} - $ _____ ?

15. $\dfrac{7}{8} - \dfrac{5}{8} = $ _____ ?

16. $\begin{array}{r} \frac{11}{12} \\ -\frac{7}{12} \\ \hline \end{array}$

17. $\begin{array}{r} \frac{7}{8} \\ -\frac{4}{8} \\ \hline \end{array}$

18. $\begin{array}{r} \frac{9}{12} \\ -\frac{2}{12} \\ \hline \end{array}$

19. $\begin{array}{r} \frac{5}{8} \\ -\frac{3}{8} \\ \hline \end{array}$

20. $\begin{array}{r} \frac{8}{10} \\ -\frac{3}{10} \\ \hline \end{array}$

21. $\begin{array}{r} \frac{9}{16} \\ -\frac{7}{16} \\ \hline \end{array}$

22. $\begin{array}{r} \frac{4}{7} \\ -\frac{2}{7} \\ \hline \end{array}$

23. $\begin{array}{r} \frac{3}{4} \\ -\frac{1}{4} \\ \hline \end{array}$

24. $\begin{array}{r} \frac{7}{18} \\ -\frac{5}{18} \\ \hline \end{array}$

25. $\begin{array}{r} \frac{13}{15} \\ -\frac{8}{15} \\ \hline \end{array}$

26. $\begin{array}{r} \frac{46}{50} \\ -\frac{28}{50} \\ \hline \end{array}$

27. $\begin{array}{r} \frac{9}{11} \\ -\frac{3}{11} \\ \hline \end{array}$

28. $\begin{array}{r} \frac{15}{20} \\ -\frac{3}{20} \\ \hline \end{array}$

29. $\begin{array}{r} \frac{26}{48} \\ -\frac{19}{48} \\ \hline \end{array}$

30. $\begin{array}{r} \frac{2}{10} \\ -\frac{1}{10} \\ \hline \end{array}$

31. $\begin{array}{r} \frac{8}{15} \\ -\frac{3}{15} \\ \hline \end{array}$

32. $\begin{array}{r} \frac{5}{8} \\ -\frac{2}{8} \\ \hline \end{array}$

33. $\begin{array}{r} \frac{5}{6} \\ -\frac{1}{6} \\ \hline \end{array}$

Copy the exercises. Write + and − in each to make a true sentence.

★ 34. $\dfrac{8}{10}$ ▨ $\dfrac{4}{10}$ ▨ $\dfrac{7}{10} = \dfrac{1}{2}$

★ 35. $\dfrac{2}{6}$ ▨ $\dfrac{3}{6}$ ▨ $\dfrac{1}{6} = \dfrac{2}{3}$

★ 36. $\dfrac{5}{8}$ ▨ $\dfrac{2}{8}$ ▨ $\dfrac{3}{8} = \dfrac{3}{4}$

★ 37. $\dfrac{7}{16}$ ▨ $\dfrac{4}{16}$ ▨ $\dfrac{5}{16} = \dfrac{1}{2}$

★ 38. $\dfrac{6}{9}$ ▨ $\dfrac{5}{9}$ ▨ $\dfrac{2}{9} = \dfrac{1}{3}$

★ 39. $\dfrac{9}{15}$ ▨ $\dfrac{4}{15}$ ▨ $\dfrac{5}{15} = \dfrac{2}{3}$

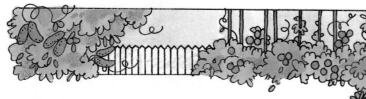

PROBLEM SOLVING • APPLICATIONS

Write the answers in lowest terms.

★ 40. Ramón picks vegetables in the garden for $\dfrac{1}{5}$ hour on Monday. He picks vegetables for $\dfrac{3}{5}$ hour on Tuesday. How much longer does he work on Tuesday than on Monday?

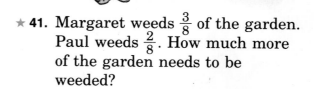

★ 41. Margaret weeds $\dfrac{3}{8}$ of the garden. Paul weeds $\dfrac{2}{8}$. How much more of the garden needs to be weeded?

Adding Fractions with Unlike Denominators

Charles ran $\frac{5}{6}$ of a lap on Tuesday. He ran $\frac{1}{10}$ of a lap on Wednesday. What part of a lap did he run in all?

$\frac{5}{6} + \frac{1}{10} = ?$

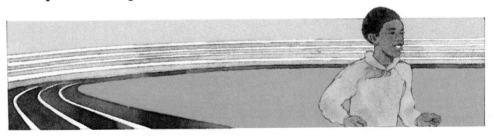

When the denominators are not the same, you can use equivalent fractions that have the same denominator. Use the least common denominator.

Step 1
Find the least common denominator.

$$\frac{5}{6} = \frac{}{30}$$
$$+\frac{1}{10} = \frac{}{30}$$

Step 2
Write equivalent fractions.

$$\frac{5}{6} = \frac{5 \times 5}{5 \times 6} = \frac{25}{30}$$
$$+\frac{1}{10} = \frac{3 \times 1}{3 \times 10} = \frac{3}{30}$$

Step 3
Add. Write the answer in lowest terms.

$$\frac{5}{6} = \frac{25}{30}$$
$$+\frac{1}{10} = \frac{3}{30}$$
$$\frac{28}{30} = \frac{14}{15}$$

Charles ran $\frac{14}{15}$ of a lap in all.

Add: $\frac{4}{5} + \frac{2}{3}$.

$$\frac{4}{5} = \frac{12}{15}$$
$$+\frac{2}{3} = \frac{10}{15}$$
$$\frac{22}{15} = 1\frac{7}{15}$$

> Write a mixed number.

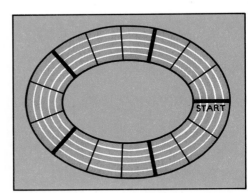

Practice • Find the least common denominator.

1. $\frac{3}{4}, \frac{1}{8}$　　　　2. $\frac{1}{3}, \frac{2}{5}$　　　　3. $\frac{1}{2}, \frac{3}{12}$　　　　4. $\frac{5}{6}, \frac{3}{8}$

Add. Write the answers in lowest terms.

5. $\frac{1}{4}$
$+\frac{3}{8}$

6. $\frac{1}{3}$
$+\frac{2}{6}$

7. $\frac{2}{5}$
$+\frac{4}{10}$

8. $\frac{1}{2}$
$+\frac{5}{7}$

9. $\frac{1}{4}$
$+\frac{4}{6}$

10. $\frac{7}{15}$
$+\frac{4}{5}$

Mixed Practice • Add. Write the answers in lowest terms.

11. $\dfrac{3}{4}$
$+\dfrac{1}{8}$

12. $\dfrac{1}{3}$
$+\dfrac{2}{5}$

13. $\dfrac{1}{2}$
$+\dfrac{3}{12}$

14. $\dfrac{5}{6}$
$+\dfrac{3}{8}$

15. $\dfrac{1}{4}$
$+\dfrac{3}{16}$

16. $\dfrac{8}{15}$
$+\dfrac{3}{5}$

17. $\dfrac{2}{3}$
$+\dfrac{2}{9}$

18. $\dfrac{3}{5}$
$+\dfrac{2}{10}$

19. $\dfrac{5}{9}$
$+\dfrac{1}{2}$

20. $\dfrac{5}{8}$
$+\dfrac{3}{16}$

21. $\dfrac{2}{5}$
$+\dfrac{1}{10}$

22. $\dfrac{3}{4}$
$+\dfrac{1}{3}$

23. $\dfrac{1}{4}$
$+\dfrac{5}{10}$

24. $\dfrac{4}{10}$
$+\dfrac{7}{10}$

25. $\dfrac{2}{6}$
$+\dfrac{1}{4}$

26. $\dfrac{4}{10}$
$+\dfrac{3}{5}$

27. $\dfrac{5}{12}$
$+\dfrac{1}{3}$

28. $\dfrac{4}{12}$
$+\dfrac{3}{12}$

★ 29. $\dfrac{1}{2}$
$\dfrac{2}{3}$
$+\dfrac{5}{6}$

★ 30. $\dfrac{3}{8}$
$\dfrac{1}{4}$
$+\dfrac{3}{16}$

★ 31. $\dfrac{1}{4}$
$\dfrac{5}{6}$
$+\dfrac{1}{3}$

★ 32. $\dfrac{5}{6}$
$\dfrac{1}{2}$
$+\dfrac{5}{12}$

★ 33. $\dfrac{3}{5}$
$\dfrac{7}{10}$
$+\dfrac{1}{3}$

★ 34. $\dfrac{3}{8}$
$\dfrac{1}{6}$
$+\dfrac{2}{3}$

35. $\dfrac{3}{4} + \dfrac{2}{12} = \underline{\quad?\quad}$

36. $\dfrac{2}{4} + \dfrac{1}{3} = \underline{\quad?\quad}$

37. $\dfrac{3}{8} + \dfrac{1}{4} = \underline{\quad?\quad}$

38. $\dfrac{3}{6} + \dfrac{4}{9} = \underline{\quad?\quad}$

39. $\dfrac{3}{8} + \dfrac{1}{6} = \underline{\quad?\quad}$

40. $\dfrac{2}{7} + \dfrac{3}{7} = \underline{\quad?\quad}$

★ 41. $\dfrac{3}{4} + \dfrac{1}{6} + \dfrac{1}{3} = \underline{\quad?\quad}$

★ 42. $\dfrac{2}{8} + \dfrac{2}{6} + \dfrac{2}{3} = \underline{\quad?\quad}$

★ 43. $\dfrac{3}{10} + \dfrac{2}{5} + \dfrac{4}{5} = \underline{\quad?\quad}$

PROBLEM SOLVING • APPLICATIONS

Write the answers in lowest terms.

44. Louisa works for $\dfrac{7}{12}$ hour making awards. Michael works for $\dfrac{2}{3}$ hour. How much time do they spend making awards?

★ 45. Running in the relay race are $\dfrac{1}{8}$ of the people in the class. The three-legged race has $\dfrac{5}{6}$ of the class running. The rest of the class does not race. What part of the class does not run in these races?

Skills Maintenance

1. $3.50
   $+ 1.96$

2. $6.75
   $+ 4.80$

3. $ .91
   $+ 3.40$

4. $7.25
   $+ 2.36$

5. $5.60
   $+ .48$

6. $7.85
   $+ 2.75$

7. $5.31
   $+ 4.27$

8. $7.28
   $+ 2.46$

9. $6.37
   $+ .81$

10. $3.00
    $+ 2.06$

Subtracting Fractions with Unlike Denominators

Dan has $\frac{3}{4}$ of a can of red paint. He has $\frac{1}{3}$ of a can of blue paint.
How much more red paint does he have than blue paint?

$$\frac{3}{4} - \frac{1}{3} = ?$$

Step 1
Find the
least common denominator.

$$\frac{3}{4} = \frac{}{12}$$
$$-\frac{1}{3} = \frac{}{12}$$

Step 2
Write
equivalent fractions.

$$\frac{3}{4} = \frac{9}{12}$$
$$-\frac{1}{3} = \frac{4}{12}$$

Step 3
Subtract.

$$\frac{3}{4} = \frac{9}{12}$$
$$-\frac{1}{3} = \frac{4}{12}$$
$$\frac{5}{12}$$

Dan has $\frac{5}{12}$ of a can more red paint.

Subtract: $\frac{11}{12} - \frac{2}{3}$

$$\frac{11}{12} = \frac{11}{12}$$
$$-\frac{2}{3} = \frac{8}{12}$$
$$\frac{3}{12} = \frac{1}{4}$$

Write the answer
in lowest terms.

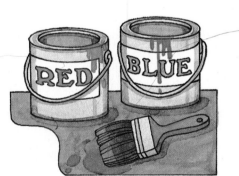

Practice • Find the least common denominator.

1. $\frac{3}{4}, \frac{3}{8}$

2. $\frac{3}{4}, \frac{5}{16}$

3. $\frac{2}{3}, \frac{1}{6}$

4. $\frac{7}{8}, \frac{1}{12}$

Subtract. Write the answers in lowest terms.

5. $\frac{15}{16}$
  $-\frac{7}{8}$

6. $\frac{11}{12}$
  $-\frac{1}{4}$

7. $\frac{13}{15}$
  $-\frac{4}{5}$

8. $\frac{5}{6}$
  $-\frac{3}{8}$

9. $\frac{8}{10}$
  $-\frac{2}{5}$

10. $\frac{2}{3}$
  $-\frac{3}{5}$

Mixed Practice • Subtract. Write the answers in lowest terms.

11. $\dfrac{3}{4}$
$-\dfrac{3}{8}$

12. $\dfrac{2}{3}$
$-\dfrac{1}{6}$

13. $\dfrac{3}{4}$
$-\dfrac{5}{16}$

14. $\dfrac{7}{8}$
$-\dfrac{1}{12}$

15. $\dfrac{13}{16}$
$-\dfrac{3}{4}$

16. $\dfrac{5}{8}$
$-\dfrac{1}{3}$

17. $\dfrac{5}{6}$
$-\dfrac{5}{8}$

18. $\dfrac{3}{4}$
$-\dfrac{2}{3}$

19. $\dfrac{3}{5}$
$-\dfrac{3}{10}$

20. $\dfrac{2}{3}$
$-\dfrac{1}{4}$

21. $\dfrac{5}{6}$
$-\dfrac{1}{4}$

22. $\dfrac{4}{5}$
$-\dfrac{2}{3}$

23. $\dfrac{11}{12}$
$-\dfrac{3}{4}$

24. $\dfrac{13}{16}$
$-\dfrac{5}{8}$

25. $\dfrac{13}{15}$
$-\dfrac{2}{3}$

26. $\dfrac{7}{10}$
$-\dfrac{1}{2}$

27. $\dfrac{11}{15}$
$-\dfrac{6}{15}$

28. $\dfrac{11}{12}$
$-\dfrac{2}{3}$

29. $\dfrac{3}{4} - \dfrac{1}{6} = \underline{\quad?\quad}$

30. $\dfrac{7}{10} - \dfrac{2}{5} = \underline{\quad?\quad}$

31. $\dfrac{7}{8} - \dfrac{3}{8} = \underline{\quad?\quad}$

32. $\dfrac{5}{6} - \dfrac{5}{12} = \underline{\quad?\quad}$

33. $\dfrac{5}{8} - \dfrac{3}{8} = \underline{\quad?\quad}$

34. $\dfrac{2}{3} - \dfrac{1}{2} = \underline{\quad?\quad}$

35. $\dfrac{11}{12} - \dfrac{5}{6} = \underline{\quad?\quad}$

36. $\dfrac{3}{4} - \dfrac{2}{5} = \underline{\quad?\quad}$

37. $\dfrac{5}{8} - \dfrac{2}{6} = \underline{\quad?\quad}$

Find the missing denominators.

★ 38. $\dfrac{5}{12} - \dfrac{3}{?} = \dfrac{1}{24}$

★ 39. $\dfrac{3}{8} - \dfrac{1}{?} = \dfrac{5}{24}$

★ 40. $\dfrac{2}{3} - \dfrac{2}{?} = \dfrac{5}{12}$

★ 41. $\dfrac{3}{?} - \dfrac{1}{5} = \dfrac{2}{15}$

★ 42. $\dfrac{3}{?} - \dfrac{3}{10} = \dfrac{1}{5}$

★ 43. $\dfrac{5}{12} - \dfrac{2}{?} = \dfrac{7}{24}$

PROBLEM SOLVING • APPLICATIONS

Write the answers in lowest terms.

44. Dan rests for $\dfrac{1}{3}$ hour in the morning. He rests for $\dfrac{1}{2}$ hour in the afternoon. How much longer does he rest in the afternoon than in the morning?

45. Hilda had $\dfrac{3}{4}$ of a tank of gas. She drove to work and back home but did not buy more gas. She had $\dfrac{1}{8}$ of a tank of gas left. What part of the tank of gas was used?

★ 46. Francisco went outside for an hour. He walked for $\dfrac{2}{6}$ of the hour and ran for $\dfrac{2}{8}$ of it. The rest of the time he sat. How much time did he spend sitting?

Adding and Subtracting Mixed Numbers with Like Denominators

Maryanne is helping to make costumes for the school play. She uses $3\frac{1}{8}$ packages of sequins for a clown costume. She uses $2\frac{3}{8}$ packages of sequins for an acrobat costume. How many packages of sequins does she use in all?

$$3\frac{1}{8} + 2\frac{3}{8} = ?$$

Step 1
Add: $\frac{1}{8} + \frac{3}{8}$.

$$\begin{array}{r} 3\frac{1}{8} \\ +2\frac{3}{8} \\ \hline \frac{4}{8} \end{array}$$

Step 2
Add: $3 + 2$.

$$\begin{array}{r} 3\frac{1}{8} \\ +2\frac{3}{8} \\ \hline 5\frac{4}{8} \end{array}$$

Step 3
Write the answer in lowest terms.

$$\begin{array}{r} 3\frac{1}{8} \\ +2\frac{3}{8} \\ \hline 5\frac{4}{8} = 5\frac{1}{2} \end{array}$$

Maryanne uses $5\frac{1}{2}$ packages of sequins in all.

Subtract: $7\frac{3}{8} - 2\frac{1}{8}$.

Step 1
Subtract: $\frac{3}{8} + \frac{1}{8}$.

$$\begin{array}{r} 7\frac{3}{8} \\ -2\frac{1}{8} \\ \hline \frac{2}{8} \end{array}$$

Step 2
Subtract: $7 - 2$.

$$\begin{array}{r} 7\frac{3}{8} \\ -2\frac{1}{8} \\ \hline 5\frac{2}{8} \end{array}$$

Step 3
Write the answer in lowest terms.

$$\begin{array}{r} 7\frac{3}{8} \\ -2\frac{1}{8} \\ \hline 5\frac{2}{8} = 5\frac{1}{4} \end{array}$$

Practice • Add. Write the answers in lowest terms.

1. $\begin{array}{r} 3\frac{1}{5} \\ +6\frac{2}{5} \\ \hline \end{array}$

2. $\begin{array}{r} 6\frac{1}{4} \\ +2\frac{1}{4} \\ \hline \end{array}$

3. $\begin{array}{r} 8\frac{3}{10} \\ +9\frac{1}{10} \\ \hline \end{array}$

4. $\begin{array}{r} 4\frac{3}{8} \\ +5 \\ \hline \end{array}$

5. $\begin{array}{r} 7\frac{1}{3} \\ +6\frac{1}{3} \\ \hline \end{array}$

Subtract. Write the answers in lowest terms.

6. $\begin{array}{r} 10\frac{3}{4} \\ -2\frac{1}{4} \\ \hline \end{array}$

7. $\begin{array}{r} 7\frac{3}{5} \\ -4\frac{2}{5} \\ \hline \end{array}$

8. $\begin{array}{r} 9\frac{5}{8} \\ -3 \\ \hline \end{array}$

9. $\begin{array}{r} 2\frac{9}{10} \\ -1\frac{7}{10} \\ \hline \end{array}$

10. $\begin{array}{r} 8\frac{2}{3} \\ -3\frac{1}{3} \\ \hline \end{array}$

Mixed Practice • Add. Write the answers in lowest terms.

11. $9\frac{3}{5}$
$+4\frac{1}{5}$

12. $4\frac{1}{4}$
$+5\frac{2}{4}$

13. $8\frac{3}{10}$
$+2\frac{3}{10}$

14. $1\frac{9}{16}$
$+5\frac{3}{16}$

15. $7\frac{7}{8}$
$+11$

16. $8\frac{7}{10}$
$+1\frac{1}{10}$

17. $5\frac{5}{16}$
$+6\frac{7}{16}$

18. $6\frac{1}{10}$
$+3\frac{7}{10}$

19. $9\frac{2}{5}$
$+7\frac{2}{5}$

20. $2\frac{1}{8}$
$+9\frac{5}{8}$

21. $8\frac{4}{7} + 7\frac{2}{7} = $ _____

22. $12\frac{2}{9} + 2\frac{1}{9} = $ _____

23. $\frac{5}{8} + \frac{2}{8} = $ _____

24. $10\frac{5}{16} + 5\frac{7}{16} = $ _____

25. $\frac{5}{10} + \frac{9}{10} = $ _____

26. $4\frac{13}{100} + 7\frac{7}{100} = $ _____

★ 27. $7\frac{3}{8} + 9\frac{?}{8} = 16\frac{3}{4}$

★ 28. $18\frac{3}{16} + 1\frac{?}{16} = 19\frac{3}{4}$

★ 29. $10\frac{7}{12} + $ _____ $ = 16\frac{7}{12}$

Subtract. Write the answers in lowest terms.

30. $12\frac{2}{4}$
$- 4\frac{1}{4}$

31. $11\frac{9}{10}$
$- 6\frac{4}{10}$

32. $9\frac{7}{12}$
$-8\frac{5}{12}$

33. $4\frac{7}{8}$
-4

34. $6\frac{11}{16}$
$-3\frac{3}{16}$

35. $4\frac{4}{5}$
$-2\frac{1}{5}$

36. $9\frac{9}{16}$
-7

37. $\frac{3}{8}$
$-\frac{2}{8}$

38. $15\frac{17}{20}$
$- 8\frac{11}{20}$

39. $19\frac{7}{10}$
$-4\frac{3}{10}$

40. $10\frac{14}{15} - 6\frac{7}{15} = $ _____

41. $\frac{11}{16} - \frac{10}{16} = $ _____

42. $17\frac{7}{9} - 8\frac{5}{9} = $ _____

43. $8\frac{3}{7} - 4\frac{2}{7} = $ _____

44. $9\frac{6}{8} - 2\frac{5}{8} = $ _____

45. $\frac{11}{12} - \frac{5}{12} = $ _____

★ 46. $6\frac{2}{5} - $ _____ $ = 3\frac{2}{5}$

★ 47. $5\frac{23}{100} - 1\frac{?}{100} = 4\frac{2}{50}$

★ 48. $7\frac{5}{8} - 4\frac{?}{8} = 3\frac{1}{4}$

PROBLEM SOLVING • APPLICATIONS

Write the answers in lowest terms.

49. Karen pulls $2\frac{1}{4}$ dozen scarves from her right sleeve. She pulls $1\frac{1}{4}$ dozen from her left sleeve. How many dozen scarves does she pull in all?

50. Karen uses two rabbits, Rita and Ralph, in her magic act. She has had Rita for $3\frac{1}{2}$ years and Ralph for 2 years. How much longer has she had Rita?

★ 51. Karen has $5\frac{3}{4}$ bags of grain. She feeds the rabbits $1\frac{1}{4}$ bags each day. How much grain is left after 3 days?

Adding Mixed Numbers with Unlike Denominators

Grandpa Hastings and Robert go fishing for $4\frac{1}{3}$ hours on Friday. On Saturday they fish for $2\frac{4}{5}$ hours. How long do they fish on both days?

$$4\frac{1}{3} + 2\frac{4}{5} = ?$$

Step 1
Write equivalent fractions.

$$4\frac{1}{3} = 4\frac{5}{15}$$
$$+2\frac{4}{5} = 2\frac{12}{15}$$

Step 2
Add: $\frac{5}{15} + \frac{12}{15}$.
Add: $4 + 2$.

$$4\frac{1}{3} = 4\frac{5}{15}$$
$$+2\frac{4}{5} = 2\frac{12}{15}$$
$$6\frac{17}{15}$$

Step 3
Since $\frac{17}{15} > 1$, regroup as $1\frac{2}{15}$.
Add: $6 + 1$.

$$4\frac{1}{3} = 4\frac{5}{15}$$
$$+2\frac{4}{5} = 2\frac{12}{15}$$
$$6\frac{17}{15} = 7\frac{2}{15}$$

They fish for $7\frac{2}{15}$ hours on both days.

More Examples

$$3\frac{6}{8}$$
$$+4\frac{5}{8}$$
$$7\frac{11}{8} = 8\frac{3}{8}$$

$$9\frac{7}{10} = 9\frac{21}{30}$$
$$+4\frac{5}{6} = 4\frac{25}{30}$$
$$13\frac{46}{30} = 14\frac{16}{30} = 14\frac{8}{15}$$

Practice • Add. Write the answers in lowest terms.

1. $5\frac{2}{3}$
$+6\frac{1}{4}$

2. $8\frac{3}{5}$
$+9\frac{7}{10}$

3. $16\frac{2}{7}$
$+ 3\frac{1}{2}$

4. $7\frac{1}{2}$
$+6\frac{5}{8}$

5. $14\frac{1}{4}$
$+ 8\frac{3}{8}$

6. $6\frac{3}{4}$
$+8\frac{1}{3}$

7. $12\frac{3}{4}$
$+ 5\frac{5}{6}$

8. $7\frac{2}{5}$
$+4\frac{7}{10}$

9. $13\frac{4}{5}$
$+ 8\frac{2}{3}$

10. $8\frac{7}{10}$
$+9\frac{4}{5}$

202

Mixed Practice • Add. Write the answers in lowest terms.

11. $4\frac{9}{12}$
$+7\frac{1}{6}$

12. $9\frac{1}{3}$
$+7\frac{7}{9}$

13. $4\frac{1}{5}$
$+6\frac{1}{4}$

14. $3\frac{1}{2}$
$+5\frac{2}{3}$

15. $2\frac{1}{2}$
$+4\frac{2}{5}$

16. $4\frac{11}{12}$
$+8\frac{5}{6}$

17. $2\frac{3}{4}$
$+6\frac{11}{16}$

18. $6\frac{2}{3}$
$+5\frac{5}{6}$

19. 8
$+3\frac{2}{3}$

20. $1\frac{4}{5}$
$+2\frac{3}{5}$

★21. $6\frac{3}{4}$
$8\frac{1}{3}$
$+1\frac{1}{4}$

★22. $8\frac{1}{2}$
$9\frac{2}{3}$
$+5$

★23. $6\frac{3}{5}$
$2\frac{1}{3}$
$+5\frac{1}{5}$

★24. $8\frac{1}{8}$
$4\frac{5}{12}$
$+3\frac{1}{2}$

★25. $7\frac{1}{6}$
$9\frac{1}{3}$
$+7\frac{1}{2}$

26. $3\frac{7}{12} + 9\frac{1}{12} = \underline{?}$

27. $5\frac{7}{8} + 7\frac{5}{8} = \underline{?}$

28. $12\frac{1}{2} + 2\frac{7}{9} = \underline{?}$

29. $17\frac{3}{8} + 4\frac{5}{16} = \underline{?}$

30. $8\frac{5}{7} + 3\frac{2}{3} = \underline{?}$

31. $15\frac{7}{9} + 6\frac{1}{4} = \underline{?}$

★32. $18\frac{5}{6} + 7\frac{7}{8} + 8 = \underline{?}$

★33. $6\frac{9}{10} + 5\frac{3}{10} + 6 = \underline{?}$

★34. $18\frac{4}{9} + 12\frac{5}{6} + 9 = \underline{?}$

PROBLEM SOLVING • APPLICATIONS

Write the answers in lowest terms.

35. During their stay at the lake, Donna catches $3\frac{1}{2}$ dozen fish and Albert catches $2\frac{2}{3}$ dozen fish. How many dozen fish do they catch in all?

★36. Sidney is $11\frac{1}{2}$ years old. His sister, Cleo, is $2\frac{1}{3}$ years older. His oldest sister, René, is $2\frac{1}{4}$ years older than Cleo. How old is René?

Midchapter Review

Add or subtract. Write the answers in lowest terms.

1. $\frac{1}{7}$
$+\frac{5}{7}$

2. $\frac{4}{9}$
$+\frac{2}{9}$

3. $\frac{5}{6}$
$+\frac{3}{4}$

4. $3\frac{5}{8}$
$+8\frac{1}{8}$

5. $4\frac{1}{2}$
$+3\frac{3}{8}$

6. $\frac{5}{8}$
$-\frac{3}{8}$

7. $\frac{3}{4}$
$-\frac{2}{3}$

8. $5\frac{3}{4}$
$-1\frac{1}{4}$

9. $12\frac{4}{5}$
$-6\frac{1}{3}$

10. $9\frac{5}{6}$
$-1\frac{1}{2}$

Subtracting Mixed Numbers with Unlike Denominators

Tony is training for a race. On Monday he runs $4\frac{1}{2}$ laps around the track. On Wednesday he runs $2\frac{1}{3}$ laps around the track. How many more laps does Tony run on Monday than on Wednesday?

$$4\frac{1}{2} - 2\frac{1}{3} = ?$$

Step 1
Write equivalent fractions.

$$4\frac{1}{2} = 4\frac{3}{6}$$
$$-2\frac{1}{3} = 2\frac{2}{6}$$

Step 2
Subtract: $\frac{3}{6} - \frac{2}{6}$.

$$4\frac{1}{2} = 4\frac{3}{6}$$
$$-2\frac{1}{3} = 2\frac{2}{6}$$
$$\frac{1}{6}$$

Step 3
Subtract: $4 - 2$.

$$4\frac{1}{2} = 4\frac{3}{6}$$
$$-2\frac{1}{3} = 2\frac{2}{6}$$
$$2\frac{1}{6}$$

Tony runs $2\frac{1}{6}$ laps more on Monday.

Practice • Subtract. Write the answers in lowest terms.

1. $4\frac{7}{10}$
$-3\frac{2}{5}$

2. $9\frac{3}{4}$
$-5\frac{1}{3}$

3. $11\frac{7}{8}$
$-6\frac{5}{6}$

4. $7\frac{3}{4}$
$-2\frac{2}{5}$

5. $9\frac{7}{12}$
$-4\frac{1}{4}$

6. $7\frac{2}{3}$
$-5\frac{1}{2}$

7. $14\frac{5}{8}$
$-9\frac{1}{4}$

8. $6\frac{4}{5}$
$-1\frac{2}{3}$

9. $8\frac{11}{12}$
$-4\frac{2}{3}$

10. $9\frac{5}{6}$
$-4\frac{3}{4}$

Mixed Practice • Subtract. Write the answers in lowest terms.

11. $15\frac{4}{5}$
$-11\frac{3}{10}$

12. $9\frac{3}{4}$
$-5\frac{1}{8}$

13. $8\frac{11}{16}$
$-2\frac{1}{4}$

14. $14\frac{1}{2}$
$-6\frac{1}{4}$

15. $20\frac{3}{4}$
$-13\frac{2}{3}$

16. $13\frac{3}{4}$
$-\ 9\frac{1}{2}$

17. $21\frac{4}{5}$
$-\ 7\frac{3}{4}$

18. $11\frac{7}{8}$
$-\ 6\frac{5}{16}$

19. $18\frac{5}{6}$
$-\ 9\frac{3}{8}$

20. $16\frac{3}{5}$
$-\ 7\frac{1}{3}$

21. $17\frac{1}{2}$
$-\ 8\frac{2}{5}$

22. $19\frac{3}{5}$
$-13\frac{1}{10}$

23. $9\frac{7}{9}$
$-6\frac{2}{3}$

24. $8\frac{7}{8}$
$-7\frac{1}{8}$

25. $10\frac{5}{6}$
$-\ 5\frac{2}{3}$

26. $10\frac{11}{16}$
$-\ 3\frac{3}{8}$

27. $24\frac{7}{12}$
$-\ 6\frac{5}{12}$

28. $19\frac{5}{6}$
$-\ 9\frac{1}{2}$

29. $6\frac{7}{9}$
$-3\frac{1}{2}$

30. $35\frac{7}{12}$
$-27\frac{1}{4}$

31. $15\frac{9}{10} - 7\frac{2}{5} =$ __?__

32. $12\frac{9}{16} - 6\frac{3}{16} =$ __?__

33. $14\frac{7}{8} - 6\frac{2}{3} =$ __?__

34. $17\frac{3}{5} - 9\frac{1}{4} =$ __?__

35. $24\frac{5}{6} - 6\frac{1}{3} =$ __?__

36. $32\frac{4}{5} - 17\frac{1}{4} =$ __?__

★**37.** $21\frac{7}{9} - 8\frac{?}{9} = 13\frac{2}{3}$

★**38.** $16\frac{3}{5} - 7\frac{?}{10} = 9\frac{1}{2}$

★**39.** $28\frac{6}{7} - \underline{\quad}\frac{2}{3} = 13\frac{4}{21}$

PROBLEM SOLVING • APPLICATIONS

Write the answers in lowest terms.

Tony, Leonard, and Randy keep a record of the number of hours they practice for the race.

Hours of Practice			
Runner	**Mon.**	**Tues.**	**Wed.**
Tony	$1\frac{1}{2}$	$1\frac{5}{6}$	$2\frac{1}{3}$
Leonard	$1\frac{1}{4}$	2	$2\frac{1}{6}$
Randy	$1\frac{3}{4}$	$1\frac{1}{2}$	$2\frac{2}{3}$

40. How much longer does Tony practice on Tuesday than on Monday?

41. How much longer does Randy practice on Wednesday than on Tuesday?

42. Find the total number of hours each runner practices.

★ **43.** Which runner spends the greatest number of hours practicing?

Subtraction with Regrouping

Mrs. Drake spent 5 hours weaving and $3\frac{2}{3}$ hours sewing. How much longer did she spend weaving than sewing?

$$5 - 3\frac{2}{3} = ?$$

Step 1
Write 5 as $4 + 1$.
Then $4 + \frac{3}{3} = 4\frac{3}{3}$.

$$\begin{array}{r} 5 = 4\frac{3}{3} \\ -3\frac{2}{3} = 3\frac{2}{3} \\ \hline \end{array}$$

Step 2
Subtract.

$$\begin{array}{r} 5 = 4\frac{3}{3} \\ -3\frac{2}{3} = 3\frac{2}{3} \\ \hline \frac{1}{3} \end{array}$$

Step 3
Subtract.

$$\begin{array}{r} 5 = 4\frac{3}{3} \\ -3\frac{2}{3} = 3\frac{2}{3} \\ \hline 1\frac{1}{3} \end{array}$$

Mrs. Drake spent $1\frac{1}{3}$ hours longer weaving than sewing.

Subtract: $6\frac{1}{4} - 2\frac{3}{4}$.

Step 1
$\frac{3}{4} > \frac{1}{4}$.
Regroup $6\frac{1}{4}$ as
$5 + 1 + \frac{1}{4}$.
Then $5 + \frac{4}{4} + \frac{1}{4}$
$= 5 + \frac{5}{4} = 5\frac{5}{4}$.

$$\begin{array}{r} 6\frac{1}{4} = 5\frac{5}{4} \\ -2\frac{3}{4} = 2\frac{3}{4} \\ \hline \end{array}$$

Step 2
Subtract.

$$\begin{array}{r} 6\frac{1}{4} = 5\frac{5}{4} \\ -2\frac{3}{4} = 2\frac{3}{4} \\ \hline 3\frac{2}{4} \end{array}$$

Step 3
Write the answer in lowest terms.

$$\begin{array}{r} 6\frac{1}{4} = 5\frac{5}{4} \\ -2\frac{3}{4} = 2\frac{3}{4} \\ \hline 3\frac{2}{4} = 3\frac{1}{2} \end{array}$$

Practice • Regroup.

1. $6 = 5\frac{?}{4}$ 2. $9\frac{3}{10} = 8\frac{?}{10}$ 3. $7\frac{3}{8} = \underline{\quad}\frac{?}{8}$ 4. $3 = \underline{\quad}\frac{?}{5}$ 5. $17\frac{1}{6} = \underline{\quad}\frac{?}{6}$

Subtract. Write the answers in lowest terms.

6. $7\frac{1}{8}$
   $-2\frac{5}{8}$

7. $5\frac{1}{5}$
   $-\ \ \frac{3}{5}$

8. 10
   $-\ 5\frac{3}{4}$

9. 15
   $-\ 7\frac{1}{3}$

10. $6\frac{4}{9}$
    $-4\frac{5}{9}$

Mixed Practice • Subtract. Write the answers in lowest terms.

11. $16\frac{2}{7}$
$-\ 9\frac{3}{7}$

12. 16
$-\ 9\frac{8}{15}$

13. 7
$-6\frac{1}{4}$

14. $13\frac{7}{12}$
$-\ \frac{11}{12}$

15. $5\frac{3}{8}$
$-1\frac{7}{8}$

16. $15\frac{3}{10}$
$-\ 6\frac{9}{10}$

17. 17
$-\ 6\frac{9}{10}$

18. $12\frac{3}{5}$
$-\ 3\frac{4}{5}$

19. 12
$-\ 8\frac{5}{6}$

20. 8
$-5\frac{7}{8}$

21. $16\frac{2}{5}$
$-\ 4\frac{3}{5}$

22. 15
$-\ 9\frac{1}{2}$

23. $9\frac{7}{12}$
$-7\frac{5}{12}$

24. $14\frac{5}{8}$
$-\ 4\frac{7}{8}$

25. $6\frac{1}{3}$
$-2\frac{2}{3}$

26. 8
$-6\frac{7}{10}$

27. $20\frac{7}{9}$
$-16\frac{2}{9}$

28. 14
$-\ 9\frac{9}{16}$

29. $8\frac{1}{8}$
$-7\frac{7}{8}$

30. 23
$-14\frac{4}{5}$

31. $5 - 3\frac{2}{5} =$ ___?___

32. $6\frac{4}{7} - 2\frac{5}{7} =$ ___?___

33. $17 - 6\frac{3}{8} =$ ___?___

34. $9\frac{1}{6} - 3\frac{5}{6} =$ ___?___

★ 35. $5\frac{3}{8} - 1\frac{?}{8} = 3\frac{1}{2}$

★ 36. $13\frac{1}{5} - 6\frac{?}{5} = 6\frac{4}{5}$

PROBLEM SOLVING • APPLICATIONS

37. It takes Tom $1\frac{2}{5}$ hours to walk to school. He stopped at Bob's house after walking for $\frac{4}{5}$ hour. How much longer must he walk to get to school?

38. Penelope has $5\frac{3}{8}$ pails of wax. After making candles she has $2\frac{5}{8}$ pails left. How much wax is used in making the candles?

39. The weight of a tub of butter including the weight of the tub is $48\frac{1}{4}$ pounds. The tub weighs $9\frac{3}{4}$ pounds. What is the weight of the butter?

★ 40. Mr. Morrow has 17 acres of land. He plants $4\frac{3}{10}$ acres with wheat and $11\frac{3}{10}$ acres with corn. How many acres are left unplanted?

Skills Maintenance

1. $4.95
$-\ 2.53$

2. $2.87
$-\ 1.98$

3. $6.84
$-\ 5.97$

4. $1.20
$-\ .95$

5. $4.65
$-\ 2.89$

6. $18.50
$-\ 3.75$

7. $35.72
$-\ 18.56$

8. $12.09
$-\ 8.45$

9. $37.25
$-\ 9.67$

10. $22.73
$-\ 18.48$

Subtraction with Regrouping Twice

A city planner meets with his staff for $3\frac{1}{5}$ hours. They spend $2\frac{2}{3}$ hours talking about where the new hospital will be built. How many hours do they spend on other business?

$3\frac{1}{5} - 2\frac{2}{3} = ?$

Step 1
Write equivalent fractions.

$$3\frac{1}{5} = 3\frac{3}{15}$$
$$-2\frac{2}{3} = 2\frac{10}{15}$$

Step 2
Since $\frac{10}{15} > \frac{3}{15}$, regroup $3\frac{3}{15}$ as $2\frac{18}{15}$.

$$3\frac{1}{5} = 3\frac{3}{15} = 2\frac{18}{15}$$
$$-2\frac{2}{3} = 2\frac{10}{15} = 2\frac{10}{15}$$

Step 3
Subtract.
$2\frac{18}{15} - 2\frac{10}{15}$.

$$3\frac{1}{5} = 3\frac{3}{15} = 2\frac{18}{15}$$
$$-2\frac{2}{3} = 2\frac{10}{15} = 2\frac{10}{15}$$
$$\frac{8}{15}$$

They spend $\frac{8}{15}$ hour on other business.

Practice • Subtract. Write the answers in lowest terms.

1. $8\frac{1}{5}$
   $-4\frac{1}{2}$

2. $10\frac{1}{4}$
   $-3\frac{5}{8}$

3. $14\frac{1}{4}$
   $-8\frac{2}{3}$

4. $7\frac{2}{5}$
   $-4\frac{2}{3}$

5. $8\frac{1}{2}$
   $-2\frac{5}{8}$

6. $9\frac{1}{4}$
   $-2\frac{1}{2}$

7. $3\frac{1}{3}$
   $-1\frac{3}{4}$

8. $6\frac{3}{5}$
   $-4\frac{2}{3}$

9. $17\frac{1}{6}$
   $-4\frac{1}{4}$

10. $5\frac{3}{8}$
    $-3\frac{2}{3}$

Mixed Practice • Subtract. Write the answers in lowest terms.

11. $4\frac{2}{7}$
    $-3\frac{1}{2}$

12. $9\frac{1}{6}$
    $-8\frac{2}{3}$

13. $10\frac{2}{9}$
    $-3\frac{2}{3}$

14. $13\frac{3}{5}$
    $-7\frac{7}{10}$

15. $6\frac{1}{3}$
    $-4\frac{5}{6}$

16. $21\frac{1}{2}$
$-\ 7\frac{7}{8}$

17. $9\frac{5}{6}$
$-6\frac{7}{8}$

18. $5\frac{3}{10}$
$-4\frac{3}{5}$

19. $16\frac{1}{4}$
$-\ 7\frac{7}{8}$

20. $11\frac{1}{3}$
$-\ 2\frac{4}{5}$

21. $13\frac{3}{10}$
$-\ 8\frac{4}{5}$

22. $11\frac{5}{9}$
$-\ 4\frac{5}{6}$

23. $9\frac{3}{4}$
$-7\frac{7}{8}$

24. $20\frac{5}{12}$
$-14\frac{1}{6}$

25. $6\frac{3}{7}$
$-3\frac{2}{3}$

26. $18\frac{7}{20} - 9\frac{9}{10} = \underline{\ ?\ }$

27. $9\frac{4}{5} - 5\frac{9}{10} = \underline{\ ?\ }$

28. $15\frac{6}{7} - 6\frac{2}{3} = \underline{\ ?\ }$

29. $11\frac{3}{8} - 3\frac{3}{4} = \underline{\ ?\ }$

30. $13\frac{5}{7} - 9\frac{1}{3} = \underline{\ ?\ }$

31. $12\frac{1}{8} - 9\frac{2}{3} = \underline{\ ?\ }$

32. $28\frac{3}{4} - 17\frac{1}{5} = \underline{\ ?\ }$

33. $14\frac{5}{8} - 6\frac{2}{3} = \underline{\ ?\ }$

34. $22\frac{7}{10} - 8\frac{3}{4} = \underline{\ ?\ }$

★ **35.** Fill in the circles.

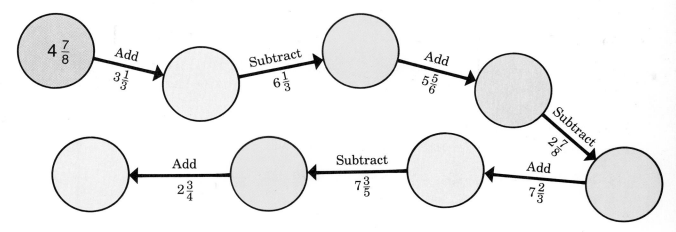

PROBLEM SOLVING • APPLICATIONS

Write the answers in lowest terms.

36. One wall of a room is decorated with fancy bricks. John orders $32\frac{1}{4}$ dozen bricks. He uses $29\frac{1}{2}$ dozen bricks. How many dozen bricks are left over?

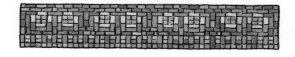

★ **37.** An architect spends $15\frac{1}{3}$ hours planning the Central Bank project. She spends $8\frac{1}{2}$ hours planning the Beekman Insurance Building and $6\frac{3}{4}$ hours planning the Middle Bank. How much longer does she spend planning the banks than the insurance building?

209

PROBLEM SOLVING · STRATEGIES

Missing Information

Some problems give you enough information to solve them. Others may not. In which problem below is information missing?

A cow gives $2\frac{1}{2}$ gallons of milk in the morning and $1\frac{1}{4}$ gallons in the evening. How much milk does the cow give in all?

Gallons in the morning	Gallons in the evening	Gallons in all
$2\frac{1}{2}$ +	$1\frac{1}{4}$ =	?

The cow gives $3\frac{3}{4}$ gallons in all.

A large cow eats $6\frac{8}{10}$ bags of grain each day. She also eats many bags of silage and hay. How much does she eat in all?

Bags of grain	Bags of silage and hay	Total
$6\frac{8}{10}$ +	? =	?

Information is missing. You do not know how many bags of silage and hay are eaten.

Do you have enough information? Write YES or NO.

1. A cow is milked for $2\frac{1}{2}$ minutes in the morning. She is milked for $2\frac{1}{4}$ minutes in the evening. How many minutes is that in all?

> Write a number sentence to help you decide if information is missing.

2. Of all milk sold, $\frac{3}{4}$ is Grade A. One store sells many cases of milk each day. How many cases of Grade A does the store sell?

What other information do you need to solve these problems?

3. The Bellaire Dairy Farm lets its cows graze for 2 hours each day. Today they have grazed for some time. How much longer should they graze?

4. The herd is being brought into the barn. If $\frac{2}{3}$ of them are already at their places, how many cows are at their places?

5. By 2:00 P.M. one cow drank $17\frac{5}{10}$ liters of water. Later she drank more water. How many liters did she drink in all?

Read the question. Think: What information do I need?

---

6. It takes a dairy worker $6\frac{1}{2}$ minutes to milk a cow by hand. How much less time does it take to milk the cow by machine?

7. The veterinarian spends $4\frac{1}{2}$ hours examining cows. Then she talks to the farm owner. How much time does she spend at Bellaire Dairy Farm in all?

8. A cow's diet is made up of hay, silage, and grain. If $\frac{1}{5}$ of her diet is grain, how much is grain?

9. Tillary works at the dairy for $5\frac{3}{4}$ hours each day. How many hours does she work in one month?

10. One supermarket sells 50 cases of Bellaire Dairy Farm milk. The supermarket also sells Blue Grass Dairy milk. How many more cases of Blue Grass Dairy milk are sold?

★**11.** Cases of milk are being loaded onto a delivery truck. Of the cases, $\frac{1}{2}$ are going to George's Market, and $\frac{1}{4}$ are going to the Value Market. How many cases of milk are going to George's Market?

★**12.** Brian spends $2\frac{1}{2}$ hours a day feeding cows. He also gathers hay for $1\frac{1}{2}$ hours in the morning and for 1 hour in the afternoon. How many hours a week does he spend feeding the cows?

REVIEW

Add. Write the answers in lowest terms. (pages 192–193, 196–197, 200–203)

1. $\frac{1}{3}$
$+\frac{1}{3}$

2. $\frac{17}{20}$
$+\frac{6}{20}$

3. $\frac{2}{3}$
$+\frac{1}{6}$

4. $\frac{4}{5}$
$+\frac{3}{10}$

5. $1\frac{1}{5}$
$+1\frac{2}{5}$

6. $2\frac{3}{8}$
$+3\frac{1}{8}$

7. $3\frac{3}{4}$
$+1\frac{3}{4}$

8. $1\frac{5}{8}$
$+6\frac{7}{8}$

9. $5\frac{1}{3}$
$+2\frac{4}{5}$

10. $8\frac{7}{10}$
$+3\frac{5}{6}$

11. $7\frac{1}{2}$
$+8\frac{3}{7}$

12. $4\frac{1}{4}$
$+2\frac{2}{3}$

Subtract. Write the answers in lowest terms. (pages 194–195, 198–201, 204–209)

13. $\frac{4}{5}$
$-\frac{1}{5}$

14. $\frac{7}{10}$
$-\frac{3}{10}$

15. $\frac{3}{4}$
$-\frac{1}{2}$

16. $\frac{7}{8}$
$-\frac{2}{3}$

17. $4\frac{9}{10}$
$-1\frac{7}{10}$

18. $8\frac{11}{12}$
$-5\frac{7}{12}$

19. $6\frac{5}{8}$
$-2\frac{1}{2}$

20. $7\frac{11}{12}$
$-1\frac{2}{3}$

21. $3\frac{3}{8}$
$-1\frac{7}{8}$

22. 6
$-4\frac{2}{3}$

23. $7\frac{2}{3}$
$-5\frac{3}{4}$

24. $4\frac{3}{10}$
$-2\frac{1}{2}$

Solve. Write the answers in lowest terms.

25. The Lyons family has been driving for $2\frac{1}{3}$ hours. They have to drive $3\frac{1}{2}$ hours more to reach their vacation house. How many hours will they have driven in all? (p. 202)

26. Karin and David spend $3\frac{1}{6}$ hours fishing the first day. The next day they fish for 5 hours. How much more time do they spend fishing the second day? (p. 206)

PROJECT

Triangular and Square Numbers

Numbers can be shown as a series of dots.
For some numbers the dots form a triangle.
These are the first three triangular numbers.
Draw the next three numbers in the pattern.

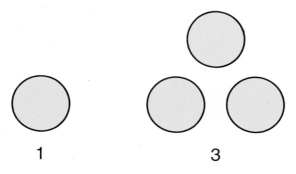

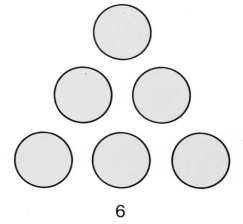

1   3   6

For other numbers the dots form a square.
These are the first three square numbers.
Draw the next three numbers in the pattern.

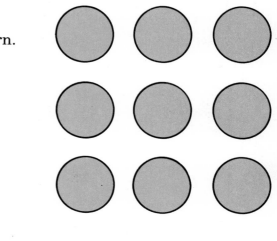

1   4   9

Draw and cut out the first and second triangular numbers.
Put them together to form a square.
Now try this with the second and third triangular numbers.
See how many other square numbers you can make from two
triangular numbers.

TEST

Add. Write the answers in lowest terms.

1. $\dfrac{2}{12}$
$+\dfrac{3}{12}$

2. $\dfrac{5}{6}$
$+\dfrac{2}{6}$

3. $\dfrac{3}{10}$
$+\dfrac{1}{5}$

4. $\dfrac{3}{4}$
$+\dfrac{5}{8}$

5. $2\dfrac{2}{7}$
$+1\dfrac{4}{7}$

6. $3\dfrac{1}{10}$
$+4\dfrac{7}{10}$

7. $1\dfrac{3}{5}$
$+3\dfrac{3}{5}$

8. $2\dfrac{3}{8}$
$+4\dfrac{7}{8}$

9. $5\dfrac{3}{4}$
$+1\dfrac{7}{12}$

10. $6\dfrac{3}{8}$
$+2\dfrac{3}{4}$

11. $1\dfrac{4}{5}$
$+3\dfrac{1}{2}$

12. $7\dfrac{2}{3}$
$+5\dfrac{4}{5}$

Subtract. Write the answers in lowest terms.

13. $\dfrac{3}{8}$
$-\dfrac{1}{8}$

14. $\dfrac{8}{9}$
$-\dfrac{2}{9}$

15. $\dfrac{3}{5}$
$-\dfrac{1}{10}$

16. $\dfrac{1}{2}$
$-\dfrac{1}{3}$

17. $5\dfrac{6}{8}$
$-2\dfrac{1}{8}$

18. $8\dfrac{3}{4}$
$-4\dfrac{1}{4}$

19. $6\dfrac{2}{3}$
$-3\dfrac{1}{6}$

20. $4\dfrac{4}{5}$
$-1\dfrac{1}{4}$

21. $4\dfrac{1}{6}$
$-2\dfrac{5}{6}$

22. 7
$-1\dfrac{4}{5}$

23. $5\dfrac{1}{2}$
$-2\dfrac{7}{8}$

24. $6\dfrac{3}{4}$
$-1\dfrac{9}{10}$

Solve. Write the answers in lowest terms.

25. Jim lives $2\dfrac{1}{2}$ blocks from school. How far does he walk each day to and from school?

26. Suki is walking home from school. She lives 6 blocks from school. She stops at a bookstore $2\dfrac{1}{4}$ blocks from school. How far is her home from the bookstore?

Stock Market

Here is how stock market prices are reported in newspapers.

The dollar value of a share of stock is shown as a whole number or a mixed number.

Stock Prices			
Stock	**Today's High**	**Today's Low**	**Today's Last**
Alimo	$41\frac{3}{8}$	$38\frac{3}{8}$	$41\frac{3}{8}$
Bralim	$41\frac{1}{4}$	$36\frac{1}{4}$	$40\frac{3}{8}$
Crinco	43	$40\frac{1}{2}$	$41\frac{3}{4}$
Euras	$40\frac{3}{8}$	$39\frac{1}{8}$	$39\frac{1}{2}$
Int G	$56\frac{1}{8}$	$38\frac{1}{4}$	$39\frac{3}{4}$

Use the table. Write the prices in order from least to greatest.

1. Today's High

2. Today's Low

3. Today's Last

What is the difference between Today's High and Today's Low for each stock?

4. Alimo

5. Bralim

6. Crinco

7. Euras

8. Int G

COMPUTER

Computer History

The history of the computer is a truly international story. A calculator called the abacus has been used in the Orient for 5,000 years.

 **John Napier** (Scottish) multiplied and divided by mechanical means in 1617.

 **Blaise Pascal** (French) built the first digital adding machine in 1642.

Gottfried Leibniz (German) multiplied and divided by machine in 1671.

 **Joseph-Marie Jacquard** (French) invented a cloth-weaving loom that was controlled by holes punched in cards.
When the holes in the cards were changed, the loom produced a different pattern in the cloth. It was 1801.

Charles Babbage (British) planned the first true digital computer in 1835. His "Analytical Machine" was based on Jacquard's punched-card loom. The Analytical Machine was the first computer designed to change its own program.

 Lady Lovelace (British) planned the first computer program in 1840. Because the Analytical Machine was never built, Lady Lovelace never got to write her program.

All of these computers were *mechanical* devices, designed before electricity.

 **Herman Hollerith** (American) used the idea of Jacquard's punched cards to build a computer for the 1880 U.S. census. This computer used electricity. In 1911 Hollerith formed a company that later became known as IBM. Workers at IBM and Harvard University built the **Automatic Sequence Controlled Calculator** in 1944. It was partly electrical and partly mechanical. This enormous machine stood eight feet high and was fifty feet long.

ACE (Automatic Computing Engine) was built by **Alan Turing** in London in 1945. **ENIAC** (Electronic Numerical Integrator and Calculator) was completed in 1946. This was the first general-purpose digital computer that was all electric.

In 1947 **John von Neumann** (Hungarian), working in the United States, designed **EDVAC**. EDVAC was the first true stored-program computer.

The invention of the **transistor** in 1948 permitted high speeds in tiny devices. At last the computer began to move into "modern" history.

UNIVAC, the first commercial computer, was being sold in America in 1950. In that year there were only ten to fifteen computers in the United States. The fastest computer could perform 1,000 calculations per second. During the next ten years, many computers were built and operated by computer companies. Most businesses could not afford to buy costly computers, and so they rented time at about $10 per minute at computer service centers.

Improved integrated circuits, invented in 1960, increased speeds. Computers took up less space. The relative cost per size fell continually. More and more companies bought their own computers for their own projects. Some of these projects included designing better and faster computers. As computers became more available, their success led to a demand for more powerful, more efficient, and less expensive computers.

By 1966 there were 35,000 computers in the United States valued at $8 billion. A calculation that took one hour in 1950 took half a second in 1966. Computers doubled in complexity each year between 1950 and 1977.

The first personal computers were sold in 1975. More than 1,000,000 exist now. By 1977 a microcomputer costing $300 was 30,000 times smaller, 10,000 times cheaper, 1,000 times more reliable, and 20 times faster than ENIAC. If jet aircraft had evolved at the rate of computers, a jet would cost $500 and fly around the world in twenty minutes on five gallons of fuel.

Now more than a million computers are made each year. Most companies and schools have one or more computers. Many individuals own computers that start below $100 in price. As calculators increase in power, computers decrease in price. It is hard to draw a line between computers and calculators. Computers will soon be as common as clocks and watches. Computers have changed the world in which we live. The effects of computers on our lives are only beginning.

Copy and complete.

1. The history of computers involved six countries: _____.

2. Higher speeds were possible by the 1948 invention of _____.

3. The first commercial computer, _____, was being sold in the year _____.

4. Higher speeds were made possible by the 1960 invention of _____

_____.

5. A 1966 computer was how many times faster than a 1950 computer? _____.

6. About how much did ENIAC cost? _____.

Choose the correct answers.

1. Write the expanded form.

2,463

A. 2,000 + 460 + 30
B. 2,000 + 400 + 60 + 3
C. 20,000 + 4,000 + 60 + 3
D. not here

2. Estimate. Round to the nearest hundred.

486
+314

A. 800
B. 700
C. 900
D. not here

3. Add.

$6 + (4 + 9) = \underline{\ ?\ }$

A. 78
B. 18
C. 19
D. not here

4. Add.

$56.29
+   8.97

A. $64.15
B. $65.26
C. $65.16
D. not here

5. Subtract.

$7,106 - 569 = \underline{\ ?\ }$

A. 6,537
B. 6,647
C. 6,675
D. not here

6. Divide.

$64\overline{)4,657}$

A. 81 r56
B. 72 r60
C. 73 r6
D. not here

7. Find the least common multiple.

9, 18

A. 2   **B.** 18
C. 72   **D.** not here

8. Write an equivalent fraction.

$\frac{2}{3} = \frac{?}{12}$

A. 4   **B.** 6
C. 8   **D.** not here

9. Add. Write the answer in lowest terms.

$6\frac{1}{2} + 3\frac{4}{5} = \underline{\ ?\ }$

A. $9\frac{3}{10}$ **B.** $10\frac{3}{10}$
C. $9\frac{7}{15}$ **D.** not here

10. Pedro has 26 cartons of carpet tiles. There are 48 tiles in each carton. How many carpet tiles does he have?

A. 686   **B.** 1,008
C. 1,248   **D.** not here

11. Cy works three days each week. He works 8 hours on Monday, $4\frac{1}{2}$ hours on Wednesday, and $5\frac{1}{2}$ hours on Friday. How many hours does Cy work in all?

A. 10   **B.** 17
C. 18   **D.** not here

Fractions: Multiplication and Division

Finding Parts • Multiplying Fractions • Multiplying Fractions and Whole Numbers • Multiplying Fractions and Mixed Numbers • Problem Solving: Using Recipes • Reciprocals • Dividing Fractions

Finding Parts

One-half of a garden is planted with vegetables.
One-fourth of the vegetable garden is planted with beans.
How much of the garden is planted with beans?

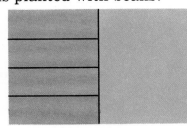

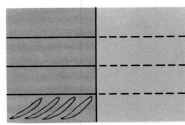

The garden is separated into 2 equal parts.

$\frac{1}{2}$

The vegetable garden is separated into 4 equal parts.

$\frac{1}{4}$ of $\frac{1}{2}$

1 part is 1 of 8 equal parts.

$\frac{1}{4}$ of $\frac{1}{2}$ is $\frac{1}{8}$.

What number is $\frac{2}{3}$ of $\frac{1}{4}$?

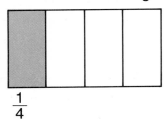

$\frac{1}{4}$

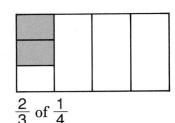

$\frac{2}{3}$ of $\frac{1}{4}$

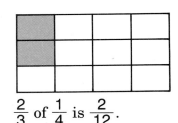

$\frac{2}{3}$ of $\frac{1}{4}$ is $\frac{2}{12}$.

What number is $\frac{3}{4}$ of $\frac{2}{3}$?

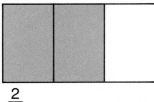

$\frac{2}{3}$

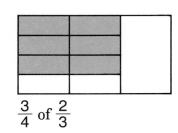

$\frac{3}{4}$ of $\frac{2}{3}$

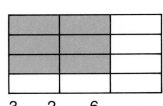

$\frac{3}{4}$ of $\frac{2}{3}$ is $\frac{6}{12}$.

Practice • Use the drawing to complete each sentence.

1.

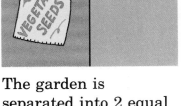

$\frac{1}{2}$ of $\frac{1}{3}$ is ___?___

2.

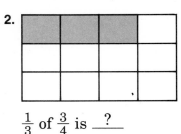

$\frac{1}{3}$ of $\frac{3}{4}$ is ___?___

3.

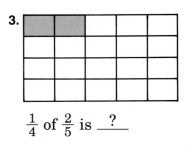

$\frac{1}{4}$ of $\frac{2}{5}$ is ___?___

Mixed Practice • Use the drawing to complete each sentence.

4.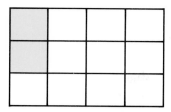

$\frac{2}{3}$ of $\frac{1}{4}$ = ___?___

5.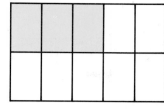

$\frac{1}{2}$ of $\frac{3}{5}$ = ___?___

6.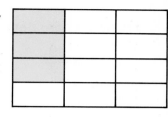

$\frac{3}{4}$ of $\frac{1}{3}$ = ___?___

7.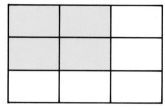

$\frac{2}{3}$ of $\frac{2}{3}$ = ___?___

8.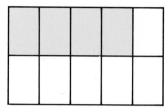

$\frac{1}{2}$ of $\frac{4}{5}$ = ___?___

9.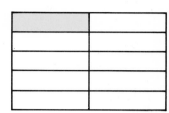

$\frac{1}{5}$ of $\frac{1}{2}$ = ___?___

10.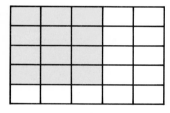

$\frac{4}{5}$ of $\frac{3}{5}$ = ___?___

11.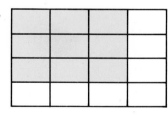

$\frac{3}{4}$ of $\frac{3}{4}$ = ___?___

12.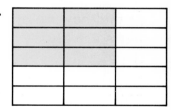

$\frac{3}{5}$ of $\frac{2}{3}$ = ___?___

Draw a picture. Then complete the sentences.

★**13.** $\frac{1}{3}$ of $\frac{2}{3}$ = ___?___

★**14.** $\frac{1}{4}$ of $\frac{4}{5}$ = ___?___

★**15.** $\frac{1}{5}$ of $\frac{5}{6}$ = ___?___

★**16.** $\frac{2}{5}$ of $\frac{2}{7}$ = ___?___

★**17.** $\frac{2}{3}$ of $\frac{3}{5}$ = ___?___

★**18.** $\frac{3}{4}$ of $\frac{5}{8}$ = ___?___

PROBLEM SOLVING • APPLICATIONS

Draw a picture to solve each problem.

★**19.** Maria planted $\frac{2}{3}$ of the garden with fruit. If $\frac{1}{2}$ of the fruit is strawberries, how much of the garden is planted with strawberries?

★**20.** Mr. Jones planted $\frac{3}{4}$ of his garden with flowers. If $\frac{2}{3}$ of the flowers are petunias, what part of the garden is planted with petunias?

Multiplying Fractions

The drawing shows:

$$\frac{3}{4} \text{ of } \frac{3}{5} = \frac{9}{20}$$

You can also multiply to find the answer.

$$\frac{3}{4} \times \frac{3}{5} = ?$$

Multiply the numerators to find how many parts are blue.

$$3 \times 3 = 9$$

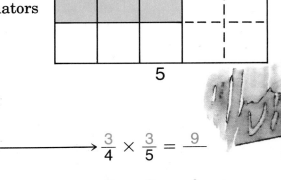

Multiply the denominators to find how many parts in all.

$$4 \times 5 = 20$$

To multiply fractions:

Step 1
Multiply the numerators. $\longrightarrow$ $\frac{3}{4} \times \frac{3}{5} = \frac{9}{}$

Step 2
Multiply the denominators. $\longrightarrow$ $\frac{3}{4} \times \frac{3}{5} = \frac{9}{20}$

Practice • Multiply. Write the answers in lowest terms.

1. $\frac{1}{8} \times \frac{2}{3} = \underline{\quad?\quad}$

2. $\frac{1}{2} \times \frac{4}{5} = \underline{\quad?\quad}$

3. $\frac{2}{5} \times \frac{1}{4} = \underline{\quad?\quad}$

4. $\frac{4}{7} \times \frac{3}{8} = \underline{\quad?\quad}$

5. $\frac{2}{3} \times \frac{1}{2} = \underline{\quad?\quad}$

6. $\frac{9}{10} \times \frac{3}{4} = \underline{\quad?\quad}$

Mixed Practice • Multiply. Write the answers in lowest terms.

7. $\frac{3}{5} \times \frac{2}{3} =$ ___?___

8. $\frac{5}{6} \times \frac{3}{4} =$ ___?___

9. $\frac{3}{9} \times \frac{1}{2} =$ ___?___

10. $\frac{3}{4} \times \frac{1}{9} =$ ___?___

11. $\frac{5}{9} \times \frac{3}{5} =$ ___?___

12. $\frac{6}{7} \times \frac{1}{2} =$ ___?___

13. $\frac{4}{5} \times \frac{2}{10} =$ ___?___

14. $\frac{1}{2} \times \frac{4}{9} =$ ___?___

15. $\frac{2}{3} \times \frac{3}{6} =$ ___?___

16. $\frac{7}{8} \times \frac{2}{5} =$ ___?___

17. $\frac{3}{5} \times \frac{4}{7} =$ ___?___

18. $\frac{2}{3} \times \frac{3}{10} =$ ___?___

19. $\frac{7}{8} \times \frac{5}{7} =$ ___?___

20. $\frac{1}{10} \times \frac{5}{6} =$ ___?___

21. $\frac{1}{8} \times \frac{4}{7} =$ ___?___

22. $\frac{2}{3} \times \frac{3}{8} =$ ___?___

23. $\frac{6}{10} \times \frac{5}{12} =$ ___?___

24. $\frac{3}{4} \times \frac{4}{5} =$ ___?___

25. $\frac{5}{8} \times \frac{2}{3} =$ ___?___

26. $\frac{3}{4} \times \frac{3}{8} =$ ___?___

27. $\frac{4}{5} \times \frac{5}{6} =$ ___?___

Find the missing factors. The products are given in lowest terms.

★ 28. $\frac{3}{5} \times$ ___?___ $= \frac{4}{15}$

★ 29. $\frac{2}{7} \times$ ___?___ $= \frac{3}{28}$

★ 30. ___?___ $\times \frac{3}{8} = \frac{5}{24}$

★ 31. $\frac{9}{10} \times$ ___?___ $= \frac{1}{2}$

★ 32. ___?___ $\times \frac{5}{9} = \frac{7}{36}$

★ 33. $\frac{1}{3} \times$ ___?___ $= \frac{2}{15}$

PROBLEM SOLVING • APPLICATIONS

Write the answers in lowest terms.

34. Suits make up $\frac{1}{2}$ of the inventory at Triglo Shop. If $\frac{3}{5}$ of the suits are for women, what part of the store's inventory is suits for women?

35. John works in the sports department. Each year $\frac{3}{8}$ of the stock he sells is from the tennis section. If $\frac{2}{3}$ of this stock is tennis rackets, what part of the stock sold is tennis rackets?

Multiplying Fractions and Whole Numbers

John practices the guitar
$\frac{3}{4}$ hour every day.
He practices 6 days a week.
How many hours does
he practice each week?

$6 \times \frac{3}{4} = ?$

Step 1
Write the whole number as a fraction.

$\frac{6}{1} \times \frac{3}{4}$

Step 2
Multiply the numerators.

$\frac{6}{1} \times \frac{3}{4} = \frac{18}{}$

Step 3
Multiply the denominators.

$\frac{6}{1} \times \frac{3}{4} = \frac{18}{4}$

Step 4
Write a mixed number for the answer.

$\frac{6}{1} \times \frac{3}{4} = \frac{18}{4} = 4\frac{1}{2}$

John practices $4\frac{1}{2}$ hours a week.

Practice • Multiply. Write the answers in lowest terms.

1. $4 \times \frac{3}{4} = $ ___?___

2. $6 \times \frac{2}{8} = $ ___?___

3. $\frac{2}{5} \times 7 = $ ___?___

4. $\frac{4}{8} \times 7 = $ ___?___

5. $8 \times \frac{5}{6} = $ ___?___

6. $\frac{1}{3} \times 5 = $ ___?___

More Practice • Multiply. Write the answers in lowest terms.

7. $3 \times \frac{4}{5} = $ ___?___

8. $9 \times \frac{5}{6} = $ ___?___

9. $8 \times \frac{2}{3} = $ ___?___

10. $\frac{2}{3} \times 4 = $ ___?___

11. $7 \times \frac{4}{6} = $ ___?___

12. $5 \times \frac{5}{8} = $ ___?___

13. $9 \times \frac{2}{4} = $ ___?___

14. $\frac{3}{5} \times 6 = $ ___?___

15. $\frac{4}{6} \times 8 = $ ___?___

16. $\frac{3}{4} \times \frac{7}{8} =$ ___?___

17. $3 \times \frac{5}{6} =$ ___?___

18. $\frac{5}{8} \times 4 =$ ___?___

19. $3 \times \frac{3}{8} =$ ___?___

20. $\frac{3}{4} \times 5 =$ ___?___

21. $6 \times \frac{5}{6} =$ ___?___

22. $\frac{2}{6} \times 5 =$ ___?___

23. $\frac{4}{5} \times \frac{3}{6} =$ ___?___

24. $\frac{3}{4} \times 3 =$ ___?___

★**25.** $21 \times \frac{3}{8} =$ ___?___

★**26.** $19 \times \frac{7}{10} =$ ___?___

★**27.** $\frac{7}{8} \times 24 =$ ___?___

PROBLEM SOLVING • APPLICATIONS

Write the answers in lowest terms.

28. The chorus practices for $\frac{3}{4}$ hour each school day. How many hours do they practice each week?

29. The school has 40 instruments. Of these, $\frac{3}{8}$ are percussion instruments, and $\frac{1}{5}$ are wind instruments. How many are percussion instruments? How many are wind instruments?

★**30.** There are 18 boys and 17 girls in the music class. The clarinet is played by $\frac{1}{5}$ of the students. How many students do not play the clarinet?

★**31.** The music class buys 15 tickets to a concert. If $\frac{2}{3}$ of the tickets are orchestra seats, how many are not orchestra seats?

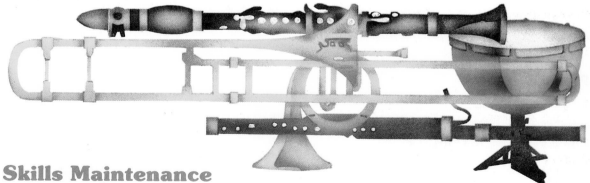

Skills Maintenance

1. $3.56
× 8

2. $4.09
× 3

3. $6.75
× 4

4. $9.32
× 5

5. $8.15
× 6

6. $17.45
× 23

7. $10.50
× 60

8. $96.25
× 56

9. $54.39
× 45

10. $75.00
× 71

Multiplying Fractions and Mixed Numbers

Alice owns a bakery.
She works $7\frac{1}{2}$ hours every day.
$\frac{5}{6}$ of this time she bakes.
The rest of the time she
serves customers. How many
hours a day does she bake?

$\frac{5}{6} \times 7\frac{1}{2} = ?$

Step 1
Write the mixed number as a fraction.

$\frac{5}{6} \times \frac{15}{2}$

Step 2
Multiply the numerators.

$\frac{5}{6} \times \frac{15}{2} = \frac{75}{}$

Step 3
Multiply the denominators.

$\frac{5}{6} \times \frac{15}{2} = \frac{75}{12}$

Step 4
Write a mixed number for the answer.

$\frac{5}{6} \times \frac{15}{2} = \frac{75}{12} = 6\frac{3}{12} = 6\frac{1}{4}$

Alice bakes for $6\frac{1}{4}$ hours every day.

Practice • Multiply. Write the answers in lowest terms.

1. $3\frac{2}{3} \times \frac{5}{6} = $ _____?_____

2. $\frac{2}{5} \times 5\frac{1}{2} = $ _____?_____

3. $2\frac{1}{6} \times \frac{3}{4} = $ _____?_____

4. $5\frac{1}{3} \times \frac{3}{7} = $ _____?_____

5. $4\frac{1}{4} \times \frac{2}{3} = $ _____?_____

6. $\frac{2}{5} \times 5\frac{5}{6} = $ _____?_____

More Practice • Multiply. Write the answers in lowest terms.

7. $\frac{3}{4} \times 4\frac{1}{4} = $ _____?_____

8. $8\frac{1}{2} \times \frac{3}{4} = $ _____?_____

9. $9\frac{1}{3} \times \frac{2}{6} = $ _____?_____

10. $\frac{3}{5} \times 6\frac{1}{3} = $ _____?_____

11. $\frac{3}{4} \times 8\frac{2}{3} = $ _____?_____

12. $\frac{7}{8} \times 7\frac{1}{4} = $ _____?_____

13. $\frac{5}{8} \times 4\frac{2}{3} = \underline{\quad ? \quad}$

14. $\frac{3}{8} \times 3\frac{1}{2} = \underline{\quad ? \quad}$

15. $5\frac{1}{3} \times \frac{5}{6} = \underline{\quad ? \quad}$

16. $\frac{4}{5} \times 9\frac{1}{2} = \underline{\quad ? \quad}$

17. $\frac{2}{5} \times 8 = \underline{\quad ? \quad}$

18. $6\frac{1}{2} \times \frac{2}{6} = \underline{\quad ? \quad}$

19. $2\frac{1}{4} \times \frac{5}{8} = \underline{\quad ? \quad}$

20. $3\frac{3}{4} \times \frac{2}{6} = \underline{\quad ? \quad}$

21. $\frac{5}{8} \times 9\frac{3}{4} = \underline{\quad ? \quad}$

22. $\frac{3}{5} \times 7\frac{1}{2} = \underline{\quad ? \quad}$

23. $\frac{7}{8} \times 4\frac{1}{2} = \underline{\quad ? \quad}$

24. $3 \times \frac{3}{5} = \underline{\quad ? \quad}$

★ 25. $\frac{4}{5} \times 15\frac{3}{8} = \underline{\quad ? \quad}$

★ 26. $\frac{2}{5} \times 17\frac{2}{3} = \underline{\quad ? \quad}$

★ 27. $\frac{5}{6} \times 29\frac{2}{3} = \underline{\quad ? \quad}$

PROBLEM SOLVING • APPLICATIONS

Write the answers in lowest terms.

28. A recipe calls for $\frac{3}{4}$ cup of flour. Luis makes $3\frac{1}{2}$ times the recipe. How much flour does he need?

29. Sonia works 6 hours a day for a bakery. She delivers orders in 2 villages. She spends $\frac{5}{8}$ of her time making deliveries in one village. How many hours is this?

★ 30. On Monday the bakery has $12\frac{1}{2}$ dozen hard rolls. The bakery sells $\frac{2}{3}$ of them. How many dozen rolls are sold? How many rolls is this?

Midchapter Review

1. $\frac{1}{2} \times \frac{3}{4} = \underline{\quad ? \quad}$

2. $\frac{4}{7} \times \frac{2}{3} = \underline{\quad ? \quad}$

3. $5 \times \frac{3}{8} = \underline{\quad ? \quad}$

4. $3 \times \frac{2}{9} = \underline{\quad ? \quad}$

5. $\frac{5}{8} \times 4 = \underline{\quad ? \quad}$

6. $\frac{3}{4} \times 2\frac{1}{2} = \underline{\quad ? \quad}$

7. $4\frac{2}{3} \times \frac{2}{5} = \underline{\quad ? \quad}$

8. $\frac{1}{2} \times 3\frac{3}{5} = \underline{\quad ? \quad}$

Multiplying Mixed Numbers

Chris and Leslie are baking.
The recipe calls for $2\frac{1}{2}$ cups
of flour. Chris and Leslie want
to make $1\frac{1}{2}$ times the recipe.
How much flour should they use?

$1\frac{1}{2} \times 2\frac{1}{2} = ?$

Step 1
Write the mixed numbers as fractions.

$\frac{3}{2} \times \frac{5}{2}$

Step 2
Multiply the numerators.

$\frac{3}{2} \times \frac{5}{2} = \frac{15}{}$

Step 3
Multiply the denominators.

$\frac{3}{2} \times \frac{5}{2} = \frac{15}{4}$

Step 4
Write a mixed number for the answer.

$\frac{3}{2} \times \frac{5}{2} = \frac{15}{4} = 3\frac{3}{4}$

They should use $3\frac{3}{4}$ cups of flour.

Practice • Multiply. Write the answers in lowest terms.

1. $2\frac{1}{2} \times 1\frac{2}{3} = \underline{}$

2. $4\frac{1}{2} \times 1\frac{7}{8} = \underline{}$

3. $3\frac{1}{2} \times 1\frac{2}{6} = \underline{}$

4. $3\frac{2}{5} \times 4\frac{1}{2} = \underline{}$

5. $2\frac{1}{2} \times 1\frac{1}{10} = \underline{}$

6. $1\frac{2}{3} \times 3\frac{3}{4} = \underline{}$

Mixed Practice • Multiply. Write the answers in lowest terms.

7. $3\frac{1}{3} \times 1\frac{3}{5} =$ _____?_____

8. $2\frac{1}{3} \times 1\frac{7}{8} =$ _____?_____

9. $4\frac{2}{3} \times 3\frac{5}{8} =$ _____?_____

10. $1\frac{4}{5} \times 2\frac{3}{4} =$ _____?_____

11. $3\frac{2}{3} \times 3\frac{5}{6} =$ _____?_____

12. $2\frac{2}{3} \times 2\frac{3}{4} =$ _____?_____

13. $2\frac{1}{4} \times 2\frac{2}{6} =$ _____?_____

14. $4\frac{2}{3} \times 2\frac{2}{5} =$ _____?_____

15. $\frac{3}{8} \times \frac{2}{3} =$ _____?_____

16. $3\frac{1}{3} \times 2\frac{5}{6} =$ _____?_____

17. $2\frac{1}{3} \times 1\frac{3}{5} =$ _____?_____

18. $4\frac{1}{4} \times 1\frac{3}{4} =$ _____?_____

19. $3\frac{1}{4} \times 3\frac{4}{5} =$ _____?_____

20. $3 \times 2\frac{3}{8} =$ _____?_____

21. $2\frac{1}{3} \times 3\frac{5}{6} =$ _____?_____

22. $4\frac{3}{4} \times 2\frac{3}{8} =$ _____?_____

23. $2\frac{3}{5} \times 4\frac{1}{2} =$ _____?_____

24. $3\frac{3}{4} \times 1 =$ _____?_____

★ **25.** $26\frac{4}{5} \times \frac{2}{3} =$ _____?_____

★ **26.** $21\frac{7}{8} \times 3\frac{1}{3} =$ _____?_____

★ **27.** $31\frac{3}{5} \times 4\frac{3}{5} =$ _____?_____

★ **28.** Fill in the circles.

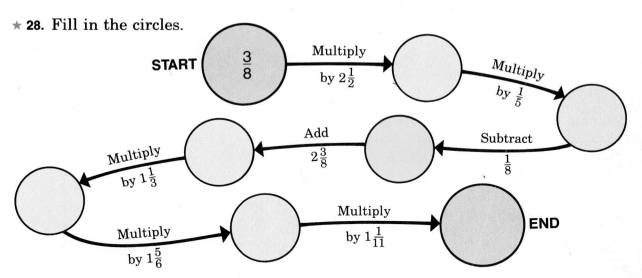

PROBLEM SOLVING • APPLICATIONS

Write the answers in lowest terms.

29. Randy works $2\frac{1}{3}$ hours on Wednesday. On Saturday he works $2\frac{1}{2}$ times as long. How many hours does he work on Saturday?

★ **30.** William buys $2\frac{1}{2}$ dozen rolls. How many rolls does William buy?

229

PROBLEM SOLVING • STRATEGIES

Using Recipes

When you are cooking for one person or for many people, you must know how to decrease or increase the number of servings a recipe will make. To adjust the recipe correctly, you must change the amount of each ingredient.

A salad recipe calls for $1\frac{1}{2}$ cups of wax beans.
The recipe makes 6 servings.
Suppose you want to make 3 servings.

Think: $\dfrac{\text{servings}}{\text{servings}} \dfrac{3}{6} = \dfrac{1}{2}$

Multiply the amount of wax beans by $\frac{1}{2}$.

$$\frac{1}{2} \times 1\frac{1}{2} = \frac{1}{2} \times \frac{3}{2} = \frac{3}{4}$$

You need $\frac{3}{4}$ cup wax beans for 3 servings.

How many cups of wax beans are needed for 9 servings?

Think: $\dfrac{\text{servings}}{\text{servings}} \dfrac{9}{6} = 1\frac{1}{2}$

Multiply the amount of wax beans by $1\frac{1}{2}$.

$$1\frac{1}{2} \times 1\frac{1}{2} = \frac{3}{2} \times \frac{3}{2} = \frac{9}{4} = 2\frac{1}{4}$$

You need $2\frac{1}{4}$ cups of wax beans for 9 servings.

Read each problem and answer the questions below it.

A recipe for meat loaf uses $\frac{3}{4}$ pound of ground veal. The recipe makes 8 servings. Suppose you want to make a different number of servings. How many pounds of ground veal do you need to make

1. 4 servings?

2. 16 servings?

3. 10 servings?

Remember to reduce each fraction to lowest terms.

You need $2\frac{3}{4}$ cups of oatmeal to make 6 servings. How many cups of oatmeal do you need to make

4. 8 servings?

5. 3 servings?

6. 12 servings?

Solve.

A casserole recipe calls for $1\frac{2}{3}$ cups of cracker crumbs. The casserole serves 8 people. How many cups of cracker crumbs do you need to make

7. 2 servings?

8. 4 servings?

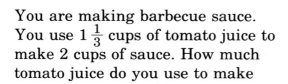

9. 16 servings?

You are making barbecue sauce. You use $1\frac{1}{3}$ cups of tomato juice to make 2 cups of sauce. How much tomato juice do you use to make

10. 1 cup of sauce?

11. 4 cups of sauce?

12. 6 cups of sauce?

When increasing or decreasing the number of servings, remember to change each ingredient in the recipe. Remember to write your answer in lowest terms.

To make 4 servings of turkey salad you use $\frac{2}{3}$ cups mayonnaise. How much mayonnaise do you use to make

13. 8 servings?

14. 2 servings?

15. 6 servings?

Pineapple Dessert

$15\frac{1}{2}$ oz crushed pineapple with juice
1 cup boiling water
1 tsp vanilla
$1\frac{1}{2}$ tsp concentrated lemon juice
2 envelopes unflavored gelatin
$1\frac{1}{3}$ cups powdered milk
$\frac{1}{4}$ tsp butter flavoring
Cinnamon

Mix pineapple and gelatin in blender at medium speed until smooth. Add boiling water and blend. Gradually add powdered milk, blending until well mixed. Add vanilla, butter flavoring, and lemon juice. Pour into 8 dessert dishes. Sprinkle with cinnamon. Chill until firm.

How much of each ingredient would you need to make

★ **16.** 4 servings?

★ **17.** 6 servings?

Reciprocals

$\frac{1}{5} \times \frac{5}{1} = \frac{5}{5} = 1$ $\frac{2}{3} \times \frac{3}{2} = \frac{6}{6} = 1$

$\frac{7}{6} \times \frac{6}{7} = \frac{42}{42} = 1$ $\frac{8}{1} \times \frac{1}{8} = \frac{8}{8} = 1$

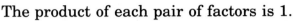

The product of each pair of factors is 1.
Two numbers are **reciprocals** when their product is 1.

Find the reciprocal of $\frac{4}{5}$, of $3\frac{5}{6}$, and of 9.

To find the reciprocal of:	$\frac{4}{5}$	$3\frac{5}{6}$	9
Step 1 Write the number as a fraction.	$\frac{4}{5}$	$\frac{23}{6}$	$\frac{9}{1}$
Step 2 Exchange the numerator and the denominator.	$\frac{5}{4}$	$\frac{6}{23}$	$\frac{1}{9}$
Step 3 Multiply the reciprocals to check. The product is 1.	$\frac{5}{4} \times \frac{4}{5} = \frac{20}{20} = 1$	$\frac{6}{23} \times \frac{23}{6} = \frac{138}{138} = 1$	$\frac{1}{9} \times \frac{9}{1} = \frac{9}{9} = 1$

Practice • Multiply. Write the answers in lowest terms.

1. $\frac{4}{6} \times \frac{6}{4} = \underline{\quad?\quad}$ 2. $1\frac{2}{9} \times \frac{9}{11} = \underline{\quad?\quad}$ 3. $\frac{1}{4} \times 4 = \underline{\quad?\quad}$

Find each reciprocal.

4. $\frac{1}{2}$ 5. 9   6. $\frac{6}{9}$ 7. $3\frac{3}{4}$ 8. $\frac{8}{2}$ 9. $3\frac{3}{8}$

Mixed Practice • Multiply. Write the answers in lowest terms.

10. $\frac{3}{4} \times 1\frac{1}{3} = \underline{\quad?\quad}$ 11. $\frac{1}{10} \times 10 = \underline{\quad?\quad}$ 12. $\frac{6}{5} \times \frac{5}{6} = \underline{\quad?\quad}$

13. $\frac{8}{2} \times \frac{2}{8} =$ _____ ?

14. $\frac{3}{8} \times 2\frac{2}{3} =$ _____ ?

15. $\frac{7}{5} \times \frac{5}{7} =$ _____ ?

16. $1\frac{2}{7} \times \frac{7}{9} =$ _____ ?

17. $3\frac{4}{7} \times \frac{7}{25} =$ _____ ?

18. $2\frac{4}{5} \times \frac{5}{14} =$ _____ ?

Find each reciprocal.

19. $2\frac{1}{5}$ 　　 **20.** $\frac{3}{5}$ 　　 **21.** $\frac{12}{14}$ 　　 **22.** 28 　　 **23.** $5\frac{1}{2}$ 　　 **24.** $\frac{8}{4}$

25. $1\frac{3}{10}$ 　　 **26.** $\frac{6}{6}$ 　　 **27.** $\frac{1}{18}$ 　　 **28.** $\frac{5}{8}$ 　　 **29.** $\frac{10}{5}$ 　　 **30.** $3\frac{1}{4}$

Find the missing factors.
Write answers greater than 1 as mixed numbers.

31. $4\frac{1}{2} \times$ _____ ? $= 1$

32. $\frac{11}{12} \times$ _____ ? $= 1$

33. _____ ? $\times \frac{3}{6} = 1$

34. _____ ? $\times \frac{9}{10} = 1$

35. _____ ? $\times 3\frac{3}{5} = 1$

36. $1\frac{3}{8} \times$ _____ ? $= 1$

37. $1\frac{5}{9} \times$ _____ ? $= 1$

38. _____ ? $\times \frac{10}{30} = 1$

39. $\frac{5}{14} \times$ _____ ? $= 1$

Solve without multiplying.

★ **40.** $\frac{1}{4} \times \frac{4}{1} = 1$, so $3 \times \left(\frac{1}{4} \times \frac{4}{1} \right) =$ _____ ?　　 ★ **41.** $\frac{1}{5} \times 5 = 1$, so $6 \times \left(\frac{1}{5} \times 5 \right) =$ _____ ?

PROBLEM SOLVING • APPLICATIONS

What are the next two numbers in the pattern?

★ **42.**

| $\frac{1}{2}$ | $\frac{1}{4}$ | $\frac{1}{8}$ | ? | ? |

★ **43.**

| $\frac{3}{4}$ | $\frac{6}{12}$ | $\frac{12}{36}$ | ? | ? |

Skills Maintenance

1. $4\overline{)\$6.00}$ 　　 **2.** $6\overline{)\$9.00}$ 　　 **3.** $5\overline{)\$6.75}$ 　　 **4.** $8\overline{)\$7.92}$ 　　 **5.** $3\overline{)\$8.46}$

6. $7\overline{)\$66.64}$ 　　 **7.** $6\overline{)\$19.74}$ 　　 **8.** $6\overline{)\$22.50}$ 　　 **9.** $8\overline{)\$96.72}$ 　　 **10.** $9\overline{)\$157.50}$

Dividing Fractions

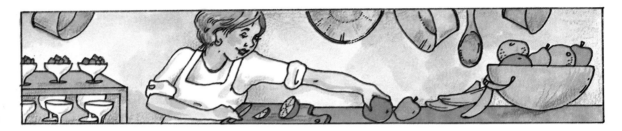

There are 4 oranges.
How many $\frac{1}{2}$s are in 4?
(Count to find how many.)

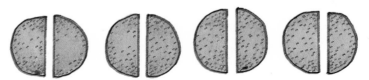

$$4 \div \frac{1}{2} = 8 \qquad 4 \times \frac{2}{1} = 8$$

reciprocals

There are $4\frac{1}{2}$ apples.
How many $\frac{3}{4}$s in $4\frac{1}{2}$?
(Count to find how many.)

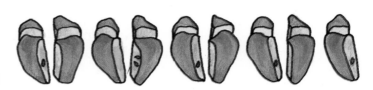

$$\frac{9}{2} \div \frac{3}{4} = 6 \qquad \frac{9}{2} \times \frac{4}{3} = 6$$

reciprocals

To divide fractions, multiply by the reciprocal of the divisor.

$$\frac{3}{4} \div \frac{5}{8} = \frac{3}{4} \times \frac{8}{5} = 1\frac{1}{5}$$

reciprocals

Practice • Complete.

1. $\frac{1}{2} \div \frac{2}{3} = \frac{1}{2} \times \frac{3}{2} = $ _____

2. $3 \div \frac{4}{9} = \frac{3}{1} \times \frac{9}{4} = $ _____

3. $\frac{4}{5} \div \frac{1}{3} = \frac{4}{5} \times \frac{?}{?} = $ _____

4. $\frac{2}{3} \div \frac{3}{4} = \frac{2}{3} \times \frac{?}{?} = $ _____

Divide. Write the answers in lowest terms.

5. $\frac{1}{8} \div \frac{4}{3} = $ _____

6. $\frac{6}{7} \div \frac{7}{6} = $ _____

7. $\frac{3}{8} \div \frac{1}{4} = $ _____

234

Mixed Practice • Divide. Write the answers in lowest terms.

8. $6 \div \frac{3}{8} =$ _____?_____

9. $\frac{5}{10} \div \frac{2}{3} =$ _____?_____

10. $\frac{10}{3} \div \frac{5}{6} =$ _____?_____

11. $\frac{3}{4} \div \frac{1}{2} =$ _____?_____

12. $\frac{7}{8} \div \frac{1}{4} =$ _____?_____

13. $\frac{5}{4} \div \frac{3}{2} =$ _____?_____

14. $\frac{7}{2} \div \frac{3}{2} =$ _____?_____

15. $\frac{3}{4} \div \frac{3}{5} =$ _____?_____

16. $\frac{1}{2} \div \frac{2}{3} =$ _____?_____

17. $\frac{5}{6} \div \frac{3}{4} =$ _____?_____

18. $\frac{5}{9} \div \frac{3}{2} =$ _____?_____

19. $\frac{3}{8} \div \frac{3}{4} =$ _____?_____

20. $10 \div \frac{5}{8} =$ _____?_____

21. $\frac{1}{5} \div \frac{2}{3} =$ _____?_____

22. $\frac{7}{2} \div \frac{3}{8} =$ _____?_____

23. $\frac{3}{2} \div \frac{2}{3} =$ _____?_____

24. $\frac{7}{12} \div \frac{1}{6} =$ _____?_____

25. $12 \div \frac{3}{4} =$ _____?_____

★ 26. $\frac{7}{3} \div \frac{?}{6} = 2\frac{4}{5}$

★ 27. $\frac{11}{3} \div \frac{5}{?} = 4\frac{2}{5}$

★ 28. $\frac{?}{11} \div \frac{3}{22} = 6$

Use the numbers in the INPUT column. Follow the rule. List the OUTPUTS. Write the answers in lowest terms.

29. Multiply by $\frac{2}{3}$

INPUT	OUTPUT
$\frac{1}{4}$	$\frac{1}{6}$
$\frac{3}{5}$	?
$\frac{7}{8}$	?
$\frac{4}{9}$	?

★ 30. Multiply by $\frac{3}{4}$

INPUT	OUTPUT
$\frac{1}{8}$	?
?	$\frac{9}{16}$
?	$\frac{27}{40}$
$\frac{5}{8}$	?

★ 31. Multiply by $\frac{1}{5}$

INPUT	OUTPUT
$\frac{1}{6}$	?
?	$\frac{4}{25}$
$\frac{7}{100}$	?
?	$\frac{3}{80}$

PROBLEM SOLVING • APPLICATIONS

Write the answers in lowest terms.

32. There is $\frac{5}{8}$ of a salad mold left on a plate. One serving is $\frac{1}{16}$ of the mold. How many servings can be made from what is left on the plate?

★ 33. The Seashore Restaurant serves melon for dessert. Each serving is $\frac{1}{3}$ of a melon. How many servings can be made from 6 melons? From 7 melons?

Multiply. Write the answers in lowest terms. (pages 222–229)

1. $\frac{1}{4} \times \frac{1}{3} =$ ___?___

2. $\frac{1}{2} \times \frac{2}{5} =$ ___?___

3. $\frac{2}{3} \times \frac{7}{10} =$ ___?___

4. $\frac{1}{8} \times \frac{4}{5} =$ ___?___

5. $\frac{2}{3} \times \frac{1}{9} =$ ___?___

6. $\frac{5}{6} \times \frac{8}{15} =$ ___?___

7. $\frac{1}{4} \times 6 =$ ___?___

8. $3 \times \frac{7}{12} =$ ___?___

9. $\frac{3}{8} \times 8 =$ ___?___

10. $9 \times \frac{5}{6} =$ ___?___

11. $6 \times \frac{7}{8} =$ ___?___

12. $\frac{5}{6} \times 4 =$ ___?___

13. $1\frac{3}{4} \times \frac{1}{3} =$ ___?___

14. $\frac{2}{8} \times 3\frac{1}{8} =$ ___?___

15. $2\frac{4}{7} \times \frac{1}{2} =$ ___?___

16. $\frac{5}{6} \times 2\frac{1}{2} =$ ___?___

17. $3\frac{1}{4} \times \frac{4}{5} =$ ___?___

18. $9\frac{3}{4} \times \frac{8}{9} =$ ___?___

19. $2\frac{1}{4} \times 1\frac{1}{7} =$ ___?___

20. $3\frac{2}{3} \times 2\frac{5}{8} =$ ___?___

21. $2\frac{3}{8} \times 1\frac{1}{3} =$ ___?___

22. $1\frac{4}{5} \times 4\frac{2}{3} =$ ___?___

23. $4\frac{1}{2} \times 2\frac{5}{6} =$ ___?___

24. $6\frac{1}{2} \times 4\frac{4}{5} =$ ___?___

Divide. Write the answers in lowest terms. (pages 234–235)

25. $\frac{1}{4} \div \frac{1}{5} =$ ___?___

26. $\frac{7}{8} \div \frac{1}{2} =$ ___?___

27. $8 \div \frac{4}{5} =$ ___?___

28. $\frac{4}{9} \div \frac{5}{3} =$ ___?___

29. $2 \div \frac{2}{5} =$ ___?___

30. $\frac{3}{4} \div \frac{3}{5} =$ ___?___

Solve. Write the answers in lowest terms.

31. A frozen pizza takes 16 minutes to cook at a certain temperature. It takes $\frac{3}{4}$ of that time at a higher temperature. How long does it take to cook the pizza at the higher temperature? (p. 224)

32. Each slice of pizza is $\frac{1}{8}$ of the pizza. How many slices are there in 3 pizzas? (p. 234)

PROJECT

Magic Squares

In a **magic square,** the sum of the numbers in each row, column, and diagonal is the same. This sum is called the **magic sum.**

1. Find the magic sum for this magic square.

   The magic sum is _____.

$1\frac{2}{3}$	$\frac{3}{4}$	$1\frac{1}{6}$	$1\frac{7}{12}$
$1\frac{1}{2}$	$1\frac{1}{4}$	$\frac{2}{3}$	$1\frac{3}{4}$
$\frac{11}{12}$	$1\frac{5}{6}$	$1\frac{5}{12}$	1
$1\frac{1}{12}$	$1\frac{1}{3}$	$1\frac{11}{12}$	$\frac{5}{6}$

Use the magic square in Exercise 1 to make a new square for each square on the right.

2. Divide each number by $1\frac{2}{3}$.
   Write the numbers in lowest terms.

   Is this a magic square? _____
   If your answer is yes,
   what is the magic sum? _____

1			

3. Multiply each number by $1\frac{3}{4}$.
   Write the numbers in lowest terms.

   Is this a magic square? _____
   If your answer is yes,
   what is the magic sum? _____

$2\frac{11}{12}$			

Multiply. Write the answers in lowest terms.

1. $\frac{1}{3} \times \frac{1}{3} = $ _____?_____

2. $\frac{1}{2} \times \frac{5}{8} = $ _____?_____

3. $\frac{3}{4} \times \frac{5}{6} = $ _____?_____

4. $\frac{3}{4} \times \frac{2}{5} = $ _____?_____

5. $\frac{5}{6} \times \frac{3}{8} = $ _____?_____

6. $\frac{3}{5} \times \frac{2}{3} = $ _____?_____

7. $5 \times \frac{2}{3} = $ _____?_____

8. $\frac{1}{2} \times 8 = $ _____?_____

9. $8 \times \frac{3}{4} = $ _____?_____

10. $8 \times \frac{1}{6} = $ _____?_____

11. $9 \times \frac{2}{3} = $ _____?_____

12. $2\frac{1}{2} \times \frac{3}{5} = $ _____?_____

13. $\frac{1}{4} \times 3\frac{3}{8} = $ _____?_____

14. $7\frac{1}{3} \times \frac{3}{8} = $ _____?_____

15. $\frac{2}{3} \times 1\frac{1}{2} = $ _____?_____

16. $3\frac{1}{3} \times \frac{1}{5} = $ _____?_____

17. $2\frac{3}{8} \times 2\frac{2}{3} = $ _____?_____

18. $4\frac{1}{2} \times \frac{2}{9} = $ _____?_____

19. $2\frac{1}{2} \times 3\frac{1}{4} = $ _____?_____

20. $3\frac{1}{2} \times 5\frac{2}{3} = $ _____?_____

21. $2\frac{2}{3} \times 2\frac{1}{4} = $ _____?_____

22. $3\frac{3}{4} \times 4\frac{5}{6} = $ _____?_____

23. $4\frac{2}{3} \times 3\frac{1}{6} = $ _____?_____

24. $2\frac{1}{5} \times 3\frac{1}{3} = $ _____?_____

Divide. Write the answers in lowest terms.

25. $\frac{1}{5} \div \frac{3}{4} = $ _____?_____

26. $4 \div \frac{2}{3} = $ _____?_____

27. $\frac{3}{10} \div \frac{1}{2} = $ _____?_____

28. $9 \div \frac{6}{7} = $ _____?_____

29. $\frac{8}{5} \div \frac{2}{5} = $ _____?_____

30. $\frac{3}{8} \div \frac{6}{4} = $ _____?_____

Solve. Write the answers in lowest terms.

31. The school band is having a picnic. There are 24 students in the band, and $\frac{3}{4}$ of the students are wearing shorts. How many students are wearing shorts?

32. The band has 12 packages of apple juice mix. For each pitcher of apple juice they use $\frac{1}{2}$ of a package. How many pitchers of apple juice can they make using the 12 packages?

Neither or Nor

There are 24 pages of coins in one of Angela's coin albums. Old pennies fill 6 pages. Old nickels fill 8 pages. How many pages contain *neither* pennies *nor* nickels?

1. Find the number of pages of pennies and nickels. $\longrightarrow$ $6 + 8 = 14$

2. Find the number of pages of other kinds of coins. $\longrightarrow$ $24 - 14 = 10$

10 pages contain neither pennies nor nickels.

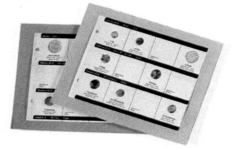

Solve the problems.

1. There are 36 pages in a coin album. Two-cent pieces fill 3 pages. One-cent pieces fill 8 pages. How many pages contain neither two-cent nor one-cent pieces?

2. There are 148 pages in a coin album. 36 pages contain silver dimes. 28 pages contain silver dollars. How many pages contain neither silver dimes nor silver dollars?

3. There are 378 coins in a collection. 45 are Indian-head pennies. 52 are buffalo nickels. 25 are eagle pennies. How many are not Indian-head pennies, buffalo nickels, or eagle pennies?

4. There are 580 old coins in a collection. 83 are two-cent pieces. 28 are half-cent pieces. 10 are one-cent pieces. How many are not two-cent pieces, half-cent pieces, or one-cent pieces?

COMPUTER

Computer Speed

The speed of a computer depends on its cycle time. **Cycle time** is the amount of time for one tick of the computer's internal clock. The faster the cycle time, the faster the computer is. The usefulness of a computer depends on its ability to work very fast. For this reason, reducing cycle time is the single most important job of computer designers.

How fast can a computer's internal clock tick? At each internal clock tick, data moves from place to place inside the computer. In the time of one internal clock tick, a bit can turn from on to off.

A **microprocessor** is the central processing unit (CPU) of a microcomputer. The rectangle you see here is as big as a microelectronic circuit that has 6,200 transistors. This circuit, the actual size of the CPU of a microcomputer, performs 770,000 calculations per second. Although it is certainly very small and very fast, it is not as small or as fast as possible.

0.16″
←0.22″

One method used to increase speed is **parallel processing**. When a computer has many circuits working at the same time, it is performing parallel processing. An **8-bit computer** works with units of one byte (eight bits). The CPU has eight circuits that move eight bits in one internal clock tick. A **16-bit computer** works with two bytes (sixteen bits) each internal clock tick. **Supercomputers** are the world's fastest computers today. They are 64-bit computers, in which circuits are repeated 64 times. These computers are very expensive—about $15 million. Only 100 to 200 of these supercomputers are expected to be sold in the next five years.

Computer engineers and designers are devoting most of their efforts to improving the speeds of the middle-range, 16-bit computer. But there is an upper limit to the speed of data movement. In the past, scientists thought that light moved instantly from place to place. Now we know that light, while fast, has a definite *speed*. No data can travel as fast as the speed of light, which is 30,000,000,000 centimeters per second.

Data move through metals called **conductors**. At room temperature all conductors offer **resistance** to data. In 1962 **Brian Josephson** did research on how metals behave at very low temperatures. At very cold temperatures (about −269°C) conductors become superconductors.

Because the resistance vanishes, the data move much faster. However, a superconducting computer the size of a dime would need a cooling unit as large as a refrigerator to keep temperatures in the superconducting range.

In the design of the very small supercomputer, speed is the most important thing. Research on ways to make computers faster is expanding areas of knowledge in physics, chemistry, and engineering.

Josephson junctions are switches that change states 167,000,000,000 times per second. In the time of one change of state, data can travel only 1.8 millimeters. (This line, _, is 1.8 millimeters long.) For data to be useful, the computer itself must be small. Otherwise a Josephson junction would change state, and some distant part of the computer would not have enough time to receive the message. Therefore, microprocessors that have Josephson junctions will be smaller and fifty times faster than the microprocessor that was discussed on page 240.

Write TRUE or FALSE after the following statements.

1. Data are sent from place to place within a microprocessor by messengers.

2. Data are sent through metals called conductors.

3. At very low temperatures, conductors become supercomputers.

4. A Josephson junction could change state 200 times in the time it takes light to travel from this page to your eyes, about 36 centimeters. (Hint: Remember that 10 millimeters equal one centimeter.)

5. A computer that has many circuits working at the same time is doing parallel processing.

6. Two computers are exactly equal except that computer A is an 8-bit computer and computer B is a 16-bit computer. Computer A is faster than computer B.

7. Speed is the most important factor in the design of supercomputers.

Choose the correct answers.

1. What number does the blue digit name?

14,607,962,175

- **A.** 600 thousand
- **B.** 600 million
- **C.** 60 billion
- **D.** not here

2. Compare.

698 ● 689

- **A.** >
- **B.** <
- **C.** =
- **D.** not here

3. Add.

762
45
176
+897

- **A.** 1,770
- **B.** 1,876
- **C.** 1,880
- **D.** not here

4. Subtract.

$20.00
− 16.50

- **A.** $4.50
- **B.** $14.50
- **C.** $36.50
- **D.** not here

5. Multiply.

427
× 89

- **A.** 35,903
- **B.** 38,003
- **C.** 42,614
- **D.** not here

6. Divide.

$64\overline{)89,104}$

- **A.** 1,296 r41
- **B.** 1,487 r52
- **C.** 1,392 r16
- **D.** not here

7. Write the number as a product of prime factors.

24

- **A.** $4 \times 3 \times 2$
- **B.** $12 \times 2 \times 1$
- **C.** $2 \times 3 \times 2 \times 2$
- **D.** not here

8. Subtract. Write the answer in lowest terms.

9
$-6\frac{3}{8}$

- **A.** $3\frac{3}{8}$
- **B.** $2\frac{5}{8}$
- **C.** $15\frac{3}{8}$
- **D.** not here

9. Multiply. Write the answer in lowest terms.

$8 \times \frac{9}{10} = \underline{\quad?\quad}$

- **A.** $8\frac{9}{10}$
- **B.** $7\frac{1}{5}$
- **C.** $7\frac{1}{10}$
- **D.** not here

10. The Mt. Cisco Volleyball Team played 4 games. The team scored 21, 17, 18, and 20 points. What is the team's average score?

- **A.** 17
- **B.** 19
- **C.** 20
- **D.** not here

11. Sparrow eggs hatch in about 12 days. It takes 5 times that long for penguin eggs. How long does it take for penguin eggs to hatch?

- **A.** 60 days
- **B.** 50 days
- **C.** 2 weeks
- **D.** not here

Measurement

**Centimeter and Millimeter • Meter, Decimeter, and Kilometer
• Perimeter • Area of Rectangles • Area of Triangles
• Volume • Problem Solving: Problems Without Numbers
• Milliliter and Liter • Gram and Kilogram • Degrees Celsius
Time • Customary Units of Length • Finding Perimeter, Area, Volume
• Customary Units of Capacity • Customary Units of Weight
• Degrees Fahrenheit • Operations with Measures**

Centimeter and Millimeter

A **centimeter (cm)** is a metric unit of length.

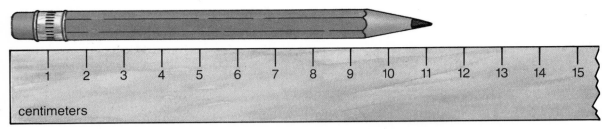

The length of this pencil is between 11 centimeters and 12 centimeters.
It is nearer to 11 centimeters.
The length is 11 centimeters to the nearest centimeter.

Each centimeter unit can be separated into 10 smaller units.
Each smaller unit is a **millimeter (mm).**

10 millimeters (mm) = 1 centimeter (cm)

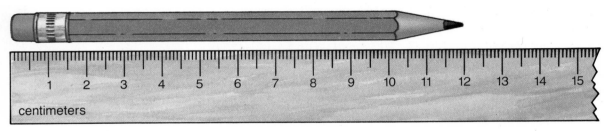

The length of this pencil is 12 centimeters.
To find the length in millimeters, multiply the number of centimeters
by 10. The length is 120 millimeters.

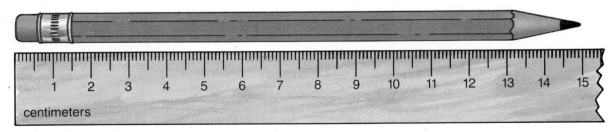

The length of this pencil is 150 millimeters.
To find the length in centimeters, divide by 10.
The length is 15 centimeters.

Practice • Estimate the length in centimeters. Then measure to
the nearest centimeter.

1.

2.

Estimate the length in millimeters.
Then measure to the nearest millimeter.

3.    **4.**

Mixed Practice • Estimate the length in centimeters. Then measure to the nearest centimeter.

5.

6.

7.

Estimate the length in millimeters. Then measure to the nearest millimeter.

8.

9.

10.

Use a ruler. Draw a picture of

11. a pencil 95 millimeters long.   **12.** a paintbrush 16 centimeters long.

Complete.

13. 10 mm = __?__ cm   **14.** 30 mm = __?__ cm   **15.** 60 mm = __?__ cm

16. 120 mm = __?__ cm   **17.** 240 mm = __?__ cm   **18.** 470 mm = __?__ cm

19. __?__ mm = 2 cm   **20.** __?__ mm = 7 cm   **21.** __?__ mm = 10 cm

22. __?__ mm = 34 cm   **23.** __?__ mm = 56 cm   **24.** __?__ mm = 85 cm

PROBLEM SOLVING • APPLICATIONS

Estimate the length in millimeters. Then measure to the nearest millimeter.
Find the difference between your estimate and the measurement.

★**25.** a piece of chalk   ★**26.** a pen   ★**27.** a crayon

Meter, Decimeter, and Kilometer

1 decimeter

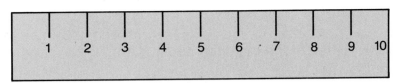

The length of this strip is 10 centimeters, or 1 **decimeter (dm)**.
Make 10 of these strips. Tape them together.
The length of your new strip is one **meter (m)**.

10 decimeters (dm) = 1 meter (m)
100 centimeters (cm) = 1 meter (m)

Use your meter strip to measure to the nearest meter.
About how high is your desk? About how high is a door?

Suppose you made 1,000 meter strips and taped them together.
The length of your new strip would be one **kilometer (km)**.

1,000 meters (m) = 1 kilometer (km)

You can walk a distance of one kilometer in about 12 minutes.
The distance between San Francisco and New York City is about
4,115 kilometers.

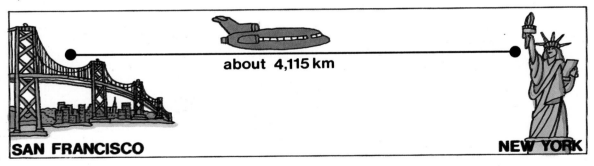

about 4,115 km

SAN FRANCISCO   NEW YORK

Practice • Which unit of measure would you use?
Write CENTIMETER, METER, or KILOMETER.

1. the length of a room

2. the height of an apartment building

3. the length of a ship

4. the distance between Miami and Dallas

5. your height

6. the length of the Mississippi River

Mixed Practice • Which unit of measure would you use?
Write CENTIMETER, METER, or KILOMETER.

7. the coastline of Texas

8. the width of a traffic sign

9. the length of a city block

10. the distance around the earth

Complete. 10 dm = 1 m

11. 40 dm = __?__ m

12. 70 dm = __?__ m

13. 170 dm = __?__ m

14. __?__ dm = 8 m

15. __?__ dm = 10 m

16. __?__ dm = 12 m

Complete. 100 cm = 1 m

17. 200 cm = __?__ m

18. 400 cm = __?__ m

19. 1,600 cm = __?__ m

20. __?__ cm = 5 m

21. __?__ cm = 10 m

22. __?__ cm = 14 m

Complete. 1,000 mm = 1 m

23. 2,000 mm = __?__ m

24. 12,000 mm = __?__ m

25. __?__ mm = 5 m

Complete. 1,000 m = 1 km

26. 8,000 m = __?__ km

27. 18,000 m = __?__ km

28. __?__ m = 10 km

★**29.** 500 m = __?__ cm

500 m = __?__ mm

★**30.** 600 m = __?__ dm

600 m = __?__ cm

PROBLEM SOLVING • APPLICATIONS

What is the distance in centimeters? 1 km = 100,000 cm

31. From Atlanta, Georgia, to
Houston, Texas: 1,128 km

32. From Phoenix, Arizona, to
Cleveland, Ohio: 2,815 km

What is the distance in millimeters? 1 km = 1,000,000 mm

★**33.** From Portland, Oregon, to
Washington, D.C.: 3,788 km

★**34.** From Chicago, Illinois, to
Miami, Florida: 1,912 km

Perimeter

The Sunshine Resort has a swimming area with 3 pools. Find the distance around the swimming area.

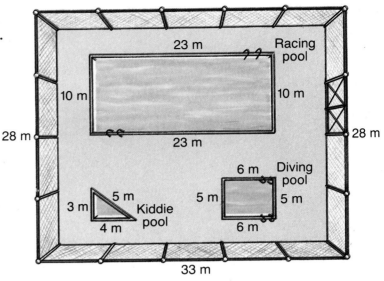

The distance around a figure is its **perimeter.**

> *The perimeter of a figure is the sum of the lengths of the sides.*

Find the perimeter of the swimming area.

Step 1
Find the measure of each side.

Step 2
Find the sum of the measures.

$$33 + 28 + 33 + 28 = 122$$

The distance around the swimming area is 122 meters.

Practice • Find the perimeter of

1. the racing pool.

2. the kiddie pool.

3. the diving pool.

Mixed Practice • Find the perimeter of each figure.

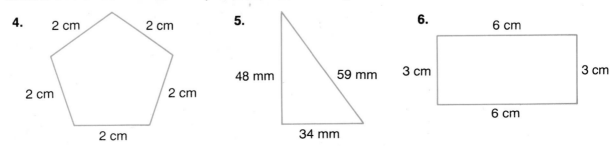

4. 2 cm 2 cm 2 cm 2 cm 2 cm

5. 48 mm 59 mm 34 mm

6. 6 cm 3 cm 3 cm 6 cm

248

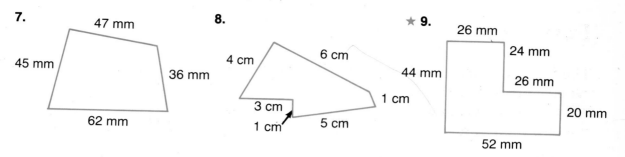

7. 47 mm, 45 mm, 36 mm, 62 mm

8. 4 cm, 6 cm, 3 cm, 1 cm, 5 cm, 1 cm

★ 9. 26 mm, 24 mm, 26 mm, 44 mm, 20 mm, 52 mm

Measure the sides to find the perimeter

10. to the nearest centimeter.

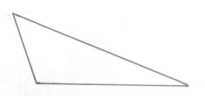

11. to the nearest millimeter.

PROBLEM SOLVING • APPLICATIONS

12. The resort has a miniature golf course. The lengths of the sides of the course are 35 meters, 20 meters, 18 meters, 43 meters, and 8 meters. How much fencing is needed to go around the golf course?

The outline of a figure may be curved. To find the perimeter place a string around the figure. Then measure the string.

★ 13. The resort is on a piece of property that has 5 sides. The lengths of the sides are 150 meters, 213 meters, 306 meters, .308 kilometers, and 436 meters. What is the perimeter of the piece of land?

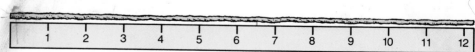

★ 14. Use a piece of string to find the perimeter of the figure.

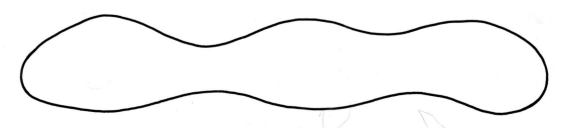

Area of Rectangles

The number of square units that cover a surface is the **area** of the surface.

A **square centimeter (sq cm)** is a unit of area.

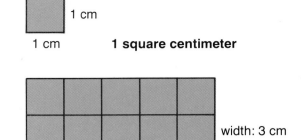

1 cm

1 cm   **1 square centimeter**

You can count to find the area of the rectangle.
It is 15 square centimeters.

width: 3 cm

length: 5 cm

You can also multiply to find the area of a rectangle.

$$\text{Area} = \text{length} \times \text{width}$$
$$= 5 \times 3$$
$$= 15$$

The area equals 15 square centimeters.

Other metric units of area are the **square millimeter (sq mm), square meter (sq m),** and **square kilometer (sq km).**

Practice • Count to find the area in square centimeters.

1.
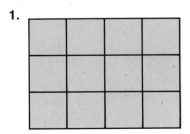

2.

3.
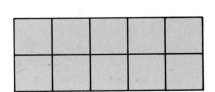

Find the area of each figure.

4.
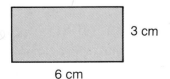
3 cm

6 cm

5.

5 cm

9 cm

6.
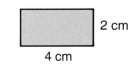
2 cm

4 cm

250

Mixed Practice • Find the area of each figure.

7.
4 cm
7 cm

8.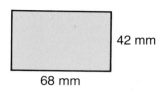
37 mm
26 mm

9.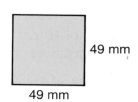
49 mm
49 mm

10.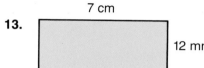
5 cm
7 cm

11.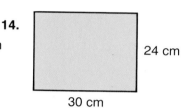
42 mm
68 mm

12.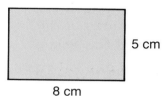
5 cm
8 cm

13.
12 mm
32 mm

14.
24 cm
30 cm

15.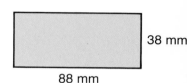
38 mm
88 mm

The length (*l*) and width (*w*) are given. Find the area.

16. $l = 7$ cm, $w = 3$ cm

17. $l = 8$ cm, $w = 4$ cm

18. $l = 6$ cm, $w = 9$ cm

19. $l = 5$ cm, $w = 8$ cm

20. $l = 21$ mm, $w = 33$ mm

21. $l = 18$ mm, $w = 48$ mm

★**22.** $l = 19$ mm, $w = 56$ cm

★**23.** $l = 42$ mm, $w = 29$ cm

Choose three rectangles in your classroom. Measure the length and the width. Record the measurements with the correct unit. Then multiply to find the area in square units.

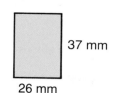

Rectangle	length (l)	width (w)	area (A)
★**24.**			
★**25.**			
★**26.**			

PROBLEM SOLVING • APPLICATIONS

27. The Johnsons are putting carpeting in their family room. The length of the room is 5 meters. The width of the room is 4 meters. How many square meters of carpeting are needed?

★**28.** The area of the floor of a rectangular room is 42 square meters. The length of the room is 7 meters. What is the width of the room?

Area of Triangles

The **base** of this triangle is 4 centimeters.
It is the same as the length of the rectangle.

The **height** of this triangle is 3 centimeters.
It is the same as the width of the rectangle.

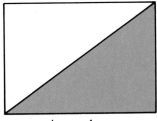

height: 3 cm

base: 4 cm

The area of the triangle is $\frac{1}{2}$ the area of the rectangle.
Find the area of the triangle.

Area of rectangle: $4 \times 3 = 12$
12 square centimeters

Area of triangle: $\frac{1}{2}$ of $12 = 6$

The area of the triangle is 6 square centimeters.

Find the area of the triangle.

$$\text{Area} = \frac{1}{2} \text{ of } (\textbf{length of base} \times \textbf{height})$$

$$= \frac{1}{2} \text{ of } (5 \times 8)$$

$$= \frac{1}{2} \text{ of } 40$$

$$= 20$$

Area equals 20 square centimeters.

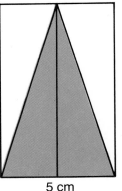

8 cm

5 cm

Practice • Find the area of each figure.

1.

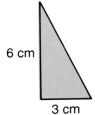

6 cm

3 cm

2.

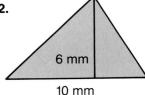

6 mm

10 mm

3.

2 cm

2 cm

Mixed Practice • Find the area of each figure.

4.

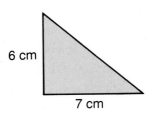

6 cm

7 cm

5.

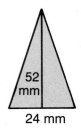

52 mm

24 mm

6.

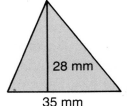

28 mm

35 mm

252

7.

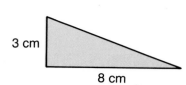

3 cm

8 cm

8.

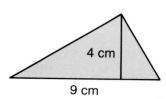

4 cm

9 cm

9.

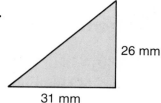

26 mm

31 mm

10.

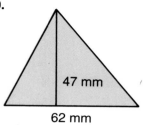

47 mm

62 mm

11.

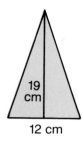

19 cm

12 cm

12.

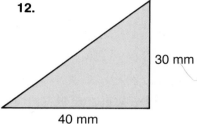

30 mm

40 mm

The base (*b*) and height (*h*) are given. Find the area.

13. $b = 8$ cm, $h = 3$ cm

14. $b = 6$ cm, $h = 8$ cm

15. $b = 5$ cm, $h = 4$ cm

16. $b = 11$ cm, $h = 14$ cm

17. $b = 10$ mm, $h = 4$ mm

18. $b = 6$ mm, $h = 16$ mm

19. $b = 24$ mm, $h = 30$ mm

20. $b = 46$ mm, $h = 53$ mm

★ **21.** Estimate the area of this lake.

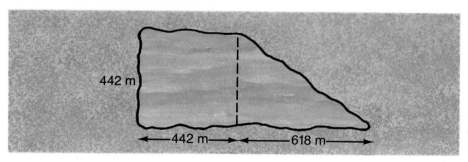

442 m

442 m — 618 m

PROBLEM SOLVING • APPLICATIONS

22. The length of the base of a triangular piece of sailcloth is 4 meters. The height is 13 meters. What is the area of the sailcloth?

★ **23.** A sailboat has two triangular sails. The base of one sail is 3 meters. The height is 8 meters. The base of the other sail is 2 meters. The height is 5 meters. How much sailcloth is used to make the two sails?

Volume

The **volume** of a box is the number of cubic units that will fit inside the box.

A **cubic centimeter (cu cm)** is a unit of volume.

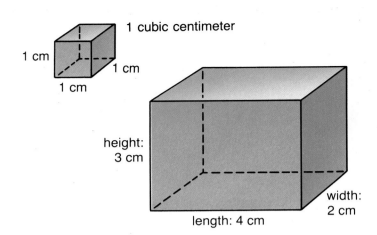

1 cubic centimeter

1 cm
1 cm
1 cm

height: 3 cm

width: 2 cm

length: 4 cm

Find the volume of the box.

Step 1
Find how many will make one layer. 4 × 2 = 8

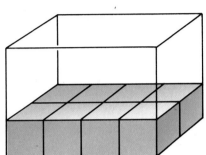

Step 2
Count the layers.
Then find how many in all.
3 × 8 = 24

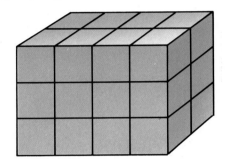

Volume = length × width × height
= 4 × 2 × 3
= 24

The volume of the box is 24 cubic centimeters.

Other metric units of volume are the **cubic millimeter (cu mm)** and the **cubic meter (cu m).**

Practice • Copy and complete the table.

	Box	Number of Cubes in 1 Layer	Number of Layers	Volume-Number of Cubes in All
1.				
2.				

Mixed Practice • Find the volume of each figure.

3.
4 cm
6 cm
2 cm

4.
20 mm
60 mm
40 mm

5.
6 cm
4 cm
3 cm

6.
10 mm
38 mm
52 mm

7.
7 cm
6 cm
2 cm

★8.
9 mm
14 mm
12 mm
31 mm
48 mm

Complete.

	Length	Width	Height	Volume
9.	4 cm	2 cm	5 cm	? cubic centimeters
10.	6 cm	7 cm	4 cm	? cubic centimeters
11.	53 mm	48 mm	17 mm	? cubic millimeters
12.	69 mm	72 mm	24 mm	? cubic millimeters
★13.	? cm	7 cm	9 cm	252 cubic centimeters
★14.	12 mm	8 mm	? mm	1,056 cubic millimeters

PROBLEM SOLVING • APPLICATIONS

15. Laverne fills this carton with children's blocks. Each block is one cubic decimeter. How many blocks fit into the carton?

★16. Laverne empties the carton. Then she puts Star building blocks into the carton. How many Star blocks fit into the carton?

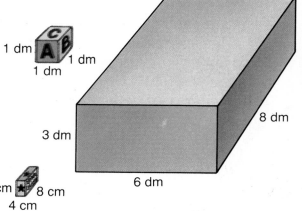

1 dm
1 dm
1 dm

3 dm
8 dm
6 dm

6 cm
8 cm
4 cm

PROBLEM SOLVING · STRATEGIES

Problems Without Numbers

You must read a problem carefully to know which operation to use to solve it.

Read the problem below. It is a problem that does not have any numbers. Which operation would you choose, and what would you do to solve it?

Juan arranges his train set on a table. He wants to put a fence around the edge of the table. He knows the table is in the shape of a rectangle. He knows the length and the width of the table. How much fencing does he need?

What operation should Juan use, and what should he do to find the amount of fencing he needs?

He knows that the distance around a figure is the perimeter.

To find the perimeter, he must use addition. He needs to find the sum of the lengths of the sides of the figure.

He should find the perimeter of the figure to solve the problem.

You cannot give an answer for these problems because you are not given numbers. Tell how you would solve the problem if you were given numbers.

1. Bob has a train set. He wants to cover his table with artificial grass before he sets up his trains. He knows the length and the width of the table. How much artificial grass does he need?

2. Richard is making shelves to display some of his trains. He knows the length of the lumber he has. He also knows how long he wants to make each shelf. How many shelves can he make if each shelf is the same size?

Try to solve the problem with easy numbers. Check to see that your answer makes sense.

256

256

3. Terry wants to decorate her train set with small trees. She knows how much each package of small trees costs. She knows how much money she can spend. How many packages can she buy?

4. Ramona wants to buy track for her train set. She knows the cost of each piece of track. She knows how many pieces she wants. How much money does she need?

5. Lucille has a recipe for papier-mâché. She wants to make a tunnel. In order to do this, she must double the recipe. How much of each ingredient does she need?

Read the question carefully. What operation should you use?

---

6. Dennis is saving money to buy a new locomotive. He is saving a certain amount each week. He knows the cost of the locomotive. How many weeks must he save to buy it?

7. Paula has a pattern for a model house. She knows how much cardboard is needed to complete the model. She also knows how much cardboard she has available. How many models can she make?

8. It takes Frances a week to set up her train set. She knows how much time she works setting up her train set each day. How much time does she spend setting up her train set?

9. Terence stores the boxes his trains were packed in. He knows how many piles of boxes there are. He knows how many boxes are in each pile. How many boxes does he have?

10. Peggy has a locomotive that makes smoke. She knows how many smoke tablets come in a box. She knows about how long each tablet will last. About how long will the whole box of smoke tablets last?

★ 11. Part of Bob's train display is a ranch. He wants to put a fence around the ranch. The ranch is in the shape of a square. He already has some fencing. He knows the length of one side of the square. How much more fencing does he need to go around the ranch?

★ 12. Frances wants to buy logs for the logging car. She plans to buy logs of different sizes. She knows how much each size log costs and how many of each size log she wants. How much money will Frances spend on the logs?

Milliliter and Liter

The **milliliter (mL)**, **metric cup (c)**, and **liter (L)** are metric units used to measure liquid capacity.

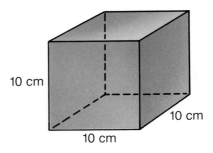

It takes 1 milliliter of water to fill 1 cubic centimeter.

The volume of a metric cup is 250 cubic centimeters. It takes 250 milliliters of water to fill a metric cup.

The volume of the cube is 1,000 cubic centimeters. It takes 4 metric cups of water to fill the cube. It takes 1,000 milliliters to fill the cube. The cube holds 1 liter.

1,000 milliliters (mL) = 1 liter (L)

Practice • Choose the correct measures.

1.

2 mL   2L

2.

36 mL   360 mL

3.

350 mL   350 L

4.

4L   40L

5.

240 mL   24L

6.
10 L   100 L

7.

4 mL   4 L

8.

25 L   250 mL

Mixed Practice • Choose the correct measures.

9.

1 L   1 mL

10.

500 L   500 mL

11.

4 L   4 mL

12.

140 L   140 mL

Complete.

13. 4,000 mL = __?__ L

14. 24,000 mL = __?__ L

15. 54,000 mL = __?__ L

16. 14,000 mL = __?__ L

17. 39,000 mL = __?__ L

18. 82,000 mL = __?__ L

19. __?__ mL = 7 L

20. __?__ mL = 45 L

21. __?__ mL = 18 L

22. __?__ mL = 72 L

23. __?__ mL = 63 L

24. __?__ mL = 51 L

Find the volume of the container in cubic centimeters.
Then find the capacity in milliliters.

★ 25.
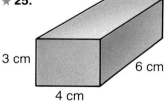
3 cm   4 cm   6 cm

★ 26.
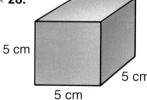
5 cm   5 cm   5 cm

★ 27.
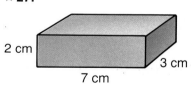
2 cm   7 cm   3 cm

Doctors often prescribe medicine in cubic centimeters rather than milliliters.
How would they prescribe these amounts using cubic centimeters?

28.

1 mL

29.

8 mL

30.

12 mL

31.

5 mL

PROBLEM SOLVING • APPLICATIONS

32. A pharmacist makes 12,000 milliliters of a special shampoo. How many 1-liter bottles can he fill?

★ 33. A container is 8 centimeters long, 4 centimeters wide, and 7 centimeters high. How many milliliters of water does it hold?

Gram and Kilogram

The **gram (g)** and the **kilogram (kg)** are metric units of mass.

1 cm 1 cm 1 cm

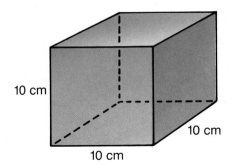

10 cm
10 cm
10 cm

The volume of the cube is 1 cubic centimeter. It holds 1 milliliter of water. 1 milliliter of water has a mass of 1 gram.

The volume of the cube is 1,000 cubic centimeters. It holds 1 liter of water. 1 liter of water has a mass of 1 kilogram.

1,000 grams (g) = 1 kilogram (kg)

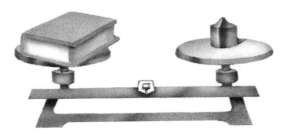

A paper clip has a mass of about 1 gram.

This book has a mass of about 1 kilogram.

Practice • Which unit would you use to find the mass of each object? Write GRAM or KILOGRAM.

1.

2.

3.

4.

Mixed Practice • Which unit would you use to find the mass of each object? Write GRAM or KILOGRAM.

5.

6.

7.

8.

Choose the correct measures.

9.

10.

11.

12.

315 g   315 kg   6 g   6 kg   500 g   500 kg   32 g   32 kg

Complete.

13. 4,000 g = __?__ kg

14. 20,000 g = __?__ kg

15. 43,000 g = __?__ kg

16. 76,000 g = __?__ kg

17. 92,000 g = __?__ kg

18. 85,000 g = __?__ kg

19. __?__ g = 8 kg

20. __?__ g = 26 kg

21. __?__ g = 48 kg

22. __?__ g = 56 kg

23. __?__ g = 82 kg

24. __?__ g = 97 kg

PROBLEM SOLVING • APPLICATIONS

25. A fish tank has the dimensions 70 centimeters by 30 centimeters by 30 centimeters. What is the mass of the water in the tank in kilograms when it is filled to the top?

26. The dimensions of a pool are 1,200 centimeters by 500 centimeters by 200 centimeters. The pool is filled with water. What is the mass of the water in kilograms?

★ **27.** The height of the fish tank in problem 25 is 30 centimeters. The water level is 10 centimeters below the top of the tank. What is the mass of water in kilograms?

Degrees Celsius

A **degree Celsius (°C)** is a metric unit used to measure temperature.

This is a **Celsius** thermometer.

Each mark stands for 2 degrees Celsius.

The thermometer shows **20 degrees Celsius above zero.**
This would be shown as **20°C.**

Temperatures can fall below zero degrees Celsius.

Suppose the temperature falls 30 degrees from 20°C.

The new temperature would be **10 degrees Celsius below zero.**
This would be shown as **⁻10°C.**

Water boils at 100°C.

Normal body temperature is 37°C.

A summer day, 25°C.

Room temperature is 20°C.

Water freezes at 0°C.

A cold winter day is ⁻10°C.

Practice • Choose the correct temperatures.

1.

30°C   −8°C

2.

50°C   10°C

3.

20°C   65°C

Mixed Practice • Give the temperatures in degrees Celsius.

4.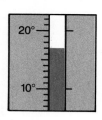

5.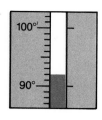

6.

7.

Complete the table.

	Temperature Before	Change	Temperature After
8.	16°C	rise of 10°C	26°C
9.	16°C	fall of 10°C	?
10.	28°C	rise of 12°C	?
11.	28°C	fall of 12°C	?
12.	−10°C	rise of 6°C	?
13.	−10°C	rise of 16°C	?
14.	0°C	fall of 12°C	?
15.	10°C	fall of 12°C	?

PROBLEM SOLVING • APPLICATIONS

16. A weather observer finds that the temperature is 13°C at 1:00 P.M. At midnight the temperature is 2°C. Did the temperature rise or fall? By how many degrees?

★ **17.** The mean temperature is the average of the high and the low temperatures for a day. Today's high is 34°C. Today's low is 18°C. Find the mean temperature for today.

Skills Maintenance

1. $\frac{3}{6} + \frac{1}{6} = $ _____?_____

2. $\frac{2}{3} + \frac{1}{3} = $ _____?_____

3. $\frac{1}{6} + \frac{7}{15} = $ _____?_____

4. $6 + \frac{1}{2} = $ _____?_____

5. $4\frac{1}{3} + 2\frac{1}{3} = $ _____?_____

6. $5\frac{3}{4} + 6\frac{3}{4} = $ _____?_____

7. $3\frac{1}{2} + 4\frac{2}{3} = $ _____?_____

8. $2\frac{1}{4} + 5\frac{2}{5} = $ _____?_____

9. $8\frac{7}{8} + 2\frac{4}{5} = $ _____?_____

Time

Ellen wakes up at [7:30] each school day.

You can read 7:30 as seven-thirty,
thirty minutes after 7, or
half past seven.

A.M. means the time from midnight until noon.

P.M. means the time from noon until midnight.
So Ellen wakes up at 7:30 A.M.

The clocks show some times during Ellen's morning.

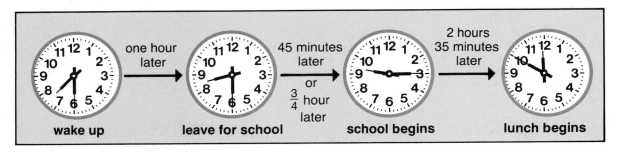

These units are used to measure time.

60 seconds (sec) = 1 minute (min)	365 days (d)	= 1 year (yr)
60 minutes (min) = 1 hour (h)	12 months (mo)	= 1 year (yr)
24 hours (h) = 1 day (d)	52 weeks (wk)	= 1 year (yr)
7 days (d) = 1 week (wk)		

**To change larger units to
smaller units, multiply.**

Think: 3 d = ? h
     1 d = 24 h
     3 × 24 = 72
     3 d = 72 h

**To change smaller units to
larger units, divide.**

Think: 420 min = ? h
     60 min = 1 h
     420 ÷ 60 = 7
     420 min = 7 h

Practice • Write the time two ways.

1.

2.

3.

4.

264

Mixed Practice • Write the time two ways.

5.

6.

7.

8.

Write A.M. or P.M.

9. Eat breakfast.

10. Eat dinner.

11. Go to school.

12. Go to morning recess.

13. Go to bed.

14. Dress for bed.

Complete.

15. 2 d = __?__ h

16. 3 min = __?__ sec

17. 6 wk = __?__ d

18. 240 sec = __?__ min

19. 49 d = __?__ wk

20. 730 d = __?__ yr

★21. $\frac{3}{4}$ yr = __?__ mo

★22. $1\frac{1}{2}$ d = __?__ h

★23. 210 min = __?__ h

What time is it?

24. 4 hours after 7:00 P.M.

25. $\frac{1}{2}$ hour before 3:00 P.M.

26. 20 minutes after 7:15 A.M.

27. $\frac{3}{4}$ hour before 12:15 P.M.

★28. 48 hours before noon

★29. 8 hours after 11:00 A.M.

PROBLEM SOLVING • APPLICATIONS

★30. On Saturday morning Sonia woke up at 8:15 A.M. She slept $9\frac{3}{4}$ hours. At what time did she go to sleep?

★31. Cindy leaves home at 6:00 A.M. on April 10. She travels to Chicago. She returns to her home at 9:45 P.M. on April 16. How many hours was she away?

Midchapter Review

1. 30 mm = __?__ cm

2. __?__ dm = 5 m

3. 2,000 mL = __?__ L

4. 6,000 g = __?__ kg

5. 3 d = __?__ h

6. __?__ sec = 3 min

Find the perimeter and area of each figure.

7.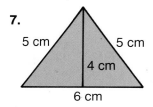

8.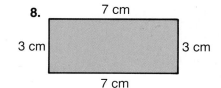

9.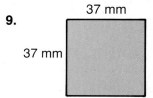

Customary Units of Length

The **inch (in.)** is a customary unit of length.
This ruler is marked in inches and parts of an inch.

The length of the ribbon is 4 inches long to the nearest inch.

It is $3\frac{1}{2}$ inches long to the nearest $\frac{1}{2}$ inch.

It is $3\frac{3}{4}$ inches long to the nearest $\frac{1}{4}$ inch.

It is $3\frac{5}{8}$ inches long to the nearest $\frac{1}{8}$ inch.

It is $3\frac{11}{16}$ inches long to the nearest $\frac{1}{16}$ inch.

A **foot (ft)**, a **yard (yd)**, and a **mile (mi)** are three other customary units of length. The table shows how they are related.

12 inches (in.) = 1 foot (ft)
3 feet (ft) = 1 yard (yd)
36 inches (in.) = 1 yard (yd)
5,280 feet (ft) = 1 mile (mi)
1,760 yards (yd) = 1 mile (mi)

To change larger units to smaller units, multiply.

Think:

$$4 \text{ ft} = ? \text{ in.}$$
$$1 \text{ ft} = 12 \text{ in.}$$
$$4 \times 12 = 48$$
$$4 \text{ ft} = 48 \text{ in.}$$

To change smaller units to larger units, divide.

Think:

$$36 \text{ in.} = ? \text{ ft}$$
$$12 \text{ in.} = 1 \text{ ft}$$
$$36 \div 12 = 3$$
$$36 \text{ in.} = 3 \text{ ft}$$

Practice • Measure the piece of cord  to the nearest

1. inch. 　2. $\frac{1}{2}$ inch. 　3. $\frac{1}{4}$ inch. 　4. $\frac{1}{8}$ inch. 　5. $\frac{1}{16}$ inch.

Which unit of measure would you use? Write INCH, FOOT, YARD, or MILE.

6. the length of a football field

7. the width of a button

8. the length of an airplane

9. the length of a rug

Mixed Practice • Which unit of measure would you use? Write INCH, FOOT, YARD, or MILE.

10. the length of a highway

11. the length of a piece of fabric

12. the length of a zipper

13. the length of a room

Estimate the length of each to the nearest $\frac{1}{2}$ inch. Then measure to check your estimate.

14.

15.

16.

Complete.

17. 36 in. = ___?___ ft

18. 12 ft = ___?___ in.

19. 60 in. = ___?___ ft

20. 6 yd = ___?___ ft

21. 9 ft = ___?___ yd

22. 20 yd = ___?___ ft

23. 27 ft = ___?___ yd

24. 4 yd = ___?___ in.

25. 10 yd = ___?___ in.

26. 108 in. = ___?___ yd

27. 252 in. = ___?___ yd

28. 3 mi = ___?___ ft

29. 7 mi = ___?___ yd

30. 5,280 yd = ___?___ mi

31. 26,400 ft = ___?___ mi

★**32.** 2 ft 3 in. = ___?___ in.

★**33.** 3 yd 2 ft = ___?___ ft

★**34.** 1 yd 5 in. = ___?___ in.

★**35.** $3\frac{1}{2}$ ft = ___?___ yd

★**36.** $4\frac{1}{3}$ yd = ___?___ in.

★**37.** $7\frac{3}{8}$ mi = ___?___ ft

PROBLEM SOLVING • APPLICATIONS

38. Jane walks $\frac{2}{3}$ mile to her sewing class. How many feet is this?

39. A piece of fabric is $\frac{3}{4}$ yard long. How many inches is this?

★**40.** Taylor buys 3 packages of seam binding. Each package contains $2\frac{1}{2}$ yards. He uses 228 inches on a tablecloth. How many inches does he have left?

Finding Perimeter, Area, and Volume

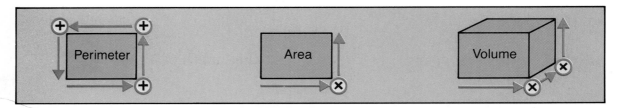

You can find the perimeter, the area, and the volume in customary units.

Find the perimeter in inches.

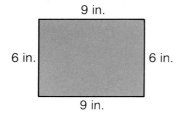

9 in.

6 in. 6 in.

9 in.

The perimeter of a figure is the sum of the lengths of its sides.

$$6 + 9 + 6 + 9 = 30$$

The perimeter is 30 inches. **(in.)**

Find the area in square yards.

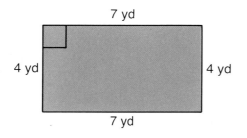

7 yd

4 yd 4 yd

7 yd

To find the area of a rectangle, multiply the length times the width.

Area = length × width
$$= 7 \times 4$$
$$= 28$$

The area is 28 square yards. **(sq yd)**

Other customary units of area are the **square inch (sq in.)**, **square foot (sq ft)**, and **square mile (sq mi)**.

Find the volume in cubic feet.

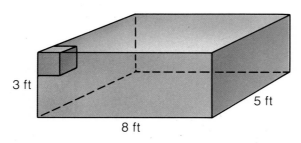

3 ft

8 ft

5 ft

To find the volume of a box, multiply the length times the width times the height.

Volume = length × width × height
$$= 8 \times 5 \times 3$$
$$= 120$$

The volume is 120 cubic feet. **(cu ft)**

Other customary units of volume are the **cubic inch (cu in.)** and **cubic yard (cu yd).**

Practice • Complete.

1.

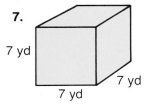

4 ft   5 ft

7 ft

2.

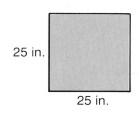

25 in.

25 in.

3.

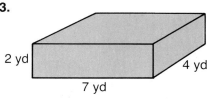

2 yd

7 yd

4 yd

Perimeter = __?__ feet   Area = __?__ square inches   Volume = __?__ cubic yards

Mixed Practice • Find the perimeter and the area of each figure.

4.

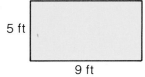

5 ft

9 ft

5.

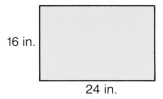

16 in.

24 in.

6.

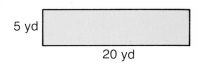

5 yd

20 yd

Find the volume of each figure.

7.

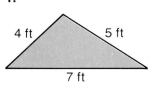

7 yd

7 yd

7 yd

8.

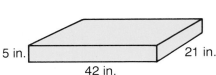

5 in.

42 in.

21 in.

9.

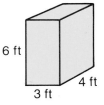

6 ft

3 ft

4 ft

PROBLEM SOLVING • APPLICATIONS

An **acre** is used to measure large areas.

     1 acre = 43,560 square feet   1 acre = 4,840 square yards

10. Mr. and Mrs. Henry buy a 5-acre farm. How many square feet is this? How many square yards?

★ **11.** A developer buys 10 acres of land. It is divided into 8 equal lots. What is the area of each lot in square yards?

12. How many square inches are in one square foot?

13. How many square feet are in one square yard?

14. How many cubic inches are in one cubic foot?

15. How many cubic feet are in one cubic yard?

★ **16.** The area of a driveway is 120 square feet. The width is 8 feet. What is the length?

★ **17.** The perimeter of a square lawn is 56 feet. What is the area?

Customary Units of Capacity

The **tablespoon (tbsp)**, **fluid ounce (fl. oz)**, **cup (c)**, **pint (pt)**, **quart (qt)**, **half gallon** ($\frac{1}{2}$ **gal**) and **gallon (gal)** are customary units used to measure liquid capacity.

| 2 tablespoons (1 fluid ounce) | 1 cup | 1 pint | 1 quart | 1 half gallon | 1 gallon |

The table shows how the units are related.

2 tablespoons (tbsp) = 1 fluid ounce (fl. oz)
8 fluid ounces (fl. oz) = 1 cup (c)
2 cups (c) = 1 pint (pt)
2 pints (pt) = 1 quart (qt)
2 quarts (qt) = 1 half gallon $\left(\frac{1}{2}\,\text{gal}\right)$
4 quarts (qt) = 1 gallon (gal)

To change larger units to smaller units, multiply.

Think: 4 pt = ? c
1 pt = 2 c
2 × 4 = 8
4 pt = 8 c

To change smaller units to larger units, divide.

Think: 16 fl. oz = ? c
8 fl. oz = 1 c
16 ÷ 8 = 2
16 fl. oz = 2 c

Practice • Complete.

1.

____?____ pt

2.

____?____ $\frac{1}{2}$ gal

3.

____?____ qt

4. 1 c = ___?___ fl. oz

5. 1 qt = ___?___ fl. oz

6. 8 c = ___?___ qt

7. 1 pt = ___?___ c

8. 16 qt = ___?___ gal

9. 1 gal = ___?___ c

Mixed Practice • Complete.

10. 1 gal = __?__ pt

11. 4 gal = __?__ $\frac{1}{2}$ gal

12. 5 gal = __?__ qt

13. 1 pt = __?__ fl. oz

14. 6 qt = __?__ pt

15. 3 pt = __?__ c

16. 8 qt = __?__ gal

17. $\frac{1}{2}$ gal = __?__ pt

18. 6 tbsp = __?__ fl. oz

19. 16 pt = __?__ gal

20. 12 qt = __?__ $\frac{1}{2}$ gal

21. 24 fl. oz = __?__ c

22. 3 qt 1 pt = __?__ pt

23. 2 c 5 fl. oz = __?__ fl. oz

24. 1 gal 1 qt = __?__ qt

25. $6\frac{1}{2}$ pt = __?__ c

26. $3\frac{1}{2}$ gal = __?__ qt

27. $1\frac{1}{2}$ c = __?__ fl. oz

Write >, <, or =.

28. 12 c ⬤ 3 qt

29. 18 fl. oz ⬤ 1 pt

30. 4 c ⬤ 2 qt

★31. 12 c + 2 qt ⬤ 4 gal

★32. 18 pts + 1 gal ⬤ 9 qts + 8 pts

★33. 7 c + 6 c ⬤ 2 qts

Choose the correct measures.

34.

12 c   12 gal

35.

1 tbsp   1 c

36.

1 qt   1 gal

PROBLEM SOLVING • APPLICATIONS

37. Valerie buys 2 gallons of apple juice for a party. How many cups is this?

38. Phil uses 48 quarts of water to fill a fish tank. How many gallons is this?

★39. Stanley buys ice cream for a party. He buys 4 pints of vanilla, 2 pints of strawberry, and 2 pints of butter pecan. How many half gallons is this?

★40. Lucy has $2\frac{1}{2}$ pints of cream. She needs one half gallon. How much more cream must she buy?

★41. One 8-ounce can of orange juice concentrate makes one quart of orange juice. How many fluid ounces of water are added?

★42. A large bottle contains 5 gallons of filtered water. How many 5-ounce drinking cups can be filled from the bottle?

271

Customary Units of Weight

The **ounce (oz)**, **pound (lb)**, and **ton (T)** are customary units of weight.

1 ounce	1 pound	about 1 ton

16 ounces (oz) = 1 pound (lb)
2,000 pounds (lb) = 1 ton (T)

To change larger units to smaller units, multiply.

Think:
3 lb = ? oz
16 oz = 1 lb
3 × 16 = 48
3 lb = 48 oz

To change smaller units to larger units, divide.

Think:
64 oz = ? lb
16 oz = 1 lb
64 ÷ 16 = 4
64 oz = 4 lb

Practice • Choose the correct measures.

1.

2 oz   2 lb

2.

6 lb   6 T

3.

12 lb   12 oz

4.

2 T   2 lb

Complete.

5. 11 lb = __?__ oz

6. 96 oz = __?__ lb

7. 10 lb = __?__ oz

8. 240 oz = __?__ lb

9. 15 lb = __?__ oz

10. 12,000 lb = __?__ T

Mixed Practice • Choose the correct measures.

11.

12.

13.

14.

1 lb 1 oz	150 lb 150 T	4 oz 4 lb	16 lb 16 oz

Complete.

15. 2 lb = ___?___ oz

16. 5 lb = ___?___ oz

17. 25 lb = ___?___ oz

18. 224 oz = ___?___ lb

19. 128 oz = ___?___ lb

20. 192 oz = ___?___ lb

21. 11 lb 6 oz = ___?___ oz

22. 2 T 700 lb = ___?___ lb

23. 5 lb 12 oz = ___?___ oz

★**24.** $3\frac{1}{2}$ lb = ___?___ oz

★**25.** $1\frac{1}{4}$ T = ___?___ lb

★**26.** $2\frac{3}{4}$ lb = ___?___ oz

Write >, <, or =.

★**27.** 12 oz ⬤ 1 lb

★**28.** 1 T ⬤ 2,100 lb

★**29.** $1\frac{1}{2}$ lb ⬤ 24 oz

★**30.** 6 lb ⬤ 89 oz

★**31.** $3\frac{1}{4}$ lb ⬤ 60 oz

★**32.** $2\frac{1}{5}$ T ⬤ 2,400 lb

PROBLEM SOLVING • APPLICATIONS

33. A can of oil weighs 2 pounds. A carton holds 24 cans. What is the total weight of the cans of oil in one carton?

★**34.** A special railroad car can carry 12 new automobiles. Each auto weighs 2,500 pounds. How many tons can the railroad car carry?

Skills Maintenance

1. $\frac{7}{8} - \frac{3}{8} =$ ___?___

2. $\frac{3}{4} - \frac{1}{4} =$ ___?___

3. $\frac{5}{8} - \frac{2}{5} =$ ___?___

4. $4\frac{2}{3} - 2\frac{1}{3} =$ ___?___

5. $6\frac{9}{10} - 2\frac{3}{4} =$ ___?___

6. $4\frac{5}{12} - 1\frac{1}{4} =$ ___?___

7. $9\frac{1}{4} - 6\frac{5}{12} =$ ___?___

8. $7 - 4\frac{3}{5} =$ ___?___

9. $2\frac{1}{2} - 1\frac{2}{3} =$ ___?___

Measure to the nearest centimeter. Then measure to the nearest millimeter. (pages 244–245, 248–251, 254–255)

1.

2.

3.

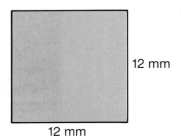

12 mm

12 mm

Perimeter = ___?___

4.

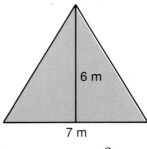

6 m

7 m

Area = ___?___

5.

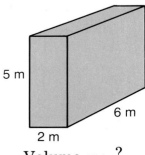

5 m

6 m

2 m

Volume = ___?___

Complete. (pages 244–247, 258–261, 264–267, 270–273)

6. 70 mm = ___?___ cm

7. ___?___ cm = 8 m

8. ___?___ m = 6 km

9. 8,000 mL = ___?___ L

10. 12,000 mL = ___?___ L

11. ___?___ mL = 9 L

12. 9,000 g = ___?___ kg

13. ___?___ g = 7 kg

14. ___?___ g = 15 kg

15. 48 h = ___?___ d

16. 240 min = ___?___ h

17. 6 yr = ___?___ wk

18. 4 yd = ___?___ ft

19. 96 in. = ___?___ ft

20. 2 mi = ___?___ ft

21. 2 pt = ___?___ c

22. 8 qt = ___?___ gal

23. 1 gal = ___?___ pt

24. 48 oz = ___?___ lb

25. 2 lb = ___?___ oz

26. 3 T = ___?___ lb

Solve.

27. The length of a family room is 20 feet. The width is 14 feet. How many square feet of carpeting are needed for this room? (p. 268)

28. At 3:00 the temperature is 0°C. In 3 hours the temperature drops 5 degrees. What is the temperature at 6:00? (p. 262)

Degrees Fahrenheit

A **degree Fahrenheit (°F)** is a customary unit used to measure temperature.

This is a **Fahrenheit** thermometer.

Each mark stands for 2 degrees Fahrenheit.

The thermometer shows **64 degrees Fahrenheit.**

This would be shown as **64°F.**

Temperatures can fall below zero degrees Fahrenheit.

Suppose the temperature falls 70 degrees from 64°F.

The new temperature would be **6 degrees Fahrenheit below zero.**

This would be shown as ⁻**6°F.**

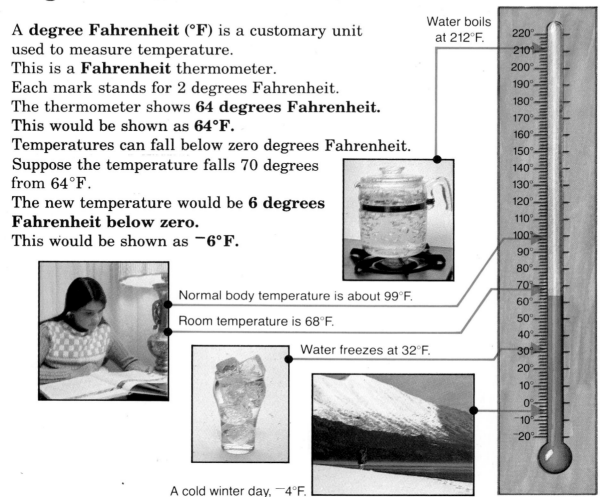

Water boils at 212°F.

Normal body temperature is about 99°F.

Room temperature is 68°F.

Water freezes at 32°F.

A cold winter day, ⁻4°F.

Use a Fahrenheit thermometer. Read the outdoor temperature three times each day for one week. Record your results. Then find the average, or mean, temperature for each time for the five days.

Time	Monday	Tuesday	Wednesday	Thursday	Friday	Average Temperature
9:00 A.M.						
12:00 noon						
3:00 P.M.						

275

Measure to the nearest centimeter. Then measure to the nearest millimeter.

1.

2.

3.

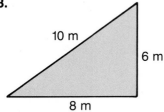

10 m

6 m

8 m

Perimeter = __?__

4.

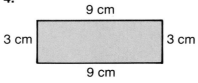

9 cm

3 cm   3 cm

9 cm

Area = __?__

5.

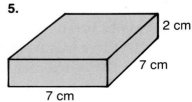

2 cm

7 cm

7 cm

Volume = __?__

Complete.

6. 40 mm = __?__ cm

7. 300 cm = __?__ m

8. __?__ m = 4 km

9. 3,000 mL = __?__ L

10. 5,000 mL = __?__ L

11. __?__ mL = 2 L

12. 5,000 g = __?__ kg

13. __?__ g = 4 kg

14. __?__ g = 12 kg

15. 3 d = __?__ h

16. 180 sec = __?__ min

17. 4 yr = __?__ wk

18. 3 yd = __?__ ft

19. 84 in. = __?__ ft

20. 3 mi = __?__ yd

21. 3 pt = __?__ c

22. 4 qt = __?__ gal

23. 2 gal = __?__ pt

24. 64 oz = __?__ lb

25. 31 lb = __?__ oz

26. 2 T = __?__ lb

Solve.

27. Jason fills a trailer with boxes. Each box is one cubic foot. The trailer is 5 feet long, 3 feet wide, and 2 feet high. How many boxes fit in the trailer?

28. Jason works for 480 minutes. How many hours is this?

Operations with Measures

Ricky works for 2 hours 40 minutes on Monday.
He works for 4 hours and 25 minutes on Tuesday.

60 min	= 1 h
12 in.	= 1 ft
3 ft	= 1 yd
16 oz	= 1 lb
4 qt	= 1 gal

Add to find how long he works on these two days.

2 h 40 min   Since 65 min > 1 h,
+4 h 25 min   you must regroup.
6 h 65 min   65 min = 1 h 5 min
              6 h + 1 h + 5 min = 7 h 5 min

Ricky works 7 hours 5 minutes on these two days.

How much longer does Ricky work on Tuesday than on Monday?

                                       3   85

4 h 25 min   Since 40 min > 25 min,   4̸ h 2̸5 min
−2 h 40 min   you must regroup.   − 2 h 40 min
                1 h = 60 min   1 h 45 min
               4 h 25 min = 3 h 85 min

Ricky works 1 hour 45 minutes longer on Tuesday than on Monday.

Add or subtract.

1.   4 ft 9 in.
     +3 ft 7 in.

2.   6 h 14 min
     +4 h 36 min

3.   7 lb 12 oz
     +6 lb 10 oz

4.   7 yd 2 ft
     +3 yd 2 ft

5.   9 h 18 min
     −4 h 33 min

6.   3 gal 2 qt
     −1 gal 3 qt

7.   6 yd 2 ft
     −3 yd 1 ft

8.   8 lb 4 oz
     −3 lb 6 oz

9.   6 gal 3 qt
     +7 gal 2 qt

10.   2 h 25 min
     +5 h 30 min

11.   12 ft 9 in.
     − 4 ft 7 in.

12.   9 h 28 min
     −6 h 43 min

Solve.

13. Ted has 4 yards of fabric. He uses 2 yards 4 inches to make banners. How much fabric is left?

14. Ricky works for 2 hours 30 minutes on Saturday. He works for 3 hours 50 minutes on Sunday. How many hours did he work this weekend?

COMPUTER

Application Programs

Each computer always operates under one specific **controlling program**. Each programmer can operate with one specific programming language at a time. **Application programs** solve a specific type of problem called an **application**. The most common application program is the word processor. It may surprise you that a word processor is not a computer. A **word processor** is an application program that enables a computer to process words easily.

Word processors can perform many document-handling jobs. Here are some of the jobs they can do.

Correct errors in spelling	Move words and paragraphs
Reorder pages and sections	Handle input/output
Combine different documents	Change spacing and format of text
Convert to different languages	Locate specific phrases
Hyphenate text	Print special symbols
Duplicate often-used phrases	Check correctness of spelling

There are many other types of application programs.

Mailing-list programs handle large-volume mailings for organizations.

Merge different mailing lists	Eliminate duplicate names
Print special mailings	Select special groups of addresses

Spread-sheet programs set up and process accounting files and tables.

Form totals and subtotals	Cross-reference different reports
Print individual sections	Maintain historical records

Games programs and **graphics programs** are also application programs. An **income-tax program** is an example of a special-application program.

Match the letter of the phrase with the number of the correct term.

1. Controlling programs   **a.** help programmers write programs for computers.

2. Programming languages   **b.** are application programs that perform document-handling jobs.

3. Application programs   **c.** are examples of special-application programs.

4. Word processors   **d.** handle large-volume mailing of organizations.

5. Mailing-list programs   **e.** solve one specific type of problem.

6. Spread-sheet programs   **f.** handle specific operations of specific computers.

7. Income-tax programs   **g.** set up and process accounting files and tables.

Choose the correct answers.

1. Add.

$$\begin{array}{r} 6{,}426 \\ 87 \\ +\ \ 359 \\ \hline \end{array}$$

A. 6,759   **B.** 6,872
C. 7,264   **D.** not here

2. Subtract.

$$1{,}609 - 978 = \underline{\ ?\ }$$

A. 631   **B.** 730
C. 1,587   **D.** not here

3. Multiply.

$$\begin{array}{r} 496 \\ \times\ \ \ 7 \\ \hline \end{array}$$

A. 3,274   **B.** 2,956
C. 3,472   **D.** not here

4. Find the remainder.

$$9\overline{)674}$$

A. 4
B. 5
C. 8
D. not here

5. Divide.

$$9{,}500 \div 50 = \underline{\ ?\ }$$

A. 19
B. 190
C. 1,900
D. not here

6. How many cars does Bill sell?

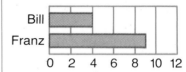

A. 4   **B.** 6
C. 9   **D.** not here

7. Find all the factors of 12.

A. 2, 4, 6, 8
B. 1, 2, 3, 4, 6, 12
C. 12, 24, 36, 48
D. not here

8. Write the fraction in lowest terms.

$$\frac{12}{15}$$

A. $\frac{6}{8}$ **B.** $\frac{3}{4}$
C. $\frac{2}{3}$ **D.** not here

9. Add. Write the answer in lowest terms.

$$\frac{1}{2} + \frac{3}{4} = \underline{\ ?\ }$$

A. $1\frac{1}{4}$ **B.** $1\frac{1}{2}$
C. $\frac{3}{8}$ **D.** not here

10. Multiply. Write the answer in lowest terms.

$$\frac{2}{3} \times \frac{5}{9} = \underline{\ ?\ }$$

A. $1\frac{1}{5}$ **B.** $\frac{10}{9}$
C. $\frac{10}{27}$ **D.** not here

11. Complete.

$$1{,}000 \text{ m} = \underline{\ ?\ } \text{ km}$$

A. 1
B. 100
C. 10
D. not here

12. Find the perimeter.

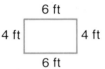

A. 24 sq ft
B. 10 sq ft
C. 20 ft
D. not here

Skills maintenance continued

Choose the correct answers.

13. Dick has saved $28.74 to buy a bicycle. The bicycle he wants to buy costs $88.95. How much more money must he save?

A. $98.70   B. $114.69
C. $60.21   D. not here

14. This morning Pio picked 29 ears of corn from the garden. Fred picked 32 ears. How many ears of corn did the two boys pick all together?

A. 3   B. 61
C. 928   D. not here

15. A cattle dealer paid $279 each for 46 steers. How much money did she spend in all?

A. $12,834   B. $13,687
C. $15,600   D. not here

16. There are 9 players on a baseball team. The Webster School has 124 students who want to play. How many complete teams can be formed?

A. 11   B. 12
C. 13   D. not here

17. Doris bought $1\frac{1}{8}$ yards of flannel to make a blanket for her dog. She used $\frac{3}{4}$ of a yard. How much flannel does she have left?

A. $\frac{1}{2}$ yd   B. $\frac{3}{8}$ yd

C. $1\frac{7}{8}$ yd   D. not here

18. The living room in Ken's house is 7 meters long and 5 meters wide. How much carpeting does Ken need to buy to cover the floor?

A. 24 meters
B. 35 meters
C. 35 square meters
D. not here

19. Cassandra uses 25,000 mL of water to fill a fish tank. How many liters is this?

A. 50   B. 250
C. 2,500   D. not here

20. Grove City buys 19 slides for its playgrounds. A total of $9,452.50 is spent. How much does each slide cost?

A. $526.10   B. $497.50
C. $485.00   D. not here

Decimals: Addition and Subtraction

CHAPTER 11

Tenths • Hundredths • Thousandths • Place Value • Comparing Decimals • Rounding Decimals • Adding Decimals • Subtracting Decimals • Problem Solving: Too Much Information • Estimating and Measuring • Using Equations to Solve Problems

Tenths

A square is divided into 10 parts of the same size. Each part is one-tenth of the square.

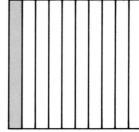

One tenth of the square is blue.

fraction $\frac{1}{10} = 0.1$ decimal

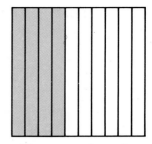

Four-tenths of the square is blue.

fraction $\frac{4}{10} = 0.4$ decimal

> For numbers less than one, write a zero before the decimal point.

You can write decimals to name **tenths**.

The number line shows that $\frac{2}{10} = 0.2$.

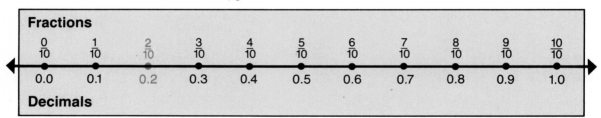

Fractions

| $\frac{0}{10}$ | $\frac{1}{10}$ | $\frac{2}{10}$ | $\frac{3}{10}$ | $\frac{4}{10}$ | $\frac{5}{10}$ | $\frac{6}{10}$ | $\frac{7}{10}$ | $\frac{8}{10}$ | $\frac{9}{10}$ | $\frac{10}{10}$ |

| 0.0 | 0.1 | 0.2 | 0.3 | 0.4 | 0.5 | 0.6 | 0.7 | 0.8 | 0.9 | 1.0 |

Decimals

Students on a school picnic eat $42\frac{7}{10}$ cheese pies.

You can use place value to show tenths.

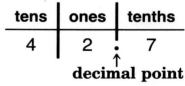

tens	ones	tenths
4	2	7

↑ decimal point

Read: ⟶ forty-two **and** seven-tenths
Write: ⟶ **42.7**

Practice • Write the decimals that tell how much is blue.

1.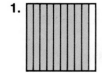

2.

3.

Write the decimals.

4. $\frac{3}{10}$

5. $\frac{9}{10}$

6. $1\frac{7}{10}$

7. $6\frac{1}{10}$

8. $17\frac{2}{10}$

9. eight-tenths

10. five-tenths

11. eleven and two-tenths

282

Mixed Practice • Write the decimals that tell how much is blue.

12.

13.

14.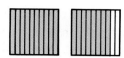

15.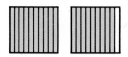

16.

17.

Write the decimals.

18. $\frac{1}{10}$ **19.** $\frac{4}{10}$ **20.** $\frac{5}{10}$ **21.** $3\frac{8}{10}$ **22.** $5\frac{2}{10}$

23. $8\frac{3}{10}$ **24.** $9\frac{7}{10}$ **25.** $21\frac{4}{10}$ **26.** $78\frac{7}{10}$ **27.** $86\frac{9}{10}$

28. $3\frac{4}{10}$ **29.** $8\frac{5}{10}$ **30.** $\frac{9}{10}$ **31.** $45\frac{6}{10}$ **32.** $98\frac{1}{10}$

33. $56\frac{2}{10}$ **34.** $87\frac{9}{10}$ **35.** $68\frac{8}{10}$ **36.** $25\frac{7}{10}$ **37.** $81\frac{3}{10}$

38. twenty-three and eight-tenths

39. fifty-nine and three-tenths

40. seventy-eight and two-tenths

41. fifteen and one-tenth

42. thirty-eight and five-tenths

43. sixty-seven and four-tenths

Complete the patterns.

44. 2.3, 3.5, 4.7, ___?___, ___?___, ___?___, ___?___

45. 17.2, 20.3, ___?___, ___?___, ___?___, ___?___

PROBLEM SOLVING • **APPLICATIONS**

46. Amata was counting by tenths. She started with one-tenth. What were the next five numbers that she counted?

★ **47.** Jake was counting by tenths, too. He only counted every other number. If he started with one-tenth, what were the next four numbers that he counted?

Hundredths

Exactly 100 pennies are worth 1 dollar. Each cent is $\frac{1}{100}$ of a dollar. The decimal for $\frac{1}{100}$ is 0.01.

The digit 1 is in the **hundredths** place.

$$\frac{1}{100} = 0.01$$

one-hundredth

There are 100 pennies here. A ring has been drawn around 32 pennies.

$$\frac{32}{100} = 0.32$$

thirty-two hundredths

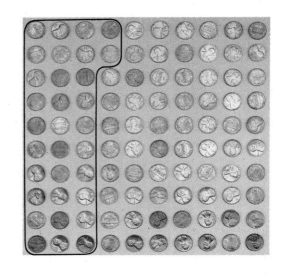

Suppose you have a check for 76 dollars and 28 cents. This is worth $76\frac{28}{100}$ dollars. The decimal for $76\frac{28}{100}$ is 76.28.

$$76\frac{28}{100} = 76.28$$

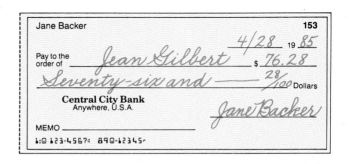

You can use place value to show hundredths.

tens	ones	tenths	hundredths
7	6	2	8

↑
decimal point

Read: ⟶ seventy-six **and** twenty-eight hundredths
Write: ⟶ 76.28

Practice • Write the decimals that tell how much is blue.

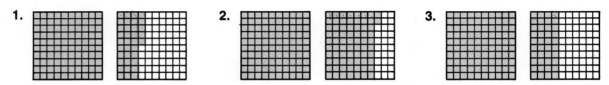

1. 2. 3.

Write the decimals.

4. $\frac{65}{100}$ 5. $\frac{90}{100}$ 6. $1\frac{17}{100}$ 7. $24\frac{46}{100}$ 8. $35\frac{4}{100}$

Mixed Practice • Write the decimals that tell how much is blue.

9.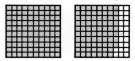

10.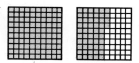

11.

12.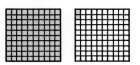

13.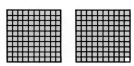

14.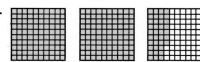

Write the decimals.

15. $\frac{6}{10}$ 16. $\frac{50}{100}$ 17. $\frac{37}{100}$ 18. $\frac{3}{10}$ 19. $\frac{2}{100}$

20. $1\frac{2}{100}$ 21. $3\frac{40}{100}$ 22. $6\frac{8}{10}$ 23. $7\frac{85}{100}$ 24. $2\frac{7}{100}$

25. $34\frac{5}{10}$ 26. $29\frac{60}{100}$ 27. $43\frac{8}{100}$ 28. $150\frac{7}{10}$ 29. $651\frac{59}{100}$

30. $\frac{9}{100}$ 31. $4\frac{75}{100}$ 32. $62\frac{4}{100}$ 33. $747\frac{78}{100}$ 34. $24\frac{5}{10}$

35. three hundredths

36. six and twenty-nine hundredths

37. fifty-two and seventy-one hundredths

38. seventeen and twenty-six hundredths

39. ninety-eight and forty-five hundredths

40. one hundred thirty-nine and four hundredths

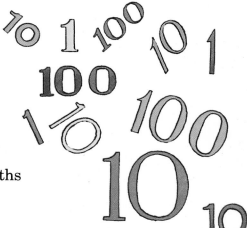

PROBLEM SOLVING • APPLICATIONS

A book is 23 centimeters wide. A centimeter is one-hundredth meter. So the book is 0.23 meter wide.

41. Chris needs a piece of wood 248 centimeters long. How many meters of wood does he need?

★ 42. Jayne went to the store to buy 5 pieces of copper tubing. Each piece had to be 136 centimeters long. How many meters long did each piece have to be?

Thousandths

There are 1,000 bulbs in the sign. The elephant's eye is $\frac{1}{1,000}$ of the bulbs. The decimal for $\frac{1}{1,000}$ is 0.001. 1 is in the **thousandths** place.

$$\frac{1}{1,000} = 0.001$$

one thousandth

Last month 125 of the bulbs burned out.

What part had to be replaced?

$$\frac{125}{1,000} = 0.125$$

one hundred twenty-five thousandths

You can use place value to show thousandths.

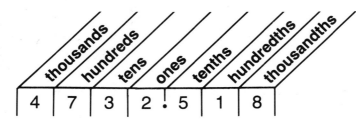

Read: ⟶ four thousand, seven hundred thirty-two **and** five hundred eighteen thousandths

Write: ⟶ 4,732.518

Practice • Write the decimals.

1. $\frac{463}{1,000}$ 2. $4\frac{172}{1,000}$ 3. $29\frac{42}{1,000}$ 4. $78\frac{14}{1,000}$ 5. $\frac{5}{1,000}$

6. nine and seventy-eight thousandths

7. three hundred eight and four hundred thousandths

8. two hundred fifty-five and forty-seven thousandths

Mixed Practice • Write the decimals.

9. $\frac{238}{1,000}$ 10. $\frac{4}{10}$ 11. $\frac{4}{100}$ 12. $\frac{8}{1,000}$ 13. $\frac{47}{100}$

14. $2\frac{9}{10}$ 15. $6\frac{52}{100}$ 16. $48\frac{399}{1,000}$ 17. $83\frac{5}{1,000}$ 18. $46\frac{40}{100}$

19. $888\frac{43}{1,000}$ 20. $625\frac{83}{100}$ 21. $597\frac{138}{1,000}$ 22. $256\frac{78}{100}$ 23. $932\frac{17}{1,000}$

24. $243\frac{900}{1,000}$ 25. $1,876\frac{3}{1,000}$ 26. $4,201\frac{7}{10}$ 27. $652\frac{891}{1,000}$ 28. $7,431\frac{56}{100}$

29. four hundred twenty-seven thousandths

30. seven thousand, five hundred twenty-one and three hundred nine thousandths

31. two thousand, eight hundred fifty-six and eighty-five thousandths

★ 32. Eighty-nine thousandths of the bulbs in the sign are red.

★ 33. Two hundred forty-eight thousandths of the bulbs in the sign are blue.

PROBLEM SOLVING • APPLICATIONS

It is 32 meters from Angela's house to Alfred's house.

A meter is one thousandth of a kilometer. So their houses are 0.032 kilometer apart.

How many kilometers is the measurement?

★ 34. 4 meters   ★ 35. 8 meters   ★ 36. 26 meters

★ 37. 257 meters   ★ 38. 142 meters   ★ 39. 1,489 meters

Skills Maintenance

1. $\frac{2}{3} \times \frac{1}{3} =$ ___?___   2. $\frac{4}{5} \times \frac{2}{4} =$ ___?___   3. $\frac{9}{10} \times \frac{3}{5} =$ ___?___

4. $4 \times 1\frac{2}{3} =$ ___?___   5. $3\frac{1}{3} \times 6 =$ ___?___   6. $4\frac{1}{2} \times 2\frac{1}{4} =$ ___?___

7. $1\frac{5}{6} \times 2\frac{2}{5} =$ ___?___   8. $\frac{1}{3} \times 6\frac{1}{4} =$ ___?___   9. $5\frac{1}{6} \times 4\frac{3}{4} =$ ___?___

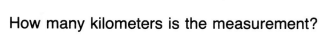

Place Value

A digit in different places names different numbers.
The chart shows how 3 can name
seven different numbers.

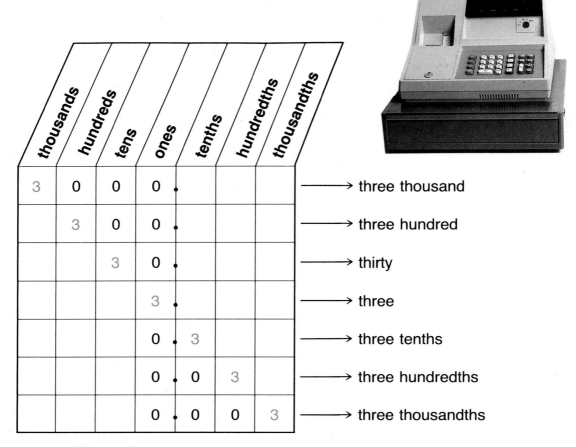

thousands	hundreds	tens	ones	tenths	hundredths	thousandths	
3	0	0	0 .				→ three thousand
	3	0	0 .				→ three hundred
		3	0 .				→ thirty
			3 .				→ three
			0 .	3			→ three tenths
			0 .	0	3		→ three hundredths
			0 .	0	0	3	→ three thousandths

Each place in a decimal number has a value
    10 times the value of the place at its right.
    $\frac{1}{10}$ the value of the place at its left.

$\frac{3}{10}$, $\frac{30}{100}$, and $\frac{300}{1,000}$ are equivalent fractions.
Decimals that name the same number are equivalent decimals.

$0.3 = 0.30 = 0.300$ $1.4 = 1.40 = 1.400$

Practice • In what place is the blue digit?

1. 21.760   **2.** 85.365   **3.** 29.246   **4.** 39.158

What number does the blue digit name?

5. 35.689   **6.** 32.478   **7.** 20.304   **8.** 72.849

Mixed Practice • In what place is the blue digit?

9. 26.498

10. 35.789

11. 53.987

12. 68.243

13. 247.633

14. 9,357.249

15. 1,175.321

16. 5,194.062

What number does the blue digit name?

17. 87.234

18. 38.423

19. 97.876

20. 49.269

21. 463.489

22. 9,836.984

23. 9,658.357

24. 3,082.175

In which numeral does the digit 3 have the greater value?

25. 23 or 2.3

26. 9.438 or 6.345

27. 12.536 or 1.253

28. 529.843 or 3.156

Complete the patterns.

29. 0.4 = 0.40 = ___?___

30. 1.8 = 1.80 = ___?___

31. ___?___ = 5.80 = 5.800

32. ___?___ = 3.10 = 3.100

33. 8.4 = ___?___ = ___?___

34. ___?___ = ___?___ = 7.900

35. 0.3, 0.4, 0.5, ___?___, ___?___

36. 0.19, 0.20, 0.21, ___?___, ___?___

★ 37. 0.07, 0.08, 0.09, ___?___, ___?___

★ 38. 3.97, 3.98, 3.99, ___?___, ___?___

Use the digits 0 through 5. Use each digit only once.

★ 39. Name the largest number possible. ____ • ____ ____ ____ ____ ____

★ 40. Name the smallest number possible. ____ ____ • ____ ____ ____ ____

PROBLEM SOLVING • APPLICATIONS

Write the decimal numbers.

41. There is a 6 in the ones place, and there is a 4 in the tenths place.

42. There is a 2 in the tens place, a 7 in the ones place, a 6 in the tenths place, and a 5 in the hundredths place.

★ 43. There is a 2 in the hundreds place, a 6 in the tenths place, and 7 in the hundredths place. The other digits are zeros.

★ 44. There is an 8 in the thousands place and an 8 in the thousandths place. The other digits are zeros.

Comparing Decimals

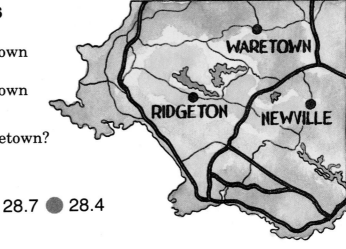

It is 28.7 kilometers from Waretown to Newville.
It is 28.4 kilometers from Waretown to Ridgeton.

Which town is farther from Waretown?

Compare the decimals.
Use >, <, or = to make the sentence true.

28.7 ● 28.4

Think:
Same number of tens.
Same number of ones.
Compare the tenths. 7 > 4   So, **28.7 > 28.4**.

Newville is farther from Waretown.

Compare the decimals.

0.8 ● 0.84

Think:
0.8 = 0.80
Compare 0.80 and 0.84.
Same number of tenths.
Compare the hundredths. 0 < 4
So 0.8 < 0.84.

More Examples

Use >, <, or = to compare.

6.75 ● 6.71	36.8 ● 39.4	8.36 ● 8.360
6.75 is greater than 6.71.	36.8 is less than 39.4.	8.36 is equal to 8.360.
6.75 > 6.71	36.8 < 39.4	8.36 = 8.360

Practice • Write >, <, or =.

1. 2.39 ● 2.47

2. 63.4 ● 63.76

3. 5.7 ● 5.70

4. 8.272 ● 8.26

5. 43.81 ● 47.23

6. 36.81 ● 36.815

7. 37.29 ● 37.290

8. 59.34 ● 58.17

9. 24.93 ● 24.5

Mixed Practice • Write >, <, or =.

10. 16.7 ⬤ 16.9

11. 2.036 ⬤ 2.03

12. 42.83 ⬤ 42.80

13. 85.6 ⬤ 83.7

14. 3.48 ⬤ 3.63

15. 9.430 ⬤ 9.43

16. 73.42 ⬤ 76.63

17. 9.65 ⬤ 9.3

18. 8.473 ⬤ 8.491

19. 27.270 ⬤ 27.27

20. 34.099 ⬤ 34.09

21. 86.42 ⬤ 87.8

22. 63.932 ⬤ 63.67

23. 77.894 ⬤ 79.996

24. 40.612 ⬤ 40.321

Which is greater?

25. 47.6 cm or 47.3 cm

26. 1.8 km or 2.7 km

27. 17.5 cm or 17.2 cm

28. 2.52 m or 2.25 m

29. 16.3 km or 17.3 km

30. 15.4 cm or 14.3 cm

Write in order from least to greatest.

⭐ 31. 3.08, 3.079, 3.107, 2.986

⭐ 32. 14.036, 1.478, 14.034, 13.976

⭐ 33. 13.064, 10.364, 12.789, 1.974

⭐ 34. 9.074, 90.001, 9.706, 9.378

⭐ 35. 24.95, 29.413, 24.509, 24.508

⭐ 36. 67.081, 67.091, 67.801, 67.901

Which is greater, 342 centimeters or 3.36 meters?

You can change m to cm: 1 m = 100 cm

So 3.36 m = 336 cm. Now compare: 342 cm or 336 cm?

342 cm is greater than 3.36 m.
Which is greater?

⭐ 37. 128 cm or 1.26 m

⭐ 38. 345 cm or 3.49 m

⭐ 39. 520 cm or 6.82 m

⭐ 40. 28 cm or 1.29 m

⭐ 41. 420 cm or 0.42 m

⭐ 42. 647 cm or 6.09 m

PROBLEM SOLVING • APPLICATIONS

Compare the decimals. Use > or < to write a true sentence.

43. John can take two bicycle paths to school. The woods path is 2.89 kilometers long. The playground path is 2.36 kilometers long. Which path is longer?

44. The road along the north shore of the lake is 19.38 kilometers. The road along the south shore is 14.38 kilometers. Which road is shorter?

Rounding Decimals

One fathom is about 1.8 meters.
1.8 is between 1 and 2. It is nearer to 2.
1.8 rounded to the nearest whole number is 2.

One scuba diver is at 5.3 fathoms.
5.3 is between 5 and 6. It is
nearer to 5. 5.3 rounded to the
nearest whole number is 5.

Another scuba diver is at 6.5
fathoms. 6.5 is halfway between
6 and 7. Round 6.5 up to 7.
6.5 rounded to the nearest whole
number is 7.

Round 17.973 to the nearest hundredth.

The digit in the hundredths place is 7.
The digit to the right of the 7 is less
than 5. Keep the digit in the hundreds
place the same.

hundredths place
↓

17.973
↑

17.973 rounded to the nearest hundredth is 17.97.

Round 17.973 to the nearest tenth.

The digit in the tenths place is 9.
The digit to the right of the 9 is greater
than 5.
Increase the digit in the tenths place by 1.

tenths place
↓

17.973
↑

17.973 rounded to the nearest tenth is 18.0.

Practice • Round to the nearest whole number.

1. 6.38   2. 9.573   3. 3.81   4. 24.66

Round to the nearest tenth.

5. 8.564   6. 53.728   7. 98.35   8. 228.77

Round to the nearest hundredth.

9. 9.482   10. 17.957   11. 83.821   12. 670.326

Mixed Practice • Round to the nearest whole number.

13. 3.6	**14.** 2.7	**15.** 97.84	**16.** 63.52
17. 42.6	**18.** 22.87	**19.** 48.53	**20.** 93.18
21. 52.58	**22.** 76.3	★ **23.** 19.9	★ **24.** 89.97

Round to the nearest tenth.

25. 68.25	**26.** 73.79	**27.** 92.06	**28.** 15.98
29. 80.38	**30.** 17.65	**31.** 79.827	**32.** 45.37
33. 56.215	**34.** 34.64	★ **35.** 27.962	★ **36.** 84.974

Round to the nearest hundredth.

37. 32.402	**38.** 68.945	**39.** 14.284	**40.** 46.729
41. 93.257	**42.** 32.674	**43.** 58.921	**44.** 73.625
45. 40.586	**46.** 62.413	★ **47.** 29.597	★ **48.** 84.095

PROBLEM SOLVING • APPLICATIONS

Round each decimal to the nearest whole number.

49. A diving bell was used to go to a depth of 9.84 fathoms.

50. An oxygen tank was used to go to a depth of 21.32 fathoms.

51. A diving suit was used to go to a depth of 56.43 fathoms.

52. Diving armor was used to descend to 69.39 fathoms.

53. Divers in a bathysphere went to a depth of 496.719 fathoms.

★ **54.** Divers in rubber suits went to a depth of 119.423 fathoms.

Midchapter Review

Write the decimals.

1. $\frac{7}{10}$ **2.** $\frac{324}{1000}$ **3.** $\frac{25}{100}$ **4.** $72\frac{4}{10}$

Write >, <, or =.

5. 2.43 ● 2.430 **6.** 18.57 ● 18.75 **7.** 42.19 ● 42.2

Round 368.274 to the

8. nearest whole number. **9.** nearest tenth. **10.** nearest hundredth.

Adding Decimals

Carmine is driving a car at 32 kilometers per hour. He sees a stoplight ahead. The car travels 6.71 meters before he is able to react and brake. The car travels 5.98 meters more before it stops. What is the total distance the car travels after Carmine sees the stop light?

6.71 + 5.98 = ?

Estimate the answer first. Think: 7 m + 6 m = 13.

Step 1
Line up the decimal points. Add the hundredths.

6.71
+5.98
___
9

Step 2
Add the tenths. Regroup.

$\overset{1}{}$
6.7 1
+ 5.9 8
___
6 9

Step 3
Add the ones. Write the decimal point.

$\overset{1}{}$
6.7 1
+ 5.9 8
___
1 2.6 9

The total distance the car travels is 12.69 meters.

Add: 7.583 + 4.92.

Step 1
Line up the decimal points.
Think: 4.92 = 4.920.
Add the thousandths.

7.583
+4.920
___
3

Step 2
Add the hundredths. Regroup.

$\overset{1}{}$
7.5 8 3
+ 4.9 2 0
___
0 3

Step 3
Add the tenths. Regroup.

$\overset{1\ 1}{}$
7.5 8 3
+ 4.9 2 0
___
5 0 3

Step 4
Add the ones. Write the decimal point.

$\overset{1\ 1}{}$
7.5 8 3
+ 4.9 2 0
___
1 2.5 0 3

Practice • Add.

1. 6.3
+3.4

2. 3.45
+7.89

3. 0.279
+9.865

4. 30.7
+ 4.93

5. 42.45
+38.3

Mixed Practice • Add.

6. 23.7
   +45.8

7. 6.7
   +9.4

8. 82.4
   + 2.2

9. 35.8
   +67.6

10. 5.6
    +4.8

11. 6.73
    +5.92

12. 6.00
    +4.79

13. 42.39
    + 8.78

14. 0.07
    +9.96

15. 27.23
    +95.97

16. 4.256
    +2.879

17. 92.078
    + 2.952

18. 3.879
    +2.603

19. 80.083
    +40.954

20. 76.067
    +84.092

21. 7.5
    +2.39

22. 0.92
    +0.8

23. 15.287
    + 4.7

24. 6.08
    +3.5

25. 68.6
    +18.758

★ 26. 2.3
       7.84
     +15.6

★ 27. 14.821
       9.7
     +26.826

★ 28. 38.38
       91.942
     +85.976

★ 29. 59.078
       55.52
     +22.6

★ 30. 63.12
       35.099
     +96.503

31. 0.96 + 0.08 = ___?___

32. 60.8 + 30.69 = ___?___

33. 43.79 + 65.28 = ___?___

34. 735 + 423.6 = ___?___

35. 2.435 + 6.89 = ___?___

36. 13.4 + 14.9 = ___?___

37. 6.789 + 4.567 = ___?___

38. 0.89 + 9.3 = ___?___

39. 75.67 + 2.7 = ___?___

PROBLEM SOLVING • APPLICATIONS

Complete the table.

	Braking Distances of Cars at Different Speeds			
	Speed (km per hour)	Reaction Distance (meters)	Braking Distance (meters)	Total Distance (meters)
40.	97	20.12	55.48	?
41.	64	13.41	21.95	?
42.	48	10.06	12.19	?

43. Carmine drives 76.7 km in the morning and 49.6 in the afternoon. How many kilometers does Carmine travel in all?

★ 44. A friend lifts three boxes of tools while helping Carmine repair his car. One box weighs 9.6 kg. The second box weighs 11.8 kg, and the third box weighs 12.9 kg. What is the total weight of the three boxes?

Subtracting Decimals

Janet buys two packages of beef for stew. The total mass is 2.73 kilograms. One package has a mass of 1.18 kilograms. What is the mass of the other package?

$2.73 - 1.18 = ?$

Estimate first.
Think: $3\,kg - 1\,kg = 2\,kg$
The answer is about 2.

Step 1
Line up the decimal points. Regroup. Subtract the hundredths.

```
    6 13
  2.7 3
- 1.1 8
      5
```

Step 2
Subtract the tenths.

```
    6 13
  2.7 3
- 1.1 8
    5 5
```

Step 3
Subtract the ones. Write the decimal point in the answer.

```
    6 13
  2.7 3
- 1.1 8
  1.5 5
```

The other package has a mass of 1.55 kilograms.

Subtract: $8.37 - 2.914$.

Step 1
Line up the decimal points.
Think: $8.37 = 8.370$.
Regroup. Subtract the thousandths.

```
      6 10
  8.3 7 0
- 2.9 1 4
        6
```

Step 2
Subtract the hundredths.

```
      6 10
  8.3 7 0
- 2.9 1 4
      5 6
```

Step 3
Regroup. Subtract the tenths.

```
  7 13 6 10
  8.3 7 0
- 2.9 1 4
    4 5 6
```

Step 4
Subtract the ones. Write the decimal point.

```
  7 13 6 10
  8.3 7 0
- 2.9 1 4
  5.4 5 6
```

Practice • Subtract.

1. 3.6
   −1.2

2. 0.21
   −0.19

3. 46.235
   − 5.454

4. 7.27
   −3.485

5. 59.76
   −15.4

296

Mixed Practice • Subtract.

6. 8.3
   −6.2

7. 7.4
   −6.8

8. 32.4
   −11.5

9. 5.47
   −4.72

10. 59.23
    − 6.45

11. 8.06
    −3.97

12. 86.07
    − 5.86

13. 6.532
    −1.713

14. 4.062
    −2.387

15. 8.194
    −7.269

16. 8.396
    −5.488

17. 5.1
    −3.29

18. 7.038
    −2.09

19. 8.3
    −2.837

20. 98.64
    − 5.293

21. 84.75 − 73.68 = __?__

22. 27.60 − 3.42 = __?__

23. 8.79 − 4.236 = __?__

24. 9.73 − 4.39 = __?__

★ 25. 6.4 − 2.38 = __?__

★ 26. 178.4 − 9__?__.7 = 81.7

★ 27. 95 − 42.5__?__ = 52.41

★ 28. 64.29 − __?__2.86 = 31.43

PROBLEM SOLVING • APPLICATIONS

29. In the summer the Wagners' cow drinks 48.7 liters of water each day. In the winter the cow drinks 36.9 liters each day. How much more does the cow drink in the summer?

30. The dairy makes 13.05 billion kilograms of milk into cheese and 8.99 billion kilograms into butter. How much more milk is used for cheese than for butter?

How much more milk is produced in

31. California than in Pennsylvania?

32. New York than in Pennsylvania?

★ 33. Wisconsin than in New York and Minnesota?

Milk Production for One Year	
State	**Billions of Liters**
Wisconsin	9.5
California	5.3
New York	4.5
Minnesota	4.2
Pennsylvania	3.5

Skills Maintenance

1. $\frac{1}{2} \div \frac{1}{4} =$ __?__

2. $6 \div \frac{1}{2} =$ __?__

3. $\frac{5}{9} \div \frac{1}{3} =$ __?__

4. $\frac{2}{5} \div \frac{3}{10} =$ __?__

5. $\frac{3}{8} \div \frac{5}{6} =$ __?__

6. $9 \div \frac{7}{8} =$ __?__

7. $10 \div \frac{6}{10} =$ __?__

8. $\frac{1}{4} \div \frac{1}{4} =$ __?__

PROBLEM SOLVING · STRATEGIES

Too Much Information

Sometimes more facts are given than are needed
to solve a problem. You must find the important facts.

Find the facts you need to answer this question.

Question: How many swimmers who are 10 or 11 years old
competed in the 45-meter freestyle race?

Facts: **A.** There are 26 races.
    B. One of the races is the 45-meter freestyle.
    C. There are 24 swimmers who are 10 years old
        entered in the 45-meter freestyle race.
    D. There are 32 swimmers who are 11 years old
        entered in the 45-meter freestyle race.
    E. The judges give out 7 gold medals.

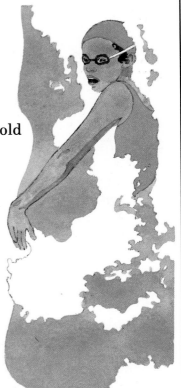

These are the facts you need: **C** and **D.**

You add to find the answer.
24 + 32 = 56
56 swimmers who are 10 or 11 years old competed in
the 45-meter freestyle race.

Write the facts you need to answer the questions.

1. How many swimmers earn a
   silver medal?

   Eileen Johnson wins the 90-
   meter freestyle race. The judges
   award 12 silver medals in the
   90-meter freestyle race. The
   judges award 8 silver medals in
   the 180-meter freestyle race.
   The second-place prize is a
   silver medal.

**Read the question carefully.
Find the facts.**

2. How many parents come to the
   swim meet?

   The swim meet lasts 5 hours.
   Some people have to travel more
   than 50 kilometers to the meet.
   There are 35 fathers and 47
   mothers at the meet. There are
   52 sisters and 46 brothers
   at the meet.

Find the facts you need. Solve.

3. How much longer does it take Laura to swim than it takes the first-place winner?

The first-place winner swims the 45-meter freestyle race in 37.959 seconds. Lizette Montgomery swims the 90-meter freestyle in 57.375 seconds. Laura Reyes swims the 45-meter freestyle race in 41.031 seconds. Elaine Ingalls swims the 180-meter freestyle in 57.956 seconds.

4. How many medals are awarded?

The judges give 48 gold medals. The judges give 48 silver medals. Eric Foran wins a gold medal and a silver medal. The judges give 48 bronze medals.

5. How much faster than the second-place winner does Kenneth swim the 22.5-meter freestyle race?

There are 63 people sitting in the front row of the balcony for the 22.5-meter freestyle race. The second-place winner in the 22.5-meter freestyle race swims the race in 16.756 seconds. Darryl Massa wins a bronze medal in the 22.5-meter freestyle race. Kenneth Ambery swims the 22.5-meter freestyle race in 15.589 seconds.

6. Who is the winner of the 45-meter freestyle race?

The Woodville Swim Club held a 45-meter freestyle race. Barbara Barrett swims the race in 33.393 seconds. Jeanine Moore swims the race in 40.948 seconds. Cathy Schaefer swims the race in 30.607 seconds.

7. How many more medals does Eloise win than Darryl?

Eloise is entered in the 22.5-meter freestyle race. Kenneth and Darryl each win 3 medals. Eloise wins 4 medals. Eloise wins 2 more medals than Frankie.

8. How many more swimmers entered the 22.5-meter freestyle race this year than last year?

Last year 18 swimmers entered the 45-meter freestyle race. This year 29 swimmers entered the 22.5-meter freestyle race. Last year Mr. Cortez coached 50 swimmers. Last year 20 swimmers entered the 22.5-meter freestyle race.

REVIEW

Write the decimals. (pages 282–287)

1. $\frac{3}{10}$ 2. $5\frac{8}{10}$ 3. $\frac{6}{100}$ 4. $32\frac{95}{100}$ 5. $9\frac{46}{1000}$

6. two and one-tenth   7. ninety-three hundredths

8. one hundred twelve thousandths   9. one and fifty-six thousandths

In what place is the 8? (pages 288–289)

10. 4.81   11. 84.961   12. 0.038

Write >, <, or =. (pages 290–291)

13. 0.3 ● 0.25   14. 0.96 ● 0.91   15. 1.8 ● 1.80

16. 14.081 ● 14.281   17. 9.24 ● 9.34   18. 3.06 ● 3.060

Round to the nearest whole number. (pages 292–293)

19. 7.94   20. 16.07   21. 24.675

Round to the nearest tenth. (pages 292–293)

22. 5.39   23. 60.41   24. 19.758

Round to the nearest hundredth. (pages 292–293)

25. 8.683   26. 52.292   27. 68.565

Add or subtract. (pages 294–297)

28. 2.13
    +5.45

29. 1.9
    −0.4

30. 0.62
    +4.093

31. 28.4
    −16.976

Solve.

32. Paul runs 100 meters in 13.6 seconds. The record is 14.9 seconds. By how much does Paul beat the record? (p. 296)

33. Marie runs the first lap of the 800-meter race in 78.5 seconds. The time for her second lap is 80.4 seconds. What is her time for the two laps? (p. 294)

PROJECT

Estimating and Measuring

Estimate the answer for each activity. Then measure in centimeters or meters. Record your results on a table like the one at the right. Compare your estimate with the actual measure.

Name	Estimate	Measure

1. Find the height in centimeters of each of four classmates. Remember to estimate first.

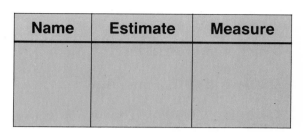

2. Have four classmates stand near a wall. Have each person reach up on the wall as high as he or she can. Find the distance in centimeters for each classmate.

3. Have each of four classmates throw a softball. Find the distance in meters for each classmate.

TEST

Write the decimals.

1. $\frac{5}{10}$ **2.** $4\frac{7}{10}$ **3.** $\frac{16}{100}$ **4.** $9\frac{8}{100}$ **5.** $6\frac{316}{1000}$

6. five and six-tenths   **7.** fifteen hundredths

8. one and thirty-one hundredths   **9.** fifty-two thousandths

In what place is the 6?

10. 13.645   **11.** 162.93   **12.** 29.026

Write >, <, or =.

13. 4.6 ⬤ 4.1   **14.** 3.6 ⬤ 36.1   **15.** 9.03 ⬤ 9.030

16. 5.847 ⬤ 5.784   **17.** 12.4 ⬤ 12.400   **18.** 65.27 ⬤ 65.275

Round to the nearest whole number.

19. 31.29   **20.** 74.578   **21.** 4.07

Round to the nearest tenth.

22. 5.64   **23.** 84.82   **24.** 23.76

Round to the nearest hundredth.

25. 18.238   **26.** 65.664   **27.** 98.261

Add or subtract.

28. $\begin{array}{r} 17.3 \\ +84.7 \\ \hline \end{array}$ **29.** $\begin{array}{r} 6.8 \\ -3.1 \\ \hline \end{array}$ **30.** $\begin{array}{r} 0.7 \\ +0.896 \\ \hline \end{array}$ **31.** $\begin{array}{r} 5.218 \\ -3.65 \\ \hline \end{array}$

Solve.

32. The average rainfall for June in Miami is 22.9 centimeters. One June, Miami had 26.4 centimeters of rain. How much more than the average rainfall did they receive?

33. One day Boston received 4.6 centimeters of rain. The next day it received 5.8 centimeters of rain. How much rain did Boston receive in the two days?

ENRICHMENT

Using Equations to Solve Problems

A furniture factory is preparing to deliver
a new line of chairs.
There are 8 trucks to load.
3 of them are loaded.
How many more trucks need to be loaded?

You can write an equation to solve the problem.

Think: 3 plus some number is 8.
Write: $3 + n = 8$

To solve the equation, find the number that makes it true.
The sum is 8. One addend is 3.
Subtract to find the other addend. $8 - 3 = ?$

$$\begin{array}{r} 8 \\ -3 \\ \hline 5 \end{array}$$

5 makes the equation true. $\qquad 3 + 5 = 8$
5 more trucks need to be loaded.

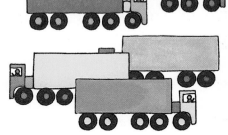

Write the equations. Then solve.

1. There are 54 folding chairs on a truck. There are 68 rocking
   chairs on the same truck. How many more rocking chairs
   are there than folding chairs?

2. Mr. Hewitt receives his shipment of tables. He receives 14
   round tables and 12 rectangular tables. How many tables
   does Mr. Hewitt receive in all?

3. Each new oak bookcase comes with 8 removable shelves. A
   truck is loaded with 50 oak bookcases. How many shelves
   should be loaded?

COMPUTER

Basic Flowcharting

A **flowchart** is a graphic method for planning anything in a step-by-step way.
A flowchart is especially useful in planning large computer systems.
Boxes of specific shapes are used to indicate specific types of functions.

 Rectangles are
process boxes. These are
things to do.

Diamonds are **decision boxes.**
Choices are given here.
Usually there are two choices.

The top flowchart on the right is an
easy way of saying this:

> If it is raining today, take your
> raincoat; then go to school.
> If it is not raining today,
> just go to school.

Decisions can lead to other decisions.
Look at the flowchart on the right.
You can go through this
flowchart in 7 different ways.
Each box is lettered from **a** to **g**.
Write the letters of the boxes for
each of the 7 different ways.
Notice that the decision box
"Are studies done?" is used twice.

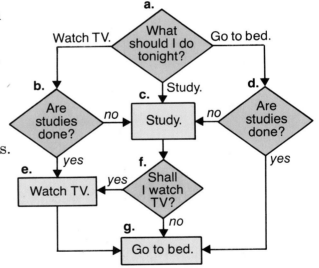

Draw a simpler flowchart by
starting with that decision box.
You might have drawn the flowchart
on the right. How many ways can
you go through this flowchart?
This flowchart is better because it
is *simpler*.
But flowcharts for computer systems
can be far more complicated than these.

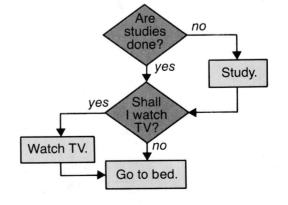

304

Many special shapes are used for program flowcharts. They tell you when put information in the computer, and when to transfer information to an output device. They also tell you how to handle the information once it is in the computer. You already know two of these boxes: the process and decision boxes. Here are three more.

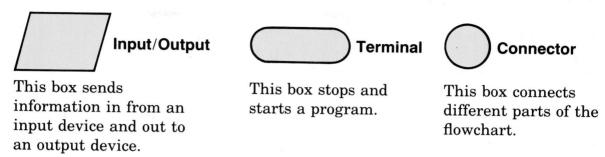

Input/Output

This box sends information in from an input device and out to an output device.

Terminal

This box stops and starts a program.

Connector

This box connects different parts of the flowchart.

The following boxes are used in systems flowcharts. They indicate the different types of devices needed in the computer operation.

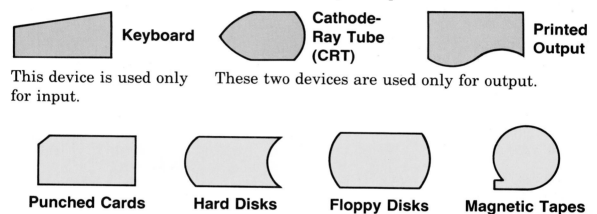

Keyboard

This device is used only for input.

Cathode-Ray Tube (CRT)

Printed Output

These two devices are used only for output.

Punched Cards   **Hard Disks**   **Floppy Disks**   **Magnetic Tapes**

These four devices can be used both for input and for output.

Copy the template below. Label every shape. Examine the systems flowchart boxes. If the box can be used for input, write the letter I. If the box can be used for output, write the letter O. If the box can be used for both, write I/O. Number 7 has been done for you.

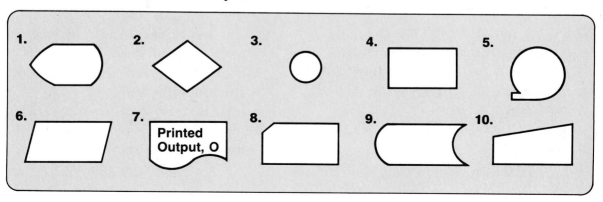

1.   2.   3.   4.   5.

6.   7. Printed Output, O   8.   9.   10.

Choose the correct answers.

1. Add.

$1{,}986 + 357 + 86 = \underline{\ ?\ }$

- **A.** 3,654
- **B.** 2,429
- **C.** 2,675
- **D.** not here

2. Subtract.

$\begin{array}{r} 652 \\ -\ 78 \\ \hline \end{array}$

- **A.** 730
- **B.** 856
- **C.** 574
- **D.** not here

3. Multiply.

$\begin{array}{r} 354 \\ \times\ 29 \\ \hline \end{array}$

- **A.** 6,475
- **B.** 8,916
- **C.** 10,624
- **D.** not here

4. Divide.

$36\overline{)\$570.60}$

- **A.** $15.85
- **B.** $18.20
- **C.** $16.45
- **D.** not here

5. Divide to find a mixed number.

$$\frac{29}{4}$$

- **A.** $6\frac{3}{4}$
- **B.** $7\frac{1}{4}$
- **C.** $7\frac{1}{2}$
- **D.** not here

6. Subtract. Write the answer in lowest terms.

$5\frac{1}{4} - 3\frac{3}{4} = \underline{\ ?\ }$

- **A.** $2\frac{1}{2}$
- **B.** 9
- **C.** $1\frac{1}{2}$
- **D.** not here

7. Find the area.

7 cm
3 cm

- **A.** 10 centimeters
- **B.** 21 cubic meters
- **C.** 21 square centimeters
- **D.** not here

8. Complete.

$2\ \text{qt} = \underline{\ ?\ }\ \text{fl. oz}$

- **A.** 32
- **B.** 64
- **C.** 88
- **D.** not here

9. Round 7.564 to the nearest tenth.

- **A.** 7.7
- **B.** 7.5
- **C.** 7.6
- **D.** not here

10. Anita drives 56.2 kilometers in the morning. She drives 87.6 kilometers in the afternoon. How far does she drive all together?

- **A.** 31.4 km
- **B.** 126.9 km
- **C.** 143.8 km
- **D.** not here

11. The average rainfall for June in Burtonsville is 17.8 centimeters. Last June, Burtonsville had 21.2 centimeters of rain. How much more than the average rainfall did they receive?

- **A.** 3.4 cm
- **B.** 39 cm
- **C.** 2.9 cm
- **D.** not here

Decimals: Multiplication and Division

CHAPTER 12

**Estimating Products • Multiplying with Decimals
• Zeros in the Product • Multiplying by 10, 100,
and 1,000 • Problem Solving: More Than One Step
• Dividing by a Whole Number • Zeros in Division
• Comparison Shopping • Checking Accounts**

Estimating Products

One tennis ball weighs 56.7 grams.
There are 24 tennis balls.
How much do the tennis balls weigh
all together?

Estimate the product. Round 56.7
to 60. Round 24 to 20. 20 × 60 = 1,200.
The answer is about 1,200.

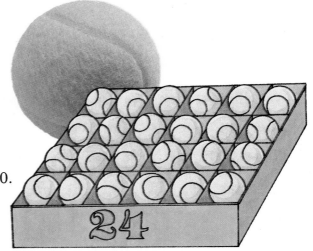

Here is the multiplication.

$$
\begin{array}{r}
56.7 \\
\times\ 24 \\
\hline
2268 \\
11340 \\
\hline
13608
\end{array}
$$

Based on your estimate, the answer
must be 1,360.8. The total weight is
1,360.8 grams.

The length of a tennis court is 23.7
meters. The width of a tennis court
is 10.9 meters. What is the area of
the tennis court?

Estimate the product. Round 23.7
to 20. Round 10.9 to 11. 11 × 20 = 220.
The answer is about 220.

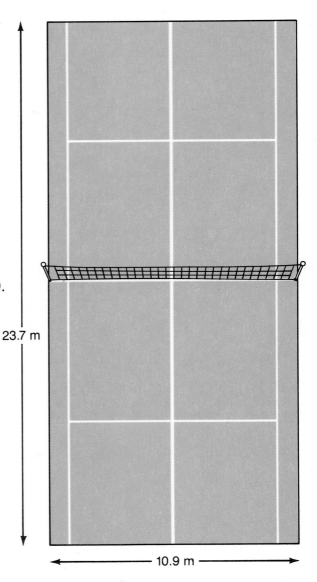

23.7 m

Here is the multiplication.

$$
\begin{array}{r}
23.7 \\
\times 10.9 \\
\hline
2133 \\
23700 \\
\hline
25833
\end{array}
$$

Based on your estimate, the answer
must be 258.33. The area of the
tennis court is 258.33 square meters.

10.9 m

Practice • Estimate to place the decimal point in the answers.

1. 47	2. 6.2	3. 9.2	4. 3.97	5. 21.9
×1.8	× 34	×3.8	× 5.2	×3.84
846	2108	3496	20644	84096

More Practice • Estimate to place the decimal point in the answers.

6. 74	7. 83	8. 237	9. 592	10. 693
×2.8	×6.5	×4.1	×2.8	×5.2
2072	5395	9717	16576	36036

11. 5.3	12. 9.4	13. 4.2	14. 9.8	15. 7.4
×7.4	×3.2	×2.4	×4.3	×9.1
3922	3008	1008	4214	6734

16. 28.6	17. 96.5	18. 63.7	19. 79.2	20. 85.6
×5.48	×4.28	×8.85	×3.86	×7.14
156728	413020	563745	305712	611184

21. 8.35	22. 68.9	23. 592	24. 5.33	25. 93.7
×72.1	×94.3	×3.87	×29.4	×4.02
602035	649727	229104	156702	376674

26. 4.63	27. 7.35	28. 9.44	29. 6.57	30. 36.2
× 3.5	× 9.8	×28.1	×43.9	×8.19
16205	72030	265264	288423	296478

31. 58.2	32. 2.95	33. 67.7	34. 29.4	35. 70.3
× 6.7	×83.1	×3.18	×19.3	×1.18
38994	245145	215286	56742	82954

Use the 3 digits and a decimal point to write 24 different numbers.

★ **36.** .3 6 4   ★ **37.** .7 8 2

PROBLEM SOLVING • APPLICATIONS

38. Terry multiplied 86.3 times 2.7. His answer without the decimal point was 23301. Where should he place the decimal point?

★ **39.** Percy multiplied 61.73 times 8.9. His answer was 54.9397. Was his answer correct? If not what should his answer have been?

Multiplying with Decimals

A wild turkey can run at a speed of 24.4 kilometers per hour. A gray fox can run 2.8 times as fast as the wild turkey. How fast can the gray fox run?

$2.8 \times 24.4 = ?$

Step 1
Multiply as if you were multiplying whole numbers.

$$
\begin{array}{r}
24.4 \\
\times\ 2.8 \\
\hline
1952 \\
488\ \ \\
\hline
6832
\end{array}
$$

Step 2
Place the decimal point in the product.
Think: Round each factor.

$3 \times 20 = 60$

The answer is about 60.

$$
\begin{array}{r}
24.4 \\
\times\ 2.8 \\
\hline
1952 \\
488\ \ \\
\hline
68\ 32
\end{array}
$$

The gray fox can run at a speed of 68.32 kilometers per hour.

Each place to the right of the decimal point is a **decimal place**. Compare the number of decimal places in the product with the total number of decimal places in the factors.

$$
\begin{array}{rl}
54.3 & \boxed{1} \\
\times\quad 7 & \boxed{0} \\
\hline
380.1 & \boxed{1}
\end{array}
\qquad
\begin{array}{rl}
2.86 & \boxed{2} \\
\times\ 1.9 & \boxed{1} \\
\hline
5.434 & \boxed{3}
\end{array}
\qquad
\begin{array}{rl}
3.58 & \boxed{2} \\
\times\ 0.6 & \boxed{1} \\
\hline
2.148 & \boxed{3}
\end{array}
$$

The number of decimal places in the product equals the sum of the number of decimal places in the factors.

Practice • Multiply.

1. $\begin{array}{r} 63.9 \\ \times\quad 7 \\ \hline \end{array}$

2. $\begin{array}{r} 24 \\ \times 0.5 \\ \hline \end{array}$

3. $\begin{array}{r} 6.35 \\ \times\ 7.4 \\ \hline \end{array}$

4. $\begin{array}{r} 259 \\ \times\ 3.9 \\ \hline \end{array}$

5. $\begin{array}{r} 3.41 \\ \times 46.8 \\ \hline \end{array}$

Mixed Practice • Multiply.

6. 2.03 × 88	7. 6.7 × 9	8. 43 ×5.5	9. 9.4 ×0.6	10. 38.15 × 6.2

11. 3.003 × 462	12. 4.44 × 400	13. 7.8 ×3.2	14. 5.9 ×0.7	15. 48.06 × 73.2

16. 5.3 ×8.6	17. 19.8 × 1.1	18. 57.3 ×0.32	19. 9.427 × 8	20. 61.25 × 4.8

Place the decimal point in each product.

21. $4.3 \times 86 = 3698$

22. $69.5 \times 0.47 = 32665$

23. $2.3 \times 6.4 = 1472$

24. $3.57 \times 59.4 = 212058$

★ **25.** Choose two decimals between 0 and 1. Find the product. $0.6 \times 0.81 = 0.486$

Is the product greater than or less than the two factors? Try other examples. Do you get the same results?

Is the product always greater than or less than the two factors? Is the product greater than or less than one?

PROBLEM SOLVING • APPLICATIONS

26. A snail travels about 0.05 kilometers per hour. A spider travels 62.4 times as fast. How fast does the spider travel?

27. A giant tortoise travels about 0.27 kilometers per hour. A rabbit runs 205.9 times as fast. How fast does the rabbit run?

★ **28.** An elephant can travel at a speed of 40 kilometers per hour. A giraffe can travel 1.28 times as fast, and a cheetah can travel 2.75 times as fast as an elephant. How many kilometers per hour faster does a cheetah travel than a giraffe?

★ **29.** An ostrich travels at a speed of 40 kilometers per hour. A jack rabbit can travel 1.125 times as fast. A gazelle can travel 1.25 as fast as an ostrich. How many kilometers per hour can a gazelle travel?

Zeros in the Product

Georgiana is making a pillow cover. She needs a piece of velvet 0.3 meters long and 0.2 meters wide. How many square meters of velvet does she need?

$0.3 \times 0.2 = ?$

Sometimes you need to write zeros in the product to locate the decimal point.

Step 1
Multiply.

$$\begin{array}{r} 0.3 \\ \times 0.2 \\ \hline 6 \end{array}$$

Step 2
Write one zero to show two decimal places. Place the decimal point. If the answer is less than one, write a zero before the decimal point.

$$\begin{array}{rl} 0.3 & \boxed{1} \\ \times 0.2 & \boxed{1} \\ \hline 0.06 & \boxed{2} \end{array}$$

Georgiana needs 0.06 square meters of velvet.

More Examples

$$\begin{array}{rl} 0.7 & \boxed{1} \\ \times 0.08 & \boxed{2} \\ \hline 0.056 & \boxed{3} \end{array}$$

$$\begin{array}{rl} 0.08 & \boxed{2} \\ \times \ \ 0.6 & \boxed{1} \\ \hline 0.048 & \boxed{3} \end{array}$$

$$\begin{array}{rl} .003 & \boxed{3} \\ \times \ \ \ 2 & \boxed{0} \\ \hline 0.006 & \boxed{3} \end{array}$$

Practice • Place the decimal point in the answers.

You may have to write zeros in the product.

1.
$$\begin{array}{r} 0.09 \\ \times \ 0.3 \\ \hline 27 \end{array}$$

2.
$$\begin{array}{r} 0.28 \\ \times \ 0.5 \\ \hline 140 \end{array}$$

3.
$$\begin{array}{r} 0.1 \\ \times 0.7 \\ \hline 7 \end{array}$$

4.
$$\begin{array}{r} 4.2 \\ \times 3.6 \\ \hline 1512 \end{array}$$

5.
$$\begin{array}{r} 0.324 \\ \times \ \ \ 57 \\ \hline 18468 \end{array}$$

Multiply.

6.
$$\begin{array}{r} 0.3 \\ \times 0.3 \end{array}$$

7.
$$\begin{array}{r} 14.4 \\ \times 0.29 \end{array}$$

8.
$$\begin{array}{r} 0.07 \\ \times 00.2 \end{array}$$

9.
$$\begin{array}{r} 461 \\ \times 0.67 \end{array}$$

10.
$$\begin{array}{r} 29.8 \\ \times 0.01 \end{array}$$

Mixed Practice • Place the decimal point in the answers.
You may have to write zeros in the product.

11. 0.005	12. 1.9	13. 0.19	14. 5.2	15. 72.4
× 3	×0.8	× .4	×.31	× 2.9
15	152	76	1612	20996

Multiply.

16. 0.07	17. 15.7	18. 0.002	19. 4.36	20. 7.285
× 0.9	×0.36	× 49	× 7.2	× 9

21. 3.7	22. 0.265	23. 0.004	24. 0.995	25. 0.94
×.02	× 58	× 21	× 87	× 0.1

26. 5.67	27. 0.03	28. 806	29. 0.07	30. 63.7
×29.6	× 0.9	×5.29	× 1.1	×8.61

31. 2.8	32. .873	33. 7.02	34. 27	35. 3.87
×0.03	× 47	× 7.9	×0.003	×47.8

36. $1.78 \times 0.6 =$ __?__   **37.** $396 \times 0.89 =$ __?__   **38.** $4.5 \times 3.84 =$ __?__

39. $1.7 \times 3.2 \times 2.5 =$ __?__   ★**40.** $0.03 \times 0.1 \times 8 =$ __?__   ★**41.** $4.8 \times 5 \times 0.003 =$ __?__

PROBLEM SOLVING • APPLICATIONS

42. The side of a red square of fabric is 0.04 meters long. The side of a blue square of fabric is 0.3 times as long. How long is the side of the blue square of fabric?

★ **43.** Norma travels 1.6 kilometers to the fabric store. Her friend Sheldon travels 0.6 times as far to meet her. How much farther does Norma travel than Sheldon?

Skills Maintenance

1. $2,000 \text{ mL} =$ __?__ L   **2.** $7,000 \text{ g} =$ __?__ kg   **3.** $3 \text{ kg} =$ __?__ g

4. $200 \text{ cm} =$ __?__ m   **5.** $88 \text{ mm} =$ __?__ cm   **6.** $150 \text{ dm} =$ __?__ m

7.

8 cm

4 cm

Perimeter = __?__

8.

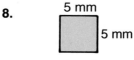

5 mm

5 mm

Area = __?__

9.

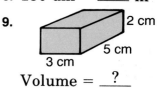

2 cm

5 cm

3 cm

Volume = __?__

313

Multiplying by 10, 100, and 1,000

Look for patterns. Watch the decimal points.

Multiply by 10.

$10 \times 0.287 = 2.87$
$10 \times 2.87 \ = 28.7$
$10 \times 28.7 \ = 287$
$10 \times 287 \ = 2,870$

Multiplying by 10 moves the decimal point one place to the right.

Multiply by 100.

$100 \times 0.394 = 39.4$
$100 \times 3.94 \ = 394$
$100 \times 39.4 \ = 3,940$
$100 \times 394 \ = 39,400$

Multiplying by 100 moves the decimal point two places to the right.

Multiply by 1,000.

$1,000 \times 0.516 = 516$
$1,000 \times 5.16 \ = 5,160$
$1,000 \times 51.6 \ = 51,600$
$1,000 \times 516 \ = 516,000$

Multiplying by 1,000 moves the decimal point three places to the right.

Practice • Multiply.

1. $10 \times 3.58 = $ __?__

2. $1,000 \times 6.159 = $ __?__

3. $100 \times 0.42 = $ __?__

4. $10 \times 0.752 = $ __?__

5. $100 \times 6.294 = $ __?__

6. $1,000 \times 8.4 = $ __?__

Mixed Practice • Multiply.

7. $10 \times 472 = $ __?__

8. $1,000 \times 0.631 = $ __?__

9. $100 \times 2,873 = $ __?__

10. $1,000 \times 358 = $ __?__

11. $100 \times 60.9 = $ __?__

12. $100 \times 564 = $ __?__

314

13. $1{,}000 \times 6.537 =$ ___?___ **14.** $100 \times 0.481 =$ ___?___ **15.** $1{,}000 \times 0.953 =$ ___?___

16. $10 \times 6.87 =$ ___?___ **17.** $1{,}000 \times 6.83 =$ ___?___ **18.** $100 \times 0.954 =$ ___?___

19. $100 \times 39.5 =$ ___?___ **20.** $1{,}000 \times 4.78 =$ ___?___ **21.** $100 \times 0.635 =$ ___?___

22. $1{,}000 \times 41.3 =$ ___?___ **23.** $10 \times 0.948 =$ ___?___ **24.** $10 \times 0.717 =$ ___?___

25. $100 \times 4.72 =$ ___?___ **26.** $1{,}000 \times 62 =$ ___?___ **27.** $1{,}000 \times 41.3 =$ ___?___

28. $100 \times 4.269 =$ ___?___ **29.** $10 \times 32.74 =$ ___?___ **30.** $100 \times 3.954 =$ ___?___

31. $1{,}000 \times 658.2 =$ ___?___ **32.** $10 \times 79.06 =$ ___?___ **33.** $100 \times 63.95 =$ ___?___

34. $10 \times 738.4 =$ ___?___ **35.** $1{,}000 \times 9.042 =$ ___?___ **36.** $1{,}000 \times 5.12 =$ ___?___

37. $100 \times 0.674 =$ ___?___ **38.** $10 \times 3.89 =$ ___?___ **39.** $10 \times 2{,}370 =$ ___?___

★**40.** ___?___ $\times 0.191 = 191$ ★**41.** $100 \times$ ___?___ $= 6$ ★**42.** $1{,}000 \times$ ___?___ $= 7870$

PROBLEM SOLVING • APPLICATIONS

Multiply to find the population.

	Population in 1900	
	City	**Number of People**
43.	Amarillo, Texas	$1{,}000 \times 1.442$
44.	Aurora, California	100×2.02
45.	Miami, Florida	$1{,}000 \times 1.681$
46.	Santa Ana, California	$1{,}000 \times 4.933$
47.	Warren, Michigan	100×3.5

48. In 1850 the population of Philadelphia was 121,376. In 1900 about 10 times as many people lived in the city. About how many people lived in Philadelphia in 1900?

Midchapter Review

1. $\begin{array}{r} 37.4 \\ \times\ \ \ 9 \\ \hline \end{array}$
  2. $\begin{array}{r} 1.26 \\ \times\ 0.4 \\ \hline \end{array}$
  3. $\begin{array}{r} 87.9 \\ \times 0.53 \\ \hline \end{array}$
  4. $\begin{array}{r} 24.5 \\ \times\ 0.08 \\ \hline \end{array}$

5. $1{,}000 \times 42.9 =$ ___?___ **6.** $100 \times 8.621 =$ ___?___ **7.** $10 \times 8.7 =$ ___?___

8. $100 \times 7.6 =$ ___?___ **9.** $1{,}000 \times 22.91 =$ ___?___ **10.** $10 \times 3.033 =$ ___?___

PROBLEM SOLVING • STRATEGIES

More Than One Step

To solve some problems, more than one step is necessary. Read the problem.

Harold and Susan are architects. They are planning a playground. They want to buy safe equipment. Flat-board swings cost $9.25 each. Animal-form swings cost $178 each. They plan to purchase 6 flat-board swings and 5 animal-form swings. How much will they cost?

It takes more than one step to solve this problem.

Step 1
Multiply to find the cost for each kind of swing.

$$\begin{array}{r} \$9.25 \\ \times \quad 6 \\ \hline \$55.50 \end{array} \qquad \begin{array}{r} \$178 \\ \times \quad 5 \\ \hline \$890 \end{array}$$

Step 2
Add to find the total cost of all the swings.

$$\begin{array}{r} \$890.00 \\ + \quad 55.50 \\ \hline \$945.50 \end{array}$$

The swings will cost $945.50.

What steps must you take to solve the problem?

1. Swing chains cost $14.50 per meter. The chains for a flat swing must be 3 meters long. Each swing needs 2 chains. How much will the chains for one swing cost?

Plan the steps you need to solve the problem.

2. Harold and Susan need 20 loads of bricks to build a field house.

Brick A sells for $130 a load. Brick B sells for $140 a load. How much will be saved if they buy Brick A?

3. A lawn area of 595 square meters needs to be made. The price to seed this area is $1.95 per square meter. The price to lay sod in this area is $4.32 per square meter. How much money will be saved if seed is used for this area?

Solve.

4. Small slides cost $110.75 each. Large slides cost $216.90 each. Susan orders 2 of each. How much will they cost?

5. A fence 12 meters long is needed in one area of the playground. A wooden fence costs $24.95 per meter. A chain-link fence costs $18.65 per meter. How much more will the wooden fence cost?

6. The playground will have 2 baseball diamonds. The bags for the first, second, and third bases cost $12.75 each. How much will the bags cost for both diamonds?

Remember to place the dollar sign and cents point in your answer when working with money.

---

7. The backstop for a baseball field costs $3,750. A side wing costs $2,500. What will be the cost for a backstop and two side wings?

8. The field house has one window with 3 panes of glass. Plate glass costs $8.23 for each pane. Unbreakable window material costs $21.45 for each pane. How much more will it cost to make the window of the field house unbreakable?

9. An evergreen screening is needed next to the road. A truckload of 45 hemlocks costs $1,935. A truckload of 45 taxus costs $3,240. How much more does each taxus cost?

10. A redwood table costs $147.85. Each bench costs $42.50. Harold orders 2 tables and 4 benches. How much will they cost?

★ 11. Harold received a bid for a blacktop parking lot and a gravel parking lot. The parking lot is 1,500 square meters. The blacktop lot would cost $18,375. The gravel lot would cost $8,685. How much more money per square meter would the blacktop lot cost?

★ 12. Trash containers cost $12.59 each. Redwood stands for the containers cost $46.87 each. The playground will have 6 containers and stands. How much more will the stands cost than the containers?

317

Dividing by a Whole Number

A stack of 9 pennies is 13.5 millimeters high.
About how thick is each penny?

$13.5 \div 9 = ?$

You can estimate to help you place the
decimal point in the quotient.

Think:
Round 13.5 to 14.
$9\overline{)14}$ is about 1. So the
quotient is about 1.

$$\begin{array}{r} 1.5 \\ 9\overline{)13.5} \end{array}$$

Here is a way to divide a decimal by a whole number.

Step 1
Place the decimal point in the
quotient directly above the
decimal point in the dividend.

$$9\overline{)13.5}$$

Each penny is 1.5 millimeters thick.

Step 2
Divide as if you were
dividing whole numbers.

$$\begin{array}{r} 1.5 \\ 9\overline{)13.5} \\ -\ 9\downarrow \\ \hline 4\ 5 \\ -4\ 5 \\ \hline 0 \end{array}$$

Practice • Write the quotients with the decimal point placed correctly.

1. $6\overline{)49.8}$ 83

2. $9\overline{)64.17}$ 713

3. $13\overline{)70.98}$ 546

4. $27\overline{)79.137}$ 2931

Divide.

5. $7\overline{)26.74}$

6. $12\overline{)94.32}$

7. $56\overline{)2,564.8}$

8. $73\overline{)39.639}$

Mixed Practice • Divide.

9. $7\overline{)19.6}$

10. $12\overline{)231.6}$

11. $6\overline{)129.48}$

12. $18\overline{)88.074}$

13. $9\overline{)160.2}$

14. $16\overline{)38.4}$

15. $3\overline{)31.482}$

16. $5\overline{)348.5}$

17. $10\overline{)72.0}$

18. $14\overline{)11.746}$

19. $8\overline{)1,004.8}$

20. $11\overline{)807.4}$

21. $48\overline{)59.424}$

22. $31\overline{)59.83}$

23. $64\overline{)17.92}$

24. $87\overline{)94.83}$

25. $76\overline{)118.56}$

26. $42\overline{)35.154}$

27. $67\overline{)109.21}$

28. $39\overline{)304.2}$

29. $52\overline{)449.28}$ ★ **30.** $73\overline{)719.561}$ ★ **31.** $93\overline{)24,049.8}$ ★ **32.** $29\overline{)11,095.4}$

33. $21.84 \div 8 = \underline{\ ?\ }$ **34.** $830.3 \div 19 = \underline{\ ?\ }$ **35.** $11.764 \div 4 = \underline{\ ?\ }$

36. $153.66 \div 26 = \underline{\ ?\ }$ **37.** $3,298.5 \div 45 = \underline{\ ?\ }$ **38.** $82.524 \div 78 = \underline{\ ?\ }$

Look for patterns. Watch the decimal points.

$2,587 \div 10 = 258.7$ $258.7 \div 10 = 25.87$ $25.87 \div 10 = 2.587$

Dividing by 10 moves the decimal point one place to the left.

$2,587 \div 100 = 25.87$ $258.7 \div 100 = 2.587$ $25.87 \div 100 = 0.2587$

Dividing by 100 moves the decimal point two places to the left.

Divide.

★ **39.** $63.92 \div 10 = \underline{\ ?\ }$ ★ **40.** $758.4 \div 100 = \underline{\ ?\ }$ ★ **41.** $297.8 \div 10 = \underline{\ ?\ }$

★ **42.** $46.9 \div 100 = \underline{\ ?\ }$ ★ **43.** $9.53 \div 10 = \underline{\ ?\ }$ ★ **44.** $876.1 \div 100 = \underline{\ ?\ }$

PROBLEM SOLVING •

45. A stack of 23 quarters is 41.4 millimeters high. How thick is each quarter?

46. If 5 bank tellers share $45.50 in nickels equally, how much money does each teller receive?

★ **47.** A bank teller has $30.00 in quarters. She puts them into rolls of 40. How many rolls of quarters does she have?

★ **48.** If 6 bank tellers share $36.60 in dimes equally, how much money does each teller receive? How many dimes does each teller receive?

Zeros in Division

A scientist lines up 8 red blood cells side by side under a microscope. The distance across the 8 cells is 0.056 millimeters. What is the distance across one red blood cell?

$0.056 \div 8 = ?$

There are not enough tenths to divide.
There are not enough hundredths to divide.
The first digit of the quotient is in the thousandths place.

Step 1
Place the decimal point.
Write zeros in the ones, tenths, and hundredths places.

$$8\overline{)0.056}$$
0.00

Step 2
Divide.

$$8\overline{)0.056}$$
0.007
-56
0

The distance across one red blood cell is 0.007 millimeters.

Sometimes you must write more zeros in the dividend in order to divide until there is a zero remainder.

Divide: $56.4 \div 24$.

Step 1
Place the decimal point.
Divide. There is a remainder of 12.

$$24\overline{)56.4}$$
2.3
$-48 \downarrow$
8 4
$-7 2$
1 2

Step 2
Think: $56.4 = 56.40$.
Write a zero in the dividend.
Divide.

$$24\overline{)56.40}$$
2.35
$-48 \downarrow$
8 4
$-7 2 \downarrow$
1 20
$-1 20$
0

Practice • Place the decimal point. Write zeros in the quotient if necessary.

1. $7\overline{)0.238}$ 34

2. $4\overline{)2.68}$ 67

3. $9\overline{)0.657}$ 73

4. $16\overline{)0.112}$ 7

Divide.

5. $8\overline{)1.96}$

6. $40\overline{)11.6}$

7. $57\overline{)36.48}$

8. $22\overline{)5.83}$

Mixed Practice • Place the decimal point in the answers.
Be sure to write zeros in the quotient if necessary.

9. $\overset{54}{8)\overline{0.432}}$

10. $\overset{86}{3)\overline{0.258}}$

11. $\overset{27}{52)\overline{1.404}}$

12. $\overset{9}{13)\overline{0.117}}$

Divide.

13. $6)\overline{1.47}$

14. $5)\overline{3.6}$

15. $35)\overline{2.17}$

16. $62)\overline{46.5}$

17. $70)\overline{2.38}$

18. $2)\overline{0.618}$

19. $48)\overline{2.928}$

20. $79)\overline{3.16}$

21. $82)\overline{36.9}$

22. $51)\overline{2.907}$

23. $28)\overline{0.252}$

24. $46)\overline{03.45}$

25. $9)\overline{6.885}$

26. $18)\overline{13.23}$

27. $44)\overline{85.8}$

28. $80)\overline{21.36}$

29. $0.78 \div 65 = \underline{\quad?\quad}$

30. $1.976 \div 8 = \underline{\quad?\quad}$

31. $2.242 \div 59 = \underline{\quad?\quad}$

★ 32. $2.418 \div \underline{\quad?\quad} = 0.026$ ★ 33. $102.6 \div \underline{\quad?\quad} = 1.35$ ★ 34. $34.03 \div \underline{\quad?\quad} = 0.415$

★ 35. Choose two decimal numbers greater than 1.
Find the product.

$1.08 \times 1.3 = 1.404$

Is the product greater than or less than the two factors?
Try other examples. Do you get the same results?

Is the product always greater than or less than the two factors?

PROBLEM SOLVING • APPLICATIONS

36. There are 7 white blood cells
side by side. The distance across
the cells is 0.084 millimeters.
What is the approximate
distance across one blood cell?

★ 37. A child who weighs 36 kilograms
has about 2.35 liters of blood.
About how many liters of blood
is there for each kilogram of
body weight? Divide to the
nearest thousandth.

Skills Maintenance

1. 24 in. = $\underline{\quad?\quad}$ ft

2. 3 yd = $\underline{\quad?\quad}$ in.

3. 4 mi = $\underline{\quad?\quad}$ ft

4. 2 qt = $\underline{\quad?\quad}$ fl. oz

5. 2 gal = $\underline{\quad?\quad}$ c

6. 3 lb = $\underline{\quad?\quad}$ oz

7. 2 ft, 2 ft

Perimeter = $\underline{\quad?\quad}$

8.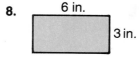

Area = $\underline{\quad?\quad}$

9.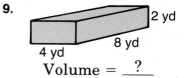

Volume = $\underline{\quad?\quad}$

Estimate to place the decimal point in the answers. (pages 308–309)

1.	6.8	2.	1.9	3.	7.28	4.	94.5
	× 6		×5.4		× 1.3		×6.27
	408		1026		9464		592515

Multiply. (pages 310–313)

5.	1.8	6.	7.03	7.	5.58	8.	39.9
	×2.5		× 9.4		× 0.7		×0.41

9.	8.2	10.	0.119	11.	9.5	12.	4.83
	×0.04		× 7		×0.08		× 0.6

Multiply. (pages 314–315)

13. $10 \times 9.53 =$ ___?___

14. $100 \times 8.36 =$ ___?___

15. $100 \times 0.167 =$ ___?___

16. $1,000 \times 0.89 =$ ___?___

Divide. (pages 318–321)

17. $3\overline{)67.2}$　　18. $7\overline{)107.8}$　　19. $23\overline{)137.08}$　　20. $59\overline{)203.55}$

21. $8\overline{)0.064}$　　22. $5\overline{)2.09}$　　23. $56\overline{)3.64}$　　24. $35\overline{)3.08}$

Solve.

25. Brian is selling wheat and honey bars. Each bar has a mass of 0.01 kilogram. He has 24 bars. What is the total mass of all the bars? (p. 310)

26. Cindy is selling nut bars. A carton of nut bars has a mass of 0.9 kilograms and contains 36 bars. What is the mass of each nut bar? (p. 320)

PROJECT

Comparison Shopping

Dale is shopping for film for his camera. Park Photo sells 3 rolls of film for $11.97. Nichols Pharmacy sells 2 rolls of the same film for $8.38. Where should Dale buy his film to get the better buy?

To find the better buy, compare **unit prices**. The unit price is the cost of 1 roll of film. To find the unit price you can divide.

Step 1
Find the unit price at Park Photo.

$$
\begin{array}{r}
\$\ 3.99 \\
3\overline{)\$11.97} \\
-9\downarrow \\
\hline
2\,9 \\
-2\,7\downarrow \\
\hline
27 \\
-27 \\
\hline
0
\end{array}
$$

1 roll of film costs $3.99 at Park Photo.

Step 2
Find the unit price at Nichols Pharmacy.

$$
\begin{array}{r}
\$4.19 \\
2\overline{)\$8.38} \\
-8\downarrow \\
\hline
3 \\
-2\downarrow \\
\hline
18 \\
-18 \\
\hline
0
\end{array}
$$

1 roll of film costs $4.19 at Nichols Pharmacy.

Step 3
Compare the unit prices.

$3.99 < $4.19

1 roll for $3.99, or 3 rolls for $11.97, is the better buy.

Dale should buy his film at Park Photo to get the better buy.

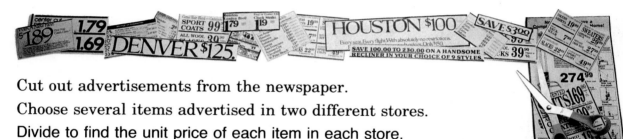

Cut out advertisements from the newspaper.

Choose several items advertised in two different stores.

Divide to find the unit price of each item in each store.

Then compare the unit prices to find the better buy.

TEST

Estimate to place the decimal point in the answers.

1.	42	2.	3.6	3.	84.2	4.	7.03
	×3.1		×5.1		× 1.9		×65.7
	1302		1836		15998		461871

Multiply.

5.	1.73	6.	84.81	7.	5.54	8.	2.76
	× 6		× 1.2		× 9.3		× 4.8

9.	0.85	10.	5.5	11.	93	12.	2.09
	× 0.1		×0.08		×0.12		× 0.6

Multiply.

13. $10 \times 2.3 =$ ___?___

14. $100 \times 5.889 =$ ___?___

15. $1,000 \times 3.292 =$ ___?___

16. $1,000 \times 0.68 =$ ___?___

Divide.

17. $2\overline{)7.08}$ 18. $8\overline{)2.696}$ 19. $35\overline{)96.25}$ 20. $61\overline{)741.15}$

21. $5\overline{)1.74}$ 22. $6\overline{)15.3}$ 23. $83\overline{)6.225}$ 24. $36\overline{)3.06}$

Solve.

25. Philip swims the length of the swimming pool 20 times. He swims a total distance of 1.5 kilometers. What is the length of the swimming pool?

26. Vicki jogs 8 laps around an oval track. Her average time for each lap is 2.5 minutes. About how many minutes does she jog in all?

ENRICHMENT

Checking Accounts

Philip bought a watch at the Clock Shop.
He paid for the watch with this check.
Philip's bank paid the Clock Shop's bank.
The money was taken from Philip's account.

Philip T. Blaine	212

July 29 19 85

Pay to the
order of _The Clock Shop_ $ _32.48_

Thirty-two and $\frac{48}{100}$ Dollars

Central City Bank
Anywhere, U.S.A.

Philip T Blaine

MEMO _____

⑈⦂0 ⦗23⦘456⦚⦂ 890⦘⦗2345⦙

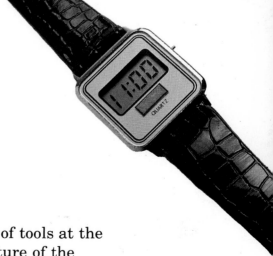

Use the check to answer the questions.

1. What is the number of this check?

2. What is the date on this check?

3. To whom is the check written?

4. What is the amount of the check?

5. Who signed this check?

6. In which bank does Philip have an account?

7. On July 31, 1985, Philip bought $84.50 worth of tools at the Fix-It-Shop. He paid with a check. Draw a picture of the completed check.

8. Last month Philip had $200.00 in his checking account. He wrote a check for $57.89. How much money did he have left in his checking account?

Philip always records the deposits that he makes to his account and the checks that he writes.

Check Number	Date	Item	Amount of Check		Amount of Deposit		Balance	
							425	40
214	8/4	B.I. Electric	27	90			397	50
215	8/31	Value Food Market	115	85			281	65
	9/2	Deposit			458	09	739	74
216	9/5	Valley Trust Bank	515	00			224	74
217	9/6	Eastern Telephone Co.	34	18				
	9/8	Deposit			327	19		
218	9/12	Water St. Furniture	98	75				
219	9/15	Hideaway Restaurant	46	50				

The balance column shows how much money is in Philip's account.

On August 31, the balance in Philip's account was $281.65.
He made a deposit on September 2 of $458.09.

Add the deposit to find the balance.

$$\begin{array}{r} \$281.65 \\ +\ \ 458.09 \\ \hline \$739.74 \end{array}$$

The balance on September 2 was $739.74.

On September 5, Philip wrote a check for $515.00.

Subtract the amount of the check.

$$\begin{array}{r} \$739.74 \\ -\ \ 515.00 \\ \hline \$224.74 \end{array}$$

The balance was $224.74.

Complete the record to show Philip's balance.

CALCULATOR

Fractions

You can use a calculator to find parts of a group. Find $\frac{2}{5}$ of 15.
Push 1 5 ÷ 5 × 2 =. The answer is 6. It may be easier to calculate
problems like $\frac{1}{2}$ of 4 in your head.

Use your calculator if you cannot find the answer in your head.

1. $\frac{8}{9}$ of 99 = __?__   2. $\frac{3}{6}$ of 24 = __?__   3. $\frac{1}{11}$ of 121 = __?__   4. $\frac{3}{4}$ of 64 = __?__

5. $\frac{1}{39}$ of 78 = __?__   6. $\frac{3}{35}$ of 70 = __?__   7. $\frac{3}{25}$ of 100 = __?__   8. $\frac{3}{2}$ of 84 = __?__

9. $\frac{2}{21}$ of 63 = __?__   10. $\frac{4}{4}$ of 86 = __?__   11. $\frac{9}{11}$ of 121 = __?__   12. $\frac{5}{47}$ of 47 = __?__

The calculator can help you find equivalent fractions.

$\frac{4}{9} = \frac{?}{279}$ Push 2 7 9 ÷ 9 =. The multiple is 31.

Push 3 1 × 4 =.   The answer is 124.

You can shorten these two steps by pushing 2 7 9 ÷ 9 × 4 =.

Again the answer is 124. This shows that $\frac{4}{9} = \frac{124}{279}$.

Find the equivalent fractions.

13. $\frac{5}{6} = \frac{?}{360}$ 14. $\frac{9}{8} = \frac{378}{?}$ 15. $\frac{0}{4} = \frac{?}{16}$ 16. $\frac{8}{9} = \frac{96}{?}$

17. $\frac{4}{6} = \frac{240}{?}$ 18. $\frac{7}{3} = \frac{?}{210}$ 19. $\frac{1}{2} = \frac{22}{?}$ 20. $\frac{3}{11} = \frac{33}{?}$

21. $\frac{6}{3} = \frac{600}{?}$ 22. $\frac{8}{7} = \frac{?}{210}$ 23. $\frac{10}{5} = \frac{440}{?}$ 24. $\frac{0}{3} = \frac{?}{287}$

25. $\frac{8}{2} = \frac{?}{422}$ 26. $\frac{4}{3} = \frac{?}{33}$ 27. $\frac{9}{4} = \frac{18}{?}$ 28. $\frac{7}{7} = \frac{?}{532}$

Choose the correct answers.

1. Add.

```
  13,657
   4,921
      87
+    699
```

- **A.** 17,653
- **B.** 19,364
- **C.** 18,707
- **D.** not here

2. Subtract.

```
 $156.02
−   99.56
```

- **A.** $65.54
- **B.** $56.46
- **C.** $112.19
- **D.** not here

3. Multiply.

$54 \times 279 = \underline{\quad?\quad}$

- **A.** 15,066
- **B.** 18,274
- **C.** 16,826
- **D.** not here

4. Name the ordered pair that locates point A.

- **A.** (0, 2)
- **B.** (3, 2)
- **C.** (2, 3)
- **D.** not here

5. Divide. Write the answer in lowest terms.

$$\frac{7}{8} \div \frac{1}{4} = \underline{\quad?\quad}$$

- **A.** $\frac{7}{32}$
- **B.** $2\frac{3}{4}$
- **C.** $4\frac{1}{2}$
- **D.** not here

6. Find the length to the nearest centimeter.

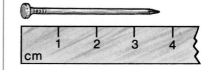

- **A.** 4
- **B.** 35
- **C.** 3
- **D.** not here

7. Find the volume.

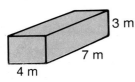

- **A.** 28 cubic centimeters
- **B.** 84 cubic meters
- **C.** 76 square meters
- **D.** not here

8. Add.

$16.42 + 9.7 = \underline{\quad?\quad}$

- **A.** 6.72
- **B.** 26.12
- **C.** 25.49
- **D.** not here

9. Subtract.

```
  4.2
−2.95
```

- **A.** 6.15
- **B.** 2.75
- **C.** 1.25
- **D.** not here

10. Mr. Hsu walks 6.8 kilometers every day. How far does he walk in one week?

- **A.** 4.76 km
- **B.** 47.6 km
- **C.** 34 km
- **D.** not here

11. Joan drove 356.5 kilometers in 4 hours. What was her average speed in kilometers per hour?

- **A.** 89.125 km/h
- **B.** 76.92 km/h
- **C.** 84.75 km/h
- **D.** not here

Geometry

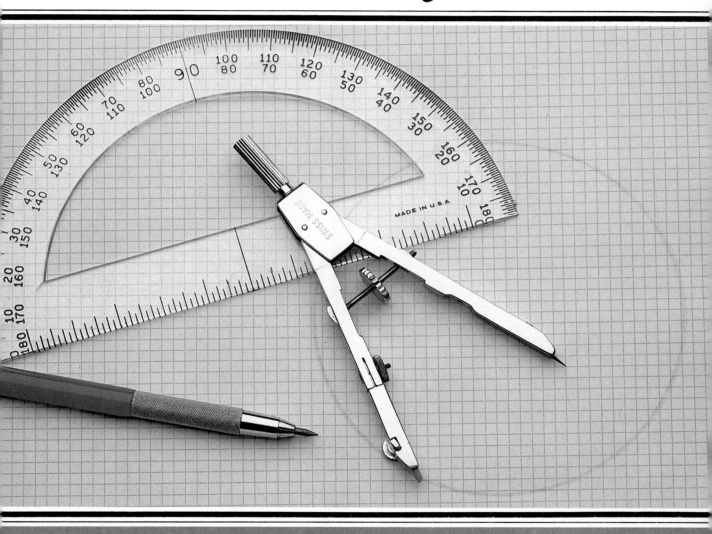

**Vocabulary of Geometry • Angles • Using a
Protractor • Parallel and Perpendicular Lines
• Problem Solving: Making a Drawing • Polygons
• Congruent Polygons • Similar Polygons
• Constructing a Circle • Lines of Symmetry
• Solid Figures • Circumference of a Circle**

Vocabulary of Geometry

A **line segment** is straight. It has two **endpoints**. A segment is named by its endpoints.

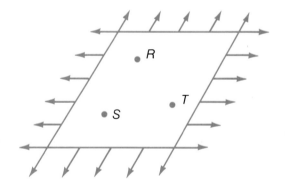

Line segment AB ($\overline{AB}$)
or Line segment BA ($\overline{BA}$)

A **line** has no endpoints. It goes on forever in both directions. A line is named by two of its points.

Line DE ($\overleftrightarrow{DE}$)
or Line ED ($\overleftrightarrow{ED}$)

A **ray** has one endpoint. It goes on forever in one direction only. Name the endpoint first.

Ray PQ ($\overrightarrow{PQ}$)

A **plane** is a flat surface that goes on forever in all directions. Points R, S, and T all lie in the same plane.

Practice • Name the figures.

1.

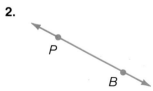

2.

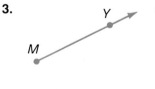

3.

4.

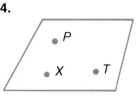

Mixed Practice • Name the figures.

5. $\overleftrightarrow{MJ}$

6. $\overline{RS}$

7. $\overrightarrow{SW}$

8. $\overrightarrow{AB}$

9. $\overrightarrow{YZ}$

10. $\overrightarrow{GH}$

11. plane *M N O*

12. $\overleftrightarrow{DE}$

Draw the figures.

13. Draw points A and B. Then draw $\overline{AB}$.

14. Draw points C and D. Then draw $\overrightarrow{CD}$.

15. Draw points E and F. Then draw $\overleftrightarrow{FE}$.

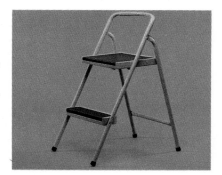

Congruent line segments have the same length.
Are the segments congruent?

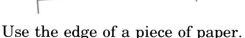

Use the edge of a piece of paper.
Make a mark at each endpoint of
one segment.

Test the other segment.
If the endpoints match, then the
segments are congruent.

Are the segments congruent? Write YES or NO.

★ **16.**

★ **17.**

PROBLEM SOLVING • APPLICATIONS

Draw points *X* and *Y*. Then answer the questions.

18. How many line segments can you draw with endpoints X and Y?

19. How many lines can you draw through points X and Y?

★ **20.** How many lines can you draw through point X?

331

Angles

Two rays that have the same endpoint form an **angle**.

The endpoint of both rays is the **vertex**.

The rays are the sides of the angle.

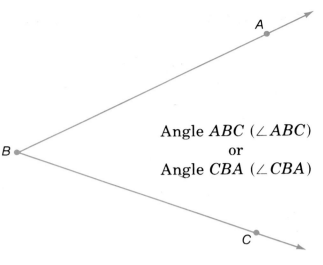

Angle *ABC* (∠*ABC*)
or
Angle *CBA* (∠*CBA*)

The unit of measure for an angle is a **degree** (1°).

One degree

The measure of a right angle is 90°.

The measure of an **acute angle** is greater than 0° and less than 90°.

The measure of an **obtuse angle** is greater than 90° and less than 180°.

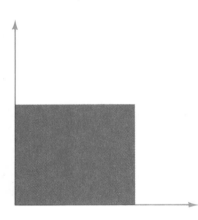

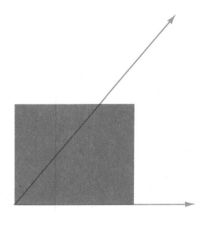

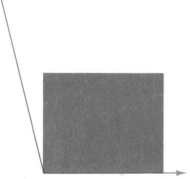

Practice • Name the angle. Write RIGHT, ACUTE, or OBTUSE.

1.

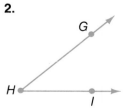

2.

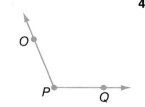

3.

4.

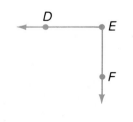

Mixed Practice • Name the angle. Write RIGHT, ACUTE, or OBTUSE.

5.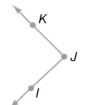

6.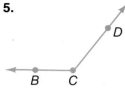

7.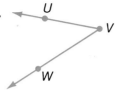

8.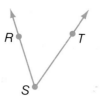

9.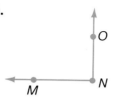

10.

11.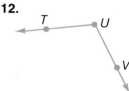

12.

The hands on a clock often form an angle.
The hands on this clock form a right angle.

What kind of angle is formed by the hands of each clock?

13.

14.

15.

16.

PROBLEM SOLVING • APPLICATIONS

Willy is standing at point *W*.
When he walks a straight path to a letter, an angle is formed.
Write RIGHT, ACUTE, or OBTUSE
for each angle named.

17. ∠*VWA*   **18.** ∠*VWB*

19. ∠*VWC*   **20.** ∠*VWD*

21. ∠*VWE*   **22.** ∠*VWF*

Skills Maintenance

1. 9.7 +1.6	**2.** 68.3 +14.9	**3.** 31.47 +56.08	**4.** 3.200 +5.560	**5.** 1.248 +8.962
6. 15.96 + 9.14	**7.** 99.78 + 0.22	**8.** 56.93 +21.46	**9.** 82.70 +19.39	**10.** 74.06 +27.93

Using a Protractor

You can use a **protractor** to measure angles.

Place the protractor so that the center mark is on the vertex of the angle and the edge is on one side of the angle. Read the scale where the other side crosses the protractor.

There are two numbers where the other side crosses the protractor. The numbers are 30 and 150. Since ∠XYZ is acute, the measure of ∠XYZ is 30°.

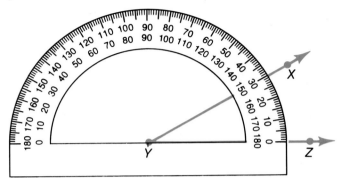

For ∠DEF, the two numbers on the scale are 120 and 60. Since ∠DEF is obtuse, the measure of ∠DEF is 120°.

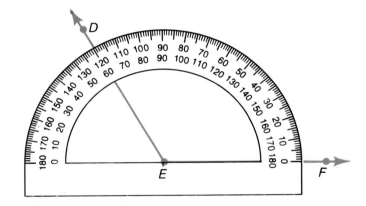

You can use a protractor to draw angles.

Follow the directions.

Draw ∠ABC with a measure of 65°.

1. Draw $\overrightarrow{BC}$.

2. Place the protractor so that the centermark is at point B.

3. Line up the 0° mark with $\overrightarrow{BC}$.

4. Locate point A at the 65° mark.

5. Draw $\overrightarrow{BA}$.

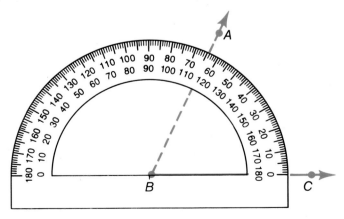

334

Practice • Measure the angles.

1.

2.

3.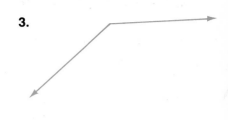

Mixed Practice • Measure the angles.

4.

5.

6.

Use a protractor to draw the angles.

7. 50°   **8.** 45°   **9.** 140°   **10.** 155°   **11.** 95°   **12.** 25°

Congruent angles have
the same measure.
The measure of ∠LMN is 60°.
The measure of ∠XYZ is 60°.
∠LMN is congruent to ∠XYZ.

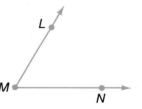

Measure each angle. Then use your protractor to draw a congruent angle.

★ **13.**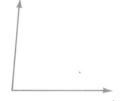

★ **14.**

★ **15.**

PROBLEM SOLVING • APPLICATIONS

★ **16.** Draw a triangle.
Measure each angle.
Add the measures.
What is the sum?
Find the sum of the angles of
several triangles. Is the sum
always the same?

★ **17.** Draw a rectangle.
Measure each angle.
Add the measures.
What is the sum?
If you draw a diagonal line
from one corner to another,
what will you have?

Parallel, Intersecting, and Perpendicular Lines

Lines that are always the same distance apart are **parallel lines**.

Parallel lines can never meet. The rails of a straight train track are parallel.

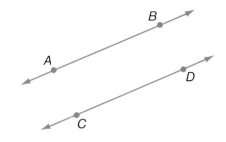

$\overleftrightarrow{AB}$ is parallel to $\overleftrightarrow{CD}$.

Lines that meet or cross each other are **intersecting lines**.

Two lines intersect at a point. The crossing guard is at the intersection of First Street and Flower Avenue.

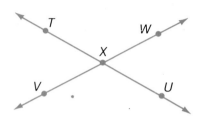

$\overleftrightarrow{TU}$ intersects $\overleftrightarrow{VW}$ at X.

Lines that intersect to form right angles are **perpendicular lines**.

Most of the time you stand perpendicular to the floor.

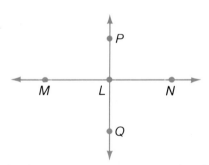

$\overleftrightarrow{PQ}$ is perpendicular to $\overleftrightarrow{MN}$.

Practice • Write PARALLEL, INTERSECTING, or PERPENDICULAR.

1.

2.

3.

4.
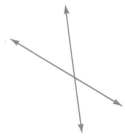

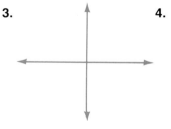

Mixed Practice • Write PARALLEL, INTERSECTING, or PERPENDICULAR.

5.

6.

7.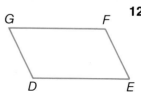

8.

Name the parallel segments. Name the perpendicular segments.

9.

10.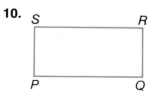

11.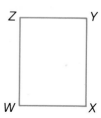

12.

PROBLEM SOLVING • APPLICATIONS

13. Draw parallel lines $\overleftrightarrow{PK}$ and $\overleftrightarrow{TR}$.

14. Draw intersecting lines $\overleftrightarrow{MJ}$ and $\overleftrightarrow{FC}$.

15. Draw perpendicular lines $\overleftrightarrow{RT}$ and $\overleftrightarrow{QZ}$.

16. Look at a wall of a room. Can you find examples of parallel lines? What about the top and the bottom edges of the wall? Find another example. Find examples of perpendicular lines.

Midchapter Review

Name the figures.

1.

2.

3.

4.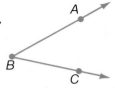

Write RIGHT, ACUTE, or OBTUSE. Then measure the angle.

Write PARALLEL, INTERSECTING, or PERPENDICULAR.

5.

6.

7.

8.

PROBLEM SOLVING • STRATEGIES

Making a Drawing

You can make a drawing to help you solve a problem.

Gretchen's horse Lightning bolts through the barn door. It gallops east 3.2 kilometers. Then it turns and trots west 1.8 kilometers. In which direction should Lightning go to take the shortest route back to the barn? How far must Lightning go?

Draw a ray going to the right. Label it 3.2 km east. Then draw a ray going to the left. Label it 1.8 km west.

The drawing shows that Lightning must continue to go west to get back to the barn.

Subtract to find out how far Lightning must go.

$$\begin{array}{r} 3.2 \\ -1.8 \\ \hline 1.4 \end{array}$$

3.2 km east

1.8 km west

Lightning must go west for 1.4 kilometers.

Make drawings to help you solve the problems.

1. A ranch hand rides out looking for Lightning. He rides north from the ranch house. After riding 4.7 kilometers, he turns and rides south for 2.1 kilometers. How far from the ranch house is he?

   Label your drawings with the correct measures.

2. Another ranch hand rides west from the ranch house for 3.2 kilometers. Then she turns east and rides 2.4 kilometers. How far from the ranch house is she?

3. Gretchen rides out to capture Lightning. She rides east 1.4 kilometers and then returns. How far does she ride in all?

Solve. Make drawings to help you.

4. The ranch manager rides southeast for a distance of 3.8 kilometers. He stops to check the shoes on his horse. Then he rides on in the same direction for another 2.7 kilometers. How far from the ranch house is he?

5. There is a fence around the edge of the ranch property. Pete rides along the fence to check it. The property is in the shape of a rectangle. It measures 4 kilometers by 2.5 kilometers How far does Pete ride?

Remember to use the correct unit of measure in your answer.

6. The barn measures 27 meters by by 15 meters. What is the area of the floor of the barn?

7. Gretchen has a flower garden behind the ranch house. It is in the shape of a square. One side is 2.8 meters long. How many square meters of garden area does she have?

8. A small corral is in the shape of a triangle. Each side measures 7.8 meters. What is the perimeter of the corral?

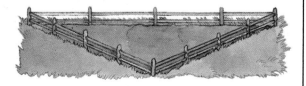

9. Butch builds a watering trough. It measures 3.2 meters by 0.54 meters by 0.4 meters. What is the volume of the trough?

10. Butch rides north for 3 hours at a rate of 10 kilometers per hour. How far is he from the ranch house?

11. The cook rides to town for supplies. He rides 5.6 kilometers west and then returns. How far did he ride in all?

★ 12. The bunkhouse measures 12 meters by 7 meters. If the walls are 20 centimeters thick, what is the area of the floor of the bunkhouse?

★ 13. A bale of hay measures 1.5 meters by 0.7 meters by 0.7 meters. The ranch stores 75 bales in part of a shed. How many cubic meters of space are used?

Polygons

The sides of a **polygon** are line segments.
The sides meet to form angles.
Line segments with the same length are **congruent**.

Names are given to polygons according to the
number of sides and the number of angles they have.
Triangles are polygons that have three sides.
Some triangles have special names.

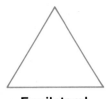 

Equilateral
There are three
congruent sides.

Isosceles
There are at least
two congruent sides.

Scalene
There are no
congruent sides.

Quadrilaterals are polygons that have four sides.
Some quadrilaterals have special names.

Parallelogram
A quadrilateral
whose opposite sides
are parallel and
congruent

Rhombus
A parallelogram
with four
congruent sides

Rectangle
A parallelogram
with four right
angles

Square
A rectangle
with four
congruent sides

Other polygons that have more than four sides and four angles are
shown below.

Pentagon
5 sides, 5 angles

Hexagon
6 sides, 6 angles

Octagon
8 sides, 8 angles

Decagon
10 sides, 10 angles

Practice • Name the polygons.

1.    2.   3.    4.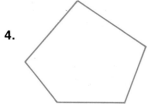

340

Mixed Practice • Name the polygons.

5.

6.

7.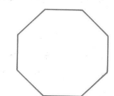

8.

9. a triangle with no congruent sides

10. a rectangle with four congruent sides

11. a parallelogram with four congruent sides

12. a triangle with only two congruent sides

13. a polygon with ten sides

How many sides does each polygon have?

14. decagon

15. parallelogram

16. pentagon

17. octagon

★ 18. Are all squares quadrilaterals?

★ 19. Are all parallelograms quadrilaterals?

★ 20. Are all rectangles parallelograms?

★ 21. Are all rectangles quadrilaterals?

Find the missing measures.

★ 22.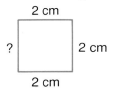
2 cm
? 2 cm
2 cm

★ 23.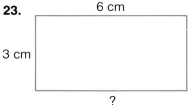
6 cm
3 cm
?

★ 24.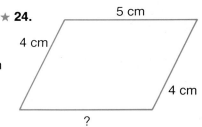
5 cm
4 cm
3 cm
4 cm
?

PROBLEM SOLVING • APPLICATIONS

A, B, C, and D are vertices of rectangle $ABCD$. A **diagonal** is a line segment that joins two vertices of a polygon but is not a side of the polygon. $\overline{AC}$ and $\overline{BD}$ are diagonals of the rectangle $ABCD$.

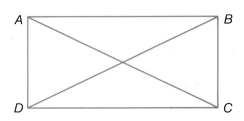

25. Trace a pentagon and a hexagon. Draw the diagonals. How many does each polygon have?

★ 26. Trace a decagon. Draw the diagonals. How many diagonals does it have?

Congruent Polygons

Congruent polygons have the same size and shape.

Is quadrilateral *ABCD* congruent to quadrilateral *WXYZ*?

Trace quadrilateral *ABCD*.
Slide and turn the tracing
to fit over quadrilateral *WXYZ*.

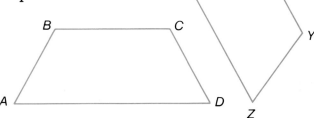

Quadrilateral *ABCD* is congruent to quadrilateral *WXYZ*.

Is triangle *MNO* congruent
to triangle *PQR*?

Trace triangle *MNO*.
Cut it out. Flip it over.
Slide it to fit on triangle *PQR*.

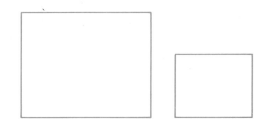

Triangle *MNO* is congruent to triangle *PQR*.

These polygons are not congruent.

These polygons look somewhat alike.
Why are they not congruent?

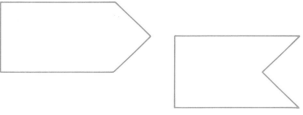

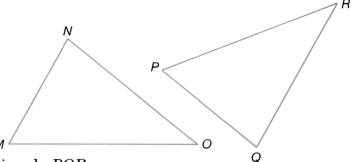

Practice • Are they congruent? Write YES or NO.

Use a tracing to help you.

1.

2.

Mixed Practice • Are they congruent? Write YES or NO.

Use a tracing to help you.

3.

4.

Find two pairs of congruent polygons.

5. a.    b.    c.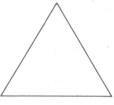

d.    e.    f.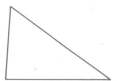

Look at the figures below.

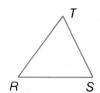 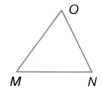

Corresponding Lines	Corresponding Angles
$\overline{MO}$ and $\overline{RT}$	$\angle OMN$ amd $\angle TRS$
$\overline{ON}$ and $\overline{TS}$	$\angle MNO$ amd $\angle RST$
$\overline{MN}$ and $\overline{RS}$	$\angle NOM$ amd $\angle STR$

Name the corresponding parts for the figures below.

6.

PROBLEM SOLVING • APPLICATIONS

Write the letter to tell where the piece fits. You can slide, turn, and flip.

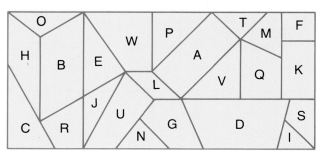

★ 7.

★ 8.

★ 9.

★ 10.

343

Similar Polygons

Similar polygons have the same shape.

Rectangle *ABCD* is similar to
rectangle *EFGH*.

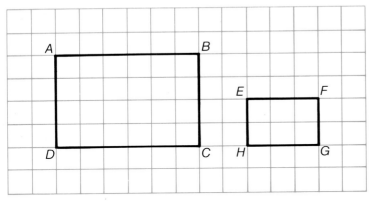

Why are these polygons not similar?

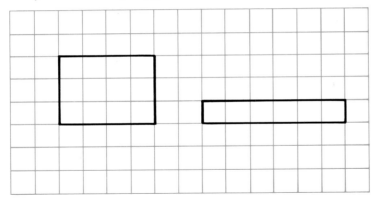

Practice • Are they similar? Write YES or NO.

1.   **2.**   **3.**

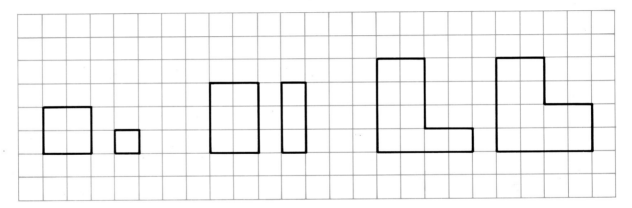

Mixed Practice • Are they similar? Write YES or NO.

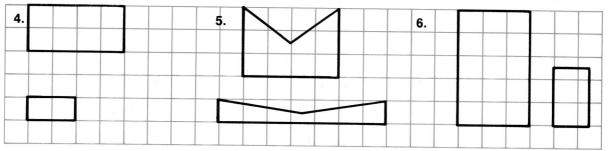

Use grid paper. Draw a polygon similar to the one shown.
Make each side twice as long.

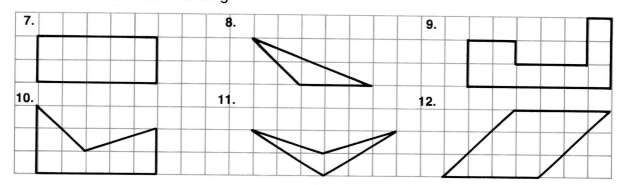

Which shape in the row is similar to the first shape?

13.

a   b   c

14.

a   b   c

★ **15.** Are congruent figures similar?   ★ **16.** Are similar figures congruent?

PROBLEM SOLVING • APPLICATIONS

Draw a polygon. Use the measures shown. Then multiply the length of each side
by 3. Draw a similar polygon using the new measures.

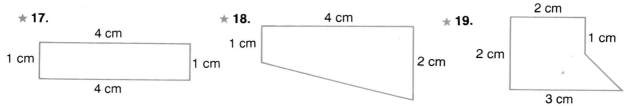

★ **17.**
1 cm   4 cm   1 cm   4 cm

★ **18.**
4 cm   1 cm   2 cm

★ **19.**
2 cm   2 cm   1 cm   3 cm

Constructing a Circle

Step 1

Use your compass. Put the metal tip on a point. Swing the pencil around.

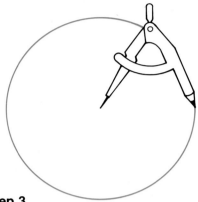

Step 2

You have constructed a circle. Point *A* is the **center**. This is circle *A*.

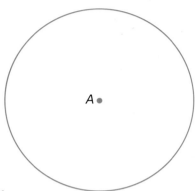

Step 3

Draw a line segment that joins the center and a point on the circle. You have drawn a **radius**. How many more could you draw?

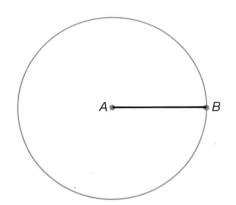

Step 4

Draw a line segment through the center that joins two points on the circle. You have drawn a **diameter**. How many more could you draw?

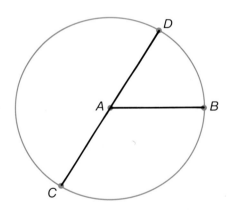

Practice • Use a centimeter ruler to measure.

1. What is the name of the circle?

2. How long is radius *AN*?

3. How long is radius *AM*?

4. If you drew another radius for Circle *A*, how long would it be?

5. How long is diameter *LN*?

6. How is the length of diameter *LN* related to the length of radius *LA*?

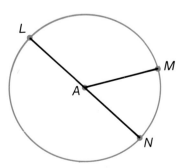

Mixed Practice • Study the circle.

7. Name the circle.

8. Name 3 radii.

9. Name a diameter.

10. Name 1 obtuse angle.

11. Name 1 acute angle.

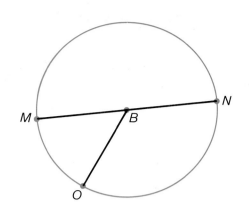

Complete the table.

	12.	13.	14.	15.	16.	17.	18.	19.
Radius	3 m	5 cm	?	?	18 cm	?	1.8 cm	?
Diameter	?	?	16 cm	22 cm	?	6.8 cm	?	9.4 cm

Draw a line segment with the length given.
Use it as a radius to construct a circle.

20. 3 cm   21. 4 cm   22. 5 cm   23. 6 cm   24. 7.5 cm

A **chord** connects two points on a circle.
$\overline{RS}$ is a chord.

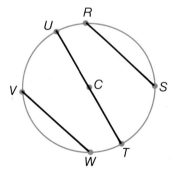

★ 25. Name the segments that are chords.

★ 26. Name the longest chord.

PROBLEM SOLVING • APPLICATIONS

★ 27. Cross out five toothpicks and
leave three squares the same size.

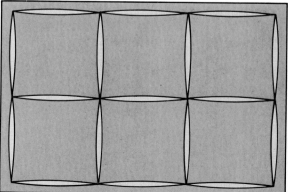

Lines of Symmetry

Trace the figure and the dotted line. Cut the figure out. Fold along the dotted line. Do the halves match?

The figure is **symmetric**. The dotted line is a **line of symmetry**. The line is a **vertical** line of symmetry.

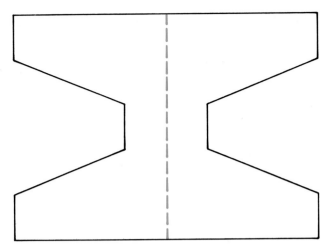

Unfold the figure. Now fold it along the line shown in the small picture. The line is a **horizontal** line of symmetry.

How many lines of symmetry have you found for this figure?

Are there other lines of symmetry for this figure?

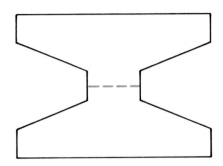

Trace the parallelogram and cut it out.

How many lines of symmetry does this figure have?

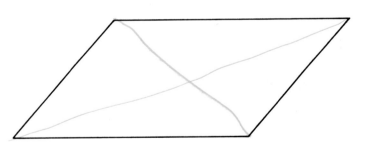

Practice • Is the dotted line a line of symmetry for the figure? Write YES or NO.

1.
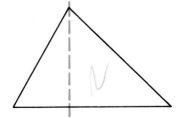

2.
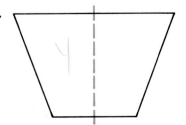

3.
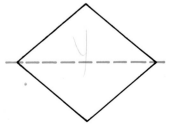

Mixed Practice • The figures have two lines of symmetry. One is shown. Trace the figures. Show the other line of symmetry.

4.

5.

6.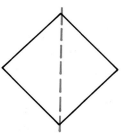

Trace the figures. Draw all the lines of symmetry.

7.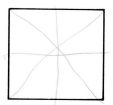

8.

9.

Trace each drawing. Then complete it to make a figure that is symmetric.

10.

11.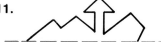

12.

PROBLEM SOLVING • APPLICATIONS

A figure can be flipped about a line of symmetry. This gives you a mirror image of the figure.

Does the picture show a mirror image? Write YES or NO.

★ 13.

★ 14.

15. Can you think of any words that have a line of symmetry?

Skills Maintenance

1. 6.8
   −0.9

2. 15.7
   − 6.8

3. 0.4
   −0.35

4. 0.91
   −0.85

5. 1.000
   −0.308

6. 78.62
   −59.55

7. 46.2
   − 8.94

8. 76.04
   −29.56

9. 54.27
   − 9.89

10. 98.16
   −89.47

Solid Figures

This solid figure is a **cube**.
Each flat surface of a cube is a **face**.
A cube has 6 faces.
The shape of each face is a square.
Two faces meet at an **edge**.
Edges meet at a **vertex**.
The cube rests on its **base**.

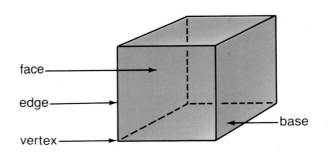

face
edge
vertex
base

The cube and these solid figures are **prisms**.
The shape of the base is used to name the prism.
What is the shape of the other faces of each of these prisms?

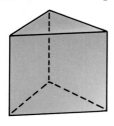
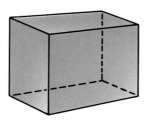
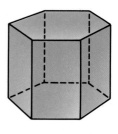

| Triangular Prism | Rectangular Prism | Hexagonal Prism |

These solid figures are **pyramids**.
The shape of the base is used to name the pyramid.
What is the shape of the other faces of each of these pyramids?

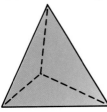
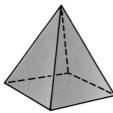
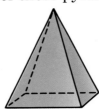
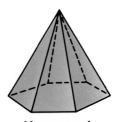

| Triangular Pyramid | Square Pyramid | Rectangular Pyramid | Hexagonal Pyramid |

Here are some other special solid figures.

Cylinder   **Cone**   **Sphere**

Practice • Name the shapes.

1.

2.

3.

4.

Mixed Practice • Name the shapes.

5.

6.

7.

8.

Complete.

	Figure	Number of Faces	Number of Edges	Number of Vertices
★ 9.	Cube	6	?	?
★ 10.	Triangular prism	?	?	?
★ 11.	Hexagonal pyramid	?	?	?
★ 12.	Hexagonal prism	?	?	?
★ 13.	Triangular pyramid	?	?	?

PROBLEM SOLVING • APPLICATIONS

Trace each pattern and cut it out. Fold along the dotted lines.
Tape the edges together. What solid figure did you make?

★ 14.

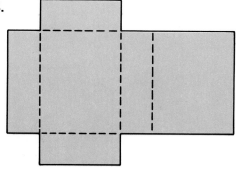

★ 15.

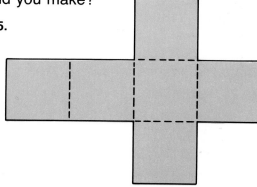

Name the figures. (pages 330–331)

1.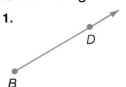

2.

3.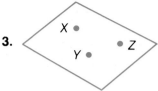

Name and measure the angles. Write RIGHT, ACUTE, or OBTUSE. (pages 332–335)

4.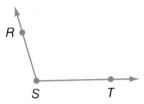

5.

6.

Write PARALLEL, INTERSECTING, or PERPENDICULAR. (pages 336–337)

7.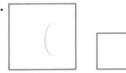

8.

9.

Name the figures. Then write CONGRUENT or SIMILAR. (pages 340–345)

10.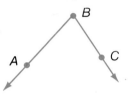

11.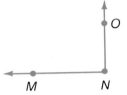

12.

Study the circle. (pages 346–347)

13. Name the center.

14. Name 3 radii.

15. Name a diameter.

Name the shapes. (pages 350–351)

16.

17.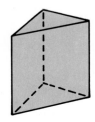

18.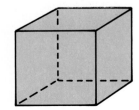

PROJECT

Printing Shapes

Here are some shapes that you have seen before.

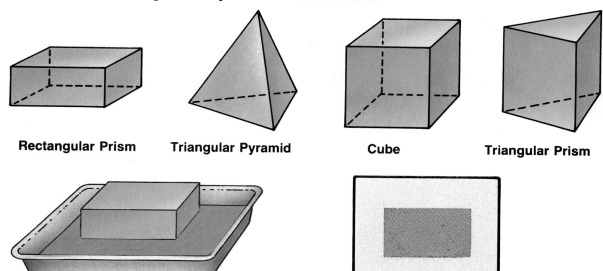

Rectangular Prism   **Triangular Pyramid**   **Cube**   **Triangular Prism**

Dip one face of a rectangular prism into poster paint. Make a print.

The print is shaped like a rectangle. What shape does the face have?

Make a print of each of the other faces of the rectangular prism. Name the shape of each face.

Make a print of each face of the other solid figures. Name the shape of each face.

On a poster arrange your prints for each solid figure.

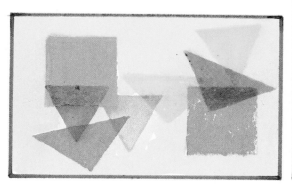

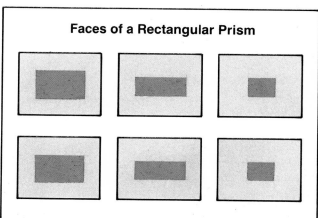

Faces of a Rectangular Prism

Name the figures.

1.

2.

3.

Name and measure the angles. Write RIGHT, ACUTE, or OBTUSE.

4.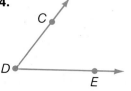

5.

6.

Write PARALLEL, INTERSECTING, or PERPENDICULAR.

7.

8.

9.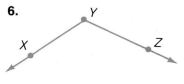

Name the figures. Then write CONGRUENT or SIMILAR.

10.

11.

12.

Study the circle.

13. Name a diameter.

14. Name a right angle.

15. Name 3 radii.

Name the shapes.

16.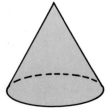

17.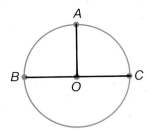

18.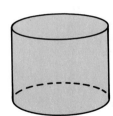

354

Circumference of a Circle

The distance around a circle is its **circumference**. You can compare the circumference of a circle to the length of its diameter.

Step 1
Place a string around a record. The length of the string is the circumference.

Step 2
Mark off on the string the diameter of the record. The string is a little longer than 3 diameters.

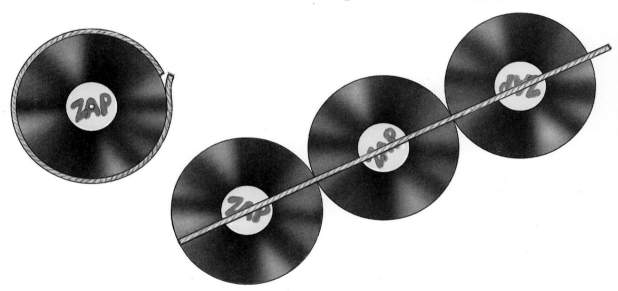

Measure the circumference and the diameter for each object listed. Measure to the nearest tenth of a centimeter.

Record your results in a chart similar to the one below.

Object	Circumference (cm)	Diameter (cm)
Quarter	?	?
Pencil holder	?	?
Roll of tape	?	?
Nickel	?	?
Cup	?	?

Compare each circumference and diameter.

Is the circumference a little longer than 3 diameters?

COMPUTER

Advanced Flowcharting

Flowcharts are very useful for planning programs in a step-by-step way.
Boxes of specific shape are used to indicate specific types of functions.

Initialization is done to set up the basic control of the program.
Input types are requested.
Specific processes are requested.
Output types are requested.
Flow direction is usually from top to bottom and from left to right.

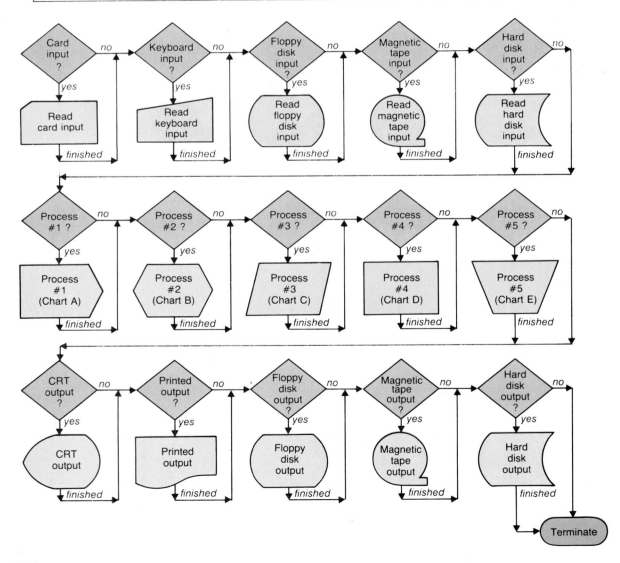

For any specific flowchart:

a. Boxes can be put in any *order* for the specific program purposes.

b. Different-shaped boxes can be added for needed program purposes.

c. Shapes that are never used can be *dropped*. If you know you always have card input, for example, you do not need a decision box for it. Just use "card input" at the start of the system.

The flowchart on page 356 could be a system flowchart since it includes input, process, and output.

Detailed flowcharts are usually needed for each process. Labels on a system flowchart indicate which processes have detailed flowcharts. Note the labels for Charts A through E on page 356.

Draw flowcharts for the following systems.

1. Card input, always two processes done, printed output

2. Card input *or* keyboard input, one process, CRT *or* printed output

3. Hard-disk input, one process, hard-disk output

4. Floppy-disk input, any of two processes, magnetic-tape output

5. Put all the following decisions and processes into proper flowchart boxes. Then arrange the boxes into a workable flowchart. You may need to use some of the boxes more than once. Use ▭ for process boxes.

Take off overcoat	Have breakfast	Get out *no* of bed	Is it cold *yes* outside?
Come back inside	Get dressed	Play outside	Put on overcoat

6. Which one box, above, can be put in different places?

7. Look for examples of flowcharts in newspapers and magazines. Copy them on paper and bring the paper to class to discuss.

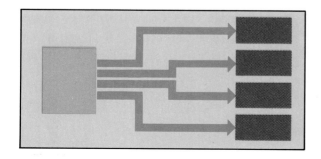

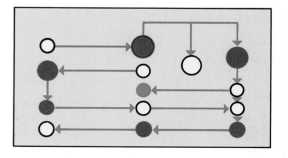

Choose the correct answers.

1. Add.

6,074 + 598 = __?__

   A. 5,476
   B. 6,672
   C. 6,592
   D. not here

2. Subtract.

$156.70
− 89.75

   A. $58.29
   B. $77.65
   C. $66.95
   D. not here

3. Multiply.

$874 \times 19 =$ __?__

   A. 16,606
   B. 15,927
   C. 160,560
   D. not here

4. Divide.

$9,427 \div 18 =$ __?__

   A. 486
   B. 508 r12
   C. 523 r13
   D. not here

5. Find the least common multiple.

4, 5

   A. 12
   B. 15
   C. 20
   D. not here

6. Add. Write the answer in lowest terms.

$$7\frac{3}{4} + 2\frac{2}{5} = \underline{\ ?\ }$$

   A. $9\frac{1}{2}$ **B.** $10\frac{3}{20}$
   C. $10\frac{2}{3}$ **D.** not here

7. Find the perimeter.

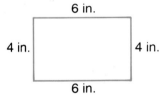

   A. 12 in.   **B.** 18 in.
   C. 24 in.   **D.** not here

8. Add.

7.272
+8.698

   A. 16.974
   B. 15.97
   C. 15.826
   D. not here

9. Name the figure.

   A. line segment
   B. line
   C. ray
   D. not here

10. Stanley buys 3 gallons of apple juice for a party. How many cups is this?

   A. 12
   B. 24
   C. 48
   D. not here

11. Paige travels 12.6 kilometers to work. Her cousin Beth travels 0.8 times as far to meet her. How far does Beth travel?

   A. 14.2 km
   B. 10.08 km
   C. 10.56 km
   D. not here

Ratio and Percent

Ratio • Equal Ratios • Ratio and Money • Time,
Rate, and Distance • Scale Drawing • Percent
• Decimals and Fractions for Percents • Problem
Solving: Circle Graphs • Probability and
Predictions • Sales Tax

Ratio

Ratio is one way of comparing numbers.

How many ducks do you see? How many owls?
The ratio of ducks to owls is 3 to 2.

Here are three ways to show the ratio.

$$3 \text{ to } 2 \qquad 3:2 \qquad \frac{3}{2}$$

There are other ways to compare the birds.

The ratio of owls to ducks is 2 to 3.
The fraction $\frac{2}{3}$ names this ratio.

The ratio of owls to birds is 2 to 5.
Which fraction names this ratio, $\frac{2}{5}$ or $\frac{5}{2}$?

The ratio of ducks to birds is 3 to 5.
Which fraction names this ratio, $\frac{3}{5}$ or $\frac{5}{3}$?

Practice • Write a fraction to show each ratio.

1. robins to canaries

2. canaries to robins

3. robins to birds

4. 7 to 8   **5.** 2 to 3   **6.** 8 to 5   **7.** 4 to 11

8. 9:16   **9.** 15:7   **10.** 5:9   **11.** 8:28

More Practice • Write a fraction to show each ratio.

12. cardinals to bluejays

13. cages to birds

14. birds to feeders

15. turkeys to chickens

16. penguins to birds

17. eagles to nests

18. 3 to 4

19. 1 to 5

20. 7 to 10

21. 6 to 3

22. 10 to 13

23. 9 to 4

24. 4 to 9

25. 8 to 1

26. 17 to 15

27. 21 to 23

28. 6 to 6

29. 24 to 27

30. 12 : 5

★ **31.** 143 : 100

★ **32.** 180 : 5

★ **33.** 166 : 100

PROBLEM SOLVING • APPLICATIONS

34. There are 4 crows and 3 worms. What is the ratio of crows to worms?

35. There are 3 eggs in a nest. What is the ratio of nests to eggs?

★ **36.** Yoshi has 4 yellow parakeets, 3 blue parakeets, and 2 cages. What is the ratio of birds to cages?

★ **37.** Marcia bought 2 kilograms of birdseed, 3 kilograms of sunflower seeds, and 1 kilogram of thistle seeds. What is the ratio of kilograms of seeds to kilograms of sunflower seeds?

★ **38.** Bleeker buys a bird feeder that costs $27. She has only $5 bills and $1 bills. She has eleven bills in all. What is the ratio of $5 bills to $1 bills?

Equal Ratios

Roland works at the Star Restaurant.

He is making turkey sandwiches.

He uses 3 slices of turkey for each 2 slices of bread.
The ratio is $\frac{3}{2}$.

There are 6 slices of turkey for each 4 slices of bread.
The ratio is $\frac{6}{4}$.

$\frac{3}{2}$ and $\frac{6}{4}$ are **equal ratios**. $\frac{3}{2} = \frac{6}{4}$

Suppose you know that the ratio of slices of turkey to
slices of bread is $\frac{3}{2}$.

You also know there are 12 slices of turkey.
How many slices of bread are there?

Think:

$$\text{turkey} \longrightarrow \frac{3}{2} = \frac{12}{?} \longleftarrow \text{turkey} \atop \longleftarrow \text{bread}$$

$4 \times 3 = 12$, and so
$4 \times 2 = 8$.

There are 8 slices of bread.
The ratio of slices of turkey to slices of bread is $\frac{3}{2}$.

There are 10 slices of bread.
How many slices of turkey are there?

Think:

$$\text{turkey} \longrightarrow \frac{3}{2} = \frac{?}{10} \longleftarrow \text{turkey} \atop \longleftarrow \text{bread}$$

$5 \times 2 = 10$, and so
$5 \times 3 = 15$.

There are 15 slices of turkey.

Practice • Complete.

1. $\frac{3}{4} = \frac{?}{12}$

2. $\frac{8}{5} = \frac{?}{20}$

3. $\frac{3}{5} = \frac{9}{?}$

4. $\frac{7}{4} = \frac{35}{?}$

5. $\frac{6}{7} = \frac{?}{49}$

6. $\frac{5}{9} = \frac{20}{?}$

7. $\frac{8}{3} = \frac{?}{18}$

8. $\frac{5}{6} = \frac{25}{?}$

Mixed Practice • Complete.

9. $\frac{4}{15} = \frac{?}{75}$

10. $\frac{9}{11} = \frac{?}{22}$

11. $\frac{1}{4} = \frac{6}{?}$

12. $\frac{7}{8} = \frac{28}{?}$

13. $\frac{21}{4} = \frac{63}{?}$

14. $\frac{9}{7} = \frac{?}{49}$

15. $\frac{2}{3} = \frac{16}{?}$

16. $\frac{5}{12} = \frac{30}{?}$

17. $\frac{7}{10} = \frac{?}{30}$

18. $\frac{8}{9} = \frac{?}{54}$

19. $\frac{5}{7} = \frac{?}{28}$

20. $\frac{1}{3} = \frac{10}{?}$

21. $\frac{2}{15} = \frac{10}{?}$

22. $\frac{5}{8} = \frac{35}{?}$

23. $\frac{4}{13} = \frac{12}{?}$

24. $\frac{14}{3} = \frac{?}{15}$

25. $\frac{6}{14} = \frac{?}{42}$

26. $\frac{8}{7} = \frac{48}{?}$

27. $\frac{12}{5} = \frac{?}{25}$

28. $\frac{11}{9} = \frac{66}{?}$

Complete the tables.

29.

cans of soup	4	?	12	?	?	24
cans of water	5	10	?	20	25	?

★ 30.

oranges	10	20	30	?	50	?
lemons	3	?	?	12	?	18

The ratio of girls to boys is 3 to 2.

★ 31. Are there more girls or more boys?

★ 32. Do you know how many girls there are?

★ 33. Suppose you know there are 12 boys. How many girls are there?

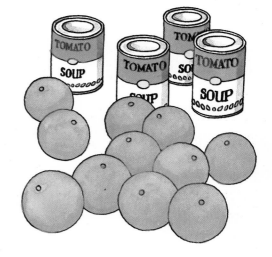

PROBLEM SOLVING • APPLICATIONS

34. The ratio of apples to bananas in a fruit salad is 4 to 7. 8 apples are used. How many bananas are used?

35. The ratio of boxes of gelatin to cups of water is 1 to 2. There are 8 cups of water. How many boxes of gelatin are there?

36. The ratio of hamburgers sold to sandwiches sold is 42 to 17. 68 sandwiches are sold. How many hamburgers are sold?

★ 37. A restaurant sells 22 ham sandwiches and 32 turkey sandwiches at lunchtime. The ratio of sandwiches sold to fruit salads sold is 9 to 2. How many fruit salads are sold?

Ratio and Money

The price of erasers
is 2 for 25¢.
Suppose you want 4.
You can use ratios
to find the cost.

erasers →	2	4
cost →	25	?

$$\frac{2}{25} = \frac{4}{?}$$

Think: $2 \times 2 = 4$, and so
$2 \times 25 = 50$.

Four erasers cost 50¢.

You can buy 4 rolls of tape for $2.50.
How many rolls can you buy for $7.50?

cellophane tape →	4	?
cost →	250	750

Think: $3 \times 250 = 750$, and so
$3 \times 4 = 12$.

You can buy 12 rolls of cellophane tape.

Practice • How much will they cost?

1. 2 for 10¢
Buy 6.

2. 3 for 25¢
Buy 9.

3. 2 for 25¢
Buy 6.

4. 4 for 20¢
Buy 12.

How many will you get?

5. 4 for 5¢
Spend 10¢

6. 2 for 25¢
Spend 75¢.

7. 2 for 15¢
Spend 45¢.

8. 3 for $1
Spend $4.

Mixed Practice • What will they cost?

9. 4 for 50¢
Buy 12.

10. 3 for 35¢
Buy 9.

11. 6 for 85¢
Buy 18.

12. 7 for 75¢
Buy 21.

13. 2 for 90¢
Buy 10.

14. 8 for 75¢
Buy 32.

15. 3 for 79¢
Buy 12.

16. 5 for $1.29
Buy 15.

How many will you get?

17. 3 for 50¢
Spend $1.50.

18. 3 for $1.00
Spend $5.00.

19. 5 for $3.00
Spend $12.00.

20. 6 for $2.75
Spend $11.00.

21. 7 for $6.00
Spend $18.00.

22. 4 for $1.25
Spend $6.25.

★ **23.** 2 for $2.99
Spend $35.88.

★ **24.** 8 for $3.49
Spend $139.60.

PROBLEM SOLVING • APPLICATIONS

25.

How much do 12 cost?

26.

How much do 6 cost?

27.

How many can you buy for $11.40?

28.

How many can you buy for $6.72?

★ **29.** Linda has only nickels and pennies. The ratio of nickels to pennies is 2 to 1. She has 11¢. How many nickels are there?

★ **30.** Tina has only dimes and pennies. The ratio of dimes to pennies is 2 to 3. She has 46¢. How many dimes are there?

Skills Maintenance

1. 67
×0.8

2. 9.6
× 7

3. 3.8
×4.5

4. 19.6
×0.81

5. 5.7
×0.09

6. 151.7
×0.08

7. 5.1
×0.98

8. 57.004
× 86

9. 4.9
×0.13

10. 2.54
× 9.6

Time, Rate, and Distance

Fred can walk 4 kilometers in 1 hour.
At this rate, how far can he walk in 3 hours?

kilometers ⟶	4	?
hours ⟶	1	3

$\frac{4}{1} = \frac{?}{3}$

Think: $3 \times 1 = 3$, and so $3 \times 4 = 12$.

Fred can walk 12 kilometers in 3 hours.

The speed limit in Fred's state is
85 kilometers per hour.
At this rate, how long will it take
to travel 340 kilometers?

kilometers ⟶	85	340
hours ⟶	1	?

$\frac{85}{1} = \frac{340}{?}$

Think: $4 \times 85 = 340$, and so $4 \times 1 = 4$.

It would take 4 hours.

Practice • How far will you go?

1. 3 km per hour
5 hours

2. 5 km per hour
7 hours

3. 64 km per hour
2 hours

How long will it take?

4. 5 km per hour
20 km

5. 50 km per hour
150 km

6. 65 km per hour
325 km

Mixed Practice • How far will you go?

7. 5 km per hour
4 hours

8. 8 km per hour
6 hours

9. 4 km per hour
2 hours

10. 35 km per hour
3 hours

11. 80 km per hour
4 hours

12. 48 km per hour
2 hours

13. 64 km per hour
5 hours

14. 96 km per hour
3 hours

15. 55 km per hour
5 hours

How long will it take?

16. 7 km per hour
21 km

17. 4 km per hour
16 km

18. 15 km per hour
75 km

19. 25 km per hour
200 km

20. 63 km per hour
441 km

21. 90 km per hour
630 km

★ **22.** 256 km per hour
2,048 km

★ **23.** 485 km per hour
2,910 km

★ **24.** 578 km per hour
2,890 km

PROBLEM SOLVING • APPLICATIONS

25. A car is traveling at an average speed of 75 kilometers per hour. At this rate, how long will it take to travel 525 kilometers?

26. A car travels 264 kilometers on 32 liters of gas. About how many kilometers will the car travel on 64 liters of gas?

★ **27.** Lin walks 5,000 meters in 2 hours. At this rate, how long will it take her to walk 25 kilometers?

★ **28.** A car travels 4 kilometers in 3 minutes. At this rate, how far can the car travel in 1 hour?

Midchapter Review

1. $\frac{2}{3} = \frac{?}{18}$

2. $\frac{7}{5} = \frac{21}{?}$

3. $\frac{9}{13} = \frac{?}{39}$

4. $\frac{15}{17} = \frac{60}{?}$

5. What will they cost?
2 for 75¢   Buy 8.

6. How many will you get?
3 for $1.50   Spend $4.50

7. How far will you go?
75 km per hour   3 hours

8. How long will it take?
45 km per hour   180 km

Scale Drawing

Marsha makes a scale drawing of the first floor of her school.

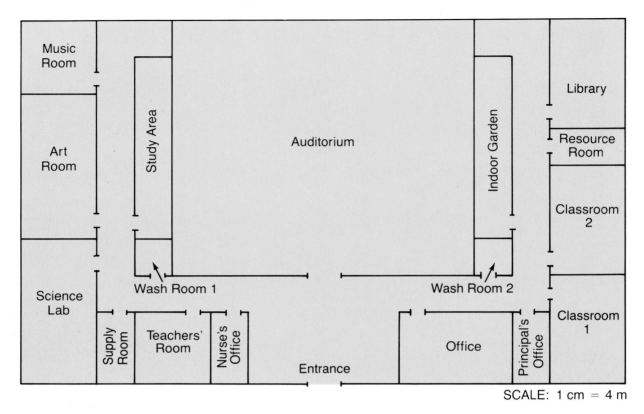

SCALE: 1 cm = 4 m

The scale at the bottom of the drawing is 1 cm = 4 m. This means that each centimeter in the scale drawing represents 4 meters in the actual school.

You can find the actual dimensions of the office.

Measure the length of the office on the drawing. It is 3 centimeters.

Use equal ratios to find the actual length of the office.

$$\text{length in drawing} \rightarrow \frac{1}{4} = \frac{3}{?} \quad \textbf{Think: } 3 \times 1 = 3, \text{ and so}$$
$$\text{actual length} \longrightarrow \qquad\qquad\qquad 3 \times 4 = 12.$$

The actual length of the office is 12 meters.

Find the actual width of the office.

$$\text{width in drawing} \rightarrow \frac{1}{4} = \frac{2}{?} \quad \textbf{Think: } 2 \times 1 = 2, \text{ and so}$$
$$\text{actual width} \longrightarrow \qquad\qquad\qquad 2 \times 4 = 8.$$

The actual width of the office is 8 meters.
The dimensions of the office are 12 meters by 8 meters.

Practice • Measure the drawing. Find the dimensions of each of these rooms.

1. Library   **2.** Supply Room   **3.** Garden

Mixed Practice • Measure the drawing. Find the dimensions of these rooms.

4. Teacher's Room   **5.** Classroom 1   **6.** Art Room

7. Principal's Office   **8.** Study Area   **9.** Science Lab

10. Washroom 1   **11.** Resource Room   **12.** Auditorium

13. Nurse's Office   **14.** Classroom 2   **15.** Music Room

16. Find the dimensions of the actual school building.

17. Name the four rooms that have the same dimensions.

PROBLEM SOLVING • APPLICATIONS

18. A pool is the shape of a rectangle. In a scale drawing the dimensions are 16 cm by 10 cm. In the drawing 2 cm represents 3 meters. Find the dimensions of the pool.

★ **19.** Suppose you are making a scale drawing of a playground. Use 1 cm to represent 8 meters. The actual dimensions of the playground are 72 m by 64 m. What will be the dimensions of the playground in the scale drawing?

★ **20.** Make a scale drawing of your classroom or of your school. Be sure to include the scale you use on the drawing. You may wish to show furniture.

Percent

Another way to show a ratio is to use **percent**.
Percent means per hundred. The symbol for percent is %.
Use a percent to show the ratio of blue blocks to all 100 blocks.

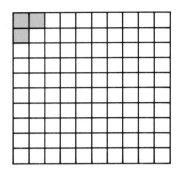 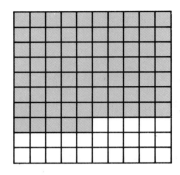 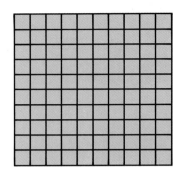

3 out of 100   75 out of 100   100 out of 100

Ratio $\frac{3}{100}$ $\frac{75}{100}$ $\frac{100}{100}$

Percent   3%   75%   100%

Practice • Write the percent that tells what part is shaded.

1. 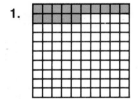   2. 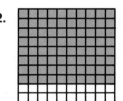   3. 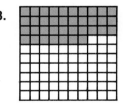   4.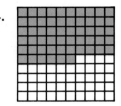

Write the percent for each ratio.

5. 8 out of 100   **6.** 42 out of 100   **7.** 76 out of 100

8. $\frac{9}{100}$ **9.** $\frac{21}{100}$ **10.** $\frac{48}{100}$ **11.** $\frac{4}{100}$ **12.** $\frac{28}{100}$ **13.** $\frac{43}{100}$

Mixed Practice • Write the percent that tells what part is shaded.

14. 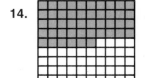   15.    16. 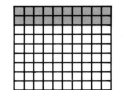   17.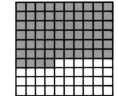

Write the percent for each ratio.

18. 6 out of 100

19. 3 out of 100

20. 24 out of 100

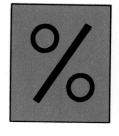

21. 30 out of 100

22. 57 out of 100

23. 92 out of 100

24. 63 per 100

25. 2 per 100

26. 55 per 100

27. $\dfrac{5}{100}$

28. $\dfrac{29}{100}$

29. $\dfrac{17}{100}$

30. $\dfrac{36}{100}$

31. $\dfrac{12}{100}$

32. $\dfrac{61}{100}$

33. $\dfrac{1}{100}$

34. $\dfrac{70}{100}$

35. $\dfrac{83}{100}$

36. $\dfrac{54}{100}$

37. $\dfrac{99}{100}$

38. $\dfrac{14}{100}$

39. $\dfrac{7}{100}$

40. $\dfrac{72}{100}$

41. $\dfrac{91}{100}$

42. $\dfrac{86}{100}$

43. $\dfrac{62}{100}$

44. $\dfrac{11}{100}$

45. $\dfrac{73}{100}$

46. $\dfrac{59}{100}$

47. $\dfrac{45}{100}$

★ **48.** $\dfrac{50}{200}$

★ **49.** $\dfrac{20}{50}$

★ **50.** $\dfrac{30}{40}$

PROBLEM SOLVING • APPLICATIONS

51. There are 100 students in the glee club. Three students are absent. What percent of the students is absent?

52. A science test is made up of 100 questions. Roseanne has 90 correct answers. What percent of the questions does she answer correctly?

★ **53.** Rory takes a test that has two parts. On the first part he correctly answers 70 out of 80 questions. On the second part he correctly answers 18 out of 20 questions. What percent of the total number of questions does Rory answer correctly?

★ **54.** Peter takes the same test as Rory. On the first part he correctly answers 56 out of 80 questions. On the second part he correctly answers 20 out of 20 questions. What was Peter's score? Who did better on the test?

Decimals and Fractions for Percents

Tickets are being sold for a concert. 35 out of 100 tickets are for seats in the balcony. This is 35% of the tickets.

Write the decimal for 35%.
Think: 35% is 35 hundredths.

$$35\% = 0.35$$

20 of the tickets are for box seats. This is 20% of the tickets.

Write the fraction for 20%.
Think: 20% is 20 hundredths.

Step 1 20% means 20 hundredths. $\longrightarrow \dfrac{20}{100}$

Step 2 Write the fraction in lowest terms. $\longrightarrow \dfrac{1}{5}$

Practice • Write the decimals for the percents.

1. 42%   2. 63%   3. 9%   4. 40%   5. 27%   6. 13%

Write the fractions for the percents. Write the answers in lowest terms.

7. 25%   8. 50%   9. 30%   10. 60%   11. 75%   12. 65%

Mixed Practice • Write the decimals for the percents.

13. 17%   14. 6%   15. 48%   16. 85%   17. 14%   18. 76%

19. 39%   20. 20%   21. 34%   22. 99%   23. 27%   24. 62%

25. 56%	26. 93%	27. 83%	28. 54%	29. 98%	30. 46%
31. 29%	32. 44%	33. 15%	34. 58%	35. 24%	36. 91%

Write the fraction for the percents. Write the answers in lowest terms.

37. 90%	38. 73%	39. 52%	40. 67%	41. 18%	42. 33%
43. 86%	44. 32%	45. 55%	46. 81%	47. 72%	48. 64%

PROBLEM SOLVING • APPLICATIONS

49. There are 100 show tickets available. If 19 of the tickets are for a musical, what percent of the tickets available are for the musical?

50. Orchestra seats make up 45% of the tickets. Write a decimal to show what part of the tickets are for orchestra seats.

51. A concert is being given, and 70% of the ticket holders arrive one hour before the concert begins. What fraction of the ticket holders arrive one hour early for the concert?

52. Only 5% of the tickets for the concert are not sold. What fraction are not sold?

★ 53. A ticket agent sells 80% of her tickets. What fraction of the tickets are left to sell?

★ 54. This year 23% of the season's concerts are sold out. Write a decimal to show what part of the concerts is not sold out.

Skills Maintenance

1. $3\overline{)22.8}$	2. $2\overline{)1.14}$	3. $6\overline{)217.2}$	4. $9\overline{)13.32}$	5. $4\overline{)0.304}$
6. $7\overline{)24.85}$	7. $15\overline{)10.8}$	8. $49\overline{)14.945}$	9. $13\overline{)16.12}$	10. $29\overline{)32.48}$

PROBLEM SOLVING • STRATEGIES

Circle Graphs

A circle graph can be used to show data given in percents.

Robin spends a total of $50.00 to take a ceramics class. The circle graph shows what percent of her money was spent for different things. How much money does she spend on tools?

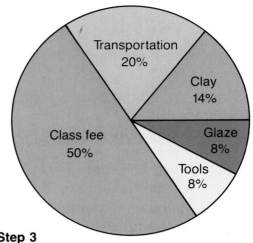

Step 1
On the graph find the percent spent on tools.

8%

Step 2
Write the percent as a decimal.

8% = 0.08

Step 3
Multiply.

$$\begin{array}{r} \$50 \\ \times 0.08 \\ \hline \$4.00 \end{array}$$

Robin spends $4.00 on tools.

Use Robin's circle graph to answer the questions.

1. What is the sum of the percents shown on the graph?

2. What percent of the $50.00 is spent on transportation?

3. On which item does Robin spend the most money?

Study the circle graph carefully to find the information you need.

---

4. Does Robin spend more money on transportation or on tools? _Trans_

5. How much money does Robin spend on the class fee? _$25_

6. What percent of the $50.00 is spent on glaze?

7. On which items does Robin spend the same amount of money? _Tool + Glaze_

8. On which item does Robin spend less money, transportation or clay? _Clay_

How much money does Robin spend on

9. transportation?

10. clay?

11. glaze?

Use the circle graphs to answer the questions.

Charles's Budget

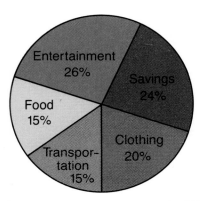

Alicia's Household Budget

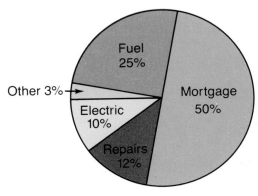

Charles has a part-time job. He makes a budget to plan how he will use his money. The circle graph shows his weekly budget.

12. What is the sum of the percents on Charles's graph?

13. What percent of Charles's money is spent on transportation?

Decide if you must change the percent to a decimal to solve the problem.

14. On which item does Charles spend the most money?

15. Does Charles spend more money on food or on savings?

In one week Charles earns $120.00. How much money does he spend on

16. entertainment?

17. savings?

18. clothing?

19. transportation

20. food?

This circle graph tells Alicia how she is budgeting her money.

21. What is the sum of the percents shown on the graph?

22. On which item is the most money spent?

23. On which item is the least money spent?

The budget allows $9,000.00 for yearly household expenses. How much money is spent on

24. fuel?

25. electricity?

26. mortgage?

★ 27. On which item is $270.00 spent?

★ 28. On which item is $1,080.00 spent?

REVIEW

Write a fraction for each ratio. (pages 360–361)

1. ○ ○ ○   ▢ ▢ ▢ ▢
   ○ ○   ▢ ▢ ▢ ▢

circles to squares

2. 7 to 1

3. $15 : 3$

Complete. (pages 362–363)

4. $\frac{1}{6} = \frac{?}{60}$

5. $\frac{7}{8} = \frac{14}{?}$

6. $\frac{3}{4} = \frac{?}{20}$

What will they cost? (pages 364–365)

7. 5 for 9¢
   Buy 10.

8. 2 for 25¢
   Buy 8.

9. 6 for $1.00
   Buy 30.

How many will you get? (pages 364–365)

10. 3 for 5¢
   Spend 25¢.

11. 7 for $1.00
   Spend $2.00.

12. 4 for $5.00
   Spend $10.00.

How far will you go? (pages 366–367)

13. 5 km per hour
   2 hours

14. 30 km per hour
   10 hours

15. 50 km per hour
   5 hours

How long will it take? (pages 366–367)

16. 2 km per hour
   6 km

17. 15 km per hour
   30 km

18. 40 km per hour
   200 km

Write the percent for each ratio. (pages 370–371)

19. 29 out of 100

20. 41 per 100

21. $\frac{5}{100}$

Write the decimals for the percents. (pages 372–373)

22. 17%

23. 2%

24. 59%

Write the fractions for the percents. Write the answers in lowest terms. (pages 372–373)

25. 40%

26. 9%

27. 99%

Solve.

28. A patio is in the shape of a rectangle. In a scale drawing the dimensions of a rectangular patio are 14 cm by 10 cm. In the drawing 2 cm represents 3 meters. Find the dimensions of the patio. (p. 368)

29. Jack will earn $350.00 this week. If he budgets 12% of this money for savings, how much will he save this week? (p. 375)

Probability and Predictions

When a coin is tossed, the probability that it will land heads is 1 out of 2. About how many times can you expect it to land heads if you toss it 2 times? 4 times? 6 times?

Complete the prediction table.

Now toss a penny.

Compare the results with your prediction.

Prediction					
Tosses	2	4	6	8	10
Heads	1	?	?	?	?

Results					
Tosses	2	4	6	8	10
Heads	?	?	?	?	?

Make 4 cards like these. Put them into a bag. The probability that you will draw a red card without looking is 1 out of 4. Complete the prediction table.

Now draw a card from the bag. Return the card to the bag after each draw. Complete the results table. Compare the results with your prediction.

Prediction					
Draws	4	8	12	16	20
Red Card	1	?	?	?	?

Results					
Draws	4	8	12	16	20
Red Card	?	?	?	?	?

When a number cube is rolled, any 1 of 6 numbers can come up. They are 1, 2, 3, 4, 5, and 6. The probability of rolling a 2 or rolling a 3 is 2 out of 6. Complete the prediction table.

Now roll the cube and complete the results table. Compare the results with your prediction.

Prediction					
Rolls	6	12	18	24	30
2 or 3	2	?	?	?	?

Results					
Rolls	6	12	18	24	30
2 or 3	?	?	?	?	?

TEST

Write a fraction for each ratio.

1.

□ △▽△

squares to triangles

2. 15 to 20

3. 30 : 1

Complete.

4. $\frac{3}{5} = \frac{?}{10}$

5. $\frac{1}{8} = \frac{5}{?}$

6. $\frac{7}{6} = \frac{21}{?}$

What will they cost?

7. 3 for 10¢
Buy 9.

8. 4 for 5¢
Buy 8.

9. 6 for 50¢
Buy 12.

How many will you get?

10. 8 for 79¢
Spend $1.58.

11. 10 for $1.00
Spend $8.00.

12. 6 for $5.00
Spend $25.00.

How far will you go?

13. 4 km per hour
5 hours

14. 20 km per hour
3 hours

15. 6 km per hour
6 hours

How long will it take?

16. 3 km per hour
15 km

17. 60 km per hour
180 km

18. 24 km per hour
240 km

Write the percent for each ratio.

19. 7 out of 100

20. 11 per 100

21. $\frac{3}{100}$

Write the decimals for the percents.

22. 8%

23. 47%

24. 98%

Write the fractions for the percents. Write the answers in lowest terms.

25. 94%

26. 58%

27. 7%

Solve.

28. In a scale drawing the length of a house is 9 cm. In the drawing 1 cm represents 3 meters. Find the actual length of the house.

29. Daisy spends 6% of her income on clothing each year. She earns $13,500.00 this year. How much does she spend on clothing?

ENRICHMENT

Sales Tax

States and cities need money for the services they provide.
One way to raise this money is to charge a **sales tax**.
This is an amount added to the cost of something you buy.

Craig wants to buy a cassette tape. It costs $5.99.
A sales tax of 7% is added to the cost.
How much does Craig need to buy the cassette?

Find the total cost of the cassette tape.

Step 1 Change 7% to a
decimal. Multiply to find
the amount of tax.

$$\begin{array}{r} \$5.99 \\ \times\ 0.07 \\ \hline \$0.4193 \end{array}$$

Step 2 Round the tax to the
next whole cent.

$0.4193 rounds to $0.42.

Step 3 Add the tax to the price.

$$\begin{array}{r} \$5.99 \\ +\ 0.42 \\ \hline \$6.41 \end{array}$$

Craig needs $6.41 to buy the cassette.

Find the amount of tax.

1. Price: $15.79
   Sales tax: 5%

2. Price: $58.99
   Sales tax: 9%

3. Price: $42.27
   Sales tax: 6%

4. Price: $27.38
   Sales tax: 7%

5. Price: $104.22
   Sales tax: 8%

6. Price: $256.83
   Sales tax: 5%

Find the total cost.

7. Price: $26.52
   Sales tax: 6%

8. Price: $93.85
   Sales tax: 8%

9. Price: $66.66
   Sales tax: 7%

10. Price: $64.45
    Sales tax: 5%

11. Price: $279.50
    Sales tax: 9%

12. Price: $735.97
    Sales tax: 8%

CALCULATOR

Calculator Percents

Some calculators have a **percent** (%) button.
If your calculator has a percent button, you can calculate sales tax using it.
Find 6% of $9.98.
Estimate: $\frac{6}{100}$ of $10 is about $.60. Push 9 . 9 8 × 6 %.
Pushing the percent button usually displays the product.
With some calculators you may need to push =.
The displayed answer is 0.5988.
Round the tax to the next whole cent.
The tax is $.60.

If your calculator has no percent button, change 6% to a decimal:
6% = 0.06. Push 9 . 9 8 × . 0 6 =. The answer is the same: 0.5988.

Find the amount of tax to the next whole cent. Use your calculator.

1. Price: $63.92
   Sales tax: 3%

2. Price: $2.45
   Sales tax: 8%

3. Price: $0.10
   Sales tax: 7%

4. Price: $17.84
   Sales tax: 1%

5. Price: $88.33
   Sales tax: 6%

6. Price: $94.21
   Sales tax: 0%

You can find the total cost using the calculator.

Price: $479.28   **Estimate:** $\frac{7}{100}$ of $500 is about $35.00.
Sales tax: 7%

Push 4 7 9 . 2 8 × 7 %
or × . 0 7 =.

The displayed answer is 33.5496. Round. Add the dollar sign and write the
tax as $33.55. Then add the price and the tax to find the total cost.

Push 4 7 9 . 2 8 + 3 3 . 5 5 =. Write the total cost as $512.83.

Find the total cost using the calculator.

7. Price: $769.23
   Sales tax: 8.2%

8. Price: $22.48
   Sales tax: 4%

9. Price: $1.00
   Sales tax: 16%

10. Price: $98.76
    Sales tax: 3%

11. Price: $55.55
    Sales tax: 0%

12. Price: $462.77
    Sales tax: 3.1%

Choose the correct answers.

1. Add.

$45.98
6.75
+ 19.95

A. $69.75
B. $84.25
C. $72.68
D. not here

2. Subtract.

$10,004 - 7,568 = \underline{\ ?\ }$

A. 2,436
B. 3,546
C. 17,572
D. not here

3. Multiply.

4,906
× 57

A. 312,932
B. 279,642
C. 285,784
D. not here

4. Divide.

$86\overline{)472,054}$

A. 5,489
B. 6,213 r6
C. 5,674 r56
D. not here

5. How many books are in Library C?

Library A	📖 📖
Library B	📖
Library C	📖 📖 📖

Each 📖 = 100

A. 100   B. 300
C. 250   D. not here

6. Multiply.

$8\frac{3}{4} \times \frac{8}{9} = \underline{\ ?\ }$

A. $8\frac{11}{36}$ B. $7\frac{1}{2}$
C. $7\frac{7}{9}$ D. not here

7. Complete.

$180 \text{ m} = \underline{\ ?\ } \text{ cm}$

A. .18
B. 18
C. 1,800
D. not here

8. Complete.

$5,000 \text{ mL} = \underline{\ ?\ } \text{ L}$

A. .5
B. 5
C. 50
D. not here

9. Subtract.

$26 - 8.97 = \underline{\ ?\ }$

A. 17.03
B. 18.86
C. 34.97
D. not here

10. Multiply.

8.96
× 0.9

A. 0.864
B. 8.064
C. 80.64
D. not here

11. Name a diameter.

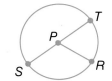

A. *PR*   B. *SP*
C. *ST*   D. not here

12. Write the percent for the ratio.

$\frac{54}{100}$

A. 100%
B. 46%
C. 54%
D. not here

Choose the correct answers.

13. Bruce buys a book for $16.95, a calendar for $6.50, and a notebook for $2.79. He gives the clerk $40. How much change should he receive?

    A. $26.24
    B. $13.76
    C. $15.25
    D. not here

14. Emilio bowls every Friday night. He plays three games and scores 200, 195, and 178. What is his average score?

    A. 185
    B. 19
    C. 191
    D. not here

15. It takes Barbara $1\frac{1}{2}$ hours to walk to school. She leaves home for school. She stops at Anne's house after walking $\frac{2}{3}$ hour. How much longer must she walk before she arrives at school?

    A. $\frac{5}{6}$ hours   **B.** $\frac{1}{2}$ hour
    C. $\frac{3}{4}$ hour   **D.** not here

16. A pool has the dimensions 60 cm by 20 cm by 25 cm. What is the mass of the water in the tank when it is filled to the top?

    A. 3 kg
    B. 300 g
    C. 30 kg
    D. not here

17. At 2:00 the temperature is 0°C. In 4 hours it drops 6 degrees. What is the temperature at 6:00?

    A. 0°C
    B. −4°C
    C. 4°C
    D. not here

18. Pennsylvania produced 3.5 billion liters of milk one year. Minnesota produced 4.2 billion liters of milk the same year. How many more liters of milk did Minnesota produce?

    A. 0.7 billion L   **B.** 0.5 billion L
    C. 7.7 billion L   **D.** not here

19. Miki jogs 11 laps around the track. It takes her a total of 27.5 minutes. What is her average time per lap?

    A. 1.9 min   **B.** 2.5 min
    C. 2.2 min   **D.** not here

20. There are 100 tickets available at a ticket booth. There are 25 tickets for a play. What percent of the available tickets are for a play?

    A. 50%   **B.** 75%
    C. 25%   **D.** not here

Extra Practice

Set 1   (pages 2–7)

Write the numbers.

1. eight hundred seventy-four
2. six thousand, five hundred eighty
3. three thousand, twelve
4. 700 + 90 + 5
5. 9,000 + 600 + 6
6. 8,000 + 40 + 9

Write the expanded forms. Then write the number in words.

7. 319
8. 2,490
9. 6,007

What number does the blue digit name?

10. 5,342
11. 72,607
12. 398,511
13. 417,030

Write the numbers.

14. 162 million, 571 thousand, 809
15. 69 billion, 331 million, 47 thousand
16. 275 billion, 18 million, 760 thousand, 54
17. thirteen billion, eight hundred three thousand, ninety

Set 2   (pages 8–11)

Use >, <, or = to write a true sentence.

1. 1,084 ● 10,084
2. 6,513,722 ● 6,513,722
3. 749,603 ● 746,903

Write in order from least to greatest.

4. 653; 365; 536
5. 8,214; 4,309; 1,597
6. 26,490; 26,049; 26,904

Round to the nearest ten.

7. 1,932
8. 4,618

Round to the nearest hundred.

9. 3,856
10. 9,927

Round to the nearest thousand.

11. 36,498
12. 89,516

Round to the nearest ten thousand.

13. 82,116
14. 176,218

Round to the nearest hundred thousand.

15. 8,487,201
16. 7,211,999
17. 8,916,985
18. 678,476,000

Problem Solving for Chapter 1   (pages 12–13)

Solve. Use the table on page 12.

1. Which states have an area of less than 100,000 square kilometers?
2. Which state has an area of about 400,000 square kilometers?

Extra Practice

Set 3   (pages 22–31)

Add or subtract.

1. 8 + 4 = ___?___

2. 5 + 9 = ___?___

3. 7 + 6 = ___?___

4. 53 + 478 = ___?___

5. 196 + 820 = ___?___

6. 345 + 719 = ___?___

7. 9
   −5

8. 8
   −2

9. 10
   − 7

10. 13
   − 4

11. 15
   − 8

12. 11
   − 3

Estimate. Round to the nearest tens.

13. 67
    +42

14. 36
    +85

Estimate. Round to the nearest hundreds.

15. 237
    +881

16. 370
    +756

Estimate. Round to the nearest thousands.

17. 3,647
    +2,182

18. 5,385
    +8,016

19. 7,459
    +4,723

Set 4   (pages 32–39, 42–45)

Add.

1. 2,843
   +1,509

2. 4,671
   + 732

3. 8,395
   +6,187

4. 37,404
   +55,816

5. 94,658
   +72,352

6. 603,794
   +289,561

Estimate. Round to the nearest tens.

7. 56
   −43

8. 72
   −18

Estimate. Round to the nearest hundreds.

9. 490
   −225

10. 804
   −380

Estimate. Round to the nearest thousands.

11. 5,327
   −3,910

12. 9,458
   −6,285

13. 7,831
   −4,677

Subtract.

14. 40,050
    −27,661

15. 843,700
    − 59,028

16. 705,206
    −556,389

17. 667 − ___?___ = 384

18. 532 − ___?___ = 251

Problem Solving for Chapter 2   (pages 40–41, 46–47)

Solve.

1. Joan has $17.54. She earns $8.76. How much does she now have?

2. A book costs $4.95 and paper costs $1.78. You are given $10.00. What coins and bills should you give in change?

Extra Practice

Set 5   (pages 56–63)

Multiply.

1. 264
× 8

2. 956
× 2

3. 6,174
× 6

4. 9,381
× 7

5. 42,093
× 5

6. 87,206
× 4

7. 549,327
× 6

8. 290,618
× 5

9. 351,706
× 9

10. 617,294
× 7

11. $4 \times (5 \times 0) = \underline{?}$

12. $3 \times (2 \times 4) = \underline{?}$

13. $9 \times (2 \times 3) = \underline{?}$

14. $4 \times 60 = \underline{?}$

15. $6 \times 500 = \underline{?}$

16. $5 \times 3,000 = \underline{?}$

17. $4 \times 527 = \underline{?}$

18. $9 \times 315 = \underline{?}$

19. $3 \times 8,917 = \underline{?}$

20. $9 \times 7,095 = \underline{?}$

21. $2 \times 65,499 = \underline{?}$

22. $8 \times 431,874 = \underline{?}$

Set 6   (pages 64–67, 70–71)

Multiply.

1. 4,508
× 69

2. 13,072
× 45

3. $2.73
× 481

4. $8.52
× 369

5. $62.81
× 803

6. 19,504
× 715

7. 627,948
× 79

8. 860,775
× 96

9. 74,939
× 568

10. 95,086
× 687

11. $30 \times 68 = \underline{?}$

12. $40 \times 75 = \underline{?}$

13. $60 \times 91 = \underline{?}$

14. $700 \times 849 = \underline{?}$

15. $900 \times 677 = \underline{?}$

16. $600 \times 785 = \underline{?}$

17. $97 \times 3,560 = \underline{?}$

18. $73 \times 29,118 = \underline{?}$

19. $524 \times 593 = \underline{?}$

20. $918 \times 607 = \underline{?}$

21. $285 \times 49,720 = \underline{?}$

22. $447 \times 53,092 = \underline{?}$

Problem Solving for Chapter 3   (pages 68–69, 72–73)

Solve.

1. Jake wanted to buy 4 record albums. Each album costs $7.79. How much money did he need?

2. A can of carrots costs $.49 and a can of corn costs $.37. Quinn buys 8 cans of carrots and 12 cans of corn. How much does Quinn spend?

Extra Practice

Set 7 (pages 82–89)

Divide.

1. $30 \div 6 = \underline{?}$ **2.** $45 \div 5 = \underline{?}$ **3.** $16 \div 4 = \underline{?}$ **4.** $63 \div 9 = \underline{?}$

5. $49 \div 7 = \underline{?}$ **6.** $12 \div 3 = \underline{?}$ **7.** $30 \div 5 = \underline{?}$ **8.** $54 \div 6 = \underline{?}$

Use the three numbers. Write four number sentences.

9. 4, 6, 24 **10.** 9, 3, 27 **11.** 6, 7, 42 **12.** 8, 2, 16

Divide.

13. $5 \overline{)63}$ **14.** $3 \overline{)98}$ **15.** $4 \overline{)71}$ **16.** $7 \overline{)84}$ **17.** $2 \overline{)57}$

18. $51 \div 4 = \underline{?}$ **19.** $91 \div 6 = \underline{?}$ **20.** $96 \div 8 = \underline{?}$ **21.** $88 \div 3 = \underline{?}$ **22.** $83 \div 7 = \underline{?}$

Complete.

23. $(\underline{?} \times 3) + 8 = 77$ **24.** $(\underline{?} \times 7) + 4 = 95$ **25.** $(\underline{?} \times 6) + 1 = 85$

Set 8 (pages 90–93, 96–99)

Divide.

1. $5 \overline{)731}$ **2.** $8 \overline{)987}$ **3.** $6 \overline{)2,365}$ **4.** $3 \overline{)1,990}$ **5.** $4 \overline{)3,736}$

6. $4 \overline{)22,915}$ **7.** $6 \overline{)40,526}$ **8.** $4 \overline{)33,201}$ **9.** $7 \overline{)\$496.37}$ **10.** $5 \overline{)\$270.25}$

11. $874 \div 3 = \underline{?}$ **12.** $960 \div 7 = \underline{?}$ **13.** $2,685 \div 5 = \underline{?}$ **14.** $1,769 \div 2 = \underline{?}$

15. $48,976 \div 8 = \underline{?}$ **16.** $39,640 \div 7 = \underline{?}$ **17.** $19,324 \div 5 = \underline{?}$ **18.** $\$845.10 \div 9 = \underline{?}$

19. $578 \div (2 + 5) = \underline{?}$ **20.** $4,537 \div (1 + 7) = \underline{?}$ **21.** $8,210 \div (3 + 4) = \underline{?}$

Find the averages.

22. 57, 70, 41 **23.** 31, 33, 35, 37 **24.** 13, 88, 80, 6, 3

Problem Solving for Chapter 4 (pages 94–95)

Solve.

1. Sue bought 3 vases. She spent $74.85. How much did each cost?

2. Irwin sold 3 cartons of folding chairs. Each carton contained 3 chairs. If he collected $147.24, how much did each chair cost?

Extra Practice

Set 9 (pages 108–113, 116–117)

Divide.

1. $87\overline{)609}$ 2. $70\overline{)257}$ 3. $16\overline{)141}$ 4. $48\overline{)325}$ 5. $61\overline{)171}$

6. $39\overline{)93}$ 7. $27\overline{)216}$ 8. $15\overline{)85}$ 9. $73\overline{)337}$ 10. $58\overline{)270}$

11. $80\overline{)522}$ 12. $69\overline{)621}$ 13. $38\overline{)200}$ 14. $24\overline{)95}$ 15. $52\overline{)347}$

16. $130 \div 20 = \underline{?}$ 17. $444 \div 53 = \underline{?}$ 18. $531 \div 78 = \underline{?}$ 19. $224 \div 29 = \underline{?}$

20. $302 \div 45 = \underline{?}$ 21. $280 \div 56 = \underline{?}$ 22. $616 \div 97 = \underline{?}$ 23. $145 \div 82 = \underline{?}$

Fill in the boxes with the missing numbers.

24.
```
         6 r■3
 4 ■)3 3 ■
  −2 ■ 4
    ■ 3
```

25.
```
            7 r2■
 ■ ■)6 ■ 6
  −6 ■ 5
    2 ■
```

26.
```
            9 r■8
 ■ 7)■ 3 ■
  −5 1 3
    ■ 8
```

Set 10 (pages 118–121, 124–125)

Divide.

1. $67\overline{)4,784}$ 2. $80\overline{)6,509}$ 3. $41\overline{)2,305}$ 4. $97\overline{)7,497}$ 5. $16\overline{)1,011}$

6. $51\overline{)8,262}$ 7. $32\overline{)9,400}$ 8. $69\overline{)7,913}$ 9. $25\overline{)4,548}$ 10. $47\overline{)6,380}$

11. $83\overline{)17,571}$ 12. $76\overline{)20,833}$ 13. $58\overline{)49,007}$ 14. $37\overline{)96,115}$ 15. $18\overline{)90,126}$

16. $707 \div 54 = \underline{?}$ 17. $589 \div 40 = \underline{?}$ 18. $904 \div 73 = \underline{?}$

19. $5,781 \div 99 = \underline{?}$ 20. $2,012 \div 27 = \underline{?}$ 21. $3,490 \div 56 = \underline{?}$

22. $347\overline{)18,044}$ 23. $268\overline{)58,692}$ 24. $451\overline{)240,240}$

Problem Solving for Chapter 5 (pages 114–115, 122–123)

Solve.

1. Dominick has 192 books in his library. He wants to put 16 books on each shelf in his bookcase. How many shelves does Dominick need?

2. There are 24 crayons in a box. Mrs. Gonzalez has 18 boxes of crayons for her students. All the crayons are shared equally by the 27 students in her class. How many crayons does each student get?

Extra Practice

Set 11 (pages 134–139)

Use the graph to answer questions 1 through 10.

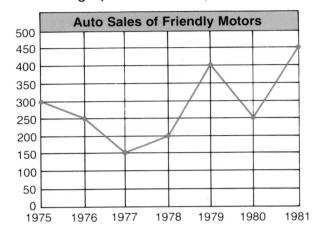

1. In which years did sales decrease from the preceding year's sales?

2. In which years did sales increase over the preceding year's sales?

Which year's sales showed more of a change from the preceding year's sales,

3. 1976 or 1977?
4. 1978 or 1981?
5. 1979 or 1980?

How many autos were sold in   **6.** 1978?   **7.** 1975?   **8.** 1980?

9. How many more autos were sold in Friendly Motors' best year than in its worst year?

10. How many more autos were sold in 1980 and 1981 than in 1975 and 1976?

Set 12 (pages 140–143)

Use the grid to answer questions 1 through 18.
What letter is at the point?

1. (8, 9)
2. (6, 0)
3. (7, 8)
4. (1, 5)
5. (3, 5)
6. (1, 8)
7. (3, 9)
8. (1, 3)
9. (5, 6)

What ordered pair tells the location of the point?

10. G
11. E
12. J
13. B
14. L
15. A
16. F
17. D
18. K

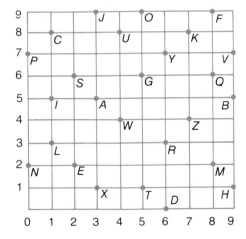

Problem Solving for Chapter 6 (pages 144–145)

Use the map on page 144 to answer the questions.

1. How many kilometers is it from Union Springs to Maplesville on Route 82?

2. It takes Lucas 2 hours to drive from Sylacauga to Troy along Highway 231. What is his average rate of speed for the trip?

388

Extra Practice

Set 13   (pages 154–163)

Find all the factors. List them in order.

1. 10   **2.** 28   **3.** 45   **4.** 63

Write PRIME or COMPOSITE.

5. 37   **6.** 87   **7.** 71   **8.** 590   **9.** 107

Write the number as a product of prime factors.
Use a factor tree.

10. 78   **11.** 69   **12.** 88   **13.** 91

Find the greatest common factor.   Find the least common multiple.

14. 32, 36   **15.** 30, 48, 54   **16.** 7, 49   **17.** 3, 7, 9

Set 14   (pages 166–181)

Complete.

1. $\frac{5}{8}$ of 64 = ____?____   **2.** $\frac{1}{3} = \frac{?}{15}$ **3.** $\frac{2}{7} = \frac{6}{?}$

Find the least common denominator. Write equivalent fractions. Write $>$, $<$, or $=$.

4. $\frac{2}{5}$ ⬤ $\frac{3}{8}$ **5.** $\frac{1}{7}$ ⬤ $\frac{1}{6}$ **6.** $\frac{11}{12}$ ⬤ $\frac{7}{8}$

Write as fractions.

7. $4\frac{2}{3}$ **8.** $1\frac{9}{10}$ **9.** $5\frac{1}{4}$ **10.** $2\frac{5}{6}$ **11.** $6\frac{4}{5}$

Divide to find the mixed numbers. Write the answers in lowest terms.

12. $\frac{32}{5}$ **13.** $\frac{26}{6}$ **14.** $\frac{33}{4}$ **15.** $\frac{42}{9}$ **16.** $\frac{78}{10}$

Problem Solving for Chapter 7   (pages 164–165, 182–183)

Choose the correct answer.

1. Mrs. Nelson spent $9.60 on jars of baby food. If each jar costs $.32, how many did she buy?   3 or 30 or 300

Use the train schedule to answer the question.

2. Giuseppe takes the train from Rome to Milan. He arrives at the station in Rome at 1:50 P.M. How long must he wait for the train to leave?

From Rome		
To Milan Leave	Arrive	Track
9:30 A.M.	11:20 A.M.	4
11:00 A.M.	1:05 P.M.	7
2:45 P.M.	4:40 P.M.	3

Extra Practice

Set 15   (pages 192–199)

Add or subtract. Write the answers in lowest terms.

1. $\frac{1}{5} + \frac{3}{5} = \underline{?}$ **2.** $\frac{1}{9} + \frac{5}{9} = \underline{?}$ **3.** $\frac{3}{8} + \frac{3}{8} = \underline{?}$ **4.** $\frac{2}{7} + \frac{4}{7} = \underline{?}$

5. $\frac{7}{10} - \frac{1}{10} = \underline{?}$ **6.** $\frac{3}{5} - \frac{2}{5} = \underline{?}$ **7.** $\frac{5}{8} - \frac{3}{8} = \underline{?}$ **8.** $\frac{8}{9} - \frac{4}{9} = \underline{?}$

Add or subtract. Write the answers in lowest terms.

9. $\begin{array}{r} \frac{2}{3} \\ +\frac{1}{4} \\ \hline \end{array}$ **10.** $\begin{array}{r} \frac{3}{10} \\ +\frac{2}{5} \\ \hline \end{array}$ **11.** $\begin{array}{r} \frac{3}{4} \\ +\frac{1}{12} \\ \hline \end{array}$ **12.** $\begin{array}{r} \frac{5}{6} \\ +\frac{1}{3} \\ \hline \end{array}$ **13.** $\begin{array}{r} \frac{4}{5} \\ -\frac{2}{15} \\ \hline \end{array}$ **14.** $\begin{array}{r} \frac{2}{3} \\ -\frac{4}{9} \\ \hline \end{array}$ **15.** $\begin{array}{r} \frac{1}{2} \\ \frac{1}{4} \\ +\frac{1}{8} \\ \hline \end{array}$

Find the missing numerators and denominators.

16. $\frac{1}{10} + \frac{?}{10} = \frac{4}{5}$ **17.** $\frac{?}{18} + \frac{5}{18} = \frac{2}{3}$ **18.** $\frac{3}{4} - \frac{7}{?} = \frac{1}{6}$

Set 16   (pages 200–209)

Add or subtract. Write the answers in lowest terms.

1. $2\frac{9}{20} + 7\frac{3}{20} = \underline{?}$ **2.** $10\frac{4}{9} + 8\frac{2}{9} = \underline{?}$ **3.** $5\frac{7}{16} + 4\frac{3}{8} = \underline{?}$

4. $3\frac{5}{6} - 2\frac{3}{4} = \underline{?}$ **5.** $6\frac{1}{5} - 1\frac{4}{5} = \underline{?}$ **6.** $8\frac{4}{15} - 4\frac{3}{5} = \underline{?}$

Find the missing numerators.

7. $6\frac{3}{20} + 5\frac{?}{20} = 11\frac{1}{2}$ **8.** $4\frac{7}{9} + 2\frac{?}{9} = 7\frac{1}{3}$ **9.** $23\frac{7}{8} - 15\frac{?}{24} = 8\frac{5}{12}$

Problem Solving for Chapter 8   (pages 210–211)

What other information do you need to solve these problems?

1. The bus trip to Kokomo takes $5\frac{1}{2}$ hours. When does the bus arrive at Kokomo?

2. Mr. Sanchez lived in New York for 23 years, New Jersey for 31 years, and the rest of his life in Florida. How many years did Mr. Sanchez live in Florida?

Extra Practice

Set 17 (pages 220–227)

Multiply. Write the answers in lowest terms.

1. $7 \times \frac{4}{7} = $ ___?___

2. $\frac{5}{6} \times 17 = $ ___?___

3. $20 \times \frac{5}{8} = $ ___?___

4. $2\frac{1}{3} \times \frac{3}{4} = $ ___?___

5. $\frac{2}{3} \times 1\frac{4}{5} = $ ___?___

6. $4\frac{1}{2} \times \frac{1}{6} = $ ___?___

7. $1\frac{1}{4} \times \frac{7}{10} = $ ___?___

8. $\frac{2}{5} \times 3\frac{1}{6} = $ ___?___

9. $5\frac{4}{9} \times \frac{3}{7} = $ ___?___

10. $4\frac{1}{6} \times \frac{9}{10} = $ ___?___

11. $\frac{4}{11} \times 8\frac{4}{5} = $ ___?___

12. $9\frac{1}{3} \times \frac{1}{4} = $ ___?___

13. $12\frac{3}{5} \times \frac{7}{9} = $ ___?___

14. $\frac{9}{20} \times 16\frac{2}{3} = $ ___?___

15. $24\frac{1}{2} \times \frac{3}{14} = $ ___?___

Set 18 (pages 228–229, 232–235)

Multiply or divide. Write the answers in lowest terms.

1. $1\frac{1}{2} \times 5\frac{1}{4} = $ ___?___

2. $1\frac{4}{11} \times 1\frac{3}{5} = $ ___?___

3. $18\frac{3}{4} \times 1\frac{12}{25} = $ ___?___

4. $\frac{2}{5} \div \frac{1}{2} = $ ___?___

5. $\frac{8}{9} \div \frac{2}{3} = $ ___?___

6. $\frac{7}{2} \div \frac{5}{12} = $ ___?___

7. $8 \div \frac{6}{5} = $ ___?___

8. $12 \div \frac{4}{7} = $ ___?___

9. $\frac{6}{5} \div \frac{?}{15} = 4\frac{1}{2}$

Find the missing factors. If the answer is greater than 1, write it as a mixed number.

10. $5\frac{1}{3} \times $ ___?___ $= 1$

11. ___?___ $\times 2\frac{2}{9} = 1$

12. $\frac{4}{15} \times $ ___?___ $= 1$

Problem Solving for Chapter 9 (pages 230–231)

To make a container of chicken salad, you mix $\frac{2}{3}$ cups of celery with $2\frac{1}{2}$ cups of diced chicken.

1. How many cups of chicken do you use to make 3 containers?

2. How many cups of celery do you use to make 2 containers?

3. How many containers can you make with 5 cups of chicken?

Extra Practice

Set 19 (pages 244–255, 258–259)

Complete.

1. 5,000 m = __?__ km
2. __?__ m = 16 km
3. 300 m = __?__ cm
4. 800 m = __?__ mm
5. 700 m = __?__ dm
6. 400 km = __?__ m

Find the perimeter.

7.

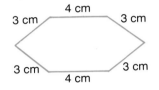

Find the volume.

8.

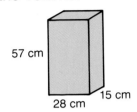

Set 20 (pages 260–273)

Complete.

1. 8,000 g = __?__ kg
2. __?__ g = 7 kg
3. 37,000 g = __?__ kg
4. 5 min = __?__ sec
5. 63 d = __?__ wk
6. 84 h = __?__ d

What time is it?

7. 5 hours before
   9:00 P.M.
8. $1\frac{1}{2}$ hours after
   8:15 A.M.
9. 4 hours before
   3:45 P.M.

Complete.

10. 17 ft = __?__ in.
11. 10,560 ft = __?__ mi
12. 9 T = __?__ lb
13. 3 lb 4 oz = __?__ oz
14. $5\frac{3}{4}$ lb = __?__ oz
15. $2\frac{2}{5}$ T = __?__ lb

Find the perimeter and the area.

16.

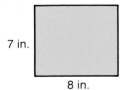

Find the volume.

17.

8 ft
5 ft
6 ft

Problem Solving for Chapter 10 (pages 256–257)

Tell how you would solve these problems if you were given numbers.

1. Mrs. Ortega is making a silk flower arrangement. She knows the cost of each silk flower. She knows how many flowers she needs. How much will it cost Mrs. Ortega to make the arrangement?

2. Sam wants to put tiles on his floor. He knows the size of his floor, the size of each tile, and the number of tiles in each box. How many boxes of tiles does Sam need?

Extra Practice

Set 21   (pages 282–289)

Write the decimals.

1. $175\frac{52}{100}$ 2. $727\frac{550}{1000}$ 3. $39\frac{5}{10}$ 4. $403\frac{1}{100}$ 5. $1,099\frac{83}{1000}$

6. six-hundredths

7. seventy-five hundredths

8. seven and two-tenths

9. nine-tenths

10. three and seven-thousandths

11. fourteen-thousandths

12. four and thirty-hundredths

13. one and eleven-hundredths

In what place is the blue digit?

14. 42.531

15. 870.739

16. 21.495

What number does the blue digit name?

17. 76.052

18. 59.261

19. 473.780

Set 22   (pages 290–297)

Write >, <, or =.

1. 39.79 ● 40.53   2. 58.640 ● 58.64   3. 81.370 ● 81.037

Round to the nearest whole number.

4. 4.7   5. 7.3   6. 51.2   7. 26.51   8. 69.88

Round to the nearest tenth.

9. 36.83   10. 21.26   11. 14.35   12. 79.018   13. 60.962

Round to the nearest hundredth.

14. 85.227   15. 19.173   16. 94.506   17. 30.848   18. 42.395

Add or subtract.

19. 9.4   20. 9.045   21. 35.607   22. 4.73   23. 7.521   24. 67.45
    $+3.92$ -1.954 $+11.8$ -3.9 -2.88 $+59.953$

25. $55.403 + 19.729 = \underline{\ ?\ }$ 26. $46.580 + 68.5 = \underline{\ ?\ }$ 27. $77.64 - 2\underline{\ ?\ }.89 = 54.75$

Problem Solving for Chapter 11   (pages 298–299)

Find the facts you need. Solve.

1. How much longer does it take William to run the mile than the first-place winner?

   The first-place winner runs the mile in 4.127 minutes. Rolando runs the mile in 4.215 minutes. William runs the mile in 4.306 minutes. Gustave runs the mile in 4.559 minutes.

2. How many seats are in the balcony of the Essex Theater?

   The Essex Theater seats 240 people. There are 185 seats in the orchestra. An orchestra seat costs $5 more than a balcony seat.

Extra Practice

Set 23   (pages 308–313)

Estimate to place the decimal point in the answers.

1. $\begin{array}{r} 1.9 \\ \times 6.5 \\ \hline 1235 \end{array}$
2. $\begin{array}{r} 25.7 \\ \times 3.82 \\ \hline 98174 \end{array}$
3. $\begin{array}{r} 5.36 \\ \times 70.3 \\ \hline 376808 \end{array}$
4. $\begin{array}{r} 6.49 \\ \times 4.41 \\ \hline 286209 \end{array}$
5. $\begin{array}{r} 8.18 \\ \times 9.27 \\ \hline 758286 \end{array}$

Multiply.

6. $\begin{array}{r} 0.37 \\ \times\ 0.2 \end{array}$
7. $\begin{array}{r} 1.8 \\ \times 0.05 \end{array}$
8. $\begin{array}{r} 00.36 \\ \times\ \ 0.7 \end{array}$
9. $\begin{array}{r} 0.69 \\ \times\ \ 41 \end{array}$
10. $\begin{array}{r} 2.4 \\ \times 0.32 \end{array}$

11. $\begin{array}{r} 0.007 \\ \times\ \ \ 14 \end{array}$
12. $\begin{array}{r} 15.3 \\ \times 0.56 \end{array}$
13. $\begin{array}{r} 2.75 \\ \times\ 0.2 \end{array}$
14. $\begin{array}{r} 4.38 \\ \times 19.7 \end{array}$
15. $\begin{array}{r} 605 \\ \times 0.784 \end{array}$

16. $39 \times 0.05 = \underline{\ ?\ }$
17. $18.2 \times 0.27 = \underline{\ ?\ }$
18. $5.7 \times 0.08 = \underline{\ ?\ }$

19. $0.2 \times 0.04 \times 9 = \underline{\ ?\ }$
20. $0.03 \times 0.5 \times 37 = \underline{\ ?\ }$
21. $2.9 \times 4.3 \times 0.6 = \underline{\ ?\ }$

Set 24   (pages 314–315, 318–321)

Multiply.

1. $10 \times 7.528 = \underline{\ ?\ }$
2. $100 \times 4{,}002 = \underline{\ ?\ }$
3. $10 \times 5.0069 = \underline{\ ?\ }$
4. $1{,}000 \times 2.5808 = \underline{\ ?\ }$
5. $100 \times 137 = \underline{\ ?\ }$
6. $1{,}000 \times 12.03 = \underline{\ ?\ }$

Divide.

7. $37.6 \div 16 = \underline{\ ?\ }$
8. $23.12 \div 85 = \underline{\ ?\ }$
9. $0.76 \div 40 = \underline{\ ?\ }$
10. $72.88 \div 10 = \underline{\ ?\ }$
11. $965.4 \div 100 = \underline{\ ?\ }$
12. $301.2 \div 10 = \underline{\ ?\ }$

Problem Solving for Chapter 12   (pages 316–317)

Solve.

1. Park tickets cost $3.95 for a child and $6.50 for an adult. The Wongs and their 4 children go to the park. How much do their tickets cost?

2. King-size mattresses cost $359.90; a queen-size costs $287.55. A shop sells 32 king-size and 41 queen-size mattresses. How much more money will the shop take in on the queen-size mattresses?

Extra Practice

Set 25 (pages 330–337, 340–341)

Use a protractor to draw the angles.

1. 100°   **2.** 55°   **3.** 30°

Measure each angle. Then use your protractor to draw a congruent angle.

4.   **5.**   **6.**

Draw two lines that are

7. parallel.   **8.** intersecting.   **9.** perpendicular.

Name the polygons.

10. a polygon with five sides
11. a quadrilateral whose opposite sides are parallel and congruent
12. a polygon with four sides
13. a triangle with no congruent sides

Set 26 (pages 342–351)

Are they congruent? Write YES or NO.
Use a tracing to help you.

1.   **2.**

Are they similar? Write YES or NO.

3.   **4.**

Study the circle.

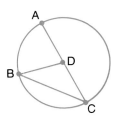

5. Name 3 radii.
6. Name 1 obtuse angle.
7. Name 2 chords.

Problem Solving for Chapter 13 (pages 338–339)

Make drawings to help you solve the problems.

1. Jeremiah walks along a straight road for 2.6 kilometers. He stops to eat his lunch. After lunch he continues walking in the same direction for another 3.7 kilometers. How far does Jeremiah walk in all?

2. A rectangular track measures 1.7 kilometers by 0.9 kilometers. Kimmara runs twice around the track. How far does she run in all?

Extra Practice

Set 27 (pages 360–367)

Write a fraction to show each ratio.

1. 13:16   **2.** 11:10   **3.** 157:50   **4.** 199:100

Complete.

5. $\frac{10}{7} = \frac{?}{35}$ **6.** $\frac{5}{16} = \frac{30}{?}$ **7.** $\frac{24}{19} = \frac{?}{76}$ **8.** $\frac{13}{18} = \frac{52}{?}$

What will they cost?   How many will you get?

9. 2 for 45¢   **10.** 6 for 80¢   **11.** 4 for $1.50   **12.** 3 for $2.75
  Buy 14.   Buy 24.   Spend $6.00.   Spend $8.25.

How far will you go?   How long will it take?

13. 11 km per hour   **15.** 26 km per hour
  8 hours   104 km

14. 70 km per hour   **16.** 317 km per hour
  5 hours   2,853 km

Set 28 (pages 368–373)

Measure the drawing. Find the dimensions of these rooms.

1. Living room
2. Kitchen
3. Bathroom

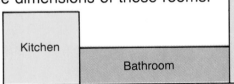

1 cm = 2 m

Living room

Kitchen

Bathroom

Write the percent for each ratio.

4. 12 per 100   **5.** 1 per 100   **6.** $\frac{76}{200}$ **7.** $\frac{17}{20}$

Write the decimals for the percents.

8. 92%   **9.** 9%   **10.** 39%   **11.** 23%

Problem Solving for Chapter 14 (pages 374–375)

1. In what does Mr. Casabueno invest the most money?

2. Does he invest more in corporate bonds or in savings bonds?

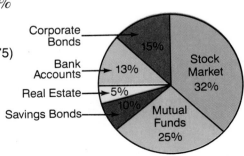

Corporate Bonds 15%
Bank Accounts 13%
Real Estate 5%
Savings Bonds 10%
Stock Market 32%
Mutual Funds 25%

TABLE OF MEASURES

Metric

Length

10 millimeters (mm) = 1 centimeter (cm)
10 centimeters (cm) = 1 decimeter (dm)
10 decimeters = 1 meter (m)
1,000 meters = 1 kilometer (km)

Area

100 square millimeters (sq mm) = 1 square
centimeter (sq cm)
10,000 square centimeters = 1 square meter
(sq m)

Volume

1,000 cubic millimeters (cu mm) = 1 cubic
centimeter (cu cm)
1,000,000 cubic centimeters = 1 cubic meter
(cu m)

Capacity

1,000 milliliters (mL) = 1 liter (L)

Mass/Weight

1,000 milligrams (mg) = 1 gram (g)
1,000 grams = 1 kilogram (kg)

United States Customary

Length

12 inches (in.) = 1 foot (ft)
36 inches ⎱
3 feet ⎰ = 1 yard (yd)
5,280 feet ⎱
1,760 yards ⎰ = 1 mile (mi)

Area

144 square inches (sq in.) = 1 square foot (sq ft)
9 square feet = 1 square yard (sq yd)

Volume

1,728 cubic inches (cu in.) = 1 cubic foot (cu ft)
27 cubic feet = 1 cubic yard (cu yd)

Capacity

1 cup (c) = 8 fluid ounces (fl. oz)
2 cups = 1 pint (pt)
2 pints = 1 quart (qt)
4 quarts = 1 gallon (gal)

Mass/Weight

16 ounces (oz) = 1 pound (lb)
2,000 pounds = 1 ton (T)

Time

60 seconds (s) = 1 minute (min)
60 minutes = 1 hour (h)
24 hours = 1 day (d)
7 days = 1 week (wk)
28 to 31 days = 1 month (mo)
12 months ⎱
52 weeks ⎰ = 1 year (yr)
100 years = 1 century (cen)

TABLE OF SYMBOLS

+	plus
−	minus
×	times
÷	divided by
=	equals or is equal to
≠	is not equal to
>	is greater than
<	is less than
≅	is congruent to
…	pattern continues without end
4 r3	four remainder three
5.2	decimal point: five and two-tenths
25%	percent: twenty-five percent
$\frac{2}{3}$	fraction: two-thirds
4:3	ratio: four to three
∟	right angle
∠ABC	angle ABC
°	degree (angle or temperature)
°C	degree Celsius
°F	degree Fahrenheit
.A	point A
$\overline{AB}$	line segment with endpoints A and B
$\overrightarrow{AB}$	ray AB with endpoint A
$\overleftrightarrow{AB}$	line through points A and B
‖	is parallel to
⊥	is perpendicular to
△ABC	triangle ABC

GLOSSARY

Acute Angle   An angle whose measure is greater than 0° and less than 90°. (p. 332)

Addend   A number that is added. (p. 22)
  Example: 8 + 7 = 15.
  The addends are 8 and 7.

Addition (+)   An operation on two numbers resulting in their sum. (p. 22)
  Example: 9 + 8 = 17. 9 and 8 are addends. 17 is the sum.

Angle   Two rays with the same endpoint. The endpoint is the vertex of the angle. (p. 332)
  Example:

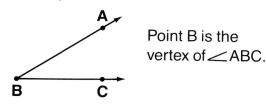

Point B is the vertex of ∠ABC.

Area   The number of square units needed to cover a surface. (p. 250)
  Examples: Some formulas to find area are:
  rectangle $A = l \times w$
  parallelogram $A = b \times h$
  triangle $A = \frac{1}{2} b \times h$

Average (mean)   The quotient found by dividing a sum by the number of addends. (p. 98)
  Example: The average of 2, 6, and 7 is 5 because 2 + 6 + 7 = 15 and 15 ÷ 3 = 5.

Bar graph   A graph with bars (rectangles) of different heights to show and compare information. (p. 136)

Capacity   The amount a container will hold when filled. (p. 258)

Chord   A line segment with endpoints on a circle. (p. 347)

Circle   A closed curve with all points an equal distance from a center point. (p. 346)

Circle graph   A graph, in the shape of a circle, used to show data given in percents. (p. 374)

Circumference   The distance around a circle. (p. 355)

399

Common denominator   A common multiple of the denominators of two or more fractions. (p. 172)
> *Example:* 12 is a common denominator for $\frac{1}{2}$ and $\frac{2}{3}$.

Common factor   A factor of two or more numbers. (p. 160)
> *Example:* 1, 2, 3, and 6 are the common factors of 6 and 12.

Composite number   A whole number greater than 1 that has more than two factors. (p. 156)
> *Example:* 6 is a composite number since its factors are 1, 2, 3, 6.

Cone   A solid with one circular face and one vertex. (p. 350)

Congruent angles   Angles that have the same measure. (p. 335)

Congruent line segments   Line segments that have the same length. (p. 331)

Congruent polygons   Polygons that have the same size and shape. (p. 342)

Coordinate graph   A drawing of numbered lines that cross at right angles and are used to name the positions of points. (p. 140)

Cube   A rectangular prism with six congruent square faces. (p. 350)
> *Example:*

Customary measurement system   A measurement system that uses inches, feet, yards, and miles as units of length; cups; pints, quarts, and gallons for liquid capacity; ounces, pounds, and tons as units of weight; and degrees Fahrenheit as units of temperature. (p. 266)

Cylinder   A solid with two bases that are congruent circles. (p. 350)

Decagon   A polygon with ten sides. (p. 340)

Decimal   A number that uses place value and a decimal point to show tenths, hundredths, thousandths, and so on. (p. 282)
> *Example:* 3.85   Read as three and eighty-five hundredths.

Degree (°)   A standard unit for measuring angles. (p. 332)

Degree Celsius (°C)   A standard unit for measuring temperature in the metric system. (p. 262)
> *Example:* Water freezes at 0°C and boils at 100°C.

Degree Fahrenheit (°F)   A standard unit for measuring temperature in the customary measurement system. (p. 275)
> *Example:* Water freezes at 32°F and boils at 212°F.

Denominator   The number below the bar in a fraction. (p. 166)
> *Example:* $\frac{3}{5}$ The denominator is 5.

Diameter A line segment through the center of a circle with endpoints on the circle. (p. 346)

Difference The answer to a subtraction problem. (p. 24)
Example: $14 - 9 = 5$
The difference is 5.

Digit Any one of the ten symbols 0, 1, 2, 3, 4, 5, 6, 7, 8, or 9. (p. 2)

Dividend The number that is divided in a division problem. (p. 82)
Example: $12 \div 4$ 12 is the dividend.

Divisible A number is divisible by another number if the quotient is a whole number and the remainder is 0. (p. 154)
Example: 15 is divisible by 3.

Division ($\overline{)}$ or $\div$) An operation on two numbers that results in a quotient and a remainder. (p. 82)

Divisor The number by which the dividend is divided. (p. 82)
Example: $5\overline{)32}^{6r2}$ The divisor is 5.

Edge The line segment where two faces of a solid meet. (p. 350)
Example:

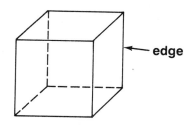

Endpoint A point at the end of a line segment or ray. (p. 330)

Equal ratios Ratios that show the same comparison. (p. 362)
Example: $\frac{1}{3}$, $\frac{2}{6}$, and $\frac{3}{9}$ are equal ratios.

Equation A number sentence that uses the symbol $=$. (p. 22)
Examples: $5 \times 4 = 20$; $8 + N = 13$

Equilateral triangle A triangle with three equal sides. Each angle measures 60°. (p. 340)

Equivalent fractions Fractions that name the same number. (p. 170)
Example: $\frac{3}{4}$ and $\frac{6}{8}$ are equivalent.

Even number A whole number that is a multiple of 2. An even number has 0, 2, 4, 6, or 8 in the ones place. (p. 154)
Examples: 4, 16, 28, 120 are even numbers.

Expanded form A way to show a number as a sum of multiples of ten. (p. 2)
Example:
$817 = 8 \times 100 + 1 \times 10 + 7 \times 1$.

Face A flat surface of a solid. (p. 350)
Example:

Factor   A factor of a number is a whole number that divides it exactly. (p. 56)
> *Example:* 1, 2, 4, and 8 are factors of 8.

Factor tree   The prime factors of a number can be found by making a factor tree. (p. 158)
> *Example:*

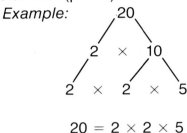

$$20 = 2 \times 2 \times 5$$

Fraction   The quotient of two whole numbers: $a \div b = \frac{a}{b}$. In the fraction $\frac{a}{b}$, a is called the numerator and b is called the denominator. (p. 166)

Graph   A drawing used to show and compare information. Some types of graphs are bar graphs, circle graphs, line graphs, and pictographs. (p. 134)

Greatest common factor (GCF)   The greatest factor that two or more numbers have in common. (p. 160)
> *Example:* 6 is the GCF of 18 and 30.

Grouping property of addition   The way in which addends are grouped does not change the sum. (p. 22)
> *Example:*
> $(7 + 5) + 6 = 7 + (5 + 6).$

Grouping property of multiplication   The way in which factors are grouped does not change the product. (p. 56)
> *Example:*
> $(3 \times 4) \times 5 = 3 \times (4 + 5).$

Hexagon   A polygon with six sides. (p. 340)

Intersecting lines   Lines that meet or cross. Intersecting lines have only one point in common. (p. 336)
> *Example:*

Isosceles triangle   A triangle with two equal sides and two equal angles. (p. 340)

Least common denominator (LCD)   The least common multiple of the denominators of two or more fractions. (p. 176)
> *Example:* 12 is the LCD for $\frac{1}{4}$ and $\frac{5}{6}$

Least common multiple (LCM)   The smallest nonzero multiple that two or more numbers have in common. (p. 162)
> *Example:* The LCM of 6 and 9 is 18.

Like fractions   Fractions with the same denominator. (p. 192)
> *Example:* $\frac{2}{5}$ and $\frac{3}{5}$ are like fractions.

Line A straight path extending in both directions with no endpoints. (p. 330)

Line graph A graph in which a line is used to show a change. (p. 138)

Line of symmetry A line that divides a figure into two congruent parts. (p. 348)

Line segment Part of a line with two endpoints. (p. 330)

Lowest terms A fraction is in lowest terms when the numerator and the denominator have no common factor greater than one. (p. 174)

Magic square The sum of the numbers in each row, column, and diagonal is the same. (p. 237)
Example:

4	3	8
9	5	1
2	7	6

Median The middle score in a distribution. (p. 129)

Metric system A measurement system that uses centimeters, meters, and kilometers as units of length; milliliters and liters as units of capacity; grams and kilograms as units of mass; and degrees Celsius as units of temperature. (p. 244)

Mixed number The sum of a whole number and a fraction. (p. 178)
Example: $5\frac{1}{4} = 5 + \frac{1}{4}$.

Multiple A number that is the product of a given number and a whole number. (p. 162)
Example: Multiples of 3: 3, 6, 9, 12, 15,…

Multiplication ($\times$) An operation on two numbers, called factors, which results in a product. (p. 56)
Example: $8 \times 9 = 72$
8 and 9 are factors and 72 is the product.

Napier's rods A method of multiplication invented by John Napier. (p. 75)

Number line A line with equally spaced points named by numbers. (p. 167)
Example:

$$-3 \;-2 \;-1 \quad 0 \quad 1 \quad 2 \quad 3$$

Numerator The number above the bar in a fraction. (p. 166)
Example: $\frac{2}{5}$ The numerator is 2.

Obtuse angle An angle whose measure is greater than 90° and less than 180°. (p. 332)

Octagon A polygon with eight sides. (p. 340)

Odd number A whole number that is not a multiple of 2. An odd number ends in 1, 3, 5, 7, or 9. (p. 154)
Examples: 5, 17, 39, 143 are odd numbers.

Order property of addition   The order in which addends are added does not change the sum. (p. 22)
  Example: $6 + 4 = 4 + 6$

Order property of multiplication   The order in which factors are multiplied does not change the product. (p. 56)
  Example: $5 \times 7 = 7 \times 5$

Ordered pair   A pair of numbers, (x, y), arranged in order so that x is first and y is second. (p. 140)

Parallel lines   Lines in the same plane that do not intersect. Parallel lines have no points in common. (p. 336)

Parallellogram   A quadrilateral with opposite sides parallel and congruent. (p. 340)

Pentagon   A polygon with five sides. (p. 340)

Percent (%)   Percent means per hundred. $P\% = \frac{P}{100}$. (p. 370)
  Example: $\frac{2}{5} = \frac{40}{100} = 40\%$

Perimeter   The sum of the lengths of the sides of a polygon. (p. 248)
  Examples: Some formulas to find perimeter are:
  rectangle $P = 2 \times (l + w)$
  square $P = 4 \times s$

Perpendicular lines   Two lines that intersect to form right angles. (p. 336)

Pictograph   A visual representation used to make comparisons. A key always appears at the bottom of a pictograph or picture graph showing how many each object represents. (p. 134)

Place value   In a decimal number, each place for a digit has a value ten times the value of the place at its right. (p. 4)
  Example: $3{,}247 = 3 \times 1{,}000$
  $+ 2 \times 100 + 4 \times 10$
  $+ 7 \times 1.$

Plane   A flat surface that extends without end in both directions. (p. 330)

Point   An exact location. A dot is often drawn to represent a point. (p. 330)

Polygon   A closed plane figure formed by three or more line segments joined at the endpoints. (p. 340)

Prime factorization   Any composite number can be factored as a product of primes. This product is called the prime factorization of that number. (p. 158)
  Examples: $24 = 2 \times 2 \times 2 \times 3$
  $45 = 3 \times 3 \times 5$
  $60 = 2 \times 2 \times 3 \times 5$

Prime number   A whole number greater than 1 that has only two factors, 1 and itself. (p. 156)
  Examples: 2, 3, 5, 7, 11, 13, 17, 19 are all prime numbers.

Prism   A solid with two parallel faces that are congruent polygons. (p. 350)

Probability   A number from 0 to 1 that tells how likely it is that an event will take place. (p. 377)

Product   The answer to a multiplication problem. (p. 56)

Property of one for multiplication   When one of the two factors is 1, the product equals the other factor. (p. 56)
   Examples: $a \times 1 = a$; $6 \times 1 = 6$.

Protractor   An instrument used to measure angles. (p. 334)

Pyramid   A solid with one face that is a polygon and three or more faces that are triangles with a common vertex. (p. 350)
   Example:

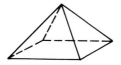

Quadrilateral   A polygon with four sides. (p. 340)

Quotient   The answer to a division problem. (p. 82)

Radius (pl. radii)   A line segment with one endpoint at the center of a circle and the other endpoint on the circle. All radii of a circle are equal. (p. 346)

Ratio   A comparison of two numbers. (p. 360)
   Example: The ratio of two to five can be written as 2 to 5, 2:5, or $\frac{2}{5}$

Ray   A part of a line that has one endpoint and extends on and on in only one direction. (p. 330)

Reciprocals   Two numbers whose product is 1. (p. 232)
   Examples: $\frac{3}{5}$ and $\frac{5}{3}$ are reciprocals.
   8 and $\frac{1}{8}$ are reciprocals.

Rectangle   A parallelogram with four right angles. (p. 340)

Remainder   The number left over in a division problem. The remainder must be less than the divisor. (p.86)
   Example: $4\overline{)39}$ with $9r3$ The remainder is 3.

Rhombus   A parallelogram with four congruent sides. (p. 340)

Right angle   An angle that measures 90°. (p. 332)

Roman numerals   Symbols used by the Romans to name numbers. Roman numeration does not use place value. (p. 17)
   Examples:

I	V	X	L	C	D	M
1	5	10	50	100	500	1,000

Rounding   Expressing a number to the nearest thousandth, hundredth, tenth, one, ten, hundred, thousand. (pp. 10 and 292)
   Example: 37.85 rounded to the nearest tenth is 37.9.

Sales tax   An amount added to the cost of an article. (p. 379)

Scale drawing   A drawing that is the same shape as an actual object, but not the same size. The scale gives the ratio of the size in the drawing to the size of the actual object. (p. 368)

Scalene triangle   A triangle with three unequal sides. (p. 340)

Similar polygons   Polygons that have the same shape. Corresponding sides of similar polygons are in proportion. Corresponding angles are congruent. (p. 344)

Sphere   A solid with all points an equal distance from the center. (p. 350)

Square   A rectangle with four congruent sides. (p. 340)

Square numbers
The numbers 1, 4, 9, 16,…
are called square numbers. (p. 213)
   Example:

   1   4   9   16

Subtraction ($-$)   An operation on two numbers resulting in a difference. (p. 24)
   Example: 25   minuend
            -8 subtrahend
            17   difference

Sum   The answer to an addition problem. (p. 24)

Symmetry (line)   A figure has line symmetry if it can be folded about a line so that the two halves of the figure are congruent. The fold line is called the line of symmetry. (p. 348)

Triangle   A polygon with three sides. (p. 252)

Triangular numbers
The numbers 1, 3, 6, 10,…
are called triangular numbers. (p. 213)
   Example:

   1   3   6   10

Triangular prism   A prism with two parallel faces that are congruent triangles. The other three faces are parallelograms. (p. 350)
   Example:

Unlike fractions   Fractions with different denominators. (p. 196)
   Example: $\frac{2}{3}$ and $\frac{3}{4}$ are unlike fractions.

Vertex (pl. vertices)   The point at which two rays of an angle, two sides of a polygon, or three or more edges of a solid meet. (p. 350)

Volume   The number of cubic units needed to fill a solid. (p. 254)
>   *Example:* Volume of a rectangular solid is $V = l \times w \times h$.

Zero property for addition   When 0 is added to any addend, the sum equals the addend. (p. 22)
>   *Examples:* $9 + 0 = 9$; $0 + 12 = 12$.

Zero property for multiplication   If 0 is a factor, the product is always 0. (p. 56)
>   *Examples:* $13 + 0 = 0$; $0 + 7 = 0$.